T0300461

# Causality in Macroeconomics

*Causality in Macroeconomics* is the first book to address the long-standing problems of causality while taking macroeconomics seriously. The practical concerns of the macroeconomist and abstract concerns of the philosopher inform each other. Grounded in pragmatic realism, the book rejects the popular idea that macroeconomics requires micro-foundations and argues that the macroeconomy is a set of structures that are best analyzed causally. Ideas originated by Herbert Simon and the Cowles Commission are refined and generalized to nonlinear systems, particularly to the nonlinear systems with cross-equation restrictions that are ubiquitous in modern macroeconomic models with rational expectations (with and without regime switching). These ideas help to clarify philosophical as well as economic issues. The structural approach to causality is then used to evaluate more familiar approaches to causality developed by Granger, by LeRoy, and by Glymour, Spirtes, Scheines, and Kelly, as well as vector autoregressions, the Lucas critique, and the exogeneity concepts of Engle, Hendry, and Richard. A constructive approach to causal inference based on patterns of stability and instability in the face of identified regime changes is developed and illustrated in two empirical case studies of the causal direction between money and prices and between taxes and spending.

Kevin D. Hoover is Professor and Chair in the Department of Economics at the University of California, Davis. He is the author of *The New Classical Macroeconomics: A Sceptical Inquiry* (1988) and the forthcoming *Applied Intermediate Macroeconomics* and *The Methodology of Empirical Macroeconomics*. Professor Hoover is also the editor of *The Legacy of Robert Lucas* (1999), *Macroeconomics: Development, Tensions and Prospects* (1995), and the three-volume *The New Classical Macroeconomics* (1992) in The International Library of Critical Writings in Economics series, and coeditor of *Real-Business-Cycle Models: A Reader* (1998, with J. Hartley and K. Salyer) and *Monetarism and the Methodology of Economics: Essays in Honour of Thomas Mayer* (1995, with S. Sheffrin). He is a Founding Member and Chair of the International Network for Economic Method, Vice President of the History of Economics Society, and Editor of the *Journal of Economic Methodology*, and he serves as an associate editor or on the editorial board of four other journals in economics and methods. Professor Hoover also served as a research associate at the Federal Reserve Bank of San Francisco and as a lecturer in economics at Balliol College and Lady Margaret Hall, Oxford.

Advance Praise for *Causality in Macroeconomics*

"Kevin Hoover uses arguments taken from philosophy to cut through the thorny problem of causation in macroeconomics. He applies his arguments to econometric methods used to test for causality in a way that will interest econometricians working on macroeconomics. In arguing for the reality of macroeconomic aggregates and causal relations between them, he challenges the current fashion for microfoundations and representative-agent models. This is a very important book, written by someone who, as a practising empirical macroeconomist trained in philosophy, is probably uniquely qualified to write it. It should interest philosophers, econometricians and macroeconomists."

– Roger E. Backhouse, *University of Birmingham*

"Kevin Hoover's *Causality in Macroeconomics* is a tour de force. Combining mastery of contemporary macroeconomics with enormous philosophical sophistication, this book is must reading for philosophers as well as economists. All those who have a serious interest in causality have a great deal to learn from this book."

– Daniel Hausman, *University of Wisconsin*

# Causality in Macroeconomics

**KEVIN D. HOOVER**

*University of California, Davis*

CAMBRIDGE
UNIVERSITY PRESS

CAMBRIDGE UNIVERSITY PRESS
Cambridge, New York, Melbourne, Madrid, Cape Town,
Singapore, São Paulo, Delhi, Tokyo, Mexico City

Cambridge University Press
The Edinburgh Building, Cambridge CB2 8RU, UK

Published in the United States of America by Cambridge University Press, New York

www.cambridge.org
Information on this title: www.cambridge.org/9780521002882

First published 2001

*A catalogue record for this publication is available from the British Library*

*Library of Congress Cataloguing in Publication Data*

Hoover, Kevin D., 1955–
    Causality in macroeconomics / Kevin D. Hoover.
       p.   cm.
    Includes bibliographical references and index.
    ISBN 0-521-45217-1 – ISBN 0-521-00288-5 (pb)
       1. Macroeconomics.   2. Macroeconomics – Philosophy.   I. Title.
HB172.5 .H658 2001
339 – dc21

                                          00–049351

ISBN 978-0-521-45217-5 Hardback
ISBN 978-0-521-00288-2 Paperback

*I dedicate this book to*
*my father,*
Charles Hoover,
*who taught me to wonder how things work,*
*and who usually could show me himself;*

*and to*
*my mother,*
Elizabeth Hoover,
*who, possessed of an inquiring mind and a discerning heart,*
*prayed that I should have them myself.*

... it is possible to tell part of the truth about the world in terms that are false, limited, and fantastic – else how should we have told it?

– Randall Jarrell

# Contents

# Preface

This book addresses questions in macroeconomics and philosophy.
There is a risk with such an enterprise of falling between two stools.
Although it requires some forbearance on each of their parts, I hope
that both economists and philosophers will find something of value
in it. A little personal history may explain how such a hybrid came
to be.

The question of the nature of causality in macroeconomics has stood
at the center of my research agenda for many years. My first degree –
from the College of William and Mary – was in philosophy. After study-
ing at Balliol College, Oxford, and taking a second bachelor's degree in
Philosophy, Politics, and Economics, I worked for two years as a research
associate at the Federal Reserve Bank of San Francisco. I arrived in
December 1979, in the wake of the famous October 6 decision to adopt
a monetary aggregate target and a nonborrowed-reserve operating procedure. Monetarism was in the air. Economists at the San Francisco Fed,
as elsewhere throughout the macroeconomics profession, were excited
by Christopher Sims's application of Granger-causality tests to the monetarist proposition that money causes prices and output. As a former
philosopher, I was at first fascinated by, and later highly skeptical of, the
claim that so fraught a question as causality could be reduced to a relatively simple econometric test. When I returned to Oxford for graduate
study at Nuffield College, I focused on the same causal questions that
had fascinated me at the Federal Reserve. I tried to work out an
approach to causal inference that would not be subject to the skeptical
objections that had been raised with respect to Granger-causality. Much
of my research over the past nearly 20 years has been devoted both to
the methodological issues (what is the proper analysis of causality in
macroeconomics? and how might one infer causal direction and measure
causal strength using macroeconomic data?) and to practical applications of the methods developed to answer these questions to monetary

and macroeconomic data. This volume is the capstone of that research program.

The book has had a long gestation. It was first proposed in a successful application for a fellowship to the National Humanities Center for the 1991–92 academic year. It has been overdue to Cambridge University Press since 1996. There are many reasons unrelated to the research itself for its slowness in reaching publication. But there are reasons related to the research as well. The longer I examined the philosophical literature on causality, the more I felt that I needed to read, the more issues seemed to require attention, before the book could achieve the level of completeness that I sought. I finally realized that publishing the book was incompatible with the desire to be comprehensive and to reach my final views on the subject; for I found that my views continued to grow, mutate, and evolve. So I made a decision to draw a line and not to consider new material until a draft was complete. The resulting volume is now offered to the reader. It is, inevitably, a snapshot extracted from a film whose plot continues to develop.

I have had the help, comments, cooperation, and support of many people in the course of writing this book and the articles that led up to it. I would like to thank and acknowledge those who have commented on and discussed with me, not only the earlier drafts of the book, but also earlier articles and papers in the same research program that helped me to form my current views. In particular, I thank Roger Backhouse, Robert Basmann, Mark Blaug, Diran Bodenhorn, Yongxin Cai, Nancy Cartwright, Thomas Cooley, Allin Cottrell, Selva Demiralp, Neil Ericsson, Charles Goodhart, Clive Granger, Clinton Greene, James Griesemer, Daniel Hammond, James Hartley, Daniel Hausman, Arthur Havenner, David Hendry, Paul Holland, Douglas Joines, Edward Leamer, Stephen LeRoy, Liang Liu, Uskali Mäki, Thomas Mayer, Mary Morgan, Peter Oppenheimer, Judea Pearl, Stephen Perez, Nicholas Ramsing, Steven Sheffrin, Mark Siegler, Peter Sinclair, Paul Teller, D. Wade Hands, Leon Wegge, James Woodward, and Nancy Wulwick. I also thank the numerous people in audiences of the various seminars and conferences at which the component parts of the book were presented. I beg the forgiveness of anyone whom I have inadvertently neglected to recall.

Throughout the writing of this book, I have had the support of the dedicated staff of the Department of Economics of the University of California, Davis, especially Kathleen Miner and Donna Raymond.

While the research program predates it, the book itself was begun on a sabbatical year at the National Humanities Center, supported by a fellowship grant from the National Endowment for the Humanities. I thank W. Robert Connor, Director, and Kent Mullikin, Associate Director, and the entire staff of the National Humanities Center for a year in the best research environment I could possibly have wished for. I also gratefully acknowledge the support of the National Science Foundation (Grant No. 9311930) and a series of Faculty Research Grants from the University of California, Davis.

I thank Patrick McCartan, the editor who first commissioned the book, and Scott Parris, the editor who has shepherded it through to final publication with good cheer and infinite patience.

Most importantly, I would like to thank my wife, Catherine, and daughters, Norah and Philippa, for their love and support over the many years that this project has been under way.

Several parts of the book are reprinted – in some cases with substantial alterations – from my own previously published work. I gratefully acknowledge the following for permitting me to use this material. Reprinted from:

- *The American Economic Review*, vol. 82, no. 2, 1992, pp. 225–248, "Causation, Spending, and Taxes: Sand in the Sandbox or Tax Collector for the Welfare State?" by permission of the American Economic Association and my coauthor, Steven Sheffrin.
- *The British Journal for the Philosophy of Science*, vol. 44, no. 4, 1993, pp. 693–710, "Causality and Temporal Order in Macroeconomics or Why Even Economists Don't Know How to Get Causes from Probabilities," by permission of Oxford University Press.
- *The Journal of Monetary Economics*, vol. 27, no. 3, 1991, pp. 381–423, "The Causal Direction Between Money and Prices: An Alternative Approach." Copyright © 1991, with permission from Elsevier Science.
- *The Monist*, vol. 78, no. 3, 1995, pp. 235–257, "Is Macroeconomics for Real?" Copyright © 1995, *The Monist*, Peru, Illinois 61354. Reprinted by permission.
- *Economics and Philosophy*, vol. 6, no. 2, 1990, pp. 207–234, "The Logic of Causal Inference: Econometrics and the Conditional Analysis of Causality," by permission of Cambridge University Press.

# 1

## The Problem of Causality in Macroeconomics

> England has not a guinea at our service; economy and Hume
> are the fashion there.
>                                    – Stendhal, *The Red and the Black*

The ultimate justification for the study of macroeconomics is a practical
one – to provide secure knowledge on which to base policy. Policy is
about influencing outcomes, about control or attempted control. The
study of causality in any particular context is the study of the particular
connections that permit control of one thing to influence another. Causal
understanding is implicit in policy discussions. The never-ending debate
over whether the Federal Reserve should raise or lower the federal funds
rate hinges on disputed causal beliefs: An increase in the rate will result
in lower inflation, higher unemployment, lower investment, and lower
stock prices.

Causal questions can be generic ("do monetary shocks or technology
shocks cause business cycles?") or singular ("did the Iraqi invasion of
Kuwait cause the 1990/91 recession in the United States?"). They can be
retrospective (as in Peter Temin's 1976 title, *Did Monetary Forces Cause
the Great Depression?*) or prospective ("will a cut in the tax rates
on capital gains cause a boom in investment?"). Causal language is
often explicit, but not always. Classic disputes in macroeconomics frequently turn on causal questions, even when causal language is explicitly
eschewed. The modern argument over monetarism is really a question
of the causal direction between money, on the one hand, and prices
and nominal income, on the other. For some participants the issues are
stated in forthrightly causal language (see, e.g., Laidler 1991); for others,
the causal issues are recast in noncausal terms (Milton Friedman 1956
prefers to talk about the stability of the demand for money). Yet, for all
participants, the question is, what happens to the economy as a result of
the money supply increasing? The question is one of control, although it

1

may be posed in every tense and mood: Did the Federal Reserve cause the Great Depression? If it had expanded the money supply in 1929, would it have caused the good times to continue and so avoided the Great Depression? Are its current policies the cause of the current boom? If it were to raise interest rates would it cause that boom to end?

It is sometimes argued that control is not the central issue, that as disinterested scientists, economists (who love to think of themselves as scientists) should be concerned with explanation. The issues of control and explanation operate on different levels. A practically minded policy-maker might want to know only what causal relations in fact obtain. That knowledge is, however, grounded in a causal explanation. A more disinterested economist might want to know why a particular causal relation holds – what is its deeper explanation? What is sought, however, is understanding of why control is possible. An adequate causal explanation provides the basis for informed attempts to control particular variables.

Causal analysis has a long history in philosophy, and causal reasoning has a long history, not only in the sciences, but in everyday life. The issue posed in this book is, what is the place of causal analysis in macroeconomics? The questions to be faced are partly philosophical ("what are causes?" and "what is the nature of causal talk?") and partly methodological ("what procedures of causal inference are suitable to macroeconomics?"). While these questions are discussed in a detached and, sometimes, abstract manner, their importance stems entirely from the practical policy orientation of macroeconomics. The last two chapters illustrate the practical lessons of the first eight.

## 1.1 THE LEGACY OF DAVID HUME

A river does not have a definite beginning. Before its stream bears a name, lakes and springs and hidden rivulets combine to supply its waters. For all that, we recognize the headwaters. Before David Hume's discussion of causality there was Aristotle and the Scholastics and Nicolas Malebranche; before Hume's account of the quantity theory of money there was Jean Bodin, John Locke, and Richard Cantillon. Yet Hume, the central figure of the philosophical school of British empiricism and the author of the definitive eighteenth-century statement of the quantity theory of money, stands at the headwaters of all modern discussions of both causality and macroeconomics. Let us begin with Hume.

### Accounting for Macroeconomics – Causally

Hume's contribution to what may be called – anachronistically – the macroeconomics of the eighteenth century was fundamental. It is found in the three essays "Of Money" (1754a), "Of Interest" (1754b), and "Of the Balance of Trade" (1754c). Explicitly and implicitly, Hume's discussions of the role of international trade and specie flows are unabashedly causal. And Hume is clear on the reason:

> But still it is of consequence to know the principle whence any phenomenon arises, and to distinguish between a cause and a concomitant effect. Besides that the speculation is curious, it may frequently be of use in the conduct of public affairs. At least, it must be owned, that nothing can be of more use than to improve, by practice, the method of reasoning on these subjects, which of all others are the most important; though they are commonly treated in the loosest and most careless manner. [Hume 1754b, p. 304]

In a word, Hume's interest in a causal account of the macroeconomy is both that of the detached philosopher (or scientist) – "the speculation is curious" – and of the would-be policy advisor for whom causal knowledge "may frequently be of use."

As the philosopher who first insisted on a sharp distinction between "is" and "ought to be" (Hume 1739, book III), Hume realized that a useful macroeconomics (normative) must begin with a successful speculation (positive) on the mechanisms of the macroeconomy.[1] Despite Hume's literary style, his three essays are recognizably economics – and the mechanisms described explicitly and implicitly causal. The quantity theory has been debated in various forms since the sixteenth century. It remains "always and everywhere controversial" (to use David Laidler's 1991 phrase), not least because of the causal issues involved. These issues are particularly clear in Hume's essays, which provide us with an excellent exemplar of the place of causal reasoning in macroeconomics – all the more excellent because, with due account for changing institutional structure, Hume's doctrines or close relatives remain central to the contemporary debate.

Five interrelated causal mechanisms dominate the three essays. The first is the *quantity theory of money* proper: The stock of money in relation to the stock of available goods causes the level of prices to be what it is. If foreign prices are given, then an increase in the stock of money causes relative prices (i.e., domestic prices relative to foreign prices) to rise. The second is the equally famous *specie-flow mechanism*: Relative prices cause money (precious metals) to vary inversely. The third is what might be called the *loanable funds doctrine*: The supply of and demand for loans are one cause of interest rates. The fourth doctrine holds that there is another causal mechanism in financial markets: Interest rates and

---

[1] The positive/normative distinction is, of course, merely the economist's translation of the distinction between "is" and "ought."

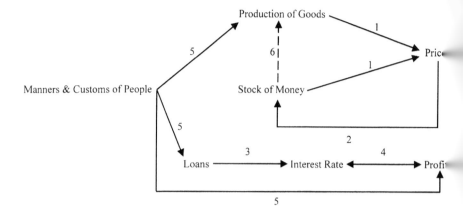

Hume's Theoretical Explanation for the Causal Links

| | |
|---|---|
| 1. Quantity Theory of Money | 4. Arbitrage Doctrine |
| 2. Specie-flow Mechanism | 5. Sociological Doctrine |
| 3. Loanable Funds Doctrine | 6. Temporary Non-neutrality of Money |

Figure 1.1

profit rates are mutually causal. This might be called the *arbitrage doctrine*. Finally, fifth, Hume maintains a crucial portmanteau mechanism, which we might regard as the ultimate *sociological doctrine*: The "manners and customs of people" cause the production and demand of goods, the supply of and demand for loans, and the rate of profits. Figure 1.1 uses arrows (each one marked to indicate which element of Hume's doctrine justifies the linkage) to show the causal influences among these macroeconomic variables as Hume understands them.[2]

A number of features of Hume's discussion are worth noting. For Hume, causation is a process. Although he refers to the time order of causes before effects relatively infrequently, the idea of causes unfolding is central. Hume dismisses money in the long run as a cause of prosperity; but, along the path to a long run in which prices have fully adjusted to increases in the money stock, increases in production and employment are important. Cause is quantitative as well. It is not just that an increase in money causes prices to rise in the long run, it is that it causes prices to rise one for one: money is "neutral" in modern terminology. (The short-run non-neutrality of money is indicated by the

---

[2] There is no reason to believe that Hume would have regarded the linkages reflected in Figure 1.1 as the complete set of causal connections in the macroeconomy, although they are the ones that receive his fullest consideration.

broken arrow running from the *Stock of Money* to the *Production of Goods* in Figure 1.1.)

Cause is asymmetrical in Hume's account. He recognizes cases of mutual causality. The quantity theory taken together with the specie-flow mechanism is a case of money causing relative prices and relative prices causing money. Hume envisages these mechanisms as separated in time and distinct. They nevertheless provide the notion of an equilibrating mechanism in which the issue of time ordering is secondary. The mutual causality of the arbitrage relationship between profits and interest rates is so direct that Hume hardly implies, much less discusses, time ordering. In the language of the modern statistician, correlation is not causation for Hume.

Correlation is not causation in another sense as well. Causes are often hidden below their surface manifestations in Hume's account. An apparent correlation between interest rates and money is explained, at least in the long run, by a common third cause: Both are the effects of the manners and customs of people. That the specie flow fails to correspond to Hume's causal mechanism is explained by a countervailing or confounding cause: Paper money displaces precious metals.

Causes are efficacious. Hume's essays are famous for a series of thought experiments: "Were all the gold in ENGLAND annihilated at once, and one and twenty shillings substituted in the place of every guinea . . ." (Hume 1754b, p. 296); or "suppose that by a miracle, every man in GREAT BRITAIN should have five pounds slipt into his pocket in one night . . ." (Hume 1754b, p. 299); or, again, "[s]uppose four-fifths of all the money in GREAT BRITAIN to be annihilated in one night . . ." (Hume 1754c, p. 311). Hume rarely reasons from a correlation, a repeated conjunction, to an effect. Instead, as with the consequences he draws from these antecedents, Hume starts with a prior, or common-sense, understanding of elementary causal connections and composes them into larger causal structures in which effects can be reliably expected to follow causes. He takes it, for example, to be obvious that money flows alter expenditure and that prices rise in the face of rising expenditure, and so concludes that money causes prices. The implicit message of Hume's thought experiments is that causation is *counterfactual* (determining "what would happen if?") and *compositive* (causes can be linked together to connect to effects in ways that are indirect and not obvious). Causes are implicitly defined by their efficacy in producing effects. This property of connecting what-is with what-is-not-yet underwrites inference beyond experience and connects Hume's positive analysis of the macroeconomy with his normative interests, in the sense that causal understanding may permit us to guide and shape future outcomes according to our goals and desires.

Hume did not hesitate to conduct causal analyses with the aim of giving policy advice. In "Of Money" Hume argued that the true cause of national prosperity was not, as the mercantilists had thought, the abundance of precious metals. In "Of Interest" he argued that the true cause of the low rates of interest was, again, not the abundance of precious metals. In each case, "a collateral effect is taken for a cause, and . . . a consequence is ascribed to the plenty of money; though it be really owing to a change in the manners and customs of the people" (Hume 1754b, p. 294). The causal direction was in fact exactly opposite to what the mercantilists believed: "when commerce is extended all over the globe, the most industrious nations always abound most with the precious metals" (Hume 1754b, p. 304). Hume provided evidence for a causal account to satisfy his philosophical curiosity and concluded "Of the Balance of Trade" with categorical policy advice:

In short, a government has great reason to preserve with care its people and its manufactures. Its money, it may safely trust to the course of human affairs, without fear or jealousy. Or, if it ever give attention to this latter circumstance, it ought only to be so far as it affects the former. [Hume 1754c, p. 326]

The ultimate rationale for macroeconomics is to give policy advice, even when the advice, as it is for Hume, is to do nothing.

Hume's discussion is remarkably fresh. Allowing for appropriate modifications to adapt to substantial institutional changes, his theories remain, in broad outlines, active in the economic debate, in large measure reflected in monetarism and the monetary approach to the balance of payments. The problems that he posed have been continuously before economists and policymakers for the past 250 years. A topical concern for current economic policy animated the debate, just as it had for Hume. Many of the issues raised in the essays – e.g., the appropriate definition of money or the quality of economic statistics – have remained important. But no issues have been as central as the questions of causal direction between money and prices and output. Let us trace the main lines of the debate from Hume to modern times.[3]

The English Bullionists of the early nineteenth century and the Currency School of a generation later supported an essentially Humean view of the monetary mechanism. On the basis of substantially improved

---

[3] Laidler (1991) provides an excellent survey of the history of quantity theory of money directed at the question of why the debate over it remains unresolved – why it is "always and everywhere controversial." A central element of Laidler's explanation is that it is principally a causal theory and the problem of inferring causal direction from empirical data remains unresolved. See also Blaug (1995a, b).

statistics, painstakingly collected, Thomas Tooke (1838–57, 1844), a leader of the Banking School (the opponents of the Currency School), argued that causality ran exclusively from prices to money – in the opposite direction of Hume's quantity-theoretic causal linkage (linkage 1 in Figure 1.1). Opinion shifted away from the quantity theory. Toward the end of the nineteenth century, it was revived by Simon Newcomb and Irving Fisher, with another classic formulation in Fisher's (1911/1931) *Purchasing Power of Money*. Fisher's understanding was clearly causal, as was that of his opponents, J. L. Laughlin among others. Paralleling Fisher's revival of the quantity theory in the United States, Alfred Marshall and the Cambridge school revived it in England. John Maynard Keynes was at first a doctrinaire quantity theorist, and in the *Treatise on Money* (1930/1971, p. 120) expressed his theoretical ambitions in explicitly causal language. By the time of *The General Theory* (1936), Keynes turned away from both the quantity theory, in which he was joined by the Stockholm school, particularly Bertil Ohlin and Gunnar Myrdal, and explicit causal argument, in which he was not. In opposition to Keynesianism, Friedman and his students and colleagues reasserted the quantity theory once more.[4] Again, the debate was implicitly causal throughout – and sometimes explicitly so. James Tobin (1970) argued that Friedman was misled by the timing of money and price and income data to conclude that money caused nominal income and prices (see Friedman 1970 for his reply).[5]

Friedman is emblematic of the fate of causal discourse in macroeconomics. The disputes over the quantity theory in which he has engaged are clearly disputes over causes. J. Daniel Hammond's (1996) book is subtitled *Causality Issues in Milton Friedman's Monetary Economics*. Yet, as Hammond (1992, pp. 91–98) documents, Friedman is reluctant to use the language of causality, preferring to talk of stable associations and functional relationships among variables. Causal language has fallen into disrepute, and Friedman, like many other modern macroeconomists, instinctively or self-consciously avoids it. Ironically – for he is himself promiscuous in talking of causes in macroeconomics – the avoidance of causal talk arises from an empiricist sensibility of which Hume is the intellectual wellspring.

[4] Especially in Friedman's edited volume *Studies in the Quantity Theory of Money*, and, in particular, his own essay in that volume (Friedman 1956). Also see Friedman and Schwartz (1963a, b; 1982), Friedman (1968).

[5] Christina Romer and David Romer (1989) have argued a position meant to parallel Friedman and Schwartz's, backed up by more sophisticated econometric evidence. Hoover and Stephen Perez (1994a) played Tobin to the Romers' Friedman and Anna J. Schwartz. Also see Romer and Romer (1994) and Hoover and Perez (1994b).

**Accounting for Causes – Economically**

The empiricist sensibility embodied in the received view of the philoso-phy of science, represented by logical positivism and its constructive critics, such as Karl Popper, Willard Quine, and Imré Lakatos, is the (often unacknowledged) background to the portrait of the economist as scientist, which economists typically paint when they engage in method-ological reflections on their discipline.[6] It is no accident that Friedman, reluctant to use causal language, is the author of the famous "Method-ology of Positive Economics" (1953), a work squarely in the tradition of the received view. The received view is one line of descent from Hume's empiricism. Hume's empiricism is presented in his essential philosophi-cal work, *A Treatise of Human Nature* (1739), and more engagingly in *An Enquiry Concerning Human Understanding* (1777).

Hume's empirical philosophy is an economical construction, animated by a single premise: All human perceptions derive from sense impres-sions. Ideas, which form the other variety of perceptions, are themselves analyzed as a faded variety of sense impression, so that every idea is ultimately resolvable into sense impressions.

The idea of cause is no different than any other idea. What sense impressions give rise to the idea of cause and effect? Hume believes that the idea of one billiard ball striking another and causing it to move resolves into three elements.[7] First, the cause is spatially contiguous with the effect (one billiard ball causes another to move when it touches it). Second, the cause precedes the effect (the ball that moves first is the cause; the other is the effect).[8] Third, the cause must be necessarily con-nected to its effect (the action of the first ball reliably sets the second into motion). (Hume (1739, pp. 77, 90–91) considers the idea of *neces-sary connection* to encompass what others mean when they refer to causes as "productive" or as having "power" or "efficacy.")

The first two elements of the idea of cause are given in sense experi-ence. But we do not directly perceive necessary connection. Still, Hume (1739, p. 77) is loath to dispense with necessary connection, arguing that it "is of much greater importance" than the other two elements. After canvassing a variety of alternative sources for the empirical basis of the idea of necessary connection, Hume concludes that it could only be the

---

[6] See Nagel (1961) for a standard account of the received view. See Blaug (1992) and Hausman (1992) for recent critical accounts with reference to economics (cf. Hoover 1995a).
[7] Hume's account of causality is developed in book I, part III of the *Treatise*. See also the *Enquiry*, sections IV–VIII.
[8] Because of worries about mental causes, Hume ultimately drops the requirement of spatial contiguity.

experience of the "constant conjunction" of cause and effect that gives us the idea of a necessary connection between them. The necessity is the "custom" or "determination" of the mind, a result of frequent repetition, to connect the cause with the effect rather than a property of the objects that are related causally (Hume 1739, p. 156).

The customary conjunction of cause and effect is, for Hume, truly constant. Laws of nature codify the exceptionless regularities between particular observables that constitute scientific knowledge. There is no chance in the world – only ignorance of real causes (Hume 1739, p. 125; 1777, p. 56). The idea of laws as exceptionless relations between facts may well predate Hume; but, after Hume, it has cast a powerful spell over philosophers and, indirectly, over the conception of a law of nature held by scientists and laymen alike. Hume has been read as dismissing necessary connection in favor of constant conjunction, so that cause becomes a mere honorific title – best dispensed with – for law-governed regularity. Famously, Bertrand Russell (1918, p. 180) dismissed causality as "a relic of a bygone age, surviving like the monarchy, only because it is erroneously supposed to do no harm."[9]

Hume's skepticism is thorough. In the course of overthrowing the notion that necessary connection resides in the causally connected objects, Hume (1739, p. 89) states the *problem of induction*: "There can be no *demonstrative* arguments to prove *that those instances, of which we have had no experience, resemble those, of which we have had experience.*" The problem of inductive warrant undermines Hume's own account of causality (Mackie 1980, p. 26). Hume wants to use the constant conjunction of cause and effect in the past to reason from causes to effects in the future, yet there can be no demonstration that the conjunction will remain constant. The philosophical tradition that includes logical positivism has taken Hume to have dismissed necessary connection and replaced it with constant conjunction. But the problem of induction has remained a festering sore on this law-based empiricism. Deeper reflection suggests further difficulties and paradoxes: If laws are statements of regularity, are all regularities lawlike? Or is there a distinction between accidental regularities and nonaccidental (lawlike) ones? If not, how is the lawlike regularity to be picked out? If conjectured laws are confirmed by their instances, what counts as a confirming instance?[10]

[9] Cartwright (1989, p. 7) directs her criticism of an acausal approach to science explicitly at Russell, rather than Hume, and so seems to agree that the standard reading misconstrues Hume.
[10] Two famous examples of paradoxes involving these questions are due to Hempel (1945, esp. p. 13 ff.) and to Goodman (1965, p. 73 ff.). Hempel's paradox is why do the numerous examples of nonblack nonravens (e.g., snow or water) not confirm the induction "all ravens are black," since it is logically equivalent to all nonblack things are non-

Hume's skepticism is a powerful solvent. He does not deny that there are powers at work behind sense impressions. He does deny that we can know anything about them. And he argues that we should not let the vague idea of them lead us astray from the clear and distinct ideas we do possess (Hume 1739, p. 68). He does not deny that there is some ultimate connection between cause and effect beyond their constant conjunction, but only that we can know what it is (Hume 1739, pp. 91–92). And he does not deny "that the operations of nature are independent of our thought and reasoning" (Hume 1739, pp. 168–169). Rather, he denies that the necessary connection of cause to effect is independent of our minds.[11] For Hume, knowledge is either knowledge of the empirically observable or of the logical and mathematical relations among ideas. (Hume (1739, book I, part II) gives an empiricist account of mathematics as well.) His inquiry into the foundations of knowledge, which began with sense impressions as the source of all knowledge, terminates in complete intellectual housecleaning:

*Does it contain any abstract reasoning concerning quantity or number?* No. *Does it contain any experimental reasoning concerning matter of fact and existence?* No. Commit it then to the flames: for it can contain nothing but sophistry and illusion. [Hume 1777, p. 165]

Hume's uncompromising empiricism inspired generations of philosophers. It is evident in the logical positivist distinctions between sense and nonsense and in the interest of Popper, Lakatos, and others, in the criteria that demarcate science from nonscience. It would be an easy surmise, but a wrong one, to think that Hume anticipated Russell and regarded causal connection as a barbarous relic – one of those bits of metaphysics that should be committed to the flames. Causality, for Hume, remains the central element in scientific understanding, whether regarded with disinterested intellectual detachment or completely practically. In the *Enquiry* he writes:

For surely, if there be any relation among objects which it imports to us to know perfectly, it is that of cause and effect. On this are founded all our reasonings concerning matter of fact or existence. By means of it alone we attain any assurance concerning objects which are removed from the present testimony of our memory and senses. The only immediate utility of all sciences, is to teach us, how

---

ravens? Goodman's paradox is why do observations of emeralds up to the present, which is before time *t*, confirm "all emeralds are green" but not "all emeralds are grue," where "grue" is defined to mean green before time *t* and blue after time *t*? While these appear to the outsider to be trivial (almost silly) puzzles, they are, in fact, difficult to resolve in a Humean framework.

[11] Hacking (1983, p. 48) writes, "Hume seldom denies that the world is run by hidden and secret causes. He denies that they are any of our business."

to control and regulate future events by their causes. [Hume 1777, p. 76; cf. p. 26 and 1739, pp. 73, 89)

The constant conjunction of cause and effect is the source of the idea of causal necessity, and it cannot, says Hume, be analyzed further: "It never gives us any insight into the internal structure or operating principle of objects, but only accustoms the mind to pass from one to another" (Hume 1739, p. 169). It is not the irreducible impression of constant conjunction, but the idea of necessary connection that it conveys, that gives casual knowledge its utility. Even if constant conjunction fails to provide insight into internal structures, causes compound to form complex structures, which are knowable through analysis:

A peasant can give no better reason for the stopping of any clock or watch than to say, that commonly it does not go right: But an artizan easily perceives that the same force in the spring or pendulum has always the same influence on the wheels; but fails of its usual effect, perhaps by reason of a grain of dust, which puts a stop to the whole movement. [Hume 1739, p. 132]

Again, while the impression of causal necessity may derive from constant conjunction, the utility of causal knowledge does not depend on repeated experiments. A single experiment properly arranged may convey particular causal knowledge, because it is supported by a complex of causal knowledge long established.

In discovering the origin of the impression of causal necessity in the constant conjunction of a cause to its effect, Hume does not seek to deny the reality of necessary connection or to replace it with regularity. For it is the necessity with which effects follow causes that permits us to know the future and to control it. The constancy of the conjunction is essential to our ability to project it into the future. A relationship that sometimes held and sometimes did not would not warrant this projection. Hume (1739, pp. 125, 171–172; 1777, p. 56) argues that such a relationship involves "chance," and chance is the antithesis of causality. Chance is pure ignorance; causality is knowledge. Where there is exceptionless universal law, knowledge is possible.

In practice, causal reasoning for Hume is only probabilistic (in a broad sense of that term). There are no genuine chances, but there are, as the example of the stopped watch makes clear, countervailing causes – often hidden, and sometimes likely to remain so. We should not expect to find *constant* conjunction in most practical cases. True causal mechanisms are often not what first impressions suggest, but are below the surface and must be discovered through reason and experiment.[12]

---

[12] Hume (1739), book I, part III, section XV, provides rules for drawing causal inferences that anticipate Mill's (1851, vol. I, p. 393 ff.) more famous rules.

With this we come full circle. Hume the economist is the artisan of public policy. He uses his causal account of the macroeconomy – based on evidence and experience, although not on repeated experiments – to reveal the grains of dust in the works, to overturn the facile first impressions of politicians and vulgar commentators as to the true sources of prosperity, and to ground antimercantilist policy.

## Causal Issues

At least four issues are evident in Hume's philosophical analysis of causality and its practical application to macroeconomics.[13] The first is conceptual: What does it mean for one thing to cause another? The second is ontological: What is the essential nature of causes, in Hume's (1739, p. 165) phrase, "in the objects"? The third is epistemological: How could we infer the existence of causal relations from observations? The fourth is pragmatic: How do we employ causal understanding as actors in the world?

In the *Enquiry* (p. 76), Hume distinguishes the concept of causality from its conditions of inference. He writes:

we may define a cause to be *an object, followed by another, and where all the objects similar to the first are followed by objects similar to the second.* Or in other words *where, if the first object had not been, the second never had existed.*

The primary meaning of causality for Hume is necessary connection, the efficacious property that permits us to connect an action with effects beyond the immediately available sense impressions. But no terms are so "obscure and uncertain" as "power," "force," "energy," and "necessary connection" (Hume 1777, p. 62). Looking behind those terms, one finds only constant conjunction as their source. There would appear to be a danger of collapsing the meaning of causation to the conditions of causal inference, a danger of conflating conceptual analysis and epistemology. But Hume is careful to avoid it. Hume distinguishes between practice and philosophical curiosity (Hume 1777, p. 38).[14] Custom and mental

---

[13] Cf. Humphreys 1989, pp. 3–4.
[14] On the difference between philosophical speculation and practical affairs, Hume (1739, pp. 268–269) writes:

But what have I here said, that reflections very refin'd and metaphysical have little or no influence upon us? This opinion I can scarce forbear retracting, and condemning from my present feeling and experience. The *intense* view of these manifold contradictions and imperfections in human reason has so wrought upon me, and heated my brain, that I am ready to reject all belief and reasoning, and can look upon no opinion even as more probable or likely than another. Where am I, or what? From what causes do I derive my existence, and to what condition shall I return? Whose favor shall I court, and whose anger must I dread? What beings surround me? and on whom have I any influence, or who have influence on me? I am confounded with all these questions, and begin to fancy myself in the most deplorable condition

habit are the guides to practice (Hume 1777, p. 44). Hume's macro-economics exemplifies his practical reasoning. In the *Essays*, he virtually never reasons directly from constant conjunctions to causes. Instead, Hume relies on established background knowledge and a few cases to construct arguments for particular causal structures. In principle, far up the causal chain, Hume supposes that the established background knowledge is grounded in constant conjunctions. Constant conjunction is the source of the idea of necessary connection, but not the touchstone for practical causal inference in the world.

Similarly, there could be a danger of conflating ontology and epistemology. But again, Hume does not fall into the trap. Careful investigation of cause and effect convinces Hume that we must be "sensible of our ignorance" of the ontology of causation and rest content with knowing that our minds are formed to make customary causal inferences irrespective of what causes may really be in the objects.

With respect to causal inference itself, we can distinguish two questions – both of which are practically illustrated in the *Essays*. The first question is the direction of causation. Hume considers questions such as, does prosperity cause money or money prosperity? The second is the question of causal strength. As we have already observed, Hume proposes quantified causal hypotheses such as, an increase in the stock of money causes an *equiproportional* increase in the level of prices. And he asserts inferential rules such as, an effect must be proportional to its cause.

In the remainder of this chapter and in later chapters, we shall return frequently to these four issues in the analysis of causality.

## 1.2 PROBABILISTIC CAUSALITY IN THE HUMEAN TRADITION

Constant conjunction is, in Hume's view, the source of the idea of causal necessity; yet, as we have seen, he downplays the importance of perceived repetition in the epistemology of the *Treatise* or the *Enquiry* and ignores it virtually completely in the practical causal inferences of the

imaginable, inviron'd with the deepest darkness, and utterly depriv'd of the use of every member and faculty.

Most fortunately it happens, that since reason is incapable of dispelling these clouds, nature herself suffices to that purpose, and cures me of this philosophical melancholy and delirium, either by relaxing this bent mind, or by some avocation, and lively impression of my senses, which obliterate all these chimeras. I dine, I play a game of back-gammon, I converse, and am merry with my friends; and when after three or four hour's amusement, I wou'd return to these speculations, they appear cold, and strain'd and ridiculous, that I cannot find in my heart to enter into them any farther.

Here then I find myself absolutely and necessarily determin'd to live, and talk, and act like other people in the common affairs of life.

*Essays.* Many modern accounts of causality, meant to be Humean in spirit, have relied nonetheless upon the criterion of constant conjunction. These may be referred to collectively as *regularity accounts.* The most important regularity account for macroeconomics is the *probability account.*

Modern probabilistic theories of causality (Suppes 1970 is the classic statement) begin with the assumption that truly constant (i.e., exceptionless) conjunction is too strong a condition to be useful. And, as we have seen, Hume would not disagree, although he would locate the reason for any exceptions in countervailing or intervening causes. Whether Hume is right or whether instead causal relations are fundamentally probabilistic or whether chances are both real and causal are questions on which probabilistic accounts are typically agnostic.[15] Rather than constant conjunction, probabilistic accounts look for relationships that tend to hold on average and for the most part. Crudely, $A$ causes $B$ on probabilistic accounts if $P(B|A) > P(B)$, where "$P(X)$" means "the probability of $X$" and "$X|Y$" means "$X$ conditional on $Y$."[16] The most prominent causal analysis in macroeconometrics, due to C. W. J. Granger (1969, 1980), falls into the class of probabilistic accounts.[17]

Probabilistic causality aims to answer questions such as, does taking aspirin cause headaches to end? This might be investigated in a controlled study in which headache sufferers are given aspirin and the results noted. The conjunction will not be constant. But aspirin will be said to cause headaches to end if the probability that one's headache will end if one takes an aspirin is greater than the probability of its ending unconditionally (i.e., whether one takes an aspirin or not). Consider an example: suppose that, in a trial using 100 patients (50 given aspirin, 50 given a placebo), the results are as reported in Table 1.1. Since P(*Headache Ending | Taking Aspirin*) = 30/50 = 3/5 > 40/100 = 2/5 = P(*Headache Ending*), the probabilistic account implies that taking aspirin causes headaches to end.

Some commentators have considered whether the inequality in the rule $A$ causes $B$ if $P(B|A) > P(B)$ should be "greater than" or simply "does not equal" (so that $A$ causes $B$ if $P(B|A) \neq P(B)$). The question is,

---

[15] Paul Humphreys (1989, p. 46) provides a classification of different varieties of theories of probabilistic causality based on how each answers such questions.

[16] This simple formulation clearly omits the nuances and qualifications that advocates of probabilistic accounts insist upon; see Suppes (1970), Cartwright (1989), Eells (1991), and Humphreys (1989) for examples of sophisticated treatments of probabilistic accounts.

[17] See Spohn (1983a), for a discussion of the relationship of Granger's analysis to other probabilistic accounts; and see Chapter 7, Section 2 in this book for a thorough discussion of so-called Granger-causality.

**Table 1.1. Results of 100 Trials**

|  |  | Treatment | |
|---|---|---|---|
|  |  | Placebo | Aspirin |
| Headache | Does Not End | 40 | 20 |
|  | Ends | 10 | 30 |

must causes increase probabilities or merely affect them?[18] Similarly, some have argued that a cause must make an event probable; that is, $A$ causes $B$ only if $P(B|A) > 50$ percent (Papineau 1985, p. 57 ff.). But these appear to be largely terminological disputes. Aspirin may increase the probability of a headache continuing (the cure is worse than the disease) or it may be relatively ineffective, but nevertheless help in some cases (e.g., $P(B|A) < 50$ percent, yet $P(B|A) > P(B)$). We can agree either way that aspirin would be *causally relevant* to headaches even if we did not wish to honor it with the name "cause." The language of causes often reflects our practical interests more than the underlying reality. Had we posed the question, does aspirin cause headaches to continue?, rather than, does it cause them to end?, the data in Table 1.1 would still be relevant, and they would tell against our hypothesis. We might, then, refer to aspirin as an "inhibitor" of headaches, rather than a cause of their ending. The tone of our description would be different, but the causal claims would have remained unchanged.

The probabilistic theory of causality in its simplest form is faced with a formidable difficulty: $P(B|A) > P(B)$ implies that $P(A|B) > P(A)$; that is, if $A$ causes $B$, then $B$ causes $A$.[19] Notice that the data in Table 1.1 show that $P(\text{Taking Aspirin} \mid \text{Headache Ending}) = 30/40 = 3/4 > 1/2 = 50/100 = P(\text{Taking Aspirin})$. According to the definition, the headache ending causes patients to take aspirin. But even the advocates of the probabilistic account naturally resist this implication.

This is an example of an important problem in econometric analysis known as *observational equivalence*.[20] The problem does not arise for Patrick Suppes (1970) or Nancy Cartwright (1989, ch. 1),

---

[18] Granger (1969, p. 376), for example, defines causality in terms of an increase in conditional over unconditional probability, while Granger (1980, p. 330) defines it as inequality between conditional and unconditional probability.

[19] Proof: $P(A, B) = P(B|A)P(A) = P(A|B)P(B)$, where $P(A, B)$ is the joint probability of $A$ and $B$, by Bayes' theorem. If $P(B|A) > P(B)$, then by substitution $P(B)P(A) < P(A|B)P(B)$, so $P(A|B) > P(A)$. QED.

[20] See Simon (1953b), Basmann (1965, 1988), Sargent (1976), and Glymour (1980, pp. 316–317).

because, following Hume, they also impose the condition that causes must precede effects. Thus, $P(B_{t+1}|A_t) > P(B_{t+1})$ does not imply that $P(A_{t+1}|B_t) > P(A_{t+1})$), where the subscripts are time indices. We rule out the conclusion that the headache ending causes the patient to receive the aspirin, because in no case does the ending of the headache precede the receiving of the aspirin.

If $A$ precedes $B$ and $P(B_{t+1}|A_t) > P(B_{t+1})$, Suppes (1970) refers to $A$ as a *prima facie cause* of $B$. $A$ is not a cause *simpliciter*, because there are clear circumstances in which we do not believe that $A$ causes $B$, even though the conditions for *prima facie* causality are fulfilled. The classic example is a falling barometer. Although it is a *prima facie* cause of a storm, we do not generally regard it as a genuine cause of a storm. Economic examples also exist. The money supply rises in late November and early December; it is a *prima facie* cause of Christmas spending; yet we do not think that the rising money supply genuinely causes Christmas spending.[21] Hume provides a similar example. Rising stocks of precious metals are *prima facie* causes of falling interest rates, yet he argues that they are not genuine causes. His reasoning carries the same form as the other two examples. In each case, a third factor is the genuine cause of both the *prima facie* cause and the *prima facie* effect.

The idea of a common third cause is illustrated in Figure 1.2. Here later times are indicated above earlier times ($t_3$ later than $t_2$ later than $t_1$) and the arrows show the true causal connections. Reichenbach (1956, pp. 158 ff.) refers to this characteristic pattern as a *conjunctive fork*. The conjunctive fork is also reflected in a characteristic pattern of conditional probabilities. While in each case in Figure 1.2 $P(B|A) > P(B)$, $P(B|A\&C) = P(B|C) > P(B)$.[22] Conditional on $C$, $A$ does not raise the probability of $B$ at all. $C$ is said to *screen off A* (see also Salmon 1984, pp. 43–45, passim). A more satisfactory definition of probabilistic cause might then be: $A$ causes $B$ if $A$ is a *prima facie* cause of $B$ and there are no $C$'s that screen $A$ off from $B$. As we shall see presently, even this is not enough.

Reichenbach (1956) places the conjunctive fork and the no-screening-off condition in the center of his causal analysis. He adopts an axiom that he calls the *common-cause principle*: "If an improbable coincidence has occurred, there must exist a common cause." So, if $A$ and $B$ are corre-

---

[21] J. Simon (1970, p. 234); Kaldor (1970, p. 6), who writes: "Nobody would suggest (not even Professor Friedman, I believe) that the increase in note circulation in December is the cause of the Christmas buying spree. But there is the question that is more relevant to the Friedman thesis: could the 'authorities' prevent the buying spree by refusing to supply additional notes and coins in the Christmas season?"

[22] Time subscripts are omitted to keep the notation uncluttered; we continue to assume that causes must precede effects.

## Time

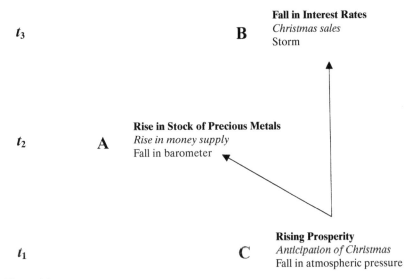

$t_3$             **B**    **Fall in Interest Rates**
*Christmas sales*
Storm

$t_2$    **A**    **Rise in Stock of Precious Metals**
*Rise in money supply*
Fall in barometer

$t_1$            **C**    **Rising Prosperity**
*Anticipation of Christmas*
Fall in atmospheric pressure

Figure 1.2

lated, either *A* causes *B*, *B* causes *A*, or they have a common third cause *C*.

The common-cause principle has been subjected to substantial criticism (e.g., see van Frassen 1977). Some of the problems are practical. For example, spurious correlations may appear in small samples that do not reflect characteristics of the population and would not appear in large samples (as Reichenbach 1956, pp. 157–158, was aware). Any two series that trend over time appear to be correlated, even though *ex hypothesi* they have no causal connection (see Chapter 7, Section 2). More substantially, Cartwright argues that the common-cause condition interpreted strictly as a screening criterion is violated whenever causes operate indeterministically, and that such indeterminism threatens the basis of any probabilistic account of causality (see Chapter 4, Section 3).[23]

The history of the probabilistic approach is one of posing counterexamples in which the probabilities violate our causal intuitions and then making adjustments to the probabilistic definition of the causal relation

---

[23] For critical discussions of the common-cause principle, see van Frassen (1977) and Humphreys (1989, pp. 66–70).

Figure 1.3

that preserve the insight of the original notion of *prima facie* cause while rendering it adequate to our intuitions.

One famous example is due to G. Hesslow (1976). Birth control pills contain chemicals that are known to clot blood, yet the probability of coronary thrombosis (i.e., blood clots in the heart) conditional on taking birth control pills is *lower* than the unconditional probability of thrombosis (i.e., $P(Thrombosis|Pills) < P(Thrombosis)$), which suggests that birth control pills do not cause thrombosis, but reduce or inhibit it. The puzzle is explained by observing that pregnancy raises the probability of thrombosis and birth control pills lower the probability of pregnancy. The observed probability of thrombosis conditional on taking birth control pills is the net result of a direct and an indirect effect as indicated in Figure 1.3. The "+" and "–" signs indicate whether the adjacent link indicates a cause that promotes (raises the probability of) or inhibits (lowers the probability of) the effect. Whether $P(Thrombosis|Pills)$ is greater or less than $P(Thrombosis)$ depends on the relative quantitative strength of the three causal linkages (cf. Cartwright 1989, pp. 99–101).

If Figure 1.3 describes the situation accurately, then the example suggests further restrictions that might be placed on the probabilistic definition of cause. First, the definition might be restricted only to direct causes with a more general *cause simpliciter* defined with relation to the causal ancestors of the effect (Cartwright 1989, p. 128).[24] But this is not quite enough, for while it clears up the linkages between birth control pills and pregnancy, and pregnancy and thrombosis, it leaves the initial puzzle unresolved. Pregnancy is not an intervening third cause in the

---

[24] This is only one of a number of strategies for dealing with issues such as those raised by Hesslow's example that Cartwright (1989, ch. 3) investigates. See also Eells (1991, ch. 4) and Chapter 4, Section 3 in this book.

sense that it will completely screen-off the effect of the birth control pills. It is a partial screen. Suppose that we were to divide women in the sample into those who became pregnant and those who did not, then for each of these subgroups $P(Thrombosis|Pills) > P(Thrombosis)$. A second restriction might then be imposed: The definition might require *contextual unanimity*; that is, the change in probability must be the same in all homogeneous backgrounds (e.g., whether pregnant or not) (Cartwright 1989, pp. 55–56, 143; Eells 1991, p. 86).

Another puzzle for probabilistic causation is known as "Simpson's paradox."[25] It can be illustrated with a simple example. Consider the problem of sex discrimination in faculty salaries.[26] Consider a cohort of male and female professors closely matched for age and professional stature. Suppose that there are 35 males with an average salary of $62,857 and 15 females with an average salary of $57,333.[27] We would be tempted to declare that female faculty were discriminated against in compensation. But now suppose that we dig deeper and divide the faculty up according to departmental affiliation. Imagine that all of the faculty are drawn either from the Engineering Department or the English Department and that the average salaries are distributed as in Table 1.2. The paradox is that, if we apply the same standard that tempted us to declare that female faculty were discriminated against in the larger pool, we would now have to declare that no individual department discriminates against its female faculty.

A typical response to the paradox is to argue that the initial evidence for discrimination was incorrect because Engineering and English professors were mixed up in the conditioning class, which confuses the probability criterion.[28] The problem is similar to Hesslow's birth control pill/thrombosis example. Consider departmental affiliation as an

---

[25] C. Simpson (1951) originally considered the case in which a positive association in subpopulations disappeared when the whole population was considered. A number of situations in which statistical dependencies that are consistent in subpopulations disappear or are reversed in whole populations have come to be referred to as Simpson's paradox, even though they are different from the case actually considered by Simpson (see Spirtes, Glymour, and Schernes 1993, pp. 64–70). Cartwright (1983, p. 24) traces the paradox back to Morris Cohen and Ernst Nagel (1934, p. 449) and Yule (1903). The paradox is also discussed *inter alia* in Cartwright (1989, pp. 55–56), Eells (1991, pp. 62–64, 72), and Irzik (1996, p. 251).

[26] The example is suggested by an actual study of graduate admissions at the University of California, Berkeley (Bickel, Hammel, and O'Connell 1975; cf. Eells 1991, pp. 62–64). It is easy to imagine other cases.

[27] The discussion is conducted here in terms of average salaries because the dispute is with respect to a continuous variable, but it could without any loss be recast into the form of conditional probabilities.

[28] Eells 1991, pp. 71 ff.; Cartwright 1983, pp. 37–38.

**Table 1.2. Salaries by Sex and Academic Department**

|  |  | Male | Female |
|---|---|---|---|
| Engineering | Salary | $80,000 | $86,000 |
|  | Number | 20 | 5 |
| English | Salary | $40,000 | $43,000 |
|  | Number | 15 | 10 |

intervening third cause. The data in Table 1.2 reverse the causal assessment.[29] There is contextual unanimity: Being female raises salaries in
both departments.

The analogy to Hesslow's example is imperfect. The third cause does
not confuse the initial assessment of probability because of the presence
of a direct and an indirect effect (at least not necessarily) in which one
link counteracts the other. Instead, it arises entirely from the lack of
homogeneity of the original conditioning class (i.e., faculty from both
departments considered together). Departmental affiliation does not
screen-off the influence of sex – even partially. Rather it interacts with
it to determine the size of salaries. The relationship can be expressed
visually as in Figure 1.4. Causal influence runs directly from both *Sex* and
*Department* to *Salary*, but *Sex* and *Department* also interact as shown by
the arrows into and out of the circle. For example, such a diagram might
represent a situation in which being an English professor, regardless of
sex, was worth $40,000 a year; while being an engineering professor,
regardless of sex, was worth $80,000 a year. Being female, regardless
of discipline, carried a premium of $3,000 a year over being male. And,
being a female engineer carried a premium of $3,000 a year in addition
to everything else. The causal possibilities are underdetermined by the
data presented; one can easily imagine other quantitative mechanisms to
generate Table 1.2. Whatever the mechanisms, the need for them reinforces the restriction (implicit in the requirement of contextual unanimity) that legitimate conditioning must be with respect to homogeneous
classes.

Notice that acceptance of a joint causal linkage of *Sex* and *Department* to *Salary* does not resolve the question of sex discrimination.
Sex and departmental affiliation are correlated, and, according to the

---

[29] Had the data shown the same average salaries for males and females (or more generally if salary conditional on departmental affiliation were probabilistically independent
of sex), then departmental affiliation would have been a screen.

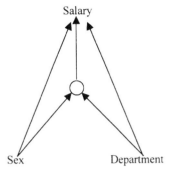

Figure 1.4

common cause principle, there ought to be a causal explanation. It may be that women more often choose English over engineering. The question of why they do so and whether invidious discrimination is involved would remain even after that causal link were established. Or it may be that engineering chooses to hire fewer women and pay they more ("tokenism") or that English chooses to hire fewer men and pay them less ("reverse discrimination"). Either way, a richer description of the causal influences and more data would be needed to resolve the issues.[30]

The present point is not to resolve the issue of sex discrimination nor to analyze the risks of drugs nor even to discover the appropriate modification of the definition of probabilistic causality. Rather it is to note the strategy through which such definitions are refined. When conditional probabilities proved to be inadequate to capture the asymmetry of causation (observational equivalence), the probabilistic account appeals to temporal ordering to impose enough structure to generate clear casual direction.[31] When *prima facie* cause proved inadequate to deal with common causes, further structure in the form of the no-screening-off condition had to be added. In the face of puzzles like Hesslow's or Simpson's paradox, even more structure in the form of

---

[30] One irony of the way in which this example is constructed is that if the Engineering Department is completely unbiased while the English Department actively discriminates in favor of women, the greater the reverse discrimination in favor of women at the departmental level, the more the overall statistics will indicate discrimination against women. For example, take the salaries in Table 1.2 as given, but assume that the Engineering Department hires men and women equally ($12\frac{1}{2}$ of each) and the English Department hires women exclusively (25 women, 0 men). The average salary for women remains $57,333, while the average salary for men rises to $80,000.

[31] Examples abound; see *inter alia* Eells (1991, pp. 118, 171) and Spohn's (1983, p. 77) observations on Suppes.

contextual unanimity and homogeneity has to be added. Relationships of regular association (if not constant conjunction) are complicated with structural restrictions in order to capture our causal intuitions.

## 1.3 THE PRIMACY OF STRUCTURE

**Implicit Structures**

The strategy of the advocates of the probabilistic account suggests its own inadequacy. Not every $A$ such that $P(B|A) > P(B)$ is regarded as a cause of $B$. As we saw in the last section, a workable probabilistic account must recognize that $A$ and $B$ might have common causes, or that third causes might intervene between them, or that probabilities might be calculated with respect to nonhomogeneous reference classes, and so forth. Much of the effort in developing probabilistic theories of causality is spent in elucidating the refinements necessary for preventing probabilistic relations like *prima facie* cause from getting it wrong. In the earlier example, despite the fact that the probabilities indicated that the ending of the headache *prima facie* caused the taking of the aspirin, the advocate of the probabilistic approach rejects the conclusion. Somehow the probabilities got it wrong. But what does it mean to get it wrong? To ask such a question is to have a strong idea of what it is to be right. Certainly, this is partly a matter of causal intuitions. But what are these "causal intuitions" intuitions of? It would appear that there is an implicit notion of causal structure involved in setting the agenda for probabilistic causality.

The puzzles and problematic cases that suggested the various refinements to *prima facie* cause appeal to descriptions of the hypothetically true causal mechanism. Often (as in Figures 1.2 and 1.3) they are clarified using path diagrams in which arrows indicate the direction of causal influence and, sometimes, parameters or "+" or "−" signs indicate the strength or at least the character of the influence. A probabilistic analysis is judged adequate only when it corresponds to the structure of such mechanisms. The primacy of these mechanisms is implicit in the very notion that a probabilistic account should resolve the various problems and puzzles that they describe.

Probabilistic accounts of causality conflate the concept of cause with the method of inferring cause. They commit what Mario Bunge (1963, p. 45) calls "the original sin of empiricism . . . the identification of *truth* with its *criterion.*" Roy Bhaskar (1975, p. 171), making the same point as Bunge, refers to the *epistemic fallacy*. The advocates of the probabilistic approach, however, find it nearly impossible to be consistent, and constantly refer to implicit causal structures. The central thesis of this book is that what is implicit in the strategy of the probabilistic approach ought to be explicitly embraced: *Causal structures are fundamental.* Probabilistic accounts are misrepresented when they are seen as elucidating the concept of causality. In fact, they are useful not for conceptual analysis, but as part of the epistemology of inferring causal structure from observations. A fuller explication and justification shall be taken up in later chapters. For the moment, a brief sketch must suffice.

**Making Structures Explicit**

The structural approach asserts that physical, social, and economic structures are real. They exist externally and independently of any (*individual*) human mind (cf. Mäki 1996 and Chapter 5 of this book). These structures possess causal powers and transmit causal efficacy. They account for the ubiquitous human experience of manipulation and control, as well as for the characteristic asymmetry of causal relations (the taking of the aspirin is the cause – not the effect – of the ending of the headache).

Hume's objection that terms like "power" and "efficacy" are merely names with no more meaning than "scarlet" has for a blind man (Hume 1739, p. 168) is based on his implausible first premise that sense impression alone is the source of all ideas. The blind man may learn much about scarlet from its role in the whole complex of his knowledge: from the reaction of bulls, from the behavior of women (see, e.g., Hardy 1874), from the electromagnetic spectrum.[32] We have no sense experience of the color ultraviolet; yet we do not doubt its reality. From the behavior of thermometers placed adjacent to the violet stripe of light refracted through a prism, to the construction of the eyes of birds and observations of their behavior (see the *Economist* 1997, pp. 71–72), to the glowing of stones under the invisible illumination of "black light," we piece together a set of relationships and capacities that are named "ultraviolet." Equally we know "power," "efficacy," "agency," "energy," "necessity," "connection," and "productive quality" (to cite the complete list of synonyms in Hume 1739, p. 157) from their functions. They are not placeholders for I-know-not-what, but placeholders for particular claims about physical and social experience – both direct and yet-to-be-observed.

---

[32] Locke (1690, book III, chapter 4, section 11) refers to "the studious blindman" who understands "scarlet" as "like the sound of a trumpet." While Locke, like Hume, emphasizes how far short the blind man falls of knowing scarlet, much knowledge is had in just such a manner.

Structural accounts reject the view that probability relations are useful in characterizing the concept of cause, although they may grant them a part in the epistemology of inferring causal structure from observations. A successful structural account must define the concept of cause differently. Causes have sometimes been regarded as necessary conditions for their effects. But this is not acceptable in its unadorned form since the same effect might be achieved from different causes – even simultaneously occurring different causes (the case known as *causal overdetermination*). Causes have sometimes been regarded as sufficient for their effects. But this will not do in its unadorned form either: For example, the match is the cause of the explosion, but only in conjunction with other necessary factors – the explosive, air, the right humidity conditions, and so forth. Many accounts of causation have tried to start either with necessity or sufficiency and add qualifications that would eliminate these obvious, as well as more sophisticated, objections. Chapter 2 develops and defends a variant of the well-known analysis of J. L. Mackie (1980) adequate to meet these objections.

Any variation on criteria of sufficiency or necessity appeals to the logic of conditional statements ("if $p$, then $q$"). Such conditionals are sometimes known as "counterfactuals" because "if $p$, then $q$" may be true even when $p$ is false.[33] To assert a counterfactual is to assert the existence of a disposition: The nature of the situation is such that $q$ is disposed to occur when $p$ does. Such dispositions need not be deterministic; $q$ may occur only with some probability. Nevertheless, invariance is implicit in counterfactuals and related dispositional claims. A counterfactual cannot be rightly asserted if, when its antecedents are fulfilled, it no longer entails (probabilistically at least) the same consequence. Invariance of this sort underwrites the intuitively appealing notion that causes are efficacious in bringing about their effects.

A causal structure can then be seen as a network of counterfactual relations that maps out the underlying mechanisms through which one thing is used to control or manipulate another. In effect, the structural account makes the empirical claim that there is something more "in the objects" than Hume's purely associative notion of causality allows. *A* causes *B* is an empirical claim that there is a real relationship through which *A* can be used to control *B*. Hume is correct that the reality is not read off the experience. Rather our knowledge of reality consists of empirically based conjectures, and is necessarily corrigible.

---

[33] More accurately they are known to philosophers as *subjunctive conditionals* (see Sanford 1989). They are distinguished from *material conditionals*, which are true whenever $p$ is false, as well as when both $p$ and $q$ are true.

The structural account needs to be fleshed out in several directions. On the one hand, the appeal to counterfactuals raises ontological issues. Truly fundamental ontological questions (e.g., about the nature of modalities such as necessity or probability) are beyond the scope of this inquiry. The question of whether macroeconomics can be given a realistic interpretation, however, is central to it and is taken up in Chapter 5. On the other hand, economically satisfactory descriptions of causal mechanisms are needed.

The probabilistic account of causality runs together the conceptual problem of defining what a cause is with the epistemological problem of inferring causes from evidence, and it does so in order to avoid making any ontological commitment to what causes are "in the objects." Thus, in Granger's analysis, to take an econometric example, causes are defined by the procedure (i.e., conditional probabilities) through which they are inferred.

Structural accounts suit economics partly because they keep the issues of definition, ontology, and epistemology distinct. Not characterizing cause by an inferential procedure, the structural account accommodates a variety of evidence, including, in the right circumstances, the evidence of conditional probabilities. Two inferential questions must be kept distinct. The first is, given *A* and *B*, what is the direction of causal influence, if any, between them? The second is, given that *A* causes *B*, what is the strength of the causal influence of *A* on *B*?

Probabilistic accounts are appealing in fields in which causal direction is implicitly known. One reason that even the advocates of probabilistic accounts resist the implication that the ending of headaches causes the receiving of aspirin, is that it is a controlled experiment in which the assignment of aspirin or placebo to patients is made independently (temporally, but more importantly) logically prior to the determination of whether their headaches ended. The causal direction is from aspirin to the end of headaches *if there is any causal connection at all*. This situation, for example, is frequent in medical research: With fairly straightforward controls probabilistic methods can be used to assess the causal efficacy of a pathogen or a treatment (implicit structural understanding, of course, informs the design of those controls).

Following on from the work of Trygve Haavelmo, the Cowles Commission in the late 1940s and early 1950s clarified the formal conditions under which systems of equations could measure causes conditional upon their accurately *identifying* the structure of causal relations (see Epstein 1987 and Morgan 1990). In the Cowles Commission analysis it is clear that, relative to the measuring exercise, identifying assumptions are *a priori* (typically theoretically grounded) assumptions. The lesson from econometrics that Cartwright (1989, ch. 1) offers for the edification of physics is that to obtain probabilistic measures of causal strength requires substantial prior knowledge of causal structure (or, at least, the pretense of it).

Unfortunately, economics does not provide convincing structural commitments (even implicitly) so well as some other fields, such as medicine, do. It is often the case that incompatible identified systems of equations are consistent with the theoretical and institutional constraints of economics. As in the example of aspirin and headaches, these alternative, identified systems are observationally equivalent in the sense that they generate the same probability distribution for the data. The nature and source of the additional structure needed to thwart observational equivalence lay at the heart of the debate over "explicit causal chain" models or "process analysis" that raged for 15 years after the late 1940s (Morgan 1991). One side of this debate (Wold 1960, Strotz and Wold 1960, and others) embraced Hume's requirement that causes occur before effects. They argued that, since causality is both logically and temporally asymmetric, econometrically estimated systems should reflect this asymmetry through the use of recursive systems of equations in which only variables dated earlier can affect variables dated later. The other side (Simon 1953b, Basmann 1965, and others) pointed out that, because of observational equivalence, the purely syntactic distinction between recursive and simultaneous systems was not enough to capture the causal asymmetry. Other fields, of course, are not immune from the problem of observational equivalence. Whether the HIV viruses cause AIDS is a question of causal direction – no different in principle than whether money causes prices or taxes cause government spending (see Chapter 9). (The heterodox view of the virologist Peter Duesberg (1996) is that HIV is simply the most common opportunistic infection of AIDS patients and not the cause of their disease.)

The estimation of identified systems of equations assumes an answer to the question of causal direction in order to pursue the question of measurement. Granger-causality assumes a temporal structure in order to address the question of causal direction using purely probabilistic methods. The approach to causal inference developed in Chapter 8 is to recognize that the very notion of structure implies that a causal structure must remain invariant to interventions in some dimensions and serve to transmit interventions in one part of the structure to other parts of the structure.

## 1.4  TAKING MACROECONOMICS SERIOUSLY

The following chapters defend and develop the structural approach to causality as the appropriate analysis for macroeconomics. Notwithstanding that Hume's illustrations of causal processes are physical – one billiard ball striking another – Hume was an historian, social critic, and economist, but not a physicist. The causal analysis of the *Essays* is certainly not social physics. Hume probably drew more upon the experience of ordinary life (albeit the life of the drawing room) than on Newtonian mechanics. Still, it is the billiard ball, not the precious metals, that have captured the imaginations of philosophers of causality. Cases drawn from physical sciences have, since Hume, dominated causal analysis. It is striking how many philosophical discussions of causality regard the adequacy of the analysis to quantum mechanics as the touchstone of its success (e.g., Bunge 1963, Redhead 1987, Cartwright 1989). I propose to take the constraints imposed by macroeconomics just as seriously as contemporary philosophers have taken those of quantum physics. Like Hume, we shall in the following chapters consider from time to time cases and analogies drawn from the physical or biological spheres, but the practical object of the investigation will be to illuminate issues relevant to macroeconomics. To take macroeconomics seriously is not to be committed to any particular theoretical development in modern macroeconomics (e.g., to real-business-cycle models), which remain the subject of intense debate; rather it is to accept the constraints imposed by the very subject matter to which all such debatable theories refer.

Chapters 2–4 develop the structural approach as a general account of causality. Although some of the examples are macroeconomic, the approach of these chapters is meant to have general relevance. Chapters 5–7 consider the particular problems of macroeconomics and the quantitative methods usually applied to them. Chapter 5 defends the idea that there is an independent macroeconomic reality to which a realist, structural approach could apply. I offer arguments against the common assumption that macroeconomic phenomena are reducible to microeconomic phenomena (the argument for microfoundations for macroeconomics). Causal relationships among macroeconomic variables are *not* best thought of as a shorthand for causal relations among microeconomic agents. Chapter 6 notes the special limitations that macroeconomics places on causal analysis. In particular, I argue that causal orderings in macroeconomics cannot usefully rely on temporal ordering as a basis for causal asymmetry. I also argue that it is necessary to defend an idea of macroeconomic structure analogous to physical structure, and that this requires a characterization of the identity conditions for such structures. Chapter 7 relates the structural approach to various attempts to provide macroeconometric analyses of causality. Chapter 8 suggests a methodology for determining causal direction that is grounded in the structural approach. Chapters 9 and 10 are two case studies in which the methods of Chapter 8 are applied to the problems of determining the causal direction between taxes and government spending and between money and prices. Finally, Chapter 11 asks where the considerations of this book leave us and what the likely direction of future research on causality in macroeconomics may be.

# 2

# The Notion of Causal Structure

> Discontented people might talk of corruption in the
> Commons, closeness in the Commons and the necessity of
> reforming the Commons, said Mr. Spenlow solemnly, in con-
> clusion; but when the price of wheat per bushel had been the
> highest, the Commons had been the busiest; and a man might
> lay his hand upon his heart, and say this to the whole world,
> – "Touch the Commons, and down comes the country!"
>
> – Charles Dickens, *David Copperfield*

Hume and his successors struggled with the two most characteristic features of causality: Causes are efficacious, they make things happen; and
causes are asymmetrical, that is, efficacy runs from cause to effect and
not from effect to cause. Hume is wrong to believe that all that we experience and the only source of our ideas – no matter how apparently
abstract – are sensations. Causal relations, though they may be misap-
prehended and are corrigible, are part of the ordinary experiences of life.
We have no genuine doubt that this is so, and we would find it hard to
conduct our lives without causal knowledge. The subjunctive mood is
largely used to describe such causal connections. Yet it is evident that
causes are, in general, neither necessary nor sufficient for their effects.
In this chapter, we begin with J. L. Mackie's (1980) conditional account
of causality, connecting it with Herbert Simon's account of causal direction, to develop an account of causal structure adequate to the problems
of efficacy and asymmetry.

## 2.1 A CONDITIONAL ANALYSIS OF CAUSALITY[1]

On Mackie's (1980, ch. 3) account, a comprehensive set of antecedent
conditions $A$ *causes* a consequence $C$ if and only if $A$ is necessary and

---

[1] Parts of this section are drawn from Hoover (1990), with permission.

sufficient for $C$. Hence, the complex proposition follows that if $A$ is true, then $C$ is also true; and if $C$ is true, $A$ is true. If it is possible by direct control to bring about $A$, then $C$ will also be brought about. Actual control is not needed. For "$A$ causes $C$" is true, sustains the counterfactual, "if $A$ had been true, then $C$ would have been true." (The term "sustains" indicates that the causal claim warrants our ordinary use of the counterfactual even though the causal claim and the counterfactual may not stand in a truth-functional relation to each other.) The set $A$ does not rule out causal overdetermination. $A$ should be taken to be the disjunction of every *minimally sufficient* subset of antecedent conditions for $C$. Each of these subsets $(A_i)$ is the conjunction of conditions, or absences of countervailing conditions, such that if the truth value of any of the conjuncts were different, it would no longer be true that $A_i$ implies $C$. If one or more of the $A_i$ are true, then $C$ is true; and, if $C$ is true, at least one of the $A_i$ is true. The comprehensive set $A$ may then be called the *full* cause, and each $A_i$ may be called a *complete* cause of $C$.

For the most part, however, we do not seem to be interested in complete causes; and any requirement that a cause be necessary *and* sufficient for $C$ seems overly strong. Necessity appears to be crucial: If $C$ is true, $A$ must be true; every consequence must have a cause. The notion of a full cause reminds us, however, that if $C$ is a skinned cat, each $A_i$ represents a different way to skin it. No one $A_i$ is necessary for $C$, although $A$ is.

Common usage suggests that we may wish to weaken the criteria for a cause still further. Any of the conjuncts of $A_i$ may be thought of as a cause; although, unless $A_i$ has only one element, this conjunct will not be sufficient for $C$. Hence, if $A_1$ consists of a certain density of water in the atmosphere and a temperature below the dew point, while $C$ is a rainstorm, not only is $A_1$ the cause of $C$; but most of us would willingly agree that the low temperature on its own was also *a* cause of the storm, although not a sufficient (or perhaps necessary) cause. In order to capture this use of "cause," Mackie proposes that an antecedent $a_j$ (an element of $A_i$) is *a* cause of $C$ if $a_j$ is an *I*nsufficient, *N*onredundant member of an *U*nnecessary but *S*ufficient set of antecedents of $C$. This he dubs the *INUS condition*.

Using the INUS condition to define "cause" should appeal to the economist faced with complex economic problems. For any economic situation that we wish to explain, we probably do not know every $A_i$. Indeed, for any $A_i$ we are unlikely to know every one of the conjuncts it comprises. And, even if we do know all or most of the conjuncts, all but a few may be of little interest to us, appearing as background or environmental considerations. The institutional structure of Wall Street may be of crucial importance in obtaining a particular yield curve for government securities; yet a reserve manager at the Open-Market Desk of the Federal Reserve Bank of New York is fully justified in referring to a particular open-market sale as *the* cause of a change in the yield curve, while ignoring the institutional structure.

We may in our minds divide up the universe of antecedent conditions of a consequence $C$ into those that are relevant, $A$, and those that are irrelevant, non-$A$. $A$ may be divided into its disjuncts, the $A_i$; and one or more may be selected for our special concern. The conjuncts of a particular $A_i$ also may be divided into particular causes (INUS conditions) that command our attention, and the remainder we relegate to the causally relevant background, which we shall call the *causal field*.[2]

The partition of a minimally sufficient subset of $A$ into a cause and a field allows us to focus our attention on some aspect of a causal problem, while not forgetting that any particular cause may be only an INUS condition. Not all partitions, however, are equally worthy. In a well-worn example, the gas leak rather than the striking of a match is most usefully considered the cause of the explosion in a house, although the reverse would be true in a gas plant. In either case, the presence of air would normally be relegated to the causal field, although not if the explosion took place on the moon. In general, the causal field contains the background circumstances and standing conditions that may be taken safely for granted.

Singling out one cause from a sufficient set may simply express a "conversational point" (Mackie 1980, p. 35). The notion of a causal field has an obvious normative or legal use. It is true that if Lincoln had not been at Ford's Theater or Booth's pistol had not been loaded, then Booth's pulling the trigger could not have caused Lincoln's death. But for attributing legal or moral blame, the first two conjuncts of the minimally sufficient set of conditions for Lincoln's death are rightly placed in the field, and our complete attention is directed to the assassin's action.

It would be wrong, however, to believe that the causal field has only a normative use. The causal field of any problem is also a pound for those standing conditions that simply do not change. Equally, although the causal field may be known to change, it may still be sufficiently stable to represent the boundary conditions for our particular causal interest.

As was pointed out in Chapter 1, Section 3, causes rendered counterfactually are implicitly general and invariant. Counterfactuals pick out dispositions – properties or characteristics that manifest themselves only under the right circumstances. It is incoherent to say that $B$ is disposed

---

[2] The notion of a causal field originates with Anderson (1938).

to follow $A$, $A$ is a sufficient condition for $B$, or $A$ is the cause of $B$ and, yet, to maintain that when $A$ is instantiated $B$ is not also instantiated. This is not to say that there cannot be circumstances or countervailing causes that prevent the instantiation of $B$ when $A$ is instantiated; but rather that, to believe in the truth of the counterfactual when $B$ fails to follow $A$, one must, at least implicitly, appeal to such circumstances or countervailing causes. The *generality* of the counterfactual relation is implicit in the comparison that counterfactuals necessarily make between cases in which their antecedents are fulfilled and cases in which they are not. The *invariance* is implicit in the fact that a true counter-factual must describe the same disposition whether that disposition is realized or not. To say that a diamond is hard except when it strikes another object or that a child is intelligent except when he has an intel-lectual task to perform is incoherent. (We shall consider the questions of generality and invariance further in Section 2.6.)

A related implication of the counterfactual account is that there is a natural distinction between dispositions (which may or may not be instantiated) and realizations (which are the instantiated or actualized).[3] As Mackie points out, causes are INUS conditions rather than necessary conditions, but this is at the level of dispositions: There is more than one combination of antecedents that imply a consequence, so no one com-bination is necessary. Nevertheless, causes play out in definite ways, so that the INUS conditions that are actually realized are *necessary in the circumstances* for their effects (Mackie 1980, p. 31). Consider a complete cause, $A_i$. It is "necessary in the circumstances" when the $a_{ij}$, the elements of $A_i$, each occur and "the circumstances" are the absences of the other $A_k$, $k \neq i$. Each element, $a_{ij}$, is also necessary in the circumstances, since each element is nonredundant. It is the notion of necessity in the cir-cumstances that captures the idea that causes compel their effects. The necessary connection is not found in the dispositional relationship but in the realizations as they actually play out.

Causal overdetermination presents a puzzle for the conditional account (see Mackie 1980, pp. 43–47 for a detailed discussion). If two suf-ficient sets of causes occur at the same time, are they both necessary in the circumstances? Are the elements of each INUS conditions?

---

[3] By "realization" I mean a particular instantiation of the variables that stand in a causal relationship. The analogy is to probability distributions governing statistical processes. The outcome of rolling a pair of dice is governed by a probability distribution in which "snake-eyes" has a 1/36 chance of occurring, and so forth. Fair dice are disposed to obey the probability distribution. A particular roll of the dice yields a particular realization of the probability distribution – one of the possible outcomes. Similarly, even in nonprob-abilistic contexts, we can refer to the particular instantiation of any general relationship as a realization.

A man is taken from a car accident that would surely cause his death, but for the emergency intervention of a surgeon. Unfortunately, the surgeon in the process of mending his heart slips and severs his aorta, killing the crash victim. Without the surgeon, the man dies; with the surgeon, the man also dies. While such cases are often considered by legal and causal theorists, this one is not particularly difficult for the conditional account. The car accident in a certain background (or field) of collateral conditions would be an INUS condition for the man's death. Equally, the actions of the surgeon in a different background of collateral conditions would be INUS conditions for the man's death. But different actions of the surgeon (not slipping with the scalpel, for instance) would have been INUS conditions for the man living. The INUS conditions in each case refer to dispositions that may or may not be realized. And, as we progress from a disposition to die as the result of the crash, to the opportunity to be saved through the surgeon's intervention, to the death through surgical error, the realizations of various dispositions change the backgrounds and render sets of conditions that were sufficient in one field insufficient in the newly realized field. We have no difficulty in seeing that while the surgeon's slip caused the man's death as events actually played out, the crash *would have* ensured that death absent the surgeon's intervention, and the intervention *would have* saved his life absent misadventure.[4]

Exact simultaneity of antecedents presents a harder case. Two villains shoot a man and the bullets lodge in his brain at precisely the same moment with fatal effect. On the assumption that each bullet would have been separately sufficient in the circumstances (excluding the other bullet), there is no problem in calling each an INUS condition of the death. But this is a dispositional claim. Can we say that each caused the death as it played out, when neither was necessary in the circumstances (which include the other bullet)? The mechanism of the death is not in doubt. Taken together, the two bullets caused his death. And since each would have done so separately, the semantic question of whether to call each "a cause" or "the cause" when they acted simultaneously is not important. For assigning legal or moral blame, issues for which intent is important, the dispositional level, at which each is an INUS condition, is decisive, especially because, unlike the example of the car crash and the

---

[4] In Hardy's *Far From the Madding Crowd*, Shepherd Oak lances the bloated stomachs of a number of sheep to release built-up gas that resulted from having eaten dangerous weeds. He saves most of the sheep from certain death; but, despite his skill and intentions, he also kills a few by puncturing something vital. The example is less contrived than the case analyzed by Eells (1991, ch. 6) in which a cat is killed in a rescue from a diabolical device, even though *ex ante* the rescue attempt raises the cat's probability of survival.

hapless surgeon, the way in which events played out did not alter background conditions in a way that changed the INUS status of the alternative routes to death.

The tricky legal and moral cases are ones that are analogous in different degrees to the case of the car crash and the surgeon. A not uncommon scenario in real life is the criminal who is saved from a murder charge merely by the good fortune (both for himself and the victim) of rapid intervention of the paramedics. The law distinguishes attempted murder from inflicting grievous bodily harm partly on the basis of unrealized dispositions – that is, on whether or not the injury was an INUS condition for death in background conditions similar to the ones that actually played out. In legal and moral cases, a clear distinction is sometimes drawn, for example, between the first bullet causing a death and a subsequent bullet desecrating a corpse. As the time between the bullets becomes closer, there no doubt comes a point at which the fact that the bullets do not strike exactly simultaneously is not considered salient and who caused the death in the final analysis is moot, because both are guilty of murder. Intentions and beliefs matter for law and morality in a way in which they are irrelevant for science.

Causal overdetermination is, perhaps, an important forensic problem. It is not practically important in macroeconomics. Nevertheless, it does force us to recognize clearly the distinction between instantiated and uninstantiated counterfactuals (dispositions and their realizations), which turns out to be important in macroeconomics.

## 2.2 CAUSAL ORDER

Cause is an asymmetrical relationship: Causes produce effects; effects do not produce causes. This is the shoal on which regularity accounts typically founder. That $A$ is regularly associated with $B$ does not tell us which is cause and which is effect. The INUS account is a sophisticated regularity account. And while $A$ is an INUS condition of $B$ need not imply that $B$ is an INUS condition for $A$, this will often be the case. The convention of representing causes using arrows aims to capture asymmetry, while restrictions that are implicitly placed on the use of the arrows aim to capture effectiveness. In general, if rain causes wheat to grow, wheat growing does not cause rain. (Mutual causation cannot be automatically ruled out, but it is not regarded as primitive.) What is more, the relationship between cause and effect cannot be rendered as a merely logical relationship. If in stating the INUS condition, we render the sufficiency of the complete cause for the effect in terms of logical (or material) implication, we face a puzzle: If rain implies that wheat grows ($R \supset W$) then we can conclude that the wheat not growing implies that the rain failed ($\sim W \supset \sim R$), yet we would be loath to conclude that the wheat not growing *caused* it not to rain. Simon and Rescher (1966, p. 323) refer to this puzzle as "the rock of contraposition." No binary relationship that contraposes can capture the directionality of causation.

Useful in many ways, INUS conditions nevertheless are not themselves adequate to capture asymmetry and effectiveness. Consider Figure 2.1, in which $C$ and $D$ are causes of $A$ and also INUS conditions for $A$; and $D$ and $E$ are causes of $B$ and also INUS conditions for $B$.[5] The figure corresponds to an example due to Mackie (1980, pp. 84–86) in which $A$ stands for the sounding of the hooters at a factory in Manchester; $B$ for Londoners leaving work at their factory; $C$ for causes other than it being five o'clock for the Manchester hooters to sound; $D$ for it being five o'clock; and $E$ causes of the Londoners leaving work other than it being five o'clock. In logical notation, we can indicate that $C$ and $D$ are INUS conditions of $A$ as $C \vee D \supset A$. Assume that each of the INUS conditions are complete causes. The definition of $C$ implies that $C$ and $D$ are the full cause of $D$ and that, therefore, the conditional can be strengthened into a biconditional:

$$C \vee D \equiv A. \tag{2.1}$$

Similarly, that $D$ and $E$ are INUS conditions of $B$ can be rendered $D \vee E \supset B$; and the definition of $E$ implies that $D$ and $E$ are the full cause of $B$, so that again the conditional can be strengthened into a biconditional:

$$D \vee E \equiv B. \tag{2.2}$$

What we wish to show is that, even though $A$ is clearly a cause neither of $D$ nor of $B$, it is nonetheless an INUS condition of them both. To be an INUS condition, we need to show that there are sets of conditions (different perhaps) that include $A$ that, while perhaps not necessary, are nonetheless sufficient for $D$ and $B$. Suppose that none of the other causes exclusive of it being five o'clock for the sounding of the hooters in Manchester occurs. Rendered symbolically, suppose $\sim C$. Together with (2.1), $\sim C$ implies (by disjunctive syllogism and conjunction):

$$\sim C \ \& \ A \equiv D. \tag{2.3}$$

$A$ is, therefore, an INUS condition for $D$. Substituting (2.3) into (2.2) yields

$$\sim C \ \& \ A \vee E \equiv B. \tag{2.4}$$

$A$ is, therefore, an INUS condition for $B$.

---

[5] Figure 2.1 and the proof in the text that $A$ is INUS for $B$ and $D$ are in the spirit of the more detailed rendering of Mackie's example provided by Cartwright (1989, pp. 26–27).

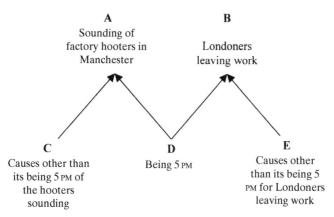

Figure 2.1

Thus, while it is implausible to believe that the sounding of the Manchester hooters either causes it to be five o'clock or causes the Londoners to leave work, the sounding of the hooters in Manchester is nevertheless an INUS condition both for the time of day and the actions of the Londoners. That *A* is an INUS condition for *B* is the deterministic analogue of spurious correlation, similar to the cases noted in Chapter 1, Section 2, of the fall in the barometer appearing on probabilistic criteria to cause the storm, or a rise of the money supply appearing to cause Christmas expenditures.

Obviously, a satisfactory account of causality must go beyond INUS conditions. There are two common strategies, which we have already met in Chapter 1. First, if one insists that causes precede effects, then *A* cannot cause *D* even though *A* is INUS for *D* (cf. Cartwright 1989, p. 26, where this assumption is explicit). This assumption will not resolve the problem of spurious correlation; for suppose that *B* occurs just a bit after *A*, the INUS relationship and the temporal order still incorrectly indicate that *A* causes *B*. The second strategy, often used in conjunction with it, is to impose a screening criterion. In this (nonprobabilistic) case, *D* screens off *A* from *B*, and *A* would not be a cause of *B*, if in the union of *D* and *A* $(D \cup A)$, *A* is not an INUS condition for *B* because it is *redundant*. In Chapter 6 I shall argue that neither of these strategies for capturing the direction and efficacy of causes can be successful given the nature of macroeconomics. For the moment, let us set that aside and concentrate, more constructively, on an alternative way of characterizing causal order.

Economists are used to the language of variables and equations. Despite the examples so far, the INUS account is not limited to events that either happen or do not happen (0/1 or true/false events). There is no bar to interpreting functional relations in terms of INUS conditions. Mackie (1980, ch. 6) distinguished between *neolithic* (or unquantified) cause and *functional* (or quantified) cause. A functional cause implies a neolithic cause: For example, the fact that dropping a ball from Carfax Tower causes it to fall at a velocity of *gt* implies that dropping a ball from Carfax Tower causes it to fall. Functional causes are more likely to be useful in economics. The identification of "functional" with "quantified" must be qualified; for functions can range over variables that are not in fact measurable (see Bunge 1963, p. 277; Katzner 1983).

Simon (1953b) offers a useful account of causal order in a system of simultaneous linear equations. One variable in such a system is said to cause another if one must know the value of the first variable in order to solve for the value of the second variable. Simon's notion of causal order is one of a hierarchy of nested subsystems in which the causes are located in the more central subsystems and the effects in the more peripheral subsystems. Causality is therefore related to (block) recursive ordering familiar in the literature on simultaneous systems in econometrics.

To illustrate Simon's analysis begin with a simple linear system:

$$p_{11}q_1 \qquad = p_{10}, \tag{2.5}$$

$$p_{21}q_1 + p_{22}q_2 \qquad = p_{20}, \tag{2.6}$$

$$p_{33}q_3 \qquad = p_{30,} \tag{2.7}$$

$$p_{42}q_2 + p_{43}q_3 + p_{44}q_4 = p_{40}, \tag{2.8}$$

where the $q_j$ are variables and the $p_{ij}$ are parameters. The distinction between variables and parameters is roughly that parameters are "variables" subject to direct control, and variables without further qualification are subject only to indirect control. This may appear to be an unusual distinction, but we postpone a more thorough discussion until after the broad outlines of Simon's analysis are clear.

Equation (2.5) is a *minimal self-contained subsystem* of equations (2.5–2.8): If one knew the values of the parameters $p_{10}$ and $p_{11}$, one could determine the value of $q_1$ in equation (2.5) without reference to any other equation. Equation (2.7) is also a minimal self-contained subsystem. Equations (2.5) and (2.6) together are also a *self-contained subsystem*, although not a minimal one: Once one knows their parameters, both $q_1$ and $q_2$ can be determined. Since the value of $q_1$ is independent of the value of $q_2$, whereas the value of $q_2$ is not independent of the value of $q_1$, $q_1$ causes $q_2$. Equations (2.5)–(2.7) are self-contained.

Similarly, equations (2.5)–(2.8) are self-contained: $q_1$ causes $q_2$, and $q_2$ and $q_3$ cause $q_4$.

Causal order is characterized here by a purely syntactic property of a formal system that expresses the relationships among variables. But, as Simon was aware, even if we restrict ourselves to linear systems, equations (2.5)–(2.8) constitute only one of an infinite number of representations that determine precisely the same values for the variables. Each has a different parameterization, and every possible causal order may be represented.

For the system to represent a definite causal order, it is necessary to make the additional stipulation that the parameters are independent in the sense that the value of one has no implications for the values of the others. To see what is at stake, consider the simpler system:

$$a_{11}x_1 + a_{12}x_2 = a_{10}, \tag{2.9}$$

$$a_{22}x_2 = a_{20}, \tag{2.10}$$

where the $a_{ij}$ are parameters and the $x_j$ are variables. In this system $x_2$ apparently causes $x_1$. Compare this with the system:

$$a_{11}x_1 + a_{12}x_2 = a_{10}, \tag{2.11}$$

$$b_{21}x_1 + b_{22}x_2 = b_{20}. \tag{2.12}$$

Here $x_1$ and $x_2$ would appear to exhibit mutual causation or simultaneity. The values of the variables, however, may be the same in each system. This is possible, for example, if either of two sets of identities holds: (A) $b_{21} = a_{11}$, $b_{22} = a_{12} + a_{22}$, and $b_{20} = a_{10} + a_{20}$, or (B) $a_{22} = (a_{11}b_{22}/b_{21}) - a_{12}$ and $a_{20} = (a_{11}b_{20}/b_{21}) - a_{10}$. Knowing which causal order actually describes the variables is then a matter of knowing whether the $a_{2j}$ or the $b_{2j}$ are the true parameters. If the $a_{2j}$ are true parameters, they may be chosen independently of each other and independently of the $a_{1j}$. But, then, no matter how the $a_{1j}$ are chosen, the $b_{2j}$ must adjust to maintain the identities (A). Equally, if the $b_{2j}$ are true parameters, they may be chosen independently of each other and the $a_{1j}$, and the $a_{2j}$ must adjust to maintain the identities (B). The problem is that there is no choosing between these forms simply on the basis of the observed values of the variables: once again, we encounter the problem of *observational equivalence*. Yet which causal order is correct makes a considerable difference. Suppose that we can intervene to alter the value of the parameter $a_{11}$. If the first ordering is correct, only the value of the $x_1$ is altered; whereas if the second order is correct, the values of both $x_1$ and $x_2$ are altered.

Simon (1953b, pp. 24–27) offers a solution to this problem. Assume that there exist experimenters (among whom nature counts as one) who can alter the parameters of a causal system. This class of interventions defines a new higher-order relation called *direct control*. If by altering a parameter, say $a_{10}$ in (2.11), the experimenter can change the value of a variable, say $x_2$ in (2.12), he has indirect control over $x_2$. The causal order is the property of the economic structure that determines which variables can be altered independently of which other variables.[6]

Causal relations on Simon's view are invariant to interventions among the parameters. Simon refers to the step up to talk of actual or hypothetical interventions as the adoption of a "metalanguage" of direct control. The point is that a distinction must be drawn between the formal representations of the causal relations and the actual causal relations that those representations are meant to capture. The fact that variables show a particular functional relationship or pattern of covariance does not capture the essence of causality. The important thing is that those relations remain stable in the face of interventions of control (actual or hypothetical). Solving the problem of observational equivalence through an appeal to interventions of control is an implicit recognition that cause is not a formal property of a model without reference to the real world, but a semantic interpretation of the world (see Simon 1955, pp. 194, 195; also see Zellner 1979, p. 25).

It is customary in many contexts, particularly in econometrics, to read effects on the left- and causes on the right-hand side of an equation or system.[7] Yet the symmetry of the equal sign encourages us to rearrange the symbols in a manner that does not respect the structure of control that is meant to be implicit in the syntax.[8] A number of causal analysts have employed graph-theoretic accounts of causation in which the causal arrows are regarded as primitive (see, for example, Glymour et al. 1987 and Pearl 1998a,b; see also Pearl 2000). The distinction between parameters and variables permits Simon to assign directionality to causes. In

---

[6] Cartwright's (1989, pp. 20–22) account of Simon concludes, I believe incorrectly, that Simon's analysis is unsuccessful in resolving the problem of observational equivalence. Her account is based on lecture notes on Simon from a class given by Clark Glymour. As reported by Cartwright, Glymour would appear to muddle the essential distinction between parameters and coefficients, which are complex combinations of parameters, and to fail to see that when Simon speaks of direct control, it is always direct control over parameters and not over the complex coefficients. Simon himself may lead readers astray by writing as if the equations were the fundamental building blocks of his system. A sympathetic reading, I believe, would take the choice of parameterization to be fundamental, as I do here.

[7] Cartwright (1989, p. 18) cites long-established precedents for this convention in physics as well as in social sciences.

[8] "Equations, merely in virtue of their form, are unfit to tell us by themselves what depends on what" (Sanford 1988, p. 398).

effect, it is the choice of parameterization that assigns the arrowheads to the causal linkages represented in a graph. If we respect that distinction, any mathematically equivalent syntax will equally well represent the same causal structure. It would reinforce the implicit semantic content, however, if a system like (2.9)–(2.10) were rendered as

$$x_1 \Leftarrow a_{10}/a_{11} - (a_{12}/a_{11})x_2, \qquad\qquad (2.9')$$

$$x_2 \Leftarrow a_{20}/a_{22}, \qquad\qquad (2.10')$$

in which the "$\Leftarrow$" (or "$\Rightarrow$") can be read as a directional equal sign. Simon stresses complete systems, that is, linear systems in which there are as many variables as equations. The distinction between variables and parameters permits us to note causal direction even in incomplete systems. We may write $w$ causes $z$ as

$$z \Leftarrow \phi w, \qquad\qquad (2.13)$$

even though it is incomplete because the causes of $w$ are unspecified, so long as we know that $\phi$ is directly controlled (and therefore independent of the choice of other parameters). In effect, any system can be formally completed in the manner that equation (2.10) completes the system (2.9)–(2.10) with an equation that says that some causal variable can be selected to take whatever value one likes in its range. Such variables could be represented themselves as parameters or, indifferently, represented as in (2.10) as selected using the parameters of their own equations. Such variables could be thought of as external causes; whereas variables whose values depend not only on the parameters of their own equations, but on the variables of causally prior equations, could be thought of as internal causes (see Chapter 3, Section 1).

Any variable that causes another in Simon's sense may be regarded as an INUS condition for that other variable (cf. Cartwright 1989, pp. 25–29). Say that $q_1$ in equations (2.5)–(2.8) takes the value 17 and $q_2$ takes the value 8. The variable $q_1$ causes $q_2$. Its being 17 is, however, insufficient for $q_2$ to be 8; that depends on the values of $p_{21}$, $p_{22}$, and $p_{20}$ as well. But given these values, $q = 17$ is nonredundant; were $q_1$ to be 18, $q_2$ would not be 8. Yet, the set of particular values of $q_1$, $p_{21}$, $p_{22}$, and $p_{20}$ is sufficient but not necessary for $q_2 = 8$; there is an infinite number of alternative sets of values for these variables that make $q_2 = 8$.

As this example illustrates, Simon's equations also capture the distinction between dispositions and instantiations. The domains of the parameters represent all the possible instantiations of antecedent conditions. The ranges of the variables represent the possible consequents.

Their relationships are in general dispositional, but any particular para-meterization represents a particular instantiation in which the causes are necessary in the circumstances for the effects.

## 2.3 PRAGMATICS

Initially at least, Mackie finds the source of causal priority precisely where Simon finds it:

The causally prior item, then, seems to be the one which we can directly control, and by which we can indirectly control the other. Causes are effective, effects are not. [Mackie 1980, p. 168][9]

But an account of causal efficacy in terms of direct control is not entirely satisfactory in Mackie's view. First, it seems hopelessly anthropomorphic. Second, it seems to argue in a circle; for what is direct control but causal efficacy. Both Mackie (1980, ch. 7) and Simon (1953a, p. 51, and 1953b, p. 12) reject temporal order as the basis of causal priority. Yet, one might think that direct control sneaks temporal priority in through the back door.

Although Mackie is right to be dissatisfied on purely philosophical grounds, I do not think that these problems need detain us long when dealing with pragmatic economics or that we need to concern ourselves with Mackie's replacement of direct control with a notion of *fixity* of causes and effects. Economics is about *human* decisions. The charge of anthropomorphism has less resonance in the social sciences than in the natural sciences. Nonhuman factors are, of course, often involved in economic processes. And many economic parameters (e.g., the aggregate marginal propensity to consume) are not within the direct control of any specific individual, even though they are the products of human choices. For pragmatic purposes, we take an anthropologist's view, which accepts the social consequences of choice as data, rather than a policy advisor's view, which seeks to shape the choices and their social consequences.

The circularity of defining causality through direct control cannot be gainsaid. The importance of this fact depends on the issue addressed. The aim of regularity theories of causality – deterministic or probabilistic – is in large measure to provide an ontological reduction of causality to something else. A definition of causality employing the notion of direct control rules out that sort of reduction. That is not troubling if, as we argued in Chapter 1, the causal relation is fundamental and the urge to reduce it to constant or probabilistic conjunction is grounded in Hume's

---

[9] Cf. Cartwright (1983, ch. 1), who stresses the effectiveness of causes.

erroneous view that only sense impressions are ultimately real and epistemologically accessible.[10]

Circularity is less troubling epistemologically than it might seem to
be ontologically. Several authors have made the point that "a causal
connection can be proved only from causal connections already known"
(Anderson 1938, p. 128).[11] Cartwright (1989, ch. 2) adopts the slogan "no
causes in, no causes out." Causal inference is possible on this view only
if a sufficient number of interfering factors have been eliminated through
direct control (the laboratory experiment is the paradigm case), so that
the observable frequencies reflect the true probabilities of individual
causal connections.[12]

The conceptual circularity of defining cause through direct control
is of little concern for epistemological issues involved in econometric
inference. It is enough to perform the thought experiment, "if we could
directly control X . . . ," to characterize a workable concept of cause and
to use the analogy, as Simon suggests, of nature with an experimenter to
glean information useful to causal inference. In economics it is often reasonable to regard some knowledge as indubitably true and not currently
at risk. In some cases, it takes neither deep theorizing nor sophisticated
econometrics to know where direct control lies. In most countries, for
instance, the central bank directly controls the monetary base. The
central bank therefore causes changes in the monetary base. Propositions

---

[10] Forster (1997a) argues that causes are in fact reducible to probabilities, but he builds
into his analysis that probabilities are a characteristic of physical structures of the sort
that we have argued support counterfactuals. While Forster's account is similar to that
endorsed here, it begs the question of whether reductionism is possible by appealing to
a much richer notion of probability than the advocates of reductionist accounts could
support.

[11] Cf. Cartwright (1989, p. 39) and Spohn (1983, p. 380).

[12] She defends the general idea of this sort of causal inference by an appeal to Glymour's
(1980) "bootstrap" methodology in which empirical evidence and maintained
assumptions deductively imply new results. ("Bootstrapping" in Glymour's sense must
not be confused with the statistical technique of bootstrapping statistics through
resampling variables or estimated errors; see Jeong and Maddala 1993. For a brief exposition of bootstrapping in Glymour's sense see Hausman 1992, pp. 310–312.) Glymour
does not regard the maintained assumptions as necessarily and finally true; rather they
are regarded as true (or true enough) given current knowledge. The maintained assumptions are not at risk in the particular inference, but they may themselves be challenged
and denied or modified on the basis of bootstrap inferences using other evidence
in other situations. Bootstrap methodology closely resembles Charles S. Peirce's theory
of empirical inquiry in which the most important inferential form is abduction
rather than induction, in which all beliefs are held to be fallible, but in which particular
beliefs are regarded temporarily and contingently as indubitable. See Harris and
Hoover (1980) and Hoover (1994c) for references and brief accounts of Peirce's theory
of inquiry.

about direct control, which may be disputable in another context, are taken to be indubitable in the process of inferring indirect causal orderings.

## 2.4 THE CAUSAL FIELD

The background conditions that we call the causal field, whether made explicit or left tacit, are essential to the study of causal structures. Our causal concerns are always more or less local, but we must consider the conditions under which we can ignore wider causal relations and how our understanding of even those relations of local concern varies with changes in the causal field.

Variables that are genuinely unchanging can always be impounded in the causal field. Such constancy can occur in two different ways. The parameters that govern a particular variable may themselves be constants. When one billiard ball causes another to land in the pocket, the force of gravity is a field condition. It is an INUS condition for the ball landing in the pocket (without it the balls would likely fly off the table), yet it is constant, because the parameters that determine it are themselves constant. A variable may also be constant because it has been controlled to be so. A boat may be held on a constant course in shifting seas only by the continual correction of the rudder (i.e., frequently changing the parameters). The constant course of a submarine may, nevertheless, be relegated to the causal field in considering the cause of a torpedo striking a warship. The variations of the rudder in themselves would matter only if they also affected the course of the torpedo or another INUS condition of the torpedo striking the ship through some other channel. Linear relations such as those analyzed by Simon rule out effects of parameters not mediated directly through a single variable. As we shall see in Section 2.5, linearity is needlessly restrictive.

As well as unchanging variables, the causal field may include variables that, although causally relevant, influence variables that interest us only through variables not relegated to the causal field. When we ask whether hot water causes an egg to cook, the means of making the water hot (electric resistance or burning gas) does not matter as the temperature of the water mediates the causal influence of the heat source.

The constancy of a variable does not alter its ontological status (cf. Humphreys 1989, p. 67). It may be an INUS condition and a cause of its effects. Yet, it poses the epistemological problem well known to econometricians of insufficient variance, sometimes called the problem of *non-excitation* (cf. Engle, Hendry, and Richard 1983, p. 285). Consider an experiment in which different objects are dropped through a constant distance, $x$, near the surface of the earth. Suppose that theory tells us that

$$x = 0.5gt^2 d^{2\theta} a^{2\mu} e^{2\varepsilon}, \tag{2.14}$$

where $g$ is the constant of acceleration due to gravity, $t$ is time, $d$ is the density of the object, $a$ is the density of the air, $e$ is the base of the natural logarithms, $\theta$ and $\mu$ are unknown constants, and $\varepsilon$ measures every omitted INUS condition of the falling object. Assume that $g$ is constant, as the experiment is conducted very near the surface of the earth. Also, $a$ is constant, as all the drops take place close to each other in time and place. Letting uppercase letters stand for the logarithms of lowercase letters and recalling that $x$ is a constant, we might estimate an ordinary least squares regression of the following form to determine the relationship between the density of the object and the time of fall:

$$T = \alpha + \beta D + \upsilon. \tag{2.15}$$

The estimate of $\beta$ measures $-\theta$, and $\upsilon$ measures $-(\varepsilon - \bar{\varepsilon})$, whereas $\alpha$ measures $0.5(\log 2x - 2\mu A - G) + \bar{\varepsilon}$. Both $a$ and $g$ can be regarded as part of the causal field. Equation (2.15) is a robust description of the relationship of object density and falling time, but only in these background conditions. Change the conditions, and the relationship changes. But in unchanged conditions, we have no way of extracting the separate roles of $a$ and $g$. In the terminology of econometrics, they are not identified. If we could conduct the experiments at different times and places, so that we could measure some variability in $A$, then we could estimate an alternative regression:

$$T = \alpha + \beta D + \delta A + \upsilon. \tag{2.16}$$

The coefficient $\delta$ measures $-\mu$. It is still not possible to disentangle $g$ from the other things captured in $\alpha$. If we know $x$ and if we assume that $\bar{\varepsilon} = 0$, then $g$ could be recovered from $\alpha$. This is an application of Mill's (1851, p. 404 ff.) "method of residues," in which a cause is identified through subtraction of all the other causes. The idea here is that equation (2.16) and the assumptions about $x$ capture the major causes, while the minor causes cancel out on average. This assumes a particular structure of the causal field. This assumption may sometimes be warranted, but there is often a lurking suspicion that a major cause has been impounded in the causal field so that $\bar{\varepsilon} \neq 0$ and the causes estimated by the method of residues are incorrectly measured. This is the essence of the "omitted variable bias" discussed in most econometrics textbooks.

Constant parameters represent *boundary conditions* for a particular causal structure. Whether to create such a boundary condition is a matter of practical judgment. It is clear that very little economics could be done without placing such limits on the range of admissible interventions. Say, for example, that inflation causes interest rates along the lines of the Fisher hypothesis. This causal ordering is dependent on a background of limited regulation. If the government were to impose regulations similar to the Federal Reserve's old Regulation Q, which prevented interest rates from moving, the boundary condition would have been violated and one would not expect the causal order to stand. Similarly, most of the causal orderings that interest us are conditional on a relatively free-market economy. Shift to a Soviet-style command economy and many causal orderings would surely change.

In both these examples, it would be possible to move the relevant boundary parameters into the parameter space and to define causal orderings that do not vary with the presence or absence of financial regulation or changes in the dominant economic system. For some problems this would be an enlightening thing to do. It is a matter of practical judgment whether we seek such enlightenment. Given the subject matter of economics, it is not possible to define causal orderings that are invariant to *all* interventions: Some parameters will always appear in the causal field; no causal ordering will ever be wholly unconditional.

Along with true constants and parameters regarded as boundary conditions, the causal field may also contain variables that are not central to our concerns. But what to impound in the causal field is not a matter of free choice. The causal field is a background of standing conditions and, within the boundaries of validity claimed for a causal relation, must be invariant to exercises of controlling the consequent by means of the particular causal relation (INUS conditions) of interest.

The possibility of control raises a distinction of greater ontological significance than the constancy of variables: the contrast between variables that belong in the causal field because they stand outside the causal network of interest and ones that belong to the causal field because their influence has been eliminated through the choice of parameterization. This distinction is one of the most common sources of puzzlement about causal structure.[13] If we regard variables and parameters as sets the elements of which are instantiated under particular parameterizations, then the difference can be clarified. Variables that stand outside the causal network that interest us are governed by parameters drawn from null sets. They do not show up in Simon's equations at all. On a causal graph,

---

[13] The need for a distinction between a parameter $\alpha$ that is an element of a nonempty set with a range of values, but which happens to equal zero in a particular case, and a parameter $\alpha$ that is an element of the null set ($\alpha \in \emptyset$), is usually not clearly articulated, but is hinted at in Woodward (1995, pp. 283–284), Pratt and Schlaifer (1984, pp. 14–16), Cartwright (1989, p. 111), Glymour and Spirtes (1988, p. 182), and Humphreys (1989, pp. 38 ff.).

the arrow connecting them is missing. Variables whose effects are eliminated through direct control are governed by particular elements of a set that represents the parameter. Consider $x$ and $y$ as causes of $z$. In the first case, in which $y$ is not part of the causal network relevant to $z$, we might have

$$z \Leftarrow \alpha x + \text{influences from the causal field.} \tag{2.17}$$

In the second case, we might have

$$z \Leftarrow \alpha x + 0y + \text{influences from the causal field.} \tag{2.18}$$

Observationally, there is no difference between (2.17) and (2.18); and, given that our concerns are limited to the case in which the parameter governing the influence of $y$ truly is zero, then there is no reason not to relegate $y$ to the causal field and to regard the two equations as causally identical. Nevertheless, the zero in (2.18) acts as a placeholder and a reminder that in the world described by (2.18) $y$ could be influential: The valve is now closed, but the pipe for which it controls the flow of water exists.

An economic example illustrates the importance of these issues. Monetarism is, in part, the doctrine that changes in the money stock cause (short-run) changes in real incomes and interest rates. It is also, in part, the doctrine that the central bank controls the stock of money. Anti-monetarists sometimes argue that money is endogenous or that the causal direction runs from the real economy to money.[14] The argument for endogenous money can be made in various ways. Most commonly it is argued that the central bank targets an interest rate; and, as a consequence, changes in real income cause changes in the stock of money. Figure 2.2 is a standard IS/LM diagram in which money is a shift variable for the LM curve and real "shocks" are a shift variable for the IS curve. Initially the equilibrium is at point A. If there is a positive shock that shifts the IS curve to IS′, the interest rate $r$ and income $Y$ would rise *ceteris paribus*. But if the central bank targets interest rates at a level $r^*$, then it supplies money shifting the LM curve to LM′. The central bank is said to *accommodate* the shock to income.

The situation can be represented causally as in Figure 2.3. $S$ represents the "shocks," $M$ the supply of money, and $P$ the price level. Assume that prices remain constant, then $P$ is part of the causal field. The solid lines represent causal connections that are given in the economic situation. The money supply is assumed to be in the direct control of the central bank. The central bank can set $M$ to any level it likes arbitrarily

---

[14] The monetarist position is set out *inter alia* in Friedman and Schwartz (1982); the anti-monetarist position in Kaldor (1982) and Moore (1988).

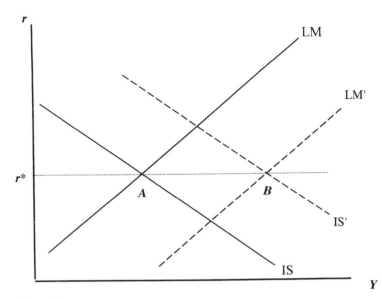

Figure 2.2

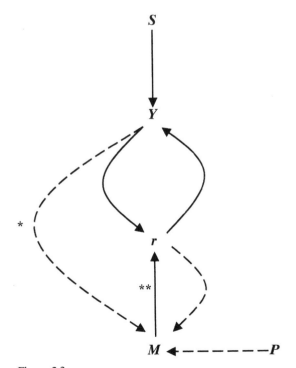

Figure 2.3

or it may react to economic conditions. The dashed lines represent possible causal connections in the bank's *policy reaction function*. The existence of reaction functions distinguishes economics from physical sciences.

The situation may be represented in a system of equations as well.

$$r \Leftarrow a_{10} + a_{11}Y + a_{12}M \tag{2.19}$$

$$Y \Leftarrow a_{20} + a_{21}r + a_{22}S \tag{2.20}$$

$$S \Leftarrow a_{30} \tag{2.21}$$

$$M \Leftarrow a_{40} + a_{41}Y + a_{42}r + a_{42}P + \ldots \tag{2.22}$$

In this system, $r$ and $Y$ are mutual causes (i.e., simultaneous), while $S$ directly causes $Y$ and $M$ directly causes $r$. $S$ is directly controlled by "nature." The inclusion of $P$ and the ellipsis points in (2.22) underlines the fact that a reaction function depends, in principle, on anything to which the agent cares to react.

The monetarist causal analysis occurs when $a_{4j} = 0$ for all $j = 1, 2, \ldots \infty$. In that case, money clearly causes interest rates and incomes and not the reverse. But suppose that the central bank chooses the reaction function

$$M \Leftarrow a_{40} + a_{41}Y. \tag{2.22'}$$

The policy of the central bank activates the causal link marked * in Figure 2.3. This can be considered to be a change in the causal field. Now suppose that the central bank sets $a_{41} = -a_{11}/a_{12}$.[15] Interest rates are now constant. Substituting (2.22') into (2.19) yields

$$r = a_{10} + a_{12}a_{40}. \tag{2.19'}$$

But it would be wrong to think that this effectively closed the causal link marked ** between money and interest rates. It is precisely the existence of that causal link that keeps rates constant. In some sense, this is implicit in the presence of $a_{40}$ in (2.19'), as this is a parameter that governs $M$. But it could be made more perspicuous if we wrote (2.19') in full as

$$\begin{aligned} r &\Leftarrow a_{10} + a_{11}Y + a_{12}(a_{40} + a_{41}Y) \\ &= (a_{10} + a_{12}a_{40}) + (a_{11} + a_{12}a_{41}Y). \end{aligned} \tag{2.19''}$$

Now it is plain that the constancy of interest rates is the result of a *particular* choice of $a_{41}$, and not a generic characterization of the causal connection.

---

[15] If the central bank knew the parameters of the true causal structure they could do this directly, or they could achieve the same result by simply aiming to stabilize $r$, just the same way that a helmsman can hold a ship on course without a quantitative knowledge of the causal connections.

If the world is truly as described in equations (2.19)–(2.22), then the antimonetarist argument is correct up to a point. There exist causal fields in which it is correct to think that income causes money. But they are wrong to think that such a causal field eliminates the causal priority of money over interest rates and, therefore, of money over income. The central bank is not eliminating that linkage but exploiting it in its policy. Even if one regarded the policy as one in which money does not cause interest rates or income, an understanding of the causal structure should lead one to say, "so what?" The causal field in which income causes money is one that has been chosen by the central bank; it has abrogated control. Still, it remains within the power of the central bank to establish control, to change the causal field and to change the variables that appear in its reaction function. As an argument against monetarism in such a world, the accommodationist position fails.[16]

### 2.5 PROBABILISTIC CAUSALITY

So far, we have considered causal structure in a deterministic framework. As Hume was well aware, constant conjunctions are not to be found in economics or other social sciences – or for that matter in most physical sciences. Probabilistic conjunctions are easily introduced into the structural account of causality. There are several routes. Although these correspond to different strategies of econometric estimation, we must be careful not to confuse the equations that we write down with the regression equations that econometricians estimate. Their problem is an epistemological one of measuring the strength of economic interrelationships (not necessarily causal). Our problem is the conceptual and ontological one of understanding the nature of causal interrelationships and representing them symbolically.

The most common econometric strategy for weakening constant conjunction is the *errors-in-equations* approach. An otherwise deterministic system such as (2.19)–(2.22′) might be made probabilistic by adding *error terms*, the $\varepsilon_j$, to each equation:

$$r \Leftarrow a_{10} + a_{11}Y + a_{12}M + \varepsilon_r \qquad (2.23)$$

$$Y \Leftarrow a_{20} + a_{21}r + a_{22}S + \varepsilon_Y \qquad (2.24)$$

$$S \Leftarrow a_{30} + \varepsilon_S \qquad (2.25)$$

---

[16] See Cagan (1965, p. 247) and Koopmans (in Hendry and Morgan 1995, p. 543). The latter writes: "A variable is called instrumental [i.e., a controlling instrument, not an "instrumental variable" in the sense used commonly in econometrics] if it is regarded as controllable by the implementation of policy decisions, even though in some past period it may either have been left uncontrolled or may have been controlled in response to endogenous variables."

$$M \Leftarrow a_{40} + a_{41}Y + \varepsilon_M \qquad\qquad (2.26)$$

The error terms might be thought to represent those INUS conditions that, though they help to determine the effects on the left-hand sides of the equations and are not constant, are not explicitly measured or modeled. So, for example, suppose that, unlike the situation in Figure 2.3, $P$ helped to determine $r$ in (2.23), but affected no other variable. The effect of $P$ would be captured in $\varepsilon_r$, as would any other variables omitted in the same way. One way in which in (2.23) differs from a regression equation is that there is no reason to assume that $\varepsilon_r$ has a mean of zero. An ordinary least squares regression imposes a zero mean on the estimated error term, and any $\bar{P} \neq 0$ would be incorporated into the estimated constant term, which will not in general correspond to $a_{10}$. The error terms might be thought of as conveying that part of the content of the causal field that is variable and affects variables of interest, but it does so in a highly restricted manner. In general, an influence can be impounded legitimately in the causal field only if the resulting $\varepsilon_j$ is not correlated with the other causal variables or with another $\varepsilon_i$, $i \neq j$. The reason is that Reichenbach's common-cause principle (see Chapter 1, Section 2), which should be regarded as, at the least, a useful heuristic, implies that such correlations indicate that some structure has been omitted from the representation, and the omitted structure might alter our assessment of the causal order. If the omitted variables meet the restrictions necessary to be included in the causal field, then the only cost of omission is the loss of efficiency in econometric estimates compared to regressions that recapitulate the complete causal order.

The causal relations in the errors-in-equation approach are made probabilistic on the assumption that the causal field contains a large number of the right sort of variables, sufficiently independent of one another that the law of large numbers can apply so that each $\varepsilon_j$ has a well-defined probability distribution. Ordinary regression equations are not usually thought of as defining probability distributions. Instead, they are usually seen as modeling the observed dependent variables. This interpretation arises from the convention of forming "fitted values" of the dependent variables through setting $\varepsilon_j$ to zero.[17] Nevertheless, the deterministic parts of such equations can be regarded as modeling the mean of the dependent variable, while $\varepsilon_j$ represents the variance (and possibly higher moments).

In the terminology developed earlier, error terms should be regarded as variables rather than as parameters. In the simplest cases, the

---

[17] The analogue for equations like (2.23)–(2.26), which, to repeat, are not regression equations, would require that $\varepsilon_j$ be set to its mean.

moments of the probability distribution governing the error terms (for example, the mean and the variance of the normal distribution) are the constant parameters (chosen by nature). In more complicated cases, these moments might be parameters chosen by policymakers (as in the central bank's reaction function (2.26)) or variables that themselves depend upon other parameters (as, for example, in models with autoregressive conditionally heteroscedastic (ARCH) errors).

The errors-in-equations approach appears to attribute the probabilistic form of the causal representation entirely to our ignorance, to variables in the causal field that are not explicitly modeled. In fact, it leaves the question of whether there is irreducible error open. We could know that there was irreducible error only after we had accounted for every possible INUS condition – and how would we know we had done that?

A second way in which errors are introduced into regressions also suggests that the source of the indeterminism is ignorance. This is the errors-in-variables approach.[18] A typical equation of the original IS/LM system above (say, (2.19)) might be written:

$$(r + \varepsilon_r) \Leftarrow a_{10} + a_{11}(Y + \varepsilon_Y) + a_{12}(M + \varepsilon_M), \qquad (2.27)$$

where the error terms are meant to reflect errors in measuring the true values of the variables (so that, for instance, only $(Y + \varepsilon_Y)$, and not $Y$ itself, is observable). This case is more complicated. Rewriting (2.27) as

$$r \Leftarrow a_{10} + a_{11}Y + a_{12}M + (a_{11}\varepsilon_Y + a_{12}\varepsilon_M - \varepsilon_r), \qquad (2.27')$$

it is obvious that the probability distribution now depends on the same parameters that govern the influences of the right-hand variables on the left-hand variables. Furthermore, since the same mismeasured variables may appear in other equations, the error terms of different equations (the weighted sums of the $\varepsilon_j$) could be correlated, violating the restrictions that we imposed for impounded errors in the causal field. (We shall consider these difficulties in greater detail in Chapter 3.)

A third method of introducing probabilities corresponds to the random coefficients model (see Theil 1971, ch. 12, section 4; Swamy and Tavlas 1995). In this case (2.19) would be rewritten:

$$r \Leftarrow \varepsilon_0 + \varepsilon_Y Y + \varepsilon_M M. \qquad (2.28)$$

While it poses some special problems for regression analysis, the case in which the $\varepsilon_j$ are independently distributed, white noise is similar to the errors-in-equations case already considered. A difference is that the variance and higher moments of the probability distribution depend on the

---

[18] See Morgan (1990, ch. 7) for a history of the debate in econometrics over the errors-in-variables and the error-in-equations approaches to econometrics.

actual values taken by the variables on the right-hand side (such as $Y$ and $M$); that is, the distribution is heteroscedastic. In more interesting cases, the $\varepsilon_j$ are themselves more complex. To illustrate, the coefficient on $Y$ might evolve over time in various ways. For example, it might evolve according to a fixed trend:

$$\varepsilon_{Y,t} = \alpha t + v_{Y,t}, \tag{2.29}$$

where $t$ is a time index, $v_Y$ a white noise random variable, and $\alpha$ a parameter. Or it might evolve as a random walk:

$$\varepsilon_{Y,t} = \varepsilon_{Y,t-1} + v_{Y,t}. \tag{2.30}$$

There are of course many other possibilities, each with implications for the causal ordering of the variables, including the $\varepsilon_j$.

A final way of introducing probabilities into causally ordered systems is suggested by Cartwright (1989, pp. 104–115). She wishes to distinguish the question of "the strength of the influence's contribution, from the question of whether the influence contributed at all" (p. 110). Her concern is a special case of the econometrics of limited dependent variables (see Theil 1971, ch. 12, section 5). In this case, probabilities are more directly modeled than in the previous case, for the probabilities themselves, rather than the value of the variable they govern, are placed on the left-hand side. Typically, the variables are discrete; for example, $x_1 = 1$ or $x_1 = 0$. So, letting $p_{x1} = \text{prob}(x_1 = 1 \mid x_2 = x_2', x_2 = x_2', \ldots)$, where the primes indicate particular values of the corresponding variables, the limited-dependent variable model can be written as:

$$p_{x1} = F(x_1, x_2, \ldots). \tag{2.31}$$

The function $F(\bullet)$ maps the variables onto the zero/one interval. Typically, $F(\bullet)$ is the cumulative normal distribution (giving the *probit* model) or a logistic function (given the *logit* model). To illustrate, the logit model in which $x_1$ depends only on $x_2$ can be written

$$p_{x1} = \left[1 + e^{-(a_{10} + a_{11}x_2)}\right]^{-1}. \tag{2.32}$$

Both the probit and logit model can be extended to systems of equations. These models correspond nicely to the probabilistic scenarios often investigated in philosophical discussions of causality in which events happen or do not with some definite probability.

Cartwright's case, however, is more closely related to the *tobit* model in which the probability distribution is truncated or censored, so that the dependent variable takes either a value of zero or a value from a range of nonzero values (see Amemiya 1985, ch. 10).[19] The standard tobit model (Amemiya 1985, p. 363) for equation (2.19) can be written:

$$r^* \Leftarrow a_{10} + a_{11}Y + a_{12}M + \varepsilon_r \qquad (2.33)$$

$$r = r^* \quad \text{if} \quad r^* > 0 \qquad (2.34)$$

$$= 0 \quad \text{if} \quad r^* \leq 0.$$

From this little system and the properties of $\varepsilon_r$, the probability of the cause operating or not and the strength of its operation can be computed. Cartwright's formulation is similar, but not identical. She treats each INUS condition as acting separately and the probability of action as not depending on the right-hand variables or the $a_{ij}$. In her case, equation (2.19) could be written:

$$r \Leftarrow \beta_{10}a_{10} + \beta_{11}a_{11}Y + \beta_{12}a_{12}M + \varepsilon_r, \qquad (2.35)$$

where the $\beta_{ij}$ are random variables that take the values of either zero or one.

Humphreys (1989, pp. 46–47), citing Deborah Rosen (1982), classifies causality involving probability into three categories. (1) A probabilistic theory of causality uses the apparatus of probability theory but does not assert that causality fundamentally involves chance. A theory of probabilistic causality could be of two types. (2) The causal relationship itself involves a probabilistic element. (3) Causes operate on the probability distributions directly. As for Papineau (1985, pp. 70–71), in case (3) it is not specific values of consequent variables that are causally determined but the chances of their taking on values within some range. Humphreys believes that type (3) is called probabilistic causality only misleadingly. Cartwright appears to believe that the introduction of probability through errors-in-variables or errors-in-equations produces theories of type (1) and that her own preferred theory is of type (2). Our analysis is agnostic as to whether probabilities are fundamental or merely, as Hume thought, expressions of our ignorance. If they are fundamental, every way of introducing probabilities that we have examined is type (3). If they are not fundamental, each collapses to type (1). Once we see the random terms as variables governed by parameters, then the causal relations themselves – even in Cartwright's preferred case – are standing conditions that transmit causal influences,

---

[19] The neologism "tobit" is a hybrid of (James) Tobin, its originator, and "probit," the limited-dependent variable model to which it is most similar. Tobin himself believes that Arthur Goldberger, who coined the name, was aware of the character named Tobit in Herman's Wouk's *The Caine Mutiny*. Wouk probably modeled Tobit on Tobin, his Harvard roommate (see McAleer 1997).

including such interacting causal influences as the $\beta_{ij}$ and $a_{ij}$ terms in equation (2.35).

The causal relation appears to some commentators to be fundamentally deterministic. But is there no room for chance governing the parameters themselves? Some parameters are chosen by human actors. The question of determinism then resolves to a question of whether their actions are determined – a question touched on in Chapter 7, Section 4. Some parameters are determined by "nature." Could it not be that these are random? If they were governed by well-defined probability distributions, we would regard them not as parameters but as variables, with the real parameters being the constants that govern those distributions. There is no reason why the randomness of the "parameters" governing a probability distribution should not be governed by random "parameters," which, in their turn, are governed by random "parameters," and so on to many higher levels. Eventually, however, we must reach the top and find the genuine parameters. Perhaps these may sometimes change, though not in a way that is governed by a well-defined probability distribution. Such changes could be thought of as whimsy or caprice or, to use Peirce's fancier term, *tychism* – the swerves taken by Lucretius' atoms that undermine determinism and introduce innovation but leave the notion of structure intact.[20]

### 2.6 ROBUSTNESS AND INVARIANCE

Both economists and philosophers frequently agree that a causal relation is an invariant relation (see Hausman 1998, ch. 11). Invariance can refer to different properties. Hume's idea of constant conjunction and the idea of exceptionless laws refer to one common notion of invariance. But it clearly will not do in a world of probabilistic causality; and it would fare even worse in a world of whimsy, caprice, or human agency (see Chapter 4). It is not just that laws are inexact, that there is some error term. Rather it is that laws manifest themselves in exceptionless pure forms only in very special cases, if at all. This is the point of experimental setups and *ceteris paribus* clauses.

Cartwright (1989, esp. ch. 4) and Woodward (1995) introduce the idea of *causal capacities* as a means of isolating those features of reality that are invariant in a way that explains the complicated flux of variable behaviors that we observe in the world around us. Capacities are dispositions to act in particular circumstances. As Cartwright (1989, p. 145) puts it:

[20] See Peirce (1934), book I, ch. 2, sect. 4.

If $C$s do ever succeed in causing $E$s (by virtue of being $C$), it must be because they have the capacity to do so. That capacity is something they can be expected to carry with them from situation to situation.

The invariance of capacities belongs to the disposition and not to its instantiations. Aspirin, Cartwright says, has the capacity to cure headaches because sometimes it cures particular headaches regardless of whether it does so frequently or reliably. This is the feature that she means to capture with her mechanism for introducing probabilities into causal relations as in equation (2.35) of the last section:

$$r \Leftarrow \beta_{10}a_{10} + \beta_{11}a_{11}Y + \beta_{12}a_{12}M + \varepsilon_r. \tag{2.35}$$

There are two dimensions of invariance here. The first is that $Y$ has the capacity to cause $r$, and does so to a degree measured invariantly by $\alpha_{11}$. The failure of constant conjunction is captured by the fact that whether it actually does so depends on whether $\beta_{11}$ takes the value 0 or 1. The second is that Cartwright expects the capacity measured by $a_{11}$ to remain constant across contexts. So suppose that in another situation, the size of the government bond stock $(B)$ also causes $r$. Then we can write:

$$r \Leftarrow \beta'_{10}a_{10} + \beta'_{11}a_{11}Y + \beta'_{12}a_{12}M + \beta'_{13}B + \varepsilon'_r. \tag{2.36}$$

The $a_{ij}$ associated with those variables that are also found in (2.35) remain the same and reflect the invariance of capacities between contexts, while the $\beta'_{ij}$ do not in general equal the associated the $\beta_{ij}$, reflecting the fact that circumstances may alter the probabilities of capacities manifesting themselves.

There is an unnecessary assumption of linearity in Cartwright's account. It is not a linearity of causes. She allows that it might be nonlinear functions, rather than the original variables, that enter into an equation such as (2.35) (it might be $Y^2$ rather than $Y$, for instance).[21] Rather, it is a linearity of causal influences: The influence of $Y$ can be added to the influence of $M$, and so forth. But linearity is unduly restrictive, and the notion of a constancy of causal influence does not do justice to Cartwright's intuitions about the distinction between a capacity and the variability of its realization in the world. A gear that forms a part of the differential in a car transmission may have the capacity to translate rotary motion from one axis to another perpendicular to it. It retains that capacity even when the differential is disassembled, although it cannot instantiate it. It carries that capacity into other circumstances, say, when it is incorporated into a drill press. It may also have other capacities to transmit other sorts of motion – or even to be used as a paperweight.

---

[21] This is the situation that econometricians think of as nonlinear in variables, but linear in parameters.

The capacity of the differential to transmit the rotation of the engine to the rotation of the wheels at possibly different speeds is a consequence of the capacities of the gear and the other parts of the differential. The organization of the differential cannot be represented as an adding up of influences nor is the manner in which the gear manifests its capacity in the context of the differential necessarily the same as the manner in which it manifests it in the drill press or some other machine or as a paperweight.

Cartwright (1997) appears to agree with these criticisms. She argues that observable laws are the products of *nomological machines*, which are highly particular organizations of components of differing capacities. The notion of additive causal influence appears to have disappeared. Scientific models on this new view are blueprints for nomological machines.[22] The relevant point in this context is that capacities compose in complex, nonlinear ways. This is consistent with an account of causality in terms of INUS conditions, which supports neither the idea that causes produce constant conjunctions nor the idea that causal influences must be additive. The causal invariance is the invariance of the disposition to act *in the right circumstances* already discussed in Section 2.1. "In the right circumstances" means in the right causal field and with the right instantiations of other INUS conditions. The key point is where the invariance lies. A law of the form "all *A*s are *B*s" need not sustain the counterfactual "if *X* were to be an *A*, then *X* would be a *B*." Rather, it sustains a counterfactual such as "if certain collateral conditions were to change, the law would continue to hold" (Hoover 1995b, p. 79; cf. Woodward 1995, pp. 20–21).

Invariance of this sort is known as *modal invariance* (Forster 1997a and Hausman 1998). It is the invariance of the causal relationship expressed in the subjunctive mood as opposed to the invariance of outcomes expressed in indicative mood. The causal relationship says what would happen in the right circumstances, not what happens in fact. Models of causal structure trace out the claims of modal invariance. Given the structures, a change in one part of the structure – i.e., a change in parameterization – is transmitted according to the causal order in a reliable way. The causal field captures the notion of "the right circumstances" by stating the limits to invariance claims.

Forster (1997a) sees modal invariance as the invariance of a probability distribution defined in a way that respects the direction of causation. Consider a causal system similar to equations (2.9) and (2.10).

$$y \Leftarrow \alpha + \beta x + \varepsilon \tag{2.37}$$

---

[22] Elsewhere, I argue that economic models are, at best, blueprints for toy nomological machines (Hoover 1997b).

$$x \Leftarrow \delta + \omega, \tag{2.38}$$

where $y$ and $x$ are variables, $\alpha$, $\beta$, and $\delta$ are parameters, and $\varepsilon$ and $\omega$ are independently distributed random-error terms. Equations (2.37) and (2.38) define a probability distribution for $x$ and $y$. Suppose that they also define the true state of the world. We might, nevertheless, consider a system of equations that simulate a causal ordering in which $y$ causes $x$:

$$x = A + By + E \tag{2.39}$$

$$y = D + W, \tag{2.40}$$

where $A = \dfrac{\delta\sigma_\varepsilon^2 - \alpha\beta\sigma_\omega^2}{\beta\sigma_\omega^2 + \sigma_\varepsilon^2}$, $B = \dfrac{\beta\sigma_\omega^2}{\beta\sigma_\omega^2 + \sigma_\varepsilon^2}$, $E \sim N\left(0, \dfrac{\sigma_\varepsilon^2\sigma_\omega^2}{\beta\sigma_\omega^2 + \sigma_\varepsilon^2}\right)$,

$D = \alpha + \delta\beta$, and $W = \varepsilon + \beta\upsilon$.[23]

If the parameters of the causally ordered, first system remain constant, then (2.39) and (2.40) also define a probability distribution for $x$ and $y$ consistent with the actual realizations of $x$ and $y$. Neither system represents constant conjunction, as the variables change with every new realization of the error terms. The probability distribution described by (2.37) and (2.38) has an invariance property not shared by the probability distribution described by (2.39) and (2.40). A change in the distribution of $y$ in (2.37) must be brought about either by a change in the parameters $\alpha$ or $\beta$ or by the suppressed parameters governing the distribution of $\varepsilon$. Such a change leaves the distribution of $x$ as described by (2.38) unchanged. The same change would alter the distribution of $y$ as described by (2.40), but it would also alter the distribution of $x$ as described by (2.39). Similarly, a change in the distribution of $x$ must be brought about either by a change in $\delta$ or in the suppressed parameters governing the distribution of $\upsilon$. These changes would leave the distribution of $y$ as described in (2.37) unaltered. Since (2.37) is conditional on $x$ already, it is only the particular realizations of $x$ that matter for the distribution of $y$ rather than the distribution of $x$ that governs the realizations. To put this another way, the value of $x$ carries all the information about the distribution of $x$ that is relevant for the distribution of $y$. It is only the particular value of $x$ that matters for $y$, not how $x$ comes to take on that particular value. The changes in parameters would also change the distribution not only of $y$ as described by (2.40), but also that of $x$ as

---

[23] The definitions of the coefficients of equation (2.39) are applications of the standard formulae for the conditional distribution of a normal distribution; cf. Chapter 8, Section 1, especially footnote 2.

described by (2.39). The second pair of equations represents a more fragile, noninvariant description of the probabilities of $x$ and $y$ than the first pair.[24]

In the illustration, equation (2.37) is (modally) invariant to changes in the distribution of $x$, although the realized values of $y$ are not invariant to changes in $x$ that arise from changing realizations of $x$. Similarly, (2.38) is (modally) invariant to changes in the distribution of $y$. But, because of the causal order, realized values of $x$ are invariant to changing realizations of $y$. The second pair of equations does not show such invariance.

Woodward (1995, pp. 34–35) argues that capacities and the causal relations that they support ought to be *robust*: "if $C$ has the capacity to cause $E$s, then, we should expect an association between $C$s and $E$s that persists over a range of changes in circumstances." Woodward views robustness as a weaker form of invariance, necessary in social sciences because there are no exceptionless laws. Here Woodward appeals to a different sort of invariance, more like constant conjunction, than the modal invariance needed to underwrite a structural account of causality. Robustness is in many circumstances a desirable property, but it is a very different property than modal invariance. Part of the appeal of capacities in Cartwright's analysis is precisely that they do not necessarily manifest themselves in a variety of circumstances or, as in her probability model (see equation (2.35)), every time relevant circumstances are repeated.

The plastic explosive C-4 can be burned or used as a baseball, and will not explode. It will explode only when triggered in a certain way. It has the capacity to explode, but only in quite particular circumstances. Some research suggests that asbestos particles have the capacity to cause asbestosis but only when present in conjunction with another aggravating factor – in particular, tobacco smoking. The particularity of the conditions that permit C-4 to explode or asbestosis to occur should not undermine the attribution of a capacity to explode or to manifest a disease any more than the failure of a gear in a disassembled differential undermines its capacity to translate linear motion. Robustness in Woodward's sense is often a desirable property for a causal relation to have – but not always. One of the advantages of C-4 over nitroglycerine is precisely that it is nonrobust in its capacity to explode. The robustness of nitroglycerine makes it an extremely dangerous instrument.

---

[24] This seems to be the essential point of Forster's (1997a, Section 7) argument that "forward-directed probabilities" are constant physical propensities, while "backward-directed probabilities" are not.

## 2.7 CAUSAL STRUCTURE

We may sum up this chapter with a restatement of the thesis that structure is the essential notion in causal analysis. The structural account of causality says that causality is a feature of the world (or the economy). It is part of the way the world is. The inference of causal structure from data about the world is a difficult – sometimes impossible – problem (see Chapters 7 and 8). We can nonetheless characterize causality satisfactorily. There are a variety of ways in which fundamental causal relations can be represented. The language of variables and parameters is, however, particularly familiar and congenial to economists. In this language, causal structure is characterized by a parameterization that governs the manner in which variables are related to each other. The fundamental concept is the independence of parameters: A parameter is a variable whose value is unrestricted by the values of other parameters or variables. The causal relationship is also one of *relative* independence. A variable causes another if its value is independent of the value of the other variable, while the value of the other variable is not independent of it. The patterns of relative independence, dependence, and interdependence among variables – the causal structure – are dictated by the parameterization.

The central idea of characterizing causal relationships through parameter independence is derived from Simon. We go further in making clear that to conjecture or assert a causal structure is to make claims about how the world or the economy really is structured, rather than to make claims about properties of a representation or model. The problem of causal inference is the problem of determining the correct structural representation on the basis of empirical observation. That problem is usually not easy to solve. It will often be the case that incompatible structural representations are consistent with the same set of data. The challenge is to find additional information that would permit us to discriminate among competing representations.

Conditional on having obtained a correct representation, however, causal relationships can be read off directly from the correct representation. Simon's account shows how to do this when relationships are linear. In the next chapter, we generalize this account to nonlinear cases as well.

# 3

# Representing Causal Structure

The worst of him is that he is much more interested in getting
on with the job than in spending time in deciding whether the
job is worth getting on with. He so clearly prefers the mazes
of arithmetic to the mazes of logic, that I must ask him to
forgive the criticisms of one whose tastes in statistical theory
have been, beginning many years ago, the other way round.

– John Maynard Keynes,
"Professor Tinbergen's Method"

Simon's original formalization of the causal relation was restricted to
linear systems of equations with independent parameters.[1] He notes that
his analysis is easily extended to nonlinear cases (Simon 1953a, p. 34).
This is fortunate as nonlinearity in parameters, as well as variables, is
pervasive in macroeconomics, especially since the advent of the rational
expectations hypothesis, threshold and switching models, increasing
returns, and chaotic dynamics.[2] The goal of this chapter is to demonstrate
that Simon's analysis can be generalized in a manner adequate to the
sorts of nonlinearity found in macroeconomics.

The first section of this chapter is formal. No formalism can solve the
puzzle of causality, but a good formalism does provide a language for
talking about causal structures and a way of representing them explicitly and characterizing models that represent them implicitly (Bunge
1963, p. 244). The reader who is willing to accept the success of the formalization may, without much loss, skip ahead to the second section in
which causal structures of illustrative models are analyzed.

---

[1] The introduction and first section of this chapter are amended versions of the appendix
to Hoover (1990), used with permission.
[2] See, for example, Hamilton (1995), Potter (1995), and any of the many surveys of the literature on rational expectations – Hoover (1988a) and Sheffrin (1996) provide accessible accounts.

### 3.1 A SET-THEORETIC FORMALIZATION OF CAUSAL STRUCTURE

Starting with Simon's analysis, Mihajlo Mesarovic (1969) proposes an extensive generalization in the context of general systems theory.[3] Our exposition extends and modifies Mesarovic in two ways. First, the notation is chosen to emphasize the close relation between the formalization and Mackie's conditional analysis of causality. Second, and more substantially, we draw a distinction between parameters and variables different from the usual distinction in the general systems literature. The reason is partly to give an explicit representation of the scope for interventions (see Chapter 2, Section 2) and partly to allow consideration of the issue of cross-equation restrictions that are important in rational expectations models (see Section 3.2 and Chapter 8, Section 2).

Consider variables in a causal structure – economic variables, such as GNP, the marginal propensity to consume, velocity of circulation, or noneconomic variables, such as mass, a patient's white-blood-cell count, or Planck's constant. Each ranges over some set of potential values. These values need not be measurable or quantifiable.[4] Variables are then sets, and each instantiation or value of a variable is an element of one of these sets. Values of variables may be indexed by time, in which case the variable is the set of the ordered pairs (the Cartesian product) that assigns each possible value to each possible time.

In keeping with the structural account of causality, variables are divided into three groups: Variables whose values are subject to direct control are called *parameters* $(P_i)$; variables in the causal field are called *field variables* $(F_i)$; and variables whose values are subject only to indirect control through control over the parameters and, therefore, are determined internally to the causal structure are called *causal structural variables* or simply *variables* $(V_i)$, without any further qualification. The distinctions among these three types follow the ideas sketched in the last chapter. Designate the complete set of parameters in any causal structure as $P^0 = \{P_i\}$, $i = 1, 2, \ldots, n$; and, similarly, the complete set of field variables as $F^0 = \{F_i\}$, $i = 1, 2, \ldots, m$; and variables as $V^0 = \{V_i\}$, $i = 1, 2, \ldots, k$.

Let

$$F = F_1 \times F_2 \times \ldots \times F_m,$$
$$P = P_1 \times P_2 \times \ldots \times P_n,$$

---

[3] For a particularly succinct and lucid account of Mesarovic's idea, see Katzner (1983, ch. 6).
[4] The measurable and the quantifiable need not be the same (see Bunge 1963, p. 277).

and

$$V = V_1 \times V_2 \times \ldots \times V_k,$$

where "×" indicates the Cartesian product. A causally ordered system $C$ can be represented as a mapping

$$C: F \times P \times V \to V.$$

This says that each combination of particular values for the inputs ($F$, $P$, and $V$) is assigned to some particular values of the outputs ($V$).

The causal structure is embodied in the mapping. The elements of $F$ and $P$ are vectors of state variables that represent restrictions on the mapping. An element of $P$ is a *parameterization*. Replacement of one element of $P$ by another is a reparameterization or an *intervention*. Thus, the set $P$ represents the scope for interventions in the causal structure. Instantiations of $F$ may include realizations of random variables that differ among different periods or different individuals. The idea that true parameters may be chosen independently is embodied in the definition of $P$ as a Cartesian product (every possible option is open) and in the fact that the mapping is one-way from $P$ to $V$ (variables and their mappings place no restrictions on the parameter space).

Let $P'$ be the Cartesian product of the elements of $P^1 \subseteq P^0$, and let $V'$ be the Cartesian product of the elements of $V^1 \subseteq V^0$. Then a causally ordered subsystem $C' \subseteq C$ is called *self-contained* if and only if:

$$C': F \times P' \times V' \to V' \qquad \text{(i)}$$

and

$$P^1 \subseteq P^0, \text{ with equality only if } V^1 = V^0. \qquad \text{(ii)}$$

Condition (i) says that a self-contained subsystem maps from a subset of the systems variables ($V^1$) into itself. Condition (ii) says that a self-contained subsystem must in general contain only a subset of the parameters of the original system.

The intersection of self-contained subsystems of $C$ is itself self-contained (Mesarovic 1969, pp. 101, 102; Katzner 1983, pp. 120, 121). And since there are a finite number of variables $V_i$, there must be *minimal self-contained* subsystems: i.e., self-contained subsystems that do not themselves contain any smaller self-contained subsystems.

The elements of $F^0$ are *external causes* of the elements of $V^0$: Each is an INUS condition of the elements of $V^0$; although by virtue of being impounded in the causal field, they are not the INUS conditions that command our immediate interest.

Consider a self-contained subsystem of $C$, $C''$ with variables $V^2$ and parameters $P^2$, such that $C' \subset C''$. Let $V''$ be the Cartesian product of the elements of $V^2 - V^1$ and $P''$ be the Cartesian product of the elements of $P^2 - P^1$. Clearly,

$$C'': F \times P' \times V' \times P'' \times V'' \rightarrow V' \times V''$$

and

$$P^1 \subset P^2 \text{ and } P^2 \subseteq P^0, \text{ with equality only if } V^2 = V^0.$$

If there is no intervening subsystem $C^*$ with parameters $P^*$ such that

$$C' \subset C^* \subset C'' \text{ and } P^1 \subset P^* \subset P^2,$$

then the elements of $V^1$ are *internal causes* of the distinct elements of $V^2$.

If $C''$ contains another distinct self-contained subsystem $C'''$, with no intervening subsystems and with elements, $V^3$, then the elements of $V^3$ are also internal causes of the distinct elements of $V^1$.

For a given instantiation of the field (i.e., for a value assigned to each $F_i$ except for the random error terms, which are realized for each case separately) and a given parameterization, the relationship between any two variables ($V_1$ and $V_2$) is ordered. There are four possibilities. Two are implied by the hierarchical relationship between self-contained subsystems: (i) $V_1$ causes $V_2$ (written $V_1 \rightarrow V_2$) or (ii) $V_2$ causes $V_1$ ($V_2 \rightarrow V_1$ or $V_1 \leftarrow V_2$).[5] Case (iii) occurs when the two variables belong to disjoint self-contained subsystems, so that neither causes the other ($V_1 \perp V_2$). Case (iv) occurs when the two belong to a minimal self-contained subsystem, so that causation is mutual ($V_1 \leftrightarrow V_2$).

Now that causal order is defined, it is easier to appreciate the initial distinctions among the types of variables. Field variables and parameters are necessarily not caused by variables. The distinction between field variables and parameters is a pragmatic one. One aspect of the distinction is that parameters can be directly controlled – hypothetically, at least. A second aspect is that, although the mapping changes with different parameterizations, the causal order does not; while, in contrast (as discussed in Chapter 2, Section 4), even the causal order may change for different instantiations of the causal field.

## 3.2 EXAMPLES OF CAUSALLY ORDERED STRUCTURES

### A Linear Case

To illustrate the application of the formalization of the last section, consider the following system of equations, which repeat equations (2.5)–(2.8) from Chapter 2, Section 2:

---

[5] The use of the arrow here to mean "causes" can be distinguished from its use in the mappings according to context.

$$p_{11}q_1 = p_{10} \tag{3.1}$$
$$p_{21}q_1 + p_{22}q_2 = p_{20} \tag{3.2}$$
$$p_{33}q_3 = p_{30} \tag{3.3}$$
$$p_{42}q_2 + p_{43}q_3 + p_{44}q_4 = p_{40} \tag{3.4}$$

$P^0 = \{p_{ij}\}$, $V^0 = \{q_j\}$ and $F^0 = \varnothing$. Equations (3.1) and (3.2) together form a self-contained subsystem: $P^1 = \{p_{11}, p_{21}, p_{22}\} \subset P^0$, and $V^1 = \{q_1, q_2\}$ is mapped into itself. It is *not* a minimal self-contained subsystem since equation (3.1) is itself self-contained (and in fact minimal). Because no subsystems intervene between equations (3.1) and the system (3.1) and (3.2) together, $q_1$ (internally) causes $q_2$: It is an INUS condition for it.

## A Rational Expectations Model

In this and the next illustration, we consider the causal structure of two models that are useful in later chapters as well. The first is a rational-expectations version of Cagan's (1956) analysis of the demand for real balances in hyperinflations.[6]

Let the demand for real balances be given by

$$m_t - p_t = \delta + \beta y_t - \alpha(r_t + (_t p^e_{t+1} - p_t)) + v_t, \tag{3.5}$$

where subscripts index time, $m_t$ is the nominal money stock, $p_t$ is the general price level, $y_t$ is real GDP, $r_t$ is the real rate of interest, $_t p^e_{t+1}$ is the expectation at time $t$ of the price level at time $t + 1$, so that $(_t p^e_{t+1} - p_t)$ is (approximately) the rate of inflation between times $t$ and $t + 1$, and $v_t$ is an independent random error term. All variables except $r_t$ are in natural logarithms, and the coefficients $\alpha$, $\beta$, $\delta \geq 0$.

Equation (3.5) is a general demand-for-money function. The special case of a hyperinflation implies that the inflation rate is so large relative to changes in real interest rates and real incomes that it would be reasonable to impound these variables as constants in a causal field. Equation (3.5) can then be rewritten as

$$m_t - p_t = \delta + \beta \bar{y} - \alpha(\bar{r} + (_t p^e_{t+1} - p_t)) + v_t, \tag{3.5'}$$

where the bars and the omission of the time subscripts indicates that the variables take on constant values. Equation (3.5′) can be written more compactly as

---

[6] This and the following example are adapted from Hamilton (1995), pp. 326–332. Similar examples, used for purposes other than demonstrating causal structure, are common in the pedagogical literature on rational expectations; see, for instance, Turner and Whiteman (1981) and Hoover (1988a), pp. 187–189.

$$m_t - p_t = \mu - \alpha(_t p_{t+1}^e - p_t) + v_t, \tag{3.5''}$$

where $\mu = \delta + \beta \bar{y} - \alpha \bar{r}$.

Assume that the central bank supplies money according to the rule

$$m_{t+1} = \lambda + m_t + \varepsilon_t, \tag{3.6}$$

where $\varepsilon$ is an independent random error. The error terms, $v$ and $\varepsilon$, are assumed to be serially uncorrelated and uncorrelated with each other and to have means of zero. The coefficient $\lambda$ can be interpreted as a constant growth rate for the money stock.

Assume that expectations are formed rationally:

$$_t p_{t+1}^e = E(p_{t+1} \mid \Xi_t), \tag{3.7}$$

where $E(\bullet)$ is the expectations operator, and $\Xi_t$ is the information available at time $t$, which is assumed to include the structure of the economy and the current and lagged values of the variables included in the model.

A reasonable conjecture of the rate of inflation is that it conforms to the rate of growth of the money stock; that is

$$(_t p_{t+1}^e - p_t) = \lambda. \tag{3.8}$$

Substituting equation (3.8) into (3.5″) and rearranging yields

$$p_t = m_t - \mu + \alpha \lambda + v_t. \tag{3.9}$$

To verify that this is the rational expectations solution, we show that, if this is in fact how the price level is determined, the mathematical expectation of the actual rate of inflation based on information available at time $t$ is $\lambda$. Using equation (3.9) at times $t$ and $t+1$,

$$
\begin{aligned}
E(p_{t+1} - p_t \mid \Xi_t) &= E(m_{t+1} - \mu + \alpha\lambda + v_{t+1} - (m_t - \mu + \alpha\lambda + v_t)) \\
&= E(m_{t+1} - m_t + v_{t+1} - v_t) \\
&= \lambda. \tag{3.10}
\end{aligned}
$$

The last step is implied by equation (3.6) and the assumption that the mean of $v_t = 0$ for all $t$.

Equations (3.6) and (3.9) form a causal structure in which money causes prices in a nonlinear manner. Whether the error terms should be interpreted as field variables or as causal structural variables depends on whether the parameters that govern their probability distributions are subject to direct control. Let us assume that they are not. Then, $F^0 = \{\bar{y}, \bar{r}, \beta, \delta, v, \varepsilon\}$, $P^0 = \{\alpha, \lambda\}$, and $V^0 = \{p, m\}$. Equation (3.6) is a self-contained subsystem. Given $F^0$ and $P^1 = \{\lambda\} \subset P^0$, equation (3.6) maps $V^1 = \{m\}$ into itself. Notice that we are treating the variable $m$ as the same variable whatever its time subscript. The notation would permit us to distinguish between a variable (at time $t$) and its lagged value (at time $t-1$), so that we could ask more temporally relativized questions. But this also raises the question of whether it makes sense to think of earlier instantiations of a variable (say, $m_{t-1}$ in equation (3.6)) causing later instantiations ($m_t$). Suffice it to say that the formalism here does not rule out this form of self-causation.

In this example, the parameters for the two equations do not form disjoint sets; $\lambda$ appears in both equations (3.6) and (3.9). This means that since the central bank can control the money stock only through setting $\lambda$, which can be interpreted as a policy rule, the conditional probability distribution described by equation (3.9) changes with every change in monetary policy. This is an example of the Lucas (1976) critique of econometric policy evaluation.[7] It arises because of the cross-equation restriction represented by the shared parameter. This is a typical feature of models with rational expectations. It illustrates how definite causal ordering presupposes neither linearity nor robustness of probability distributions among variables.

**A Regime-Switching Model**

The final illustration extends the last one. The possibility that the parameter $\lambda$ can take different values suggests to many economists that the solution to the last model is not consistent with rational expectations, except in the unlikely case that any change in $\lambda$ was completely unexpected and thought to be permanent once it had occurred. Barring that, $\lambda$ should be governed by a probability distribution. It would be a variable and not a causally significant parameter.

To keep things simple, assume that there are only two possible growth rates for the money stock: zero and a positive rate, $\lambda$.[8] The variable $s_t = 0$ when the monetary authority is in the zero growth rate regime and $= 1$ when it is in the positive growth rate regime. $s_t$ is a random variable. Its distribution over time,

$$P(s_{t+1}|s_t),\tag{3.11}$$

is described by the following transition matrix. Conditional on being in one or the other regime at time $t$, it shows the probabilities of either remaining in that regime or switching to the other regime:

---

[7] See Chapter 7, Section 4, for further discussion of the Lucas critique.
[8] Which is actually to treat $\lambda$ as a constant; the variability of the policy regime is shifted elsewhere in the notation.

|  | Regime at time $t+1$ | |
|---|---|---|
|  | $s_t = 1$ | $s_t = 0$ |
| $s_t = 1$ | $\theta$ | $1 - \theta$ |
| $s_t = 0$ | $1 - \omega$ | $\omega$ |

Regime at time $t$

The money stock can be described as

$$m_t = s_t\lambda + m_{t-1} + \varepsilon_t. \tag{3.12}$$

The model can be solved similarly to the last one. A solution for the general price level is conjectured, and then it is shown that using that conjectured solution the mathematical expectation for prices in the model (the rational expectation) is exactly that solution. The conjectured solution is

$$p_t = -\mu + \frac{\alpha\gamma(1-\omega)}{1-\phi} + m_t + \frac{\phi\gamma}{1-\phi}s_t, \tag{3.13}$$

where

$$\phi = \frac{\alpha(\theta+\omega-1)}{(1+\alpha)}.$$

Hamilton (1995, pp. 341–342) demonstrates that this solution is consistent with rational expectations.

Equations (3.11)–(3.13) form a causal structure in which it remains the case that money causes prices. $F^0 = \{\bar{y}, \bar{r}, \beta, \delta, v, \varepsilon, \lambda, s\}$, $P^0 = \{\alpha, \gamma, \theta, \omega\}$, and $V^0 = \{p, m\}$. Expression (3.11) and equation (3.12) are a minimal self-contained subsystem: for $F^0$ and $P^1 = \{\theta, \omega\} \subset P^0$, given the system (3.11)–(3.12) maps $V^1 = \{m\}$ into itself. Notice that $\lambda$ and $s$ are now impounded in the causal field; $\lambda$ because it is constant, $s$ because it is random. $\theta$ and $\omega$ are included among the parameters as they control the transition probabilities that determine the degree to which $s$, which could be regarded as a uniform random variable on a unit interval, affects $m$. In a richer model, $s$ might be treated as a structural variable. But here, as it has no causes of its own independent of the manner in which it affects $m$, there is no reason to do so.[9] Money causes prices, because (3.11)–(3.13) also form a self-contained system with no other intervening subsystems.

Again, this example illustrates that causal asymmetry can be defined formally in complex, nonlinear systems in an unambiguous manner. This example is important because it raises issues that will be addressed in later chapters. In particular, notice that the intuition that, under rational expectations, parameters cannot change, so a parameter supposedly subject to direct control should be treated as a variable determined endogenously or as a constant, merely moves the problem up one level: The questionable parameter $\lambda$ is impounded in the causal field, but only at the cost of introducing two new parameters, $\theta$ and $\omega$. Are these really constants and part of the field? Or is the intuition that motivated this elaboration of the simpler rational expectations model subject to some sort of pragmatic limitation? It turns out that this is a crucial issue for the structural account of causality, but one that we must defer until Chapters 5 and 6.

---

[9] See Chapter 4, Section 3, on the identity of structures.

# 4

## Articulating Causal Structure

> To him, the world had no order of succession, no causation,
> no precedent. Everything he saw was new-minted, and thus
> every day was a parade of wonders.
>
> – Charles Frazier, *Cold Mountain*

After Hume, the usual approach to the analysis of causality was to reduce the causal relation to something else, probabilistic relations, interpreted as indeterministic or approximate versions of natural laws, being the most frequent something. The thesis of the structural account of causality, set out in Chapter 2, is that cause is not reducible, but is in fact a fundamental building block of our understanding of the world. Cause is the name that we give to that ubiquitous feature of our experience: *directed influence*. Cause is what Hume denies that we ever can perceive: the hidden power that connects the actions of one thing to another. Hume is correct that we cannot observe these connections immediately. We can, nonetheless, infer them – conjecture their existence and check our conjectures – as well as we infer anything in ordinary life or in science that lies beyond direct sense experience.

A *direct cause* is one that is unmediated: *A* directly causes *C* if and only if there is some causal path connecting *A* to *C* in which there is no *B* that is, at once, an effect of *A* and a cause of *C*. The direction of direct causation, the property of causal asymmetry, is part of the essential notion of causality as a dispositional property, and is reflected in the analysis of the causal relationship in terms of counterfactual conditionals. It is this conditional nature that permits causal relationships to be used to control things. Control is often the source of our pragmatic interest in causal relations, but control *per se* is not part of the concept of causality itself, except insofar as hypothetical control is one way to understand the meaning of counterfactual conditionals. The direction of *indirect* causation arises from the relationships of direct causes.

69

Simon analyzes these relationships as the relationships between variables.

Causality is about how things get determined to occur. Yet, in many fields, including economics, determinism appears to be incomplete; the best understood relationships are probabilistic. The structural view accounts for probabilistic outcomes by accepting random variables and analyzing their causal relationships with reference to the parameters that govern their probability distributions.

There remain some important questions to answer about the structural account. First, can it be elaborated in a manner that suits the analytical needs of macroeconomics? Second, once elaborated, is it an adequate account of causality in general? And, finally, is it an adequate account of causality in macroeconomics? In Chapter 3, we showed that it was possible to characterize formally complex networks of interrelated variables as causally ordered. The main goal of this chapter is to examine whether the structural account succeeds in providing a good general account of causality. We shall postpone, except for passing remarks, the central discussion of the suitability of the structural account to macroeconomics. That is the subject (directly) of the next two chapters and (indirectly) of the remainder of the book.

### 4.1   TYPES AND TOKENS

The formal representations in the last chapter present a vision of causal structure in terms of the relationships among variables. The question to be addressed in this chapter is the general adequacy of that vision. As we observed in the opening paragraphs of Chapter 1, causal questions can be generic ("do monetary shocks or technology shocks cause business cycles?") or singular ("did the Iraqi invasion of Kuwait cause the 1990/91 recession in the United States?"). Philosophers refer to generic terms like "monetary shocks," "technology shocks," or "business cycles" as *types*. They refer to terms like "the Iraqi invasion of Kuwait in 1990" or the "recession in the United States in 1990/91" as instances or *tokens* of particular types. Our pragmatic interests extend to questions involving the causal relationships among both types and tokens. Accounts of causality differ in part in how they specify the relationship between causation at the level of types and at the level of tokens.

Nancy Cartwright (1989, p. 2) characterizes Hume as subscribing to two theses: First, singular causal facts (tokens) are true in virtue of generic causal facts (types); and, second, generic causal facts are regularities (cf. Chapter 1, Section 1). Cartwright challenges both theses (see Section 4.4). In partial contrast, the structural account defended here accepts that token-level causal relations obtain by virtue of type-level causal relations, but replaces Hume's second thesis with the claim that generic causal facts are causal structures.

As the conditional analysis of Chapter 2 suggests, the image of causal structure is one of dispositions or propensities. Causality itself resides in the linkages among variables.[1] Variables are intrinsically types. But variables take values. Tokens are the *instantiations* of variables or, as we shall say in the case of random variables, their *realizations*. Tokens inherit their relationships as causes and effects from the causal structure of the variables for which they are instantiations or realizations.

The structural account may be contrasted with at least two related alternatives. The first is Hume's own second thesis: type-level causal relations are regularities or constant conjunctions – i.e., invariable laws of nature. The second is the similar, but weaker, thesis, explored in Chapter 1, that type-level causal relations are probabilistic associations – sometimes glossed as stochastic laws. As we have seen, neither alternative is satisfactory. First, without substantial elaboration neither can account for the asymmetry of causation. Second, such elaborations implicitly refer to notions of causal structure. Our essential contention is that this notion of structure should be brought out of the shadows and made the center of the analysis. If we accept that no account that relies on exceptionless regularities is likely to be useful, we are then left with the question, what is primitive – probabilities or structure? We have argued that it is structure. But then the question is, where do we find such structure?

Consider the issues raised by Hume's theses: What is the relation of the singular to the generic? Which level is primitive? For the structural account, as well as for Hume and the advocates of the probabilistic accounts, the singular, token-level causal relation *exemplifies* the primitive, generic type-level causal relation. For some philosophers, J. L. Mackie and Daniel Hausman, for instance, generic, type-level relations *generalize* primitive, token-level relations.[2] We shall examine each view, starting with the accounts that are nearest to the structural account, from which it nevertheless must be distinguished.

The probabilistic accounts discussed in Chapter 1 take the level of types to be fundamental and must explain the relationship between tokens with reference to the relationships between types. Letting uppercase letters represent types and lowercase letters represent the

---

[1] Owens (1992, pp. 82–83), expresses a similar view that cause resides in the "nexus," which, however, he contrasts with objective, conditional accounts such as defended here in favor of an epistemic account that finds causal asymmetry in the asymmetry of casual explanation: The direction of causation is the direction that minimizes the number of coincidences.

[2] My current position against taking token causes as primitive is a shift from Hoover (1990, p. 219), which accepted Mackie's view.

corresponding tokens, an advocate of a probabilistic account might hold that $a$ (token-)causes $b$, when $a$ occurs and $b$ occurs and $A$ (type-)causes $B$.[3] By "type $A$ causes type $B$," probabilistic accounts mean $P(B = b|A = a) \neq P(B = b)$, adding, of course, whatever additional restrictions to the cited probabilistic relationship that, to the satisfaction of the advocate of the probabilistic account, resolve the objections to the whole notion of probabilistic causality, such as those mentioned in Chapter 1, Section 2. But what if $a$ occurs, and $b$ does not? The failure of tokens to exemplify the causal relationship does not, in itself, threaten the relationship at the level of types; for typically both $P(B = b|A = a) < 1$ and $P(B = b) < 1$. We are not dealing in sure things. There is no contradiction in token-level occurences not exemplifying type-level causality in each instance, yet if type-level causality is held to be primary, there are problematic cases in which our analysis and our intuitions may move in different directions.

A well-known example is due to the philosopher Deborah Rosen (cited in Suppes 1970, p. 41):

suppose a golfer makes a shot that hits a limb of a tree close to the green and is thereby deflected directly into the hole, for a spectacular birdie. . . . If we know something about Mr. Jones' golf we can estimate the probability of his making a birdie on this particular hole. The probability will be low, but the seemingly disturbing thing is that if we estimate the conditional probability of his making a birdie, given that the ball hit the branch, . . . we would ordinarily estimate the probability as being still lower. Yet when we see the event happen, we recognize immediately that hitting the branch in exactly the way it did was essential to the ball's going into the cup.

A similar example is due to I. J. Good (1961, p. 318):

Sherlock Holmes is at the foot of a cliff. At the top of the cliff, directly overhead, are Dr. Watson, Professor Moriarty, and a loose boulder. Watson, knowing Moriarty's intentions, realises that the best chance of saving Holmes's life is to push the boulder over the edge of the cliff, doing his best to give it enough horizontal momentum to miss Holmes. If he does not push the boulder, Moriarity will do so in such a way that it will be nearly certain to kill Holmes. Watson then makes the decision . . . to push the boulder, but his skill fails him and the boulder falls on Holmes and kills him. . . .

In both examples a type-level inhibitor or preventative (i.e., a negative cause) appears to operate: Striking the limb lowers the probability of the birdie; Watson pushing the rock lowers the probability of Holmes's death. Yet, if we focus on tokens, we are inclined to say that, in the event,

---

[3] Cf. Eells (1991, pp. 289–290), who does not agree with this view, but recounts it clearly.

the causal import is reversed: Hitting the limb caused the birdie and Watson caused Holmes's death.

The same issue arises in less contrived examples. Take the case of polio vaccines. The Salk vaccine was the first successful preventive for polio. It used a dead polio virus. Later, the Sabin vaccine supplanted the Salk vaccine. The Sabin vaccine used a live, but weakened, polio virus. The Sabin vaccine had an advantage from the perspective of public health: Because it was live, it could be passed on from a vaccinated person to an unvaccinated person; it made immunity infectious. The probability of an individual contracting polio is lower if he is vaccinated and lower, even if he is not vaccinated, the more people around him are vaccinated. Thus, even if the Sabin vaccine was no more effective (or, perhaps, even less effective) in directly conveying immunity, it reduced the overall probability of any person contracting polio more than the Salk vaccine. But there is a downside to the Sabin vaccine. Because it is a live vaccine, some people actually contract polio from the vaccine itself, which does not occur with the Salk vaccine at all. The probability of contracting polio from the vaccine is low enough that the net effect is still to lower the probability of a randomly chosen person's contracting polio. Vaccine manufacturers have been sued, nonetheless, on behalf of individual people who have contracted polio from the vaccines. The liability is argued to arise because there exists an alternative, the Salk vaccine, which, in their particular case, would not have given them polio. Clearly, the Sabin vaccine inhibits polio more effectively than the Salk vaccine for a randomly chosen individual. And the best expectation of its effect in advance of actual vaccination for an individual who, as it turns out, contracts polio was that it would convey immunity.[4]

Related examples are commonplace. An article in the *Economist* (11 July 1998, pp. 78–80) comments that, even when a technique in forensic science has been validated probabilistically, "what counts is the individual case[;] [t]hat is what convicts or acquits a defendant." Knowing that causal analysis got it right at the level of types is small comfort to the imprisoned, but innocent, man; to the child who contracts polio *because* of the vaccine, or to Sherlock Holmes, crushed beneath a boulder. The lucky golfer will not, perhaps, complain.[5]

Ellery Eells (1991, ch. 6) attempts to deal with the tension between type-level and token-level causation providing a separate analysis for

---

[4] Since I first wrote this passage, public health physicians have begun to argue for a return to the Salk vaccine. Many believe that the Sabin vaccine has proved so successful, and polio has become so rare, that the individual risk of the live vaccine is now much greater (even though still quite low) than the possible marginal external benefit.

[5] But not necessarily: Japanese golfers take out insurance against holes-in-one, which carry with them the liability of having to treat large numbers of their comrades to free drinks.

each level within a sophisticated probabilistic account. Eells maintains the independence of each level. This means, on the one hand, that a type-level causal relation may exist even where no token-level relation exists, and, on the other hand, that token-level causal relations may exist even where no type-level causal relations exist. The first point is the less puzzling. That $A$ may type-cause $B$, even though there are no tokens $a$ of $A$ or $b$ of $B$ is consistent with any dispositional or propensity account of probability, as well as with the counterfactual analysis that underlies the structural account. The second point is illustrated by the various examples cited above in which our intuitions clearly identify token-level causes that appear to be inconsistent with the type-level causes. The puzzle is to provide a probabilistic account of token-level causation that both explains the intuitions and does not conflict with the type-level account.

Eells argues (1991, pp. 288, 295–297) that we need to consider both tokens that occur *because of* type-causes and those that occur *despite* type-causes. Each of these relationships between types and tokens is explicated as an evolving probability. Take, for example, Rosen's case of the improbable birdie. Eells asks us to consider the evolution of $P_t(Birdie)$, from time $t = t_{Shot}$ to time $t = t_{Birdie}$. This is shown in Figure 4.1.[6] The token event of hitting the limb occurs at $t_{Limb}$. This immediately lowers the probability of the birdie substantially. What this means is that at $t_{Limb}$, the ball could follow an infinite number of paths with some probability of making a birdie (zero for virtually all of them); the probability shown on the diagram is the integral of these probabilities over every possible path. This is shown by the solid dot above $t_{Limb}$. The ball, of course, must follow some path; and, improbable as it is, in this case it follows a path that raises the probability for each time after $t_{Limb}$ (shown by the solid line to the right of $t_{Limb}$) at the higher level of probability. The ball continues along some higher probability (but less than certain) path until the birdie is made at $t_{Birdie}$.[7]

In this case, $P_{t \triangleright t_{Limb}}(Birdie \mid Limb) > P_{t \triangleleft t_{Limb}}(Birdie)$, which conforms to our notion that hitting the limb was a token-cause of the birdie. Still, the relationship between the conditional and unconditional probabilities in the definition of (probabilistic) type-causality was one of simple inequality ($\neq$) rather than increase ($>$). Eells suggests in another example

---

[6] Eells (1991, p. 292, fig. 6.1). Eells alters the story a bit from the way it is recounted by Suppes in that he makes the initial probability of a birdie (shown as the horizontal line starting on the left-hand side of the diagram) relatively high and recasts the intervening event as a squirrel kicking the ball after the putt on the green. We stick with the original example.

[7] As Eells (1991, p. 294) acknowledges, the path need not be one of constant probability and could even converge on $P_t(birdie) = 1$ as $t$ approached $t_{Birdie}$.

$P_t$ (Birdie)

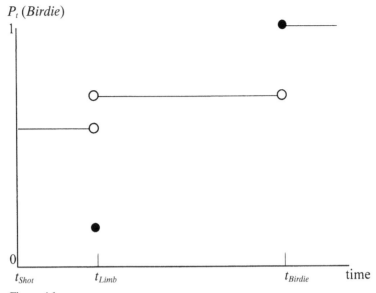

Figure 4.1

that when the inequality is specified to be a decrease, that our intuitions about token causes are different. The example is due to Cartwright (1983, pp. 28, which reprints Cartwright 1979; cf. Eells 1991, p. 290):

> I consider eradicating the poison oak at the bottom of my garden by spraying it with defoliant. The can of defoliant claims that the spray is 90 per cent effective; that is, the probability of the plant's dying given that it is sprayed is .9 and the probability of its surviving is .1. Here ... the probable outcome, and not the improbable, is explained by the spraying. One can explain why some plants died by remarking that they were sprayed with a powerful defoliant; but this will not explain why some survive.

For one of the improbable cases of a plant surviving, Eells (1991, p. 294, Fig. 6.2) plots the evolving probability of a plant sprayed at $t_{Spray}$ reaching $t_{Survive}$, the time at which we check the plants for survival, in a healthy state. This is shown in Figure 4.2. The puzzle here is that just as in the case of the birdie, the intervening event substantially lowers the probability of the final outcome and that probability is ultimately more than restored, yet in this case it seems unnatural to say that the plant survived because of the defoliant and far more natural to say that it survived in spite of the defoliant. The difference between the two cases, according to Eells, lies in the time path of the probabilities. He attempts (Eells 1991, pp. 295–308) to give a general characterization of the

$P_t$ *(Survival)*

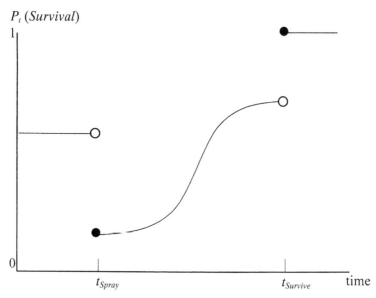

Figure 4.2

token-level relationships, *because of, in spite of, independent of,* and *autonomous of.*

Eells does not seem to have got to the heart of the matter. We think of the ball hitting the limb as a token-level cause of the birdie because it was an intermediate step in the way in which the birdie, in the event, was made. Had the ball not hit the limb, the birdie would not have been made *that* way. Cartwright's description of the defoliant does not suggest the time path shown in Figure 4.2. It could just as well be represented with appropriate changes by the time path of the birdie in Figure 4.1. The idea is that the defoliant is sprayed; and, with little or no lapse of time, the probability of the plant surviving is seen to be higher (i.e., unlike the case in Eells's scenario, in which weakened plants gradually recover their health, the defoliant appears not to weaken some plants at all). What makes this a case of surviving despite the defoliant rather than because of it, is the fate of all the other plants (counterfactually, at least) that fail to survive. Figure 4.3 modifies Figure 4.1. The time paths of the probabilities of survival of two representative plants are shown. As indicated by the circular nodes, both plants follow the same path up to $t_{Spray}$; after that the survival probability of the one plant (shown by squares) rises as in Figure 4.1, while that of the other plant (shown by triangles) falls and eventually terminates in death. The notion of surviving in spite of the defoliant is better understood as a statement that the probabi-

$P_t$ (*Survival*)

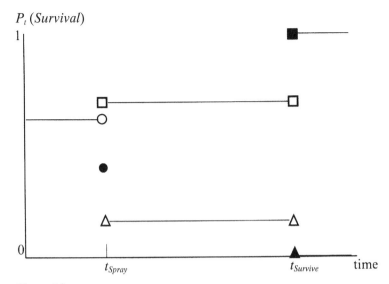

Figure 4.3

listic measure of survival paths is smaller than that of nonsurvival paths: there are many realizations of the probabilities that terminate in death after having passed through spraying (i.e., many like the triangle path) and few that terminate in health (i.e., few like the square path). While the time path of the probabilities may be of some interest, the fact that similar time paths may be given different interpretations suggests that time is not fundamental.

How would the structural account treat such cases? Consider the birdie. Figure 4.4 shows the causal structure of the case (which, incidentally, could also serve as a schematic diagram of the physical layout of the hole). Each of the variables, *Shot* (i.e., taking a shot), *Limb* (i.e., the ball striking the limb), *Birdie* (i.e., making a birdie), is defined on the set {0, 1}, where 0 indicates that it does not occur and 1 that it does. This structure can be represented as a system of two equations, each a version of the limited-dependent variable equation (2.30) in Chapter 2:

$$P(Birdie) \Leftarrow f(Shot, Limb), \tag{4.1}$$

$$P(Limb) \Leftarrow g(Shot). \tag{4.2}$$

Given this structure, *whatever the probabilities*, *Shot* causes *Limb*, and *Shot* and *Limb* cause *Birdie*. That, of course, is at the type level.

The probability of making a birdie conditional on taking a shot (whether directly or through striking the limb) is

*Birdie*

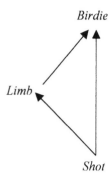

*Limb*

Figure 4.4

*Shot*

$$p_{B,S} \equiv P(Birdie = 1|Shot = 1)$$
$$= P(Birdie = 1|Shot = 1 \& Limb = 0)P(Limb = 0|Shot = 1)$$
$$+P(Birdie = 1|Shot = 1 \& Limb = 1)P(Limb = 1|Shot = 1) \qquad (4.3)$$

The probability of making the birdie conditional on taking the shot and hitting the limb is

$$p_{B,S,L} \equiv P(Birdie = 1|Shot = 1 \& Limb = 1) \qquad (4.4)$$

Making the birdie through hitting the tree limb might be against the odds: $p_{B,S,L} \ll p_{B,S}$. Yet, every event is a realization of the variables; in this case: $\langle Shot, Limb, Birdie \rangle = \langle 1, 1, 1 \rangle$. It is the fact that $Limb = 1$ in the way the shot actually played out, given that $Limb$ is a type-level cause of *Birdie*, that gives us the sense of the birdie being made because of the ball hitting the limb. It is the fact that $p_{B,S,L}$ is low that gives us the sense that this is a spectacular outcome.

We say that hitting the limb is a token-level cause of the birdie because *Limb* is a (positively relevant) type-level cause of *Birdie* and the particular realization instantiated *Limb* positively. Equally, we could say that the defoliant did not cause the survival of the plant (that the plant survived despite being sprayed) because the *Spraying* is a (negatively relevant) type-level cause of *Survival* and the particular realization instantiated *Spraying* positively and *Survival* positively. On the structural account, these judgments should be regarded as pragmatic – not features of the causation itself as it is in the structure, but evaluations made relative to our interests.

Consider Figure 4.5, which modifies Figure 4.4. *Shot* and *Birdie* remain 0/1 variables. A new variable, a triple, *Drive* = $\langle Angle, Loft, Velocity \rangle$, in which each element is continuously variable, intervenes between *Shot* and the other variables; *Limb* is now defined continuously as something

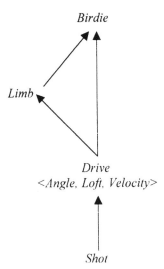

Figure 4.5

like the direction of deflection from a ball striking the limb. As before, we might imagine that the probability of a birdie is higher conditional on taking the shot (without realizing *Drive*) than it is conditional on taking the shot with the ball traveling along one of the (now infinite) paths that involve hitting the limb. Nevertheless, conditional on the particular realization of *Drive*, it is not inconsistent that only a realization that involves hitting the limb is consistent with the realization of a birdie.

Seen from the point of view of taking a shot, the birdie might be made despite hitting the limb; while, seen from the point of view of the drive leaving the club, the birdie might be made because of hitting the limb. A soldier who abandons his watch post and happens to discover the enemy in an unexpected place may, at once, be condemned for failing in his duty and seen to be the savior of the outpost. This has to do with the moral, legal, or other normative evaluations and not with positive characteristics of token-level causation. Eells's time paths of probabilities may well be relevant to these evaluations and may sometimes inform our assignment of terms like "because of" or "in spite of," even though these assignments will not usually be unique. The important positive point is that tokens may be realized against type and that this does not threaten type-level causality nor call for an independent analysis of token-level causality.

Did Watson cause Holmes's death? In one sense, obviously yes. Consider Figure 4.6. Here *Death* is a 0/1 variable. Initially, consider *Watson* to be a variable taking the value 1 if Watson pushes the rock and 0 if he

Figure 4.6

does not, and *Moriarity* to be a variable taking the value 1 if Moriarity pushes the rock and 0 if he does not. Again, this may be represented as two equations:

$$P(Death) \Leftarrow f(Watson, Moriarity), \tag{4.5}$$

$$Moriarity \Leftarrow g(Watson). \tag{4.6}$$

Here *Watson* causes *Moriarity*, and *Moriarity* and *Watson* cause *Death*. A key fact is that whenever *Watson* = 1, *Moriarity* = 0. If Watson in fact pushes the rock and Holmes dies, then Watson token-caused Holmes's death in that Watson's pushing the rock was essential to the manner in which Holmes actually died. But does any blame adhere to Watson? Probably not, if the description in Figure 4.6 and equations (4.5) and (4.6) is the most detailed possible. In that case, Watson did his best (perhaps acted heroically); Holmes's death occurred against type.

But suppose that more detail can be filled in. Instead of 0/1 variables, assume that both *Watson* and *Moriarity* are triples of the form ⟨*Push, Angle, Force*⟩, in which *Push* is 1 in *Watson* if the rock is pushed by Watson and 0 otherwise and similarly for *Moriarity*, while *Angle* and *Force* are continuous parameters chosen by Watson for *Watson* and by Moriarity for *Moriarity*. Still, if *Push* = 1 for *Watson*, *Push* = 0 for *Moriarity*. Now, the manner in which Watson pushes the rock may alter the probability of Holmes's death. Whether we blame Watson for causing Holmes's death or praise him for his heroic, but ultimately futile, effort depends on judgments about what we believe Watson could or should have done in choosing the parameters *Force* and *Angle*.

Even if the representation in equations (4.5) and (4.6) is exhaustive – that is, there are no variables impounded in the causal field other than unobservable error terms that are relevant to the probability of Holmes's death – and even if Watson has made every effort that we might morally require of him, Holmes may still be crushed: Sometimes things just happen. Here the underdetermination of the token outcomes by the type-level causal structure is ontological by construction. It is not because we are ignorant of the causes (epistemic underdetermination), it is because the situation is ultimately stochastic. When investigating token outcomes (e.g., airliner crashes), the heuristic procedure is to suppose that all underdetermination is epistemic. Yet, in the final analysis, the reason why some such questions are sometimes not answered is that sometimes no answer can be given because there is an irreducible, objective probability (luck). While the point is somewhat obscured by the habit of philosophers of using examples involving finite numbers of discrete outcomes (0/1 variables, for instance), continuous variables force us to recognize that in any indeterministic setting, not only are realizations finally due to luck, but any particular pattern of realizations is measure zero: The chances of an outcome happening exactly the way it happened were infinitesimally small.

## 4.2 VARIABLES OR TROPES?

The implications of the structural view for the relationship between type-level and token-level causation can be summarized: *Token causes are causes by virtue of their being realizations of type-level causes (i.e., of variables in a causal structure), and token-level causes do not stand in need of an independent analysis.* Cases in which token-level and type-level causes appear to work in opposite directions arise because realizations of variables may occur against type; that is, given our pragmatic perspective (determined by our interests), they are low probability outcomes that are, nonetheless, consistent with the causal structure. Some such outcomes are inevitable in structures that are ontologically indeterministic, and we may not be able to distinguish ontological from epistemic indeterminism in practice. On this view, type-level causation is primary. Hausman (1998) makes the strongest case I know against it. He argues that type-level causation cannot be primary, because causation cannot be a relationship among variables.

Hausman begins with two presumptions. First, the paradigmatic case of causality is the concrete instance of one token causing another; and, second, the essential characteristic of causality is asymmetry. The structural account agrees that asymmetry is essential. But it disagrees that examples of token-level causation are paradigmatic. The reason is found in the conditional analysis of cause (see Chapter 2, Section 1). The notion of cause is essentially counterfactual. Typically (that is, absent cases of overdetermination), if $a$ (token-) causes $b$, it must be the case that had $a$ been different, $b$ would have been different; otherwise, the relation between $a$ and $b$ is literally just coincidence. Such counterfactuals would seem to be intrinsically type-level relations. Hausman does not disagree. If a cause is an INUS condition for an effect, Hausman argues that it must be *nomic* (or lawlike) INUS condition.[8] But, Hausman argues, this does not make type-level causes primary, because laws are themselves symmetric; causal asymmetry arises from the manner in which tokens are actually instantiated in concrete systems. Here, *concrete* means fully realized or instantiated properties or variables.

Hausman's notion of the relationship between laws and causal relations can be understood through an illustration. In fact, such illustrations themselves appear to be Hausman's principal argument in support of his view (Hausman 1998, pp. 25–28). Consider the ideal gas law: *Pressure* × *Volume* = *number of moles of gas* × *constant* × *Temperature* or $PV = nRT$. This law is a relation between variables and is symmetrical: There is no causal direction among $P$, $V$, or $T$. But now consider two concrete setups: (a) A cylinder with a movable piston is filled with gas and immersed in a bath of oil maintained at a constant temperature, and (b) a cylinder with a fixed volume is surrounded by a variable heat source (cf. Simon and Rescher 1966, pp. 338–339). These are causally ordered systems. In (a) pressure applied to the piston alters the volume according to the gas law ($nRT/P \Rightarrow V$): *Pressure* causes *Volume*. In (b), changing temperature alters the pressure according to the gas law ($nRT/V \Rightarrow P$): *Temperature* causes *Pressure*. It is only in such localized and concrete cases that there is any causal order at all.

While one can agree in this case that the causal order depends on the details of the setup, it is not clear that the reference to a concrete setup reduces the causal relationship to the level of tokens; for, after all, the now causally ordered relationships are still expressed in terms of the variables, $P$, $V$, and $T$. Hausman must maintain that these variables are now generalizations from particular instantiations or values of the variables. But that seems to beg the question. Let us, nonetheless, follow his argument further.

Hausman (1998, pp. 22–23) gives good philosophical reasons for rejecting the view that token-level causality relates facts. And while he accepts that causality relates events, he argues that it is only particular aspects of the events that are causally relevant. To single out these aspects, he appeals to the notion of *simple tropes*, which are defined as *"located values of relevant variables* or *located instantiations of relevant properties"* (Hausman 1998, p. 18).[9] The asymmetry of causality arises

---

[8] Hausman's view is similar to that of the econometrician Arnold Zellner (1979), who, adopting the suggestion of Feigl (1953, p. 408), suggests that a causal relationship is one that yields predictability according to law. Cf. Marget's discussion (in Hendry and Morgan 1995, pp. 184, 185) of Oscar Morgenstern's distinction between laws as "continuous repetition" and as "rules of adequate causation."

[9] "Trope" is an odd term. The *Concise Oxford English Dictionary* defines it as the "figurative (e.g., metaphorical or ironical) use of a word." It is derived from the Greek for "turn." Hausman attributes the coinage to Donald Williams (1953).

from the relationships among tropes. Type-level causes, in Hausman's view, are generalizations of token-level causes. To paraphrase Hausman's (1998, p. 102) "Generalization View": *A* is a cause of *B* in circumstances *K* if and only if in circumstances *K* each event *a* (a token of *A*) that might occur would causes some event *b* (a token of *B*).[10]

Hausman anticipates the objection that we shall in fact make:

> One might object that the reduction of type to token causal claims puts things exactly backwards. Causal relations obtain in virtue of lawful relations among *properties*. How then can one turn around and claim ... that causal relations among the properties are generalizations of relations among the tokens?
>
> This objection rests on an equivocation. Causal relations among tokens presupposes [*sic*] *nomic* relations among properties. They do not presuppose (asymmetrical) *causal* relations among properties. It is the latter, not the former that are generalizations of relations among tokens. [Hausman 1998, p. 104]

Hausman envisages the linkages among laws and token-level and type-level causality as shown in Figure 4.7. Laws relate variables or properties, but laws are not causal. Tokens exemplify (or instantiate) laws and gain their causal asymmetry from localization (i.e., the particular manner in which the laws are expressed in a concrete system).[11] Type-level causality generalizes the individual instances of token-level causality. Both laws and type-level causality relate variables, but the asymmetry of causality, even at the type level, depends essentially on the existence of token-level causality, which relates tropes.

The structural account questions both of Hausman's linkages. Hausman denies that causality can be fundamentally a relationship among variables. The main argument against variables is that they are not located in space and time and are, therefore, not the kind of things that can be causally related. One might object to Hausman's presumption that causes are necessarily located in space and time, but we shall take it for granted that causes are local and question instead Hausman's claim that variables or properties are not local. This appears to rest entirely on a stipulative definition of *variable*. For, sometimes elliptically, sometimes explicitly, variables are often localized: *U.S.* GDP in *2010* or oil pressure *in my Dodge Caravan next week* are located variables. In general, as shown in Chapter 3, the variables that form the range on

---

[10] This is nearly a quotation from Hausman. It is modified to make it consistent with the type/token nomenclature defined earlier, and it omits reference to temporal order that is irrelevant to the present discussion.

[11] The lower left-hand box, symmetrical token relations is left empty as it does not concern us here. There is no reason, however, that laws should not have noncausal and, therefore, symmetric instances.

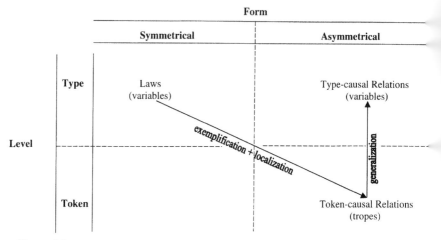

Figure 4.7

which causal structure is defined need not be simple, but can be *n*-tuples formed as the Cartesian products of simple variables, including ones representing time and space.

The idea of localized variables is similar to Eells's (1991, p. 249) idea of temporally localized properties, for example, not the property of being *blue*, but the property of being *blue* at time *t*. Hausman (1998, pp. 101–102) criticizes Eells's localized properties. He argues, first, that it is "undesirable to postulate new kinds of properties." Questions about the nature of the implied standard of desirability to one side, there is reason to doubt that Eells postulates any new kinds of properties. Entities are characterized by multiple properties. A particular scrub jay is characterized by a large number of properties, for example, color and time of existence and many others. To group them analytically as ⟨*color, time, . . .*⟩ is not to postulate new properties, but only to recognize that the properties do not float freely as Platonic forms but are found as ensembles in particular things, so that, for example, the scrub jay instantiates the ensemble ⟨*color = blue, time = t, . . .*⟩.[12] Once that is recognized, there is no principled reason not to consider partial instantiations, so that, for example, in a causal account of the determination of the jay's color we

---

[12] The elements of this *n*-tuple are themselves variables rather than properties, but nothing hangs on this. We could, for example, replace each variable with an exhaustive list of properties, so that an instantiation of the *n*-tuple indicated simply the presence or absence of the property. *Color*, for instance, could be replaced by *red, orange, yellow, green, blue, violet* (or every possible shade of these colors), which would take the value 1 if they were present and 0 otherwise, and so on for every property.

might consider the ensemble $\langle color, time = t, \ldots \rangle$, in which the failure to assign a particular instantiation to color indicates that it is a variable that might have various instantiations.

Partial instantiations of ensembles (or $n$-tuple variables) may or may not accurately capture Eells's time-dependent properties. It is not our purpose to defend Eells. They would seem, however, not to be susceptible to another of Hausman's objections to Eells's account. Hausman argues that the only way in which something could have the time-dependent property $A_t$ is if, during time $t$, it instantiates the property $A$. Therefore, if anything has the property $A_t$ it must exemplify the trope $\langle time = t, A = a \rangle$. Token-level (trope-level) causation is therefore a necessary condition for type-level causation. This objection does not touch the structural account, however, as the structural account localizes variables, not properties; potentialities, not particulars.

Hausman (1998, p. 89) also objects that Eells's "account of causal asymmetry" is "idiosyncratic and undeveloped." Eells's account appeals fundamentally to the temporal relations among time-dependent properties. The structural account, as presented in Chapters 2 and 3, has made no fundamental reference to time ordering. So far it neither endorses nor condemns the Humean axiom that causes must precede effects. Asymmetry arises, as shown in Figures 4.4–4.6 and their associated equations, from parameterizations rather than time. We shall argue in Chapter 6 that macroeconomics should not employ a concept of causality in which time order is fundamental.

On a related point, Hausman sees Eells's account as counterintuitively implying that type-level causal claims are absolute-time specific: Smoking in 1960 causes cancer in 1999. Again, whether or not that is true for Eells's account, it does not touch the structural account. Variables may be localized without absolute time or absolute position playing causal roles in themselves. And relative time (and relative position) are frequently part of type-level causal claims (even if time ordering is not fundamental): As Hausman agrees, when the Surgeon General says "smoking causes cancer," he means that smoking at an earlier time causes cancer at a later time. Time order of this sort is reflected in restrictions on the mappings between variables (functional forms) in Chapter 3, Section 1, but does not require any reference to particular instantiations of variables and, therefore, to tropes.

Hausman's second linkage is meant to establish that type-level causality as we use it is related derivatively to token-level causality. Hausman's generalization view is open to several objections. The first is that the Generalization View requires that a token $a$ causes a token $b$ in circumstances $K$. But to generalize we need to find $K$'s that are alike. It is too strong to say that all $K$'s are identical, since there are in fact no completely identical circumstances. And "alikeness" already brings types in through the back door.

Setting aside the objection that types are implicit in generalization, the Generalization View would generate a weak variety of type-level causation. Imagine that there are a number of different kinds of circumstances, $K_1, K_2, \ldots, K_n$. Each type-level causal relation formed from generalizing in one of these $K_j$ circumstances would be independent, specialized to the circumstances. They might be the same, they might not; there is no way to connect the manner in which tokens change across changing circumstances. The power of articulated causal knowledge is found in the capacity it gives us to analyze such questions. The Generalization View provides no basis for understanding that capacity.

Another weakness of the Generalization View is that it cannot adequately handle indeterminism. Each of the examples of type-level/ token-level conflict presented in Section 4.2 involves tokens that do not correspond to the presumed type-level causal relation. Generalization from such tokens to the appropriate types is impossible. The point is reinforced in cases in which outcomes are both probabilistic and defined on a continuous set. The *exact* repetition of any particular relationship between causes and effects in that case is a measure-zero result.[13] Generalization could proceed only once a judgment had been made about what class of outcomes should be grouped together – but that is a type-level claim.

One way around indeterminism would be to fill in more causal details until the indeterministic situation collapsed into a fully deterministic one (Bunge 1963, pp. 266–267). This approach takes it on faith that all underdetermination of effects by causes is epistemic. As pointed out in Section 4.2, this is both a useful heuristic approach to science and an unfulfilled promissory note. We cannot rule out ontological underdetermination and must have an analysis adequate to deal with it.

Hausman's (1998, ch. 9) strategy for dealing with indeterminism has two planks. The first is to deny that ontologically underdetermined outcomes are caused at all. The second is to shift the explanandum from outcomes to probabilities of outcomes. Probabilities themselves can be regarded as deterministically caused (cf. Papineau 1985, p. 71). This is not

---

[13] In a probabilistic world, everything is a miracle and determinism is pure faith. "[M]an – not nature – is the privileged inventor of strict (ideal) identity and recurrence; man is consequently the exclusive proprietor of boredom" (Bunge 1963, p. 266). See also Holland 1986, p. 947.

satisfactory. Consider the example of the polio vaccines. Here, when a person is vaccinated, we are asked to regard that as determining not immunity, but the probability of immunity. On the propensity view of probability, to which Hausman (1998, pp. 31–32) is sympathetic, probability cannot be regarded as a token. It is a disposition of random behavior to demonstrate a certain regularity. Frequencies are the statistical evidence for probabilities. They are assemblages of tokens. In order to be meaningfully assembled, however, tokens must be grouped. Type-level relationships govern such groupings. There is also an equivocation. When we ask whether the Sabin vaccine prevented John's polio or caused Mary's – even if we acknowledge this to be an indeterministic outcome, something that given all the causes, circumstances, and probabilities, nevertheless, in the final analysis, just happens – it is still the administration of the vaccine and the getting or not getting polio that are the tokens of interest, not the probabilities.[14]

### 4.3 SINGULAR CAUSE AND CONCRETE STRUCTURES

Hausman's account of the relationship of type-level to token-level causation is unnecessarily backhanded and complex. It requires a largely unanalyzed notion of scientific law, operating at the level of types or variables, to support token-level causal relations from which type-level causal relations are derived. The structural account provides a simpler, more direct view of the type/token/law relationship, shown in Figure 4.8. Type-level causal relations are fundamental. Token-level causal relations exemplify (instantiate or realize) type-level casual relations. Laws, if they exist at all, can be seen as abstractions from particular examples of type-level causal relations.

On this view, the two examples of the cylinders of gas can each be thought of as defining concrete causal structures, where here, unlike for Hausman, *concrete* does not imply that every variable is localized and takes a value, but rather that there is enough localization and instantiation of variables that we are able to say that it is *this* cylinder and not some other one. Given that the causal structure is concrete in this sense, it nevertheless embodies type-level causal relations in its dispositions. So, in the case of cylinder (b) in our previous example, in the manner it is actually configured, increasing the temperature would increases the pressure, whether or not the temperature were actually increased.

---

[14] Cf. Salmon's (1984, p. 272) discussion of the causal explanation of plagues.

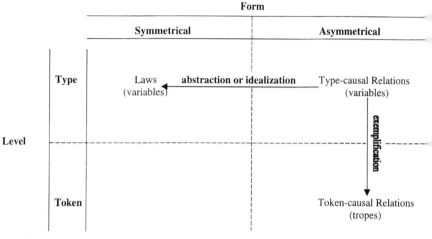

Figure 4.8

The evidence for such type-level relations is, of course, particular tokens. But, as Hume pointed out, there is no deduction from these tokens to the type; it is a conjecture or hypothesis that must be justified other than deductively. Laws are no easier to justify. In fact, the leap from token evidence to type-level causal relations is smaller than the leap from token evidence to laws. Hausman finds it necessary to invoke type-level laws, but the warrant for maintaining the existence of laws is surely weaker than the warrant for maintaining the existence of type-level causal relations.

The ideal gas laws can be seen instead to have been derived from the observation of a common relationship among type-level causes, in particular, instantiated causal structures. We notice, for instance, that if we can ignore the causal arrow in cylinder (a), (b), and related structures, the variables *P*, *V*, and *T* stand in the same (symmetrical) relationship in each case. We call this the ideal gas law. It idealizes particular causal structures by abstracting from their causal asymmetry.[15] It is derived, not primary.

Useful abstractions to lawlike relationships are not necessarily always possible, even when well-defined causal structures exist. This is no doubt true in economics, and is probably true in large areas of physical sciences

---

[15] On idealization, see Cartwright (1989), ch. 5, and Hamminga and De Marchi (1994) and the references therein.

as well. There is not necessarily a law to support every causal relation, and causal relations do not need such support.[16]

The suggestion here that scientific laws occupy a secondary status recalls the major theses of Cartwright's *How the Laws of Physics Lie* (1983) and *Nature's Capacities and Their Measurement* (1989). Yet, in the latter book, Cartwright – in apparent contrast to the position maintained here – stresses the centrality of singular (i.e., token-level) causes. The contrast is only apparent; for, whereas Hausman's claim for the primacy of token-level causes is construed here to be an ontological one, Cartwright's claim is best interpreted as an epistemological one.

Cartwright's vision is that we live in a "dappled world" (Cartwright 1999) characterized by a "patchwork of laws" (Cartwright 1994). Empirical regularities (and even more so, laws) are hard to find and limited in scope. At best, regularities are evidence for capacities. And, as discussed in Chapter 2, Section 6, capacities may themselves be instantiated only irregularly. All evidence is singular or token evidence. Even regularities taken as evidence are but collections of tokens. Frequencies are not, in themselves, probabilities. Probabilities are a model of frequencies; and, as such, are assertions about dispositions, type-level claims that go beyond the evidence (Cartwright 1989, pp. 35–36; cf. Forster 1997a). Here, as elsewhere, there is no induction interpreted as an inference from nothing but particulars to the general. Inferences from particulars to the general are possible only when we are willing to accept as beyond immediate doubt strong maintained assumptions. These assumptions stand in a web of mutual evidential support: each may be doubted separately against the background of some subset of the others. But inference from the particular to the general would not be possible if the entire web of assumptions was cast simultaneously into doubt.[17] A central thesis of *Nature's Capacities* and her later work is that, in answering causal questions, these assumptions include singular causal claims. But this is obviously an epistemological, not an ontological, point. The central category, the capacity, is dispositional in nature; it is ontologically a type.

The structural account shows that type-level relationships need not imply simple regularities (or even instances), much less laws of nature. And so it is too with Cartwright's capacities. Yet, if there were not some *conditional regularities*, at least, it would not be possible to learn about causal structure or capacities. Producing conditional regularities seems

---

[16] Francis Crick is quoted (Holt 1997) as saying "consciousness is mysterious and quantum theory is mysterious and wouldn't it be nice if one explained the other?" We could with equal justice replace "consciousness" by "causality" and "quantum theory" by "laws."

[17] See the comments on the so-called bootstrap methodology, Chapter 2, note 13.

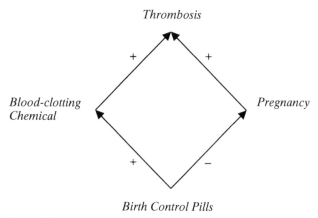

Figure 4.9

to be the point of scientific experiments, creating in a pure form phenomena that otherwise could not be directly observed in nature (see
Hacking 1983, esp. ch. 9). Experimentation famously involves particular
interventions – that is, singular causes.

Cartwright's point about the epistemological necessity of singular
causes is illustrated by her analysis of Hesslow's puzzle about birth
control pills and thrombosis (Chapter 1, Section 2; Cartwright 1989, pp.
99–103). Cartwright fleshes out the example by specifying the mechanism
through which birth control pills cause thrombosis: She posits that they
create a blood-clotting chemical. Figure 1.2 is transformed into Figure
4.9. Assuming that each causal path is independent (i.e., there is no interaction), having the chemical or pregnancy occur with some frequency in
the absence of the pill, so that in a stable set of background circumstances
there are four populations of women, {±*Chemical*, ±*Pregnancy*}, with
definite probabilities. Taking the pills shifts women among these
populations. The problem with looking at the conditional probability
P(*Thrombosis*|*Pills*) as an indicator of causality is that it mixes these four
dissimilar populations, in effect smearing or averaging out the causal
effect. As before, whether pills turn out to be a positive or negative factor
on average depends on the relative strengths of the linkages. Cartwright's
claim is that the probabilities will properly reflect the underlying causal
linkages only if one can first assign women to groups according to which
population they would have occupied in the absence of the pill. This
involves a singular causal judgment about each woman.

David Papineau (1991, pp. 404–406) argues that the multiple
regression can adequately sort out the relative strength of each channel

without appeal to singular causal judgments. Estimate a set of regressions:

$$Chemical \Leftarrow \alpha_0 + \alpha_1 Pills + \varepsilon, \tag{4.7}$$

$$Pregnancy \Leftarrow \beta_0 + \beta_1 Pills + v, \tag{4.8}$$

$$Thrombosis \Leftarrow \delta_0 + \delta_1 Chemical + \delta_2 Pregnancy + \omega, \tag{4.9}$$

where $\varepsilon$, $v$, and $\omega$ are residual error terms.[18] Although the data on which these regressions are estimated are token observations, Papineau's claim is that it is unnecessary in this context to make counterfactual assignments of particular women to groups that they would have occupied absent birth control pills. The tokens in this case are merely relative frequencies that, in turn, are interpreted as evidence of probabilities. In this sense, econometrics refines Hume's regularity account, rather than offering an alternative based on singular causes (Papineau 1991, p. 399).

Papineau (1991, p. 406) sees his conclusions as depending on the independence of the two causal channels; Cartwright, he says, may well be right to stress singular causes when intermediate causes (here *Chemical* and *Pregnancy*) interact. Interaction alone is not enough, however, to undermine Papineau's point. There is no reason that we cannot modify regression (4.9) to take the form

$$Thrombosis \Leftarrow \delta_0 + \delta_1 Chemical + \delta_2 Pregnancy$$
$$+ f(Chemical, Pregnancy) + \omega, \tag{4.9'}$$

where the function $f(\bullet)$ accounts for the interaction. This introduces another aspect of nonlinearity, but one for which there are established econometric techniques. Corresponding to this new equations, Figure 4.9 would have to show some sort of linkage between *Chemical* and *Pregnancy*. Cartwright, however, has something more subtle in mind: The only linkage is through *Pills*; and, yet, *Pills* do not screen off the correlation between *Chemical* and *Pregnancy*.[19]

---

[18] Strictly speaking, at least regressions (4.8) and (4.9) should be treated using limited-dependent variable techniques as described in Chapter 2, Section 5, and illustrated in regressions (4.1) and (4.2). These linear forms, however, serve to make Papineau's point.

[19] Humphreys (1989, p. 95) also maintains that the causal relationship depends on singular causes. He gives the example of the alligator whose eggs will develop into females if incubated at less than 30°C and into males if incubated at greater than 34°C, with the probability of any egg developing as a male increasing monotonically for temperatures

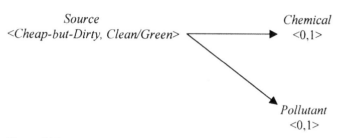

Figure 4.10

To underwrite her view that we must appeal to singular causes epistemically, Cartwright (1993) adopts the strategy of showing that there are cases in which the common-cause condition on which Papineau and others rely fails. She imagines a city trying to determine which of two chemical companies – Clean/Green and Cheap-but-Dirty – to use to provide a chemical for waste processing. During a test period, each company provides the chemical on alternate days.

Cheap-but-Dirty employs a genuinely probabilistic process to produce the chemical: the probability of actually getting it on any day the factory operates is only about 80%. So on some days the sewage does not get treated, but the method is so cheap the city is prepared to put up with that. What they object to are the terrible pollutants that are emitted as a by-product. [Cartwright 1993, p. 115]

The actual causal structure and the range of the variables is set out in Figure 4.10. If the source is Clean/Green, then only the chemical is produced. If the source is Cheap-but-Dirty, the chemical is produced with an 80 percent probability, but the pollutant is produced if, and only if, the chemical is produced. There is no direct causal linkage between *Chemical* and *Pollutant*.

After running the experiment for some time and collecting data, the city is inclined to blame Cheap-but-Dirty and place their business

greater than $30°C$ and less than $34°C$. Whether temperature causes maleness or femaleness seems to depend upon a singular cause – the precise temperature. The structural approach does not see such examples as making the case for the primacy of singular causes, but for the importance of nonlinearity. Let *Sex* = 0 if male and 1 if female. Then, $P(Sex|Temperature)$ is easily modeled using a limited-dependent variable model (like the tobit and probit models of Chapter 2, Section 5). The fundamental relationship is still one between variables, but it is not linear.

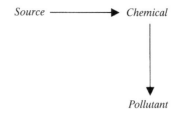

Figure 4.11

with Clean/Green. But Cheap-but-Dirty argues that the statistics do not warrant the city's conclusion. They propose an alternative theory, shown in Figure 4.11: The city's own mishandling of the chemical produces the pollution. Appealing to the principle of common cause, the city says that if *Source* causes *Pollutant*, then as a common cause it should screen off the observed correlation between *Pollutant* and *Chemical*. This can be written in terms of conditional correlations. For any variables $A, B, C$, let $r_{A,B|C}$ be the correlation of $A$ and $B$ conditional on $C$. Then Cheap-but-Dirty's claim is that for the city's view to be correct:

$$r_{Chemical,\,Pollutant|Source} = 0. \tag{4.10}$$

In fact, given the true relationships, this will not occur. Given the probabilities in the example:[20]

$$r_{Chemical,\,Pollutant|Source} = 1. \tag{4.11}$$

The common-cause condition helps Cheap-but-Dirty to criticize the city, but it is not positively supportive of its alternative theory, which suggests that *Chemical* should screen off *Pollutant* from *Source*. It does not:

$$r_{Pollutant,\,Source|Chemical} = 1. \tag{4.12}$$

Cartwright locates the failure of the common-cause condition to discriminate between the competing theories in its general failure in any case in which the common cause is irreducibly indeterministic. Once

---

[20] For three variables $A, B, C$, the conditional correlation between $A$ and $B$ conditional on $C$ is $r_{A,B|C} = \left(r_{A,B} - r_{A,C}r_{B,C}\right)\left(\sqrt{1-r_{A,C}^2}\,\sqrt{1-r_{B,C}^2}\right)^{-1}$. Letting *Source* = 1 if Cheap-but-Dirty and 0 if Clean/Green is the designated supplier, and *Chemical* and *Pollutant* = 1 if present and 0 if not, the raw correlations are $r_{Chemical,Pollutant} = 0.27$, $r_{Chemical,\,Source} = -0.33$, $r_{Source,Pollutant} = 0.82$.

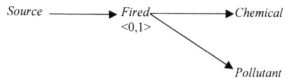

Figure 4.12

again, Cartwright is drawing a distinction between Cheap-but-Dirty's capacity to produce the chemical and the pollutant and that capacity having been exercised or having "fired" in a particular case (see Chapter 2, Section 5). Against such cases, Papineau (1991, p. 406) argues that in fact the singular cause is an illusion. There should be an intermediate variable indicating whether or not the capacity was exercised. This is shown in Figure 4.12, in which the variable *Fired* takes the value 1 when Cheap-but-Dirty actually produces and 0 when it does not. *Fired* in fact screens off *Chemical* from *Pollution*; the common-cause condition operates as expected.[21]

No one can doubt that scientific progress often consists in articulating such deterministic common causes. But Cartwright's point is that, in general, there is no guarantee that such intermediate variables exist or are observable. Existence and observability are different things. And Cartwright dismisses the principle of the common cause only in its narrowest form in which it is defined by the screening-off relationship. Reichenbach also defined the principle more broadly as a heuristic rule that all robust correlations should have a causal account. There is nothing in the case of Cheap-but-Dirty's pollution that would suggest abandoning that useful heuristic.

Still, we cannot rule out the stochastic common cause. A general pattern is set out in Figure 4.13. Here *A* and *B* have independent causes as well as a common stochastic cause (random error), ε. This case is well known to econometricians as *seemingly unrelated regressions* (*SUR*) (Johnston 1972, pp. 238–241). Figure 4.13 can be represented as

---

[21] A similar strategy is employed in the move between Figures 4.4 and 4.5. Because of the deterministic relationship between *Fired* and *Pollution*, which amounts to a failure of independence (see Section 4.4), the conditional correlation between *Chemical* and *Fired* conditional on *Pollution* is undefined as the denominator in the formula in note 12 involves division by zero. Still, it is clear that *Pollution* carries no nonredundant information about chemical, once we know that Cheap-but-Dirty is not only the designated supplier but, in fact, actually produced.

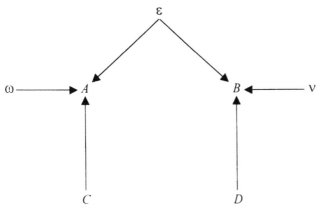

Figure 4.13

$$A \Leftarrow \alpha C + \varepsilon + \omega = \alpha C + \Omega, \tag{4.13}$$

$$B \Leftarrow \beta D + \varepsilon + \nu = \beta D + N. \tag{4.14}$$

The errors are unobservable, but estimates can be formed of $\hat{\Omega}$ and $\hat{N}$ from the separate regressions. Equations (4.13) and (4.14) are then transformed using an estimate of the covariance of the errors, $\text{cov}(\hat{\Omega}, \hat{N})$, and are then reestimated to generate new values for $\hat{V}$ and $\hat{N}$ and the coefficients $\alpha$ and $\beta$. The iterative process is repeated until the estimates converge. The properties of the common error term, $\varepsilon$, can be inferred from these efficient estimates of $\alpha$ and $\beta$ (conditional, of course, on knowledge of the causal structure).[22]

In Chapter 5, we shall consider whether macroeconomics provides cases of irreducibly stochastic common causes. In the meantime, what more can be learned from this example about the role of singular causal claims in causal inference?

Consider how the alternative theories might be investigated. The city might not simply observe the outcomes passively. If it were to purchase its chemicals only from Clean/Green for some time and then only from Cheap-but-Dirty for another period of time, then it would be clear that the pollution occurred only when using Cheap-but-Dirty's

[22] J. Simon (1970, p. 245) expresses skepticism about latent variables, saying that they make it too easy to explain correlations. Similarly, Spirtes, Glymour, and Scheines (1991) note that any correlation can be explained by some unmeasured common cause. For all that it is a useful heuristic to eschew latent variables, it is pure faith that it will always be a successful strategy.

chemicals. Notice that this manipulation of the supplies amounts to intervention over singular causes and is consistent with Cartwright's general point. It would not, however, settle the matter; for is it Cheap-but-Dirty's process or the city's handling that is the cause of the pollution?

Another way of investigating the sewage-treatment case also appears to involve singular causes fundamentally. This is the *mark method* due to Reichenbach (1956, pp. 197–205; see also Salmon 1984, ch. 5, and Cartwright 1993).[23] Reichenbach's idea is that causality should be viewed as a process involving in Salmon's (1984, p. 139) terminology *production* and *propagation*. A way of checking whether a process is causal process or a pseudocausal process is to see whether it can transmit marks. Suppose that one sees two mirror images of a man in a funhouse and one is unsure which is the real man: Does image *A* cause image *B* or the other way round? If *A* is, in fact, the real man and a fly lands on his nose, he is marked. That mark transmits to image *B*, and one is still unable to tell which is real. But if a fly lands on the mirror, right on the image of the man's nose on *B*, the fly will not transmit to image *A*. This failure of the mark to propagate from *B* to *A* clearly identifies *A* as cause and *B* as effect.

Mark propagation would seem to be a discriminating criterion when the issue involved is the direction of causation. But that it is not the question in Cartwright's example, which presupposes that, if there is a causal link between *Source* and *Chemical*, *Source* is the cause; that, if there is a causal link between *Chemical* and *Pollution*, *Chemical* is the cause; and that, if there is no such link, *Source* must cause *Pollution*. Even in this case, knowledge of mark transmission may be helpful, but only with additional detailed knowledge of causal capacities.

Suppose, for instance, that the both the chemical produced by Cheap-but-Dirty and its by-product pollution were hydrocarbons and that the carbon feedstocks could be irradiated to produce carbon-14, a radioactive, but chemically neutral, mark. Then, checking both the chemical and the pollution for radioactivity would show that both came from the same source. It might not prove that the cause could not

---

[23] Tooley (1987, pp. 220–221) objects to the mark method on the ground that it presumes the causal efficacy of the marking process. Humphreys (1989, p. 91) rightly argues that, while marks cannot define cause, because of this circularity, they can provide an effective strategy for learning about causes of which we are ignorant on the basis of causal knowledge already thought to be secure. This recalls Cartwright's slogan, "no causes in, no causes out." See also the discussion of the circularity of defining causality in terms of direct control in Chapter 2, Section 3.

have been the handling of the chemical after it was in the hands of the city – absolving Cheap-but-Dirty of the blame, even though they were ultimately the source. But, if detailed understanding of the chemistry could rule out the selfsame carbon atoms found in the chemical as constituents of the pollution, then it would absolve Cheap-but-Dirty as well. But the causal structures do not necessarily admit of marking in any particular way. Suppose instead that the pollution were sulfuric acid ($H_2SO_4$). Since the pollution molecule does not contain any carbon, even if *Source* were the cause of *Pollution*, that particular mark would not transmit.

Cartwright's two examples demonstrate that neither the common-cause principle nor mark transmission is the essence of causation.[24] Rather they are heuristically useful features that work, when they do work, because of the particular causal structure. Is this, then, to concede Hausman's point that causality is a relationship between tropes – fully instantiated variables? To see that it is not requires a fuller notion of what constitutes structure.

Reality can be characterized at any moment by the relationships among a large set of variables and by the particular values that they take. Some variables are more tightly linked than others. Particularly tightly linked variables can be thought of as objects or structures. There is some latitude in drawing the boundaries around particular structures depending on our purposes. The cow's thighbone is at once a structure and an element of a larger structure. The cow and the herd are related similarly. This latitude in demarcating structures does not threaten their reality Some demarcations do not isolate structures that enter as units into relationships with other structures. The thighbone of a cow and the thighbone of a kangaroo half-way around the world can be grouped mentally but do not enter into effective causal relationships with any other structures as a unit. Nature has joints, and such a grouping fails to take nature apart at its joints.

The identity of structures cannot depend on the complete instantiations of all their variables at any time. We see the *same* cow as she walks across a field, even though many of the variables that describe her change. Identity depends not on the constancy of every variable, but, in some cases, on the constancy of some subset of variables or, in others, on the continuity of some subset of variables. To take a hackneyed example, George Washington's original hatchet cannot be

---

[24] A point that Reichenbach (1956, pp. 157–158) explicitly acknowledges with respect to the principle of the common cause and one that is implicit in his discussion of marks as one instrument of causal investigation among others.

constructed today out of new parts. Were it preserved in a museum – perhaps decaying, but certainly changing time and location relative to its encounter with the cherry tree – we would regard it as the same object. Had it been used every twenty-second of February to chop down a cherry tree in veneration of its owner and so, over two centuries of wear and tear, had each of its parts replaced, we might regard it nonetheless – relative to some purposes and in some causal relations – as the same object.

This last example is related to Reichenbach's (1956, p. 38, 224, passim) notion of *genidentity* (cf. Humphreys 1989, p. 22). For mark transmission usefully to trace out causal relations it is necessary that the structure be changed by the mark. We identify the structure as the same structure through reference to the genesis of the final structure – an appeal to the continuity of some of the sequence of instantiations of some of its variables. The mark must alter a variable that is inessential to the continued identity of the structure, as in the case of marking Cheap-but-Dirty's feedstocks with an isotope that, though radioactive, is chemically indistinguishable from ordinary carbon.[25]

Causal relationships occur in structures, and structures are identified by definite instantiations of certain variables of a linked group. To that extent, causality is a token-level phenomenon. It is the existence or not of a movable piston or the presence or not of external temperature regulation that determines whether pressure causes volume or temperature causes pressure in the gas-law illustrations of Section 4.2. But that in no way detracts from the conclusion that the causalness of the relationship between temperature and pressure or pressure and volume is located in their relationship as types. The variables whose instantiations determine the causal structure are not the variables that themselves stand in the causal relationship of interest. This is reflected in the fact that our representations of causal relationships often elide reference to those variables (or their instantiations) that determine structure. They are part of the causal field and become important only if they change in some relevant way: The causal relationship between pressure and volume breaks down if the cylinder cracks.

---

[25] Causality is about structure. The fundamental problem of causal inference relates to the identity of structure: It is impossible to observe a mark or any change in the structure on truly the *same* structure (see Holland 1986, p. 947). Genidentity provides a notion for grouping structures that change over time as the same structure. If there were other criteria of identity, then it might be possible to group structures that differ over space as the same structure in the relevant sense as well. This is the notion that lies behind treatment and controls in experimental contexts.

The same point supports Cartwright's general contention that singular causes play an essential part in causal inference against Papineau's neo-Humean contention that multiple regression can sort causal relationships out without reference to singular causes. Systems of regression equations can sometimes be thought of as representing a structure. That is the significance of the directed equalities ($\Leftarrow$) in regressions (4.7)–(4.9). The focus of Papineau's analysis is on the type-level relations between variables, but regression can sort out these type-level relations only in the context of strong assumptions about token-level structures. This is the point of the econometric literature on identification and of Simon's solution to the problem of observational equivalence (see Chapter 2, Section 2).

Does this concede too much? Could it not be argued that in order to build structures, mark processes, conduct experiments, or otherwise intervene in the world that one must manipulate, or at least know of, singular causal relationships.

Singular facts are not reducible to generic ones, but exactly the opposite: singular facts are basic. A generic claim, such as 'Aspirins relieve headaches', is best seen as a modalized singular claim: 'An aspirin can relieve a headache'; and the surest sign that an aspirin can do so is that sometimes one does do so. Hence my claim that Hume had it just upside down. [Cartwright 1989, p 95]

But where, one asks with Hume, do singular facts declare their causal nature? We believe that an aspirin relieved a headache because of strong assumptions about surrounding conditions that make it probable that it is so. In experimental situations, these assumptions are often strong enough, and empirically warranted enough, that the single test is convincing (see Cartwright 1989, p. 2), but in ordinary life they might not stand scrutiny. As a father, I am convinced that in particular cases antibiotics have cured my daughter's ear infection. Yet, controlled scientific studies suggest that they may be ineffective and that ear infections end naturally with or without the antibiotics. Singular relations do not wear their causal nature on their faces. We assert the singular causal claims only through subsuming them to type-level claims (cf. Humphreys 1989, p. 52). The assertions involved are counterfactual and often do not involve the repeated realization of a situation – a fact about practical inference that was, as we saw in Chapter 1, well known to Hume. Rather, we assert unique casual relations because the network of type-level relations can narrow the probabilities of anything but a particular token-level cause and effect to practically zero. Yet, even in such circumstances, extremely low probability events may occur, things happen against type, which may account for cases in which airplanes crash for no discernible reason or apparent miracles occur.

That types are ontologically basic threatens neither Cartwright's experimental philosophy nor her conclusion that sometimes particular tokens must be realized if causal inferences are to be drawn. Indeed, it better suits her notion of capacities, which are intrinsically dispositional. It says that causal relations are relations among capacities and it is only in virtue of being realizations of those capacities that tokens can stand in causal relations at all.

## 4.4 CAUSALITY AND LAWS

Cartwright stresses simple capacities and their universalizable character – that is, that capacities carry their peculiar virtues from situation to situation (Cartwright 1989, pp. 3, 146–147, 191, passim). While not inconsistent with Cartwright, the structural account developed here emphasizes different features of capacities. First, as already discussed at length, capacities are dispositions. Second, there is an important aspect of *emergence* that can be underplayed in focusing on simple capacities.

Capacities can be seen as derived from structures, as emerging when the right situations are created. Mechanics is about predictable emergence. Gears, drums, springs, timers, and motors each have various capacities; and, when assembled into a washing machine, they have the capacity to wash clothes – a virtue that emerges because of the particular structure into which the parts are assembled. The organization is an element independent of the parts.

Emergence need not be predictable. Science is full of examples of assemblies of what were thought to be well-understood parts displaying capacities not derivable from the capacities of the parts separately. The usual strategy is then to seek a reduction – to show how a richer understanding of the parts or the organization would make the emergent capacity predictable. This is not always successful, although it is the abiding faith of many scientists that in the long run it must be.[26] Typically, mechanics suggests emergence as a property of orderly assemblies – washing machines, watches, radios – yet it may also be possible that mere agglomeration (e.g., the collection of molecules into an ideal gas) may also create emergent capacities (see Bunge 1963, p. 170; cf. Popper 1972, pp. 209–210, who explicitly denies the possibility).

The notion of emergence suggests a third feature of capacities – *locality*. Capacities exist only within particular structures and, as we have seen, structures are localized. Capacities are dual – at once universal and

[26] It is worth recalling Bunge's (1963, p. 156) observation that explaining emergence is the same as explaining it away.

local. This duality recommends Cartwright's vision of the "dappled world." Scientific laws in the standard view are thought to be universal, not local. But laws are difficult to find and not obvious to apply in concrete situations (Cartwright 1989, p. 8). And they are not required. It is always nice to have a law, but in economics, laws – or at least laws of any precision – are rare. And economics is not alone. Richard Feynman (1995, p. 66) gives the example of the problem of circulating or turbulent fluids:

Nobody in physics has really been able to analyze it mathematically satisfactorily in spite of its importance for sister sciences. . . . If we watch the evolution of a star, there comes a point where we can deduce that it is going to start convection; and thereafter we can no longer deduce what should happen. A few million years later the star explodes, but we cannot figure out the reason. We cannot analyze the weather. We do not know the patterns of motion there should be inside the earth. The simplest form of the problem is to take a pipe that is very long and push water through it at high speed. We ask: to push a given amount of water through the pipe, how much pressure is needed? No one can analyze it from first principles and the properties of water. If the water flows very slowly, or if we use a thick goo like honey, then we can do it nicely. You will find that in your textbook. What we really cannot do is deal with actual, wet water running through a pipe.

The structural account is at home in situations such as Feynman describes and which are ubiquitous in economics and physical sciences.

A dappled world characterized by a patchwork of laws suggests that the causal connections are not dense, that everything does not depend on everything else; rather that the world can be – indeed, must be – segmented into more or less autonomous structures and each analyzed separately. Nothing in the formalism of the last chapter implies such restriction: We can characterize causal connections howsoever dense they may be. Rather, it is an empirical fact. But is it a fact about the nature of the world or about the limitations of our minds? Pierre Laplace clearly thought that it was a limitation of our minds:

Such perfection as the human mind has been able to give astronomy affords but a feeble sketch of [an imagined intelligence capable of exact application of Newton's laws to the entire universe]. . . . All our efforts in our search for truth tend, without respite, to approximate the intelligence imagined, but our efforts will always fall infinitely short of this mark. [Laplace 1812, pp. 2–3][27]

---

[27] Laplace anticipates what I shall refer to, in Chapter 5, as the "Cournot problem." Laplace's vision of what a perfect intelligence could do is clear in his statement: "Given for one instant an intelligence which could comprehend all the forces by which nature

Since Laplace's time, some physical scientists have taken it as an article of faith that only our mental limitations stop us from comprehending that the world is completely lawlike and completely determined – and completely free of any need for a causal account. The Walrasian fantasy of economics is the analogue of the Laplacian fantasy of physics.[28] In the Walrasian model, producers and consumers, given tastes and technology, determine the amounts and prices of all goods. It is sometimes said that in such a densely connected system there is no causality among the variables. But it is also said that in such a dense system everything causes everything else.

The counterfactual nature of causality requires that things could have been different from the way they actually are. In the structural account, this amounts to there being some variables that can change (a) without affecting the identity of the structure and (b) independently of other causes. Such variables are either parameters or field variables. Require- ment (a) means that economic analysis cannot be restricted to pure com- parative static exercises in which the comparison is between structures that are not genetically connected, but that are nonetheless identical except for some particular parameters of interest. Such exercises are the stuff of typical economics texts. But in a genuine causal account, change must be a possibility for *this* structure, not reduced to pointing out a *döppelganger* with a slightly different countenance.

The notion of structure itself implies an element of indeterminism. If structures are to be distinct, yet interact, then some variables in them must not be caused within the structure itself. There are two varieties of indeterminism, which might be termed "stochastic" and "nonstochastic" indeterminism. Stochastic indeterminism corresponds to the random, probability governed elements of the causal field; while nonstochastic indeterminism corresponds to changes in the parameters, which could

is animated and the respective positions of the beings which compose it, if moreover this intelligence were vast enough to submit these data to analysis, it would embrace in the same formula both the movements of the largest bodies in the universe and those of the lightest atom; to it nothing would be uncertain, and the future as the past would be present to its eyes." That Laplace regarded this vision of a super intelligence as a fantasy is perhaps implied in his more famous exchange with Napolean. On receipt of Laplace's *Mécanique Céleste*, Napoleon is said to have remarked that he had written it without mentioning the author of the universe. To which, Laplace is said to have replied: "Sire, I have no need of that hypothesis." (Barlett's *Familiar Quotations* gives the source of this remark as Eric Temple Bell, *Men of Mathematics*, 1937).

[28] Popper (1972, p. 218) refers to the "deterministic nightmare." Hacking (1983, p. 213) refers to the "Leibnizian dream" of eliminating all free parameters. To characterize these as dreams and fantasies is not to deny the fruits of striving for their fulfillment nor to deny the utility of the tools with which the dreams are spun: Laplace's mechanics and Walras's economics are substantial, albeit limited, achievements.

conform to the laws of probability only contingently. Nonstochastic indeterminism provides the potential for control, for purposeful interventions in causal structures and for their instrumental use. Were all the
variables of a structure determined within the structure, there would be
no sense to the idea of being outside the structure and there could be
no interaction with it. Mark transmission and other features of causal
propagation depend on this distinction between variables whose values
persist or form a continuous set and those that change.

The Laplacian fantasy is that there are ultimately no field variables or
parameters. The slogan "no free parameters" is cashed out, as the physical constants of the universe turn out to be implied from first principles
and initial conditions.[29] The dynamics of every variable are governed
entirely by universal laws. The only significant changes that could exist
are ones that generate an alternative universe. Consider this universe.
For the same set of laws and different initial conditions, the past and
future of the variables would be different. While there could be such
an alternative universe, there would be no way to get there from ours,
and, indeed, no interaction between it and ours. Modern quantum
physics accepts irreducible stochastic indeterminism. A modern physicist
must, consequently, be more modest than Laplace in his claims for prediction, yet this development, as important as it is, does not undermine
the basis for the Laplacian faith. Only nonstochastic indeterminism can
do that.

Various philosophers have identified nonstochastic indeterminism as
an important feature of causality under different guises. Cartwright
(1989, ch. 1, sec. 4) argues that one can identify genuine causes in a set
of INUS conditions only if each has an open back path. An *open back
path* exists for any cause $A$ of effect $B$ if $A$ has some independent cause
that causes $B$ only through its effect on $A$. In a diagram of a causal structure, there is an open back path for $A$ if a causal arrow from $C$ points
into $A$ and there is no other path from $C$ to $B$.[30] Hausman (1998,
p. 63 ff.) bases an account of causal priority on a similar notion, which he
labels *independence*: If $A$ and $B$ (or if $A$ and $B$ are causally connected
only as effects of a common cause), then $B$ has a cause that is distinct
from $A$ and is not causally connected to $A$.[31] The implication of inde-

---

[29] Glymour and Spirtes (1988, p. 178) and Glymour (1980, p. 384) put the general case for
avoiding free parameters. Lucas (1980, esp. sec. 6) sketches a Walrasian vision for macroeconomics in which the elimination of free parameters through an appeal to first principles is the main goal.
[30] Cartwright presumes that the INUS conditions are time ordered and that the functional
relations between them are linear.
[31] This is a very close paraphrase of Hausman's definition, ignoring his restriction to token
causes.

pendence is that all effects have multiple causes and not all causes are directly or indirectly causally connected (Hausman 1998, p. 64). The point to notice is that independence arises naturally in the structural account with its emphasis on the causal field (error terms in econometric applications) and parameters (nonstochastic indeterminism).

Is independence an epistemic or an ontological requirement? Cartwright's (1989, p. 33) stipulation in her definition that "it is both true, *and known to be true*" (emphasis added) that a cause is located at the root of the open back path suggests an epistemic requirement consistent with the epistemic importance of singular causes (cf. Owens 1992, p. 108). Consider a pared down case of the Laplacian fantasy in which the independence condition fails. Imagine a universe consisting only of two neutrons orbiting around each other governed by the textbook laws of physics (Tooley 1987, p. 220). What is their causal relationship? There are at least two possible answers. First, although the two neutrons stand in a law-governed relationship, the arrangement is perfectly symmetrical and there can be no notion of cause without asymmetry. Second, the two stand in an ontologically well-defined causal order (namely mutual or reciprocal cause), but given that this is the complete universe and there are no independent channels of intervention, one could never make this inference.[32] There is no need to choose between these answers, which suggests a third possibility: The situation is pragmatically impossible; there is no situation related to any human interest or purpose that is analogous to this one.[33]

How might independence fail in economics? One possibility is through logical identity. It is not uncommon for newspapers to report that bond prices fell *causing* yields on bonds to rise. This is nonsense because, given the face value, coupon structure, and maturity of the bond, the yield and the price are related by a mathematical identity. One might object that this is not a failure of independence but a failure

---

[32] Opinions differ on which view to take. Humphreys (1989, pp. 83–85) argues that if a set of conditions is sufficient for an effect, there is no cause: The inevitable is not caused. Similarly, Mackie (1980, p. 191) argues that there is no cause in a determined universe; Sanford (1976, p. 196) disagrees with Mackie. Tooley (1987, p. 237) argues against the centrality of causal forks as defining causes, since that would imply counterintuitively that there is no causality with less than three causal relata. The structural approach permits a bivariate causal relation, but the possibility of intervention always implies a third causal element off-stage. Intervention implies nonstochastic indeterminism (see Chapter 2, Section 5). Bunge (1963, p. 181) appears to take a similar view when he argues that determinism requires freedom.

[33] Reichenbach (1956, pp. 95–96) seems to reach a similar conclusion: "We are allowed to regard even the evolution of the universe as a genuine probability chain, in which each successive step is a matter of chance, whereas the sequence as a whole is governed by statistical laws as dependable as the so-called strict causal laws of physics."

of the putative cause and effect to be distinct.[34] But this multiples categories unnecessarily. We can say that two aspects of a structure are not distinct if they cannot be separated into substructures, which means that they cannot be separated into groups of variables governed by their own parameters. Identity is just the most extreme case of a failure of independence.

Take a less extreme case – a miniature version of the Walrasian fantasy, the analogy to the two-neutron version of the Laplacian fantasy. Consider an economy of a single agent with an exogenous income ($Y$) and two goods ($A$ and $B$) supplied freely from the outside at a relative price ($P$). Clearly the exogenous variables, $P$ and $Y$, cause $A$ and $B$, but what is the causal relationship between $A$ and $B$? There are two sources of constraint. If $A$ and $B$ are chosen optimally (as in the standard neoclassical account in which demand curves are derived from utility maximization), then the choice must be coordinated. Independent of optimal choice, if there are really no other goods (or assets), then $A$ and $B$ are linked by a budget constraint.

On analogy with the two-neutron universe, consider the situation in which no parameters could possibly change. We could then regard the relationship between $A$ and $B$ as governed by the law of demand (relativized to the particular utility function), but as noncausal. Equally, and indifferently, we could regard the connection between $A$ and $B$ as causal despite the fact that the situation gives us no epistemic handle by means of which we could come to know the nature of the connection. Similarly, even if the parameters of, say, the utility function could change, we cannot distinguish observationally between different causal orders, say, Figure 4.14 in which $A$ and $B$ are directly causally independent, linked only by sharing $P$ and $Y$ as causes, and Figure 4.15 in which $A$ and $B$ are mutual causes, as well as being caused by $P$ and $Y$.[35]

We can adopt the same pragmatic response to the two options (laws without cause or cause without causal inference) in this case as in the two-neutron universe. In any case of any genuine human concern, there

---

[34] A suggestion made to me in private correspondence by Daniel Hausman.
[35] To say that parameters cannot change is not to say that variables do not have time paths, and to say that parameters can change is not to say that parameter change is required for any change of variables. Just as in Laplacian physics, economic variables can develop through time without any causally significant intervention. Consider a simple dynamic model such as the cobweb in which a supply curve, $q_t = s_0 + s_1 p_{t-1}$, interacts with a demand curve, $q_t = d_0 - d_1 p_t$, where $q$ is quantity, $p$ is price, and $t$ is a time index. The general path of prices can be described as $p_t = (d_0 - s_0)/d_1 - (s_1/d_1)p_{t-1}$. For an initial $p_0$, $p$ (and $q$) change every period, even for fixed parameters. If the parameters are chosen just right (e.g., $d_1 = s_1 = 1, s_0 = 0$), the analogy with the two-neutron universe is complete: Prices will alternate between $p_0$ and $p_1$, eternally.

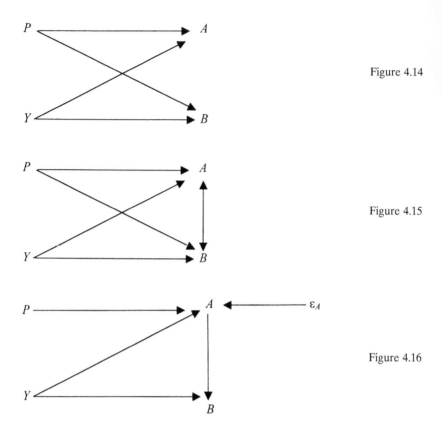

Figure 4.14

Figure 4.15

Figure 4.16

is both a parameter space and a causal field. The budget constraint still binds and reality can no longer be represented indifferently as in Figures 4.14 and 4.15. Say, for example, $A$ is chosen optimally, but the actual purchase is subject to a random implementation error ($\varepsilon_A$). To respect the budget constraint, this *must* be reflected in the actual purchases of $B$, so that a well-defined causal order between $A$ and $B$ would be as shown in Figure 4.16. Cartwright (1989, pp. 114–117) argues that there is no causality between quantities connected by a budget constraint. That could be true only in a world of Walrasian fantasy.

The Laplacian and Walrasian fantasies are inspirational and fuel the search for overarching universal laws governing the physical and social worlds. In contrast, practical physics and economics concentrates on less dense causal networks, and, therefore, on structures that stand in localized relationships, mostly less universal than the ideal scientific law.[36] On a structural account of causality, the goal of science is the articulation and isolation of capacities and causes.[37] Whether macroeconomics can be interpreted as structural is a question we take up in the next chapter.

---

[36] Simon and Rescher (1966, p. 330) offer the Postulate of Independence or the Empty World Postulate, which states that the web of causal connection is not too dense to isolate subsystems, and the Postulate of Prepotence, which states that subsystems can be isolated in which the causal influences within the subsystem are large relative to the influences on the subsystem from the outside. These postulates appear to make a similar distinction as ours between causal structure and causal field.

[37] The idea that a Walrasian account is, for practical purposes, an inspiring fantasy in which (contrary to the Empty World Postulate of fn. 36) everything is connected to everything else is what lies behind Friedman's (1955) distinction between Marshallian and Walrasian methodology. In Friedman's view, it is only when economics can focus on a tractably limited set of causal connections that it can serve as Marshall's "engine for the discovery of concrete truth." For a further discussion of Friedman's distinction, see Hoover (1984; 1988a, ch. 9) and Hammond (1996).

# 5

# The Reality of Macroeconomic Structures

All are keeping a sharp look-out in front, but none suspects
that the danger may be creeping up from behind. This shows
how real the island was.

– J. M. Barrie, *Peter Pan*

David Hume, the macroeconomist and historian, talked freely about
causes linking macroeconomic and social variables and events; David
Hume, the philosopher of causality, analyzed almost exclusively physical
causes.[1] In the preceding chapters, we have followed in Hume's footsteps,
concentrating on physical and biological examples. It is now time to
inquire, as Hume never did, into the connection between the practical
causal reasoning of macroeconomics and the general causal analysis
developed for other problems. We address two questions. First, in this
chapter, we ask, is macroeconomics a suitable subject for a structural
causal account? That is, are there macroeconomic structures analogous
to physical structures? In the next chapter, we ask, what constraints does
the nature of macroeconomics place on the details of a suitable causal
account?

The subject of these chapters (and, for that matter, of the book as a
whole) has been left up to now implicit. It might be useful to start with
a working definition. To begin at the beginning, we define the key terms.
"Macroeconomics" is sometimes thought to be the economics of broad
aggregates, and "microeconomics" the economics of individual economic
actions. Although he did not use the terms microeconomics and macroeconomics, John Maynard Keynes (1936, pp. 292–293) drew a related distinction: Microeconomics is the theory of the individual industry or firm;
macroeconomics is the theory of output and employment as a whole. As
Maarten Janssen (1993, ch. 1) shows, these alternative definitions cut in

---

[1] This chapter is a revised and slightly expanded version of Hoover (1995c). Copyright ©
1995, *The Monist*, Peru, Illinois 61354. Reprinted by permission.

somewhat different ways. They are, however, similar enough for present purposes, since any quantification of output and employment *as a whole* is bound to involve broad aggregates. Economics is a social science; but macroeconomics is remarkably dehumanized. People are at best referred to as representatives of a class; and, mostly, the talk is about variables. Macroeconomics is thus that area of economics that studies GDP, unemployment, interest rates, the flow of financial resources, exchange rates, and so forth.

The structural account of causality presupposes a realist ontology. Causes are real properties of variables in structures. It seems unproblematic to think of a billiard ball or a piston and cylinder or a disease as a real structure. It is somewhat harder to think of GDP or the general price level as structures or parts of structures. They seem to be derived from something more basic, and not to be real things at all, but creations of our minds – mere summaries for the genuinely real behaviors of individual economic actors. The recent history of macroeconomics, with the emphasis on the microfoundations of macroeconomics, reinforces these doubts.

What is meant by realism? Uskali Mäki (1996) offers a careful discussion of realism in relation to economics that might help to define the term. Mäki distinguishes between *ontological realism*, which raises questions about what there is, and *semantic realism*, which raises questions about the connection between language and what there is. Semantic realism can be analyzed further, but the central issue here is ontological: *Do macroeconomic aggregates and causal relations among them exist?* More precisely, and again using Mäki's terminology, do macroeconomic aggregates exist *externally* (i.e., independently of any *individual* human mind) and *objectively* (i.e., unconstituted by the representations of macroeconomic theory). Advocates of what might be called the *strong program of microfoundations* would reject realism with respect to macroeconomic entities in this sense and, implicitly, reject macroeconomics as a suitable subject of structural causal analysis.[2] If it could be established that macroeconomics was a suitable subject for a realist causal account, then one of the central rationales for the program of microfoundations for macroeconomics would be eliminated.

## 5.1 THE PROGRAM OF MICROFOUNDATIONS

Before the twentieth century, the most common definition of economics was epitomized by Alfred Marshall (1920, p. 1): "[A] study of mankind in

[2] The future for Lucas (1987, pp. 107–108) is one in which macroeconomics has been so thoroughly reduced to microeconomics that it will no longer be useful to use the prefix "micro" as there would be no distinction left to draw.

the ordinary business of life; [economics] examines that part of individual and social action which is most closely connected with the attainment and with the use of the material requisities of well-being." This definition, which is reasonably hospitable to macroeconomics, has now largely been supplanted by that of Lionel Robbins (1935, p. 16): "Economics is the science which studies human behaviour as a relationship between ends and scarce means which have alternative uses." On Robbins's definition, economics must be fundamentally about the individual.

Modern macroeconomics developed in the wake of Keynes's *General Theory of Employment Interest and Money* (1936). Typical elements of Keynes's analysis were the consumption function, which related aggregate consumption to aggregate national income, the investment function, which related aggregate investment to the general rate of interest, and the liquidity preference function, which related the aggregate stock of money to aggregate national income and the general rate of interest. It is easy to understand that in a profession committed to Robbins's definition of economics, such aggregate relationships were at best rather unappealing way stations on the path to an individualist economics. The program of microfoundations, as it has developed over the past 60 years, aims to explain all macroeconomic properties of the economy – *in principle*, at least – by reference to the behavior of rational economic actors such as postulated by microeconomics.[3]

Approval of the program of microfoundations is almost universal among economists. Those economists who have reflected at all deeply on the matter typically associate microfoundations with methodological individualism (e.g., Janssen 1993, pp. 26–29 passim; Boland 1979, chs. 2 and 5).[4] Mark Blaug (1992, p. 44) defines *methodological individualism* as the principle that "asserts that explanations of social, political, or economic phenomena can only be regarded as adequate if they run in terms of the beliefs, attitudes, and decisions of individuals."

Methodological individualism is a doctrine about explanation. Despite lip-service to it, it is not widely practiced by economists. The reason is what I have elsewhere labeled the "Cournot problem" after its lucid, early formulation by Augustine Cournot (1838/1927, p. 127), the nineteenth-century mathematician and economist: There are too many individuals (firms and consumers) and too many goods to be handled by direct modelling.[5] Blaug (1992, p. 46) observes that few explanations of

---

[3] See Weintraub (1979) and Janssen (1993) for general discussions of microfoundations for macroeconomics.

[4] I must be careful not to leave a false impression: Both Janssen and Boland are critics of the program of microfoundations.

[5] Hoover (1988a, p. 135). Also see Hoover (1988a, ch. 9, esp. sec. 2; ch. 10, pp. 241–244); Friedman (1955).

macroeconomic phenomena have been successfully reduced to their microfoundations, so that insistence on microfoundations would eliminate explanations of macroeconomic phenomena *tout court*. Even Lucas (1987, pp. 107–108), an important advocate of the program of microfoundations, holds up only the *hope* of the elimination of distinction between microeconomics and macroeconomics.[6]

The commitment of economists to methodological individualism is thus not grounded in successful applications. Rather it appears to be based on an instinctive belief in *ontological individualism*: the doctrine that all that exists fundamentally for the economy are individual economic actors. Lucas and his fellow new classical economists have promoted representative-agent models, a class of models in which the mathematical methods of microeconomic optimal choice are applied to a single individual who takes national income as his budget constraint and whose choices are taken to represent the aggregate choices of the economy, because they appear to achieve the reduction of macroeconomics to microeconomics as required by the program of microfoundations for macroeconomics. A. P. Kirman (1992) severely criticizes the representative-agent model, not because it aspires to methodological individualism, but because it fails to fulfill the necessary conditions for perfect aggregation, so that the representative agent in the models fails to represent actual individuals successfully.[7] Methodological individualism remains the goal. Similarly, David Levy (1985) argues that complete methodological individualism is impossible, because, given imperfect information, individual economic actors must make reference to collective entitites as part of their own decision-making processes. Nevertheless, Levy (1985, p. 107) writes: "These collectives have no real existence but are simply the product of theories." While defending macroeconomics against the strong claims of the program of microfoundations, Blaug (1992, p. 45) nevertheless writes: "ontological individualism is trivially true."

It is important to understand that there are some senses in which neither the methodological nor the ontological individualist denies the existences of aggregates, collectives, or wholes. No one denies that GDP calculations can be made and reported, or even that GDP may have some locally stable relationship to unemployment or average interest rates or some other aggregate. Similarly, no one denies the existence of

---

[6] It is because he regards the success of the program of microfoundations as a hope rather than an inevitable triumph that I have previously characterized Lucas as calling for the euthanasia of macroeconomics – a pleasant and, no doubt, incremental death – rather than for its extermination or liquidation (Hoover 1988a, p. 87).

[7] Hartley (1997) provides a detailed examination of the representative-agent model and related aggregation issues.

social organizations such as governments or firms (in the sense that talk of governments and firms conveys meaning). What is typically denied is that such aggregates or organizations are among the fundamental units from which economic reality is constructed.

Hayek (1979, ch. 4) argues that such entities are secondary, and that the role of a social science is "compositive" – that is, that it must explain these entities as arising from the fundamental individual components.[8] Hayek (1979, ch. 6) denies that the wholes that social science explains through compositive methods are subject to scientific laws. He holds up the attempt to connect them through laws as an example of Whitehead's "fallacy of misplaced concreteness." He writes, "the wholes about which we speak exist only if, and to the extent to which, the theory is correct which we have formed about the connection of the parts which they imply, and which we can explicitly state only in the form of a model built from those relationships" (Hayek 1979, p. 98). Hayek thus argues that aggregates exist, but derivatively rather than fundamentally, and that in Mäki's terminology they do not exist objectively (i.e., unconstituted by the representations of theory).[9] Still even Hayek does not endorse practicable methodological individualism, stressing the importance of a reduction to microfoundations *in principle* and himself citing the Cournot problem (Hayek 1979, pp. 74–75, esp. fn. 8).

It may come as a surprise to most economists to discover that an essentially similar debate over reductionism rages in physics. Some condensed-matter physicists are for the emergence of properties that are not reducible without loss to the behavior of the particles that constitute their substance. Some nuclear and particle physicists insist that such a reduction is fundamental. (See Cat 1998.) My position is analogous to that of the condensed-matter physicists.

## 5.2  IS MACROECONOMICS ONTOLOGICALLY PROBLEMATIC?

One might concede the main point of the last section – namely, that the drive for microfoundations is driven by ontological individualism – yet not believe that any interesting metaphysical issue is involved, because the ontology of economics is too well understood by common sense to

---

[8] While not denying that aggregates such as GDP or the general price level can be calculated, Mises (1949/1966, p. 217) goes further than Hayek in arguing that they are quite devoid of meaning (also see Lachmann 1976, p. 96).

[9] The terminology of "fundamental" or "derivative" is fraught with difficulties. It is beyond my purpose to try to sort such matters out here. It is enough for the point at hand, however, to note that Hayek does not believe that economic aggregates can be causes in their own rights. They might serve as some sort of shorthand, but he argues that there is always an adequate causal mechanism independent of that shorthand.

pose any serious puzzle. Mäki (1996), for example, contrasts *folk economics* with *scientific economics*, arguing that scientific economics merely presents modifications of the " 'ontic furniture' of the general folk views of 'man' and society." He lists some types of possible modifications: selection, abstraction, idealization, exaggeration, projection, and aggregation. But he maintains that none of these modifications or combinations thereof "accomplishes a major departure from the ontic furniture of the ordinary realm. No new *kinds* of entities or properties are introduced" (Mäki 1996). Mäki illustrates his point with a discussion of the business firm in standard neoclassical analysis, and concludes "that folk economics and neoclassical economics have real business firms as their shared referent even though they represent these firms differently."

Mäki's case for the "ontological commonsense realism" of economics in which the ontic furniture poses no special challenges to the understanding is more persuasive for some parts of economics than others. It is not particularly cogent for macroeconomics: Macroeconomic aggregates do not share a referent with folk notions. The case can be illustrated with reference to the related notions of "real GDP" (or "real income" or "real output," these terms being used almost interchangeably) and the "general price level."

On any interpretation, macroeconomics takes a larger view of the economy and deals with aggregates, which are, in turn, constructed from characteristics of individual economic actors. It is helpful to distinguish two types of aggregates.

First are what we might call *natural* aggregates: simple sums or averages. Examples of natural aggregates are the level of total employment or the average rate of interest on six-month commercial paper. These are called natural because they are measured in the same units (i.e., they have the same dimensionality) as the individual components that they comprise and, therefore, preserve a close analogy with those individual components. Employment, for instance, is measured by the number of workers or the number of labor hours at both the level of a single individual and in aggregate. The rate of interest on a bond and the average rate of interest on a group of similar maturity bonds are both expressed as a percentage yield per unit time.

A second type of aggregate, what we might call *synthetic* aggregates, are important for macroeconomics. These are called synthetic because they are fabricated out of components in a way that alters the structure of the components, so that they are dimensionally distinct from the components and so that there is no close analogy (despite their sometimes sharing a common name) with the components. The nature of the synthesis is well illustrated by the general price level. The notion of a general price level aims to capture a prescientific insight: "A dollar just ain't what it used to be!"; "when I was a lad, a penny would buy what a quarter does these days." To capture this insight, one would like to have some notion of the average level of prices. A simple average will not of course work: (10¢/orange + 20¢/apple + $27,948/Volvo station wagon)/3 does not convey any useful information. One cannot add apples and Volvos, as they say.

It might be argued that any sort of an average is altogether the wrong way to start. What is really wanted is an estimate of the price of money itself, and not the average price of goods. The price of money would, like the price of oranges, be a single number. The general price level could be defined to be its inverse $(1/p_m)$. Since relative prices of goods change because of changes in the conditions of demand and supply, there would be, at best, a rough proportionality between individual prices and the general price level. Indeed, it would permit one to isolate which changes in individual prices were the result of "real" factors and which of monetary factors.

This approach, however, does not do justice to the prescientific insight, for it does not provide us with a concept or a measurement of prices that is independent of highly particular and highly inadequate theoretical models. To see this, consider how one would actually determine the value of $p_m$. One might, for instance, write down a complete Walrasian general equilibrium model in which commodities were expressed in natural quantities, prices in terms of money, and all assets denominated in money were valued using $p_m$. Aside from the impracticality of formulating and solving such a model for an actual economy (the Cournot problem again), it is well known that $p_m$ might not be determinable in such a model, or if it is, might not be unique.[10] The essence of the problem is that the real quantity of money (i.e., the useful services that it provides), unlike the real quantities of apples or Volvos, depends fundamentally on the price of other goods. In adjusting the prices of various goods, including money, unique convergence may not be possible, because each time prices adjust to remove an excess demand or supply, the quantity of money changes – possibly in a discontinuous manner – which can increase rather than diminish some of the excess demands or supplies.

This problem in the foundations of monetary theory has yet to be satisfactorily resolved. But what if it had been? It would tie the notion of the general price level extremely closely to a particular theoretical analysis. The measurement of $p_m$ would be *derived* rather than fundamental (see Ellis 1966, ch. 8). The prescientific notion is not tied to such a deriva-

---

[10] Hahn 1965; Samuelson and Sato 1984; see Hoover 1988a, ch. 5, sec. 1 for a simple exposition.

tion. That would not pose any special problem if the general price level derived in this way correlated closely with numerous other theoretical methods of deriving it, which in turn correlated reasonably with the prescientific sense of a general rise in prices.[11] Temperature provides an example of what is wanted (Ellis 1966, ch. 6). The prescientific notion of hotter and colder is vague. The first attempts to provide quantification relied on some presuppositions – e.g., the linearity of the expansion of the various fluids used in thermometers – but were not tied to particular theories. Temperature measures can now be derived from particular theoretical understandings – e.g., from the kinetic theory of gases. Such derived measures show considerable – if necessarily imperfect – consilience with the prescientific notions of hotter and colder and with the atheoretical measurement systems. They permit the extension of temperature scales beyond ordinary experience – e.g., to the measurement of the temperature of the sun – but retain their independence from particular theories to the degree that there is consilience of measurements derived from different theoretical starting points. In contrast, the measurement of the general price level remains at the atheoretical stage, in which the makers of price index numbers, Laspeyres, Paasche, and Fisher, are the economists' Fahrenheit and Celsius.

The point of raising these difficulties in measuring the general price level is not that the existence of aggregates is tied to their measurement. Rather it is that the difficulties in measuring them help to expose what problematic entities they are and undermine the appeal of seeing them as close analogues of their components (particular prices, particular goods, and so forth). The disanalogies can be made clearer through a more detailed examination of the general price level.

The fundamental insight of the index number is that one can avoid some of the dimensional nonsense of averaging disparate prices by averaging percentage rates of change instead. A simple average, however, does not capture the common-sense feeling for the degree of price change. A change in the price of gasoline should count for more than, say, a change in the price of caviar in measuring the change in the general price level. How to weight various price changes turns out to have an irreducible degree of arbitrariness.

In general, the percentage change in the general price level, indicated as $\Delta p$ (where $p$ is the logarithm of the general price level), is related to the individual underlying prices as

$$\Delta p = f(\Delta p_1, \Delta p_2, \dots, \Delta p_n) \tag{5.1}$$

[11] Avogadro's number, for example, can be computed to take the same value from numerous theoretically independent methods (see the discussion in Hacking 1983, pp. 54–55).

where $p_j$ is the price of good $j$ for $j = 1, 2, \ldots n$. Now, the properties that theoretically restrict the functional form of $f(.)$ are very weak:

$$\Delta p \leq \max\{\Delta p_1, \Delta p_2, \ldots, \Delta p_n\},\tag{5.2}$$

$$\Delta p \geq \min\{\Delta p_1, \Delta p_2, \ldots, \Delta p_n\}.\tag{5.3}$$

Conditions (5.2) and (5.3) together imply two obvious corollaries:

if $\forall j \; \Delta p_j \gtreqless 0$, then $\Delta p \gtreqless 0$.$\tag{5.4}$

if $\Delta p_1 = \Delta p_2 = \ldots = \Delta p_n$, then $\Delta p = \Delta p_j$ for any $j$.$\tag{5.5}$

Conditions (5.2) and (5.3) say that the general price level cannot increase by more than the largest nor decrease by less than the smallest individual price change. Condition (5.4) says that if each price increases (decreases) the general price level must itself increase (decrease), and that the general price level cannot change if no individual price changes. Condition (5.5) says that if every individual price changes equiproportionally, so must the general price level. An infinite number of functions fulfill these conditions, and the range of consistent changes in the general price level, given a fixed set of underlying price changes, is wide. In practice, price indices are generally linear:

$$\Delta p = \sum_{j=1}^{m} w_j \Delta p_j, \text{ where } \sum_{j=1}^{m} w_j = 1.\tag{5.6}$$

For $m < n$, this formulation recognizes the practical fact that price indices are based on samples of selected goods. The weights $w_j$ in these indices are chosen in practice to capture the prescientific sense of the amount of a price rise. Two common weighting schemes with rationales in microeconomic consumer theory are the Laspeyres index, which chooses the weights to reflect the share of each good in base period consumption, so that the general price level effectively measures the changing cost of a fixed bundle of goods, and the Paasche index, which chooses weights to reflect the share of each good in current period consumption, so that some compensation is made for substitution from relatively more expensive to relatively cheaper goods in the face of changes in relative prices.

Neither index is "correct"; there are an infinite number of indices lying between the two, and economists have from time to time argued the case for other indices with different weighting schemes.[12] The non-uniqueness of the price index is important for the point of this chapter. It is a fundamental property. A price index is an attempt to quantify the prescien-

---

[12] Generally one expects the Laspeyres index to be greater than the Paasche index, but this can be guaranteed only if certain regularity conditions are imposed on preferences that may not always hold for individual agents.

tific insight that the value of money changes. The different admissible price indices are not, however, approximations to some true underlying general price level. The general price level is, in some fundamental sense, nonscalar, although there is no currently acceptable scientific refinement that captures that fact.[13] No similar indefiniteness attaches to any of the prices of the underlying individual goods.

The change in the general price level, $\Delta p$, may be integrated over time to generate a price level

$$\left( p_{t+n} = \int_t^{t+n} \Delta p \, dt = p'_{t+n} + c \right).$$

The constant of integration $c$ permits us to choose an arbitrary base. The base is usually $P_t = 1$ or $P_t = 100$, where $P = \exp(p)$, for some desired base period $t$ (other base values are less common, but not unknown). $P$ differs from the particular price of, say, a Volvo, not just in its intrinsic indefiniteness, but also in its dimensions. The dimensions of the price of a Volvo are dollars/Volvo; the dimensions of $P$ are period-$t$ dollars/base-period dollars. The dimensions of $P$ are not the dimensions of the price of any good. They appear to be the inverse dimensions of the price of money, taking base-period money to be the *numéraire*. Given the indefiniteness of the price index, however, it is evident that the price of money is unlike the price of other goods, and represents a substantial departure from pretheoretic notions of price. The price index is used to normalize the price of particular goods, thereby to decompose individual price changes into a common or general element and a real or relative (to the index) element. That this operation is not obvious to common sense will be evident to anyone who has taught elementary economics or read policy analysis by noneconomists.

Real GDP is another important example of a synthetic aggregate. Considered as national income, nominal GDP adds up the incomes of each individual in the economy and is an obvious extension of the accounting framework for business or personal income. In a major innovation in economic analysis, the national accounting framework since the 1930s establishes the three-way identity between the sum of all incomes, the value added in production, and the value of all final goods and services. That these other methods of computing GDP have obvious common-sense analogues is less clear. If final goods (i.e., goods that are not inputs into other production processes) are indicated by $Q_j$, then nominal GDP is

---

[13] This may be an area in which the theory of fuzzy sets would be helpful. The use of scalar indices may account for some portion of the apparently irreducible randomness in estimated macroeconomic relations.

$$Y^N = \sum_{j=1}^{n} P_j\, Q_j, \quad j=1,2,\dots,n. \tag{5.7}$$

The dimension of income is dollars/unit time. Money provides the common unit that is essential if disparate goods are to be added.

If some or all of the prices of individual goods increase, it is obvious that nominal GDP could increase without any of the individual quantities changing. In the utilitarian framework that underlies economics this is an undesirable characteristic, because the measure of income has changed without the underlying utility, which is assumed to be generated by the quantities of the goods themselves, changing. It is clearly desirable to correct for changing prices. The usual way to do this is to compute real GDP as

$$Y^R = Y^N / P. \tag{5.8}$$

Real GDP is often treated as the analogue of an individual good. It does not, however, have the dimensions of a real good. Rather its dimension is base-period dollars (not dollars/unit good). Real GDP is a derivative measurement. One gets a different measurement for it for every different admissible price index. It inherits the fundamental fuzziness of the general price level.

The analogy of real GDP to an individual good is suggested to some by the possibility of perfect aggregation. If, for example, relative prices are constant (i.e., $p_j/p_k$ is constant for all $j$ and $k$), then $\sum_{j=1}^{n} P_{j,t}Q_{j,t}$ (where the $t$ in the subscript indicates the base time period $t$) can be normalized by choosing the units for the $Q_{j,t}$ so that each $P_{j,t}=1$. Then nominal GDP at time $n$ can be written

$$\sum_{j=1}^{n} P_{j,t+n}Q_{j,t+n} = P_{t+n}\sum_{j=1}^{n} Q_{j,t+n}. \tag{5.9}$$

In this case, conditions (5.2) and (5.3) above ensure that $P$ is unique. Some conclude therefore that in this limited case, one can treat the summation in the right-hand side of equation (5.9) as a natural aggregate quantity analogous to an individual quantity. The conditions for constant relative prices are almost certainly never fulfilled, but even if they were, the summation is not analogous to an individual quantity. The general price level $P$ in equation (5.9) still has the dimension period-$n$ dollars/ period-$t$ (i.e., current period/base period) dollars. To sum heterogeneous goods, they must still be converted to a common denominator, and in this case, the summation still has the dimensions of period-$t$ dollars. This would be more perspicacious if (5.9) were written as

$$\sum_{j=1}^{n} P_{j,t+n} Q_{j,t+n} = P_{t+n} \sum_{j=1}^{n} 1_{j,t+n} Q_{j,t+n},$$ (5.10)

where the subscripted numeral 1 is a placeholder for the dimensional conversion.

The general price level and real GDP are the most important aggregates in macroeconomics. There are many others. Each mixes the characteristics of simple and synthetic aggregates to different degrees. Average interest rates were cited above as an example of a simple aggregate, but when averaging is across nonhomogeneous maturities and risk classes, interest rates, too, are complicated by the fundamental problems of index numbers. Aggregation of employment across skill or quality levels faces similar considerations. There are other derivative quantities as well. The real rate of interest is defined to be the market interest rate less the percentage change in the general level of prices ($\Delta p$). Like real GDP, the real rate of interest inherits the fundamental fuzziness of the general price level.

The history of quantitative economics demonstrates that even the use of simple averages represented a difficult conceptual leap. On the best interpretation, what is accepted to common sense is relative. To treat synthetic aggregates as mere extensions of common-sense notions appears in comparison to make a category mistake. Despite their deceptively related names, there is no simple analogy between the general price level and individual prices or between quantities of individual goods and real GDP.

## 5.3 THE SUPERVENIENCE OF MACROECONOMICS ON MICROECONOMICS

Synthetic aggregates, at least, are not direct extensions of folk ontology. It is clear, however, that, if their independent reality is to be demonstrated in a sense more fundamental than that one can always calculate them according to some algorithm, we must first show that such aggregates cannot be reduced to properties of individual economic actors. Aggregates are in fact calculated; they clearly do not exist in a separate Platonic realm; and ontological individualism has immediate appeal, because we all have first-hand experience as economic actors. Any account of the autonomy of macroeconomic aggregates must account, therefore, for the relationship of the individual to the aggregate. To deny an essential connection between individual economic behaviors and macroeconomic aggregates would be absurd. The thing to be demonstrated is rather that economic reality is necessarily characterized differently at the microeconomic and the macroeconomic levels and that one level is not reducible to the other. To sustain this claim we appeal to the philosophical literature on supervenience, to which we give an anti-reductionist twist.

Macroeconomic aggregates *supervene* upon microeconomic reality. What this means is that even though macroeconomics cannot be reduced to microeconomics, if two parallel worlds possessed exactly the same configuration of microeconomic or individual economic elements, they would also possess exactly the same configuration of macroeconomic elements. It is not the case, however, that the same configuration of macroeconomic elements implies the same configuration of microeconomic elements.

The relationship of the ideal gas laws to the kinetic theory of gases provides a simple illustration of supervenience.[14] The kinetic theory describes gases as a collection of elastic particles (molecules) with randomly distributed momenta. Pressure corresponds to the average force that these particles impart to the walls of an enclosing container. Temperature corresponds to the average translational kinetic energy per molecule. The micro level of the molecules and the macro level of pressure and temperature operate under different descriptions. Pressure and temperature are not distinct or well defined at the micro level. A single speeding molecule has a momentum and kinetic energy, but it does not have a pressure or temperature, which are properties of a collection large enough to exemplify a consistent statistical character. But temperature and pressure supervene on the micro level in the sense that any particular arrangement of molecules and their momenta corresponds to a particular pressure and temperature, and, if that arrangement is ever repeated, the same pressure and temperature would be registered. There are, however, infinitely many arrangements of molecules and their momenta that register the same pressure and temperature. The gas laws provide a classic case of supervenience. Although the kinetic-theoretic account is sometimes presented as a clear case of a successful *reduction* of the macro to the micro, in fact, something is lost in the reduction. On the one hand, there is a shift of fundamental concepts between the levels, even though there is a mapping: Temperature and pressure are not defined at the micro level. And, in order to make the reduction, the kinetic theory has to appeal to an irreducibly statistical (and, therefore, macro) postulate: Momenta are assumed to be distributed so that there is an equal probability that any molecule is moving in any direction.

A second illustration is drawn from the life sciences. Biology provides both analogies and disanalogies for economics. Alexander Rosenberg

---

[14] An account of this relationship is standard in most introductory physics textbooks. See, e.g., Weidner and Sells (1973, ch. 19, secs. 1–3).

(1985, ch. 4, sec. 8, ch. 6, sec. 3, passim) applies the notion of supervenience to the relationship of functional biology (macro) to molecular
biology (micro). To take one example, hemoglobin is an element in functional explanations of the operations of the cardiopulmonary and circu-
latory systems of higher animals (Rosenberg 1985, ch. 4, sec. 2). At the
molecular level, hemoglobin is not a single chemical, but a family of
chemicals. To be hemoglobin at the macro level, a molecule must possess
nine particular proteins at critical junctures in the molecular structure.
Across different species, the approximately 140 remaining proteins that
the hemoglobin molecule comprises vary considerably. Similarly, Rosenberg argues that Mendelian genetics supervenes on a molecular base.
Mendelian genetics uses a conceptual scheme that is not easily mapped
onto molecular features, but nevertheless identical molecular configurations produce identical genetic behavior.

The notion of supervenience was initially suggested in moral philosophy as an account of the relationship between ethical facts and
"natural" facts. The idea has been used in the philosophy of mind as a
method of retaining the dependence of the mental on the physical, while
at the same time denying psychophysical laws (see Kim 1978, p. 153).
Rosenberg draws on the analysis of Jaegwon Kim (1978). For Kim, supervenience is a relationship between two distinct realms of properties (or
relations). Consider $I_j$, which is a conjuction of properties in the micro
realm in which every one of the properties or its complement form one
of the conjuncts.[15] Each $I_j$ is then a complete characterization of a possible micro state. The disjunction of every $I_j$ is the set of all possible micro
states. Consider the $A_j$, constructed *mutatis mutandis* for the macro state.
A family of macro properties is supervenient on a family of micro properties when any objects that share the same micro properties necessarily share the same macro properties. Kim (1978, pp. 152–153) shows that
one can derive the following relationship:

For any $A_k$, there are $I_1, I_2, \ldots, I_n$ such that
$$I_1 \vee I_2 \vee \ldots \vee I_n \supset A_k, \tag{5.11}$$

where the $I_h$, $h = 1, 2, \ldots, n$, are a subset of the $I_j$.[16] Of relation (5.11),
Kim (1978, p. 153) says: "I don't see how such generalizations could fail
to be lawlike."

---

[15] The account of Kim's analysis here omits most of the technical details (these are also
reproduced in Rosenberg 1985, pp. 113–116), and changes his notation. The identification of the distinct realms of properties as "micro" and "macro" is my addition – literally ad hoc – and does not significantly affect Kim's analysis.

[16] Kim goes on to show that in some cases the implication in relation (5.11) can be strengthened to a biconditional.

Using Kim's analysis, Rosenberg argues against the autonomy of Mendelian genetics. The conceptual scheme of Mendelian genetics (the macro level) does not map easily into the conceptual scheme of molecular biology (the micro level). Mendelian genetics permits explanation of phenomena not easily explainable directly from the molecular level. However, Mendelian genetics fails to account for some phenomena within its scope. Rosenberg argues that Mendelian genetics supervenes on molecular biology, and that molecular biology is the more scientifically advanced, more fundamental and autonomous theory. Mendelian genetics is reducible in principle (that is the upshot of Kim's analysis in relation (5.11) above), but it retains heuristic power, because something like the Cournot problem prevents the practicable application of molecular biology to some phenomena in which Mendelian genetics is relatively successful. Indeed, one might argue that supervenience fails if the supervenience base is only the DNA. It holds only if the supervenience base includes the full developmental environment. In that case, the Cournot problem applies with great viciousness.

Even if supervenience implies reduction in the case of genetics, the analogous argument does not work in economics. Rosenberg (1992, p. 129) himself has argued that the intentional character of microeconomics limits its scientific development: Microeconomic "theory's prediction and explanation of the choices of individuals [cannot] exceed the precision and accuracy of commonsense explanations and predictions with which we have all been familiar since prehistory." In fact, macroeconomic explanation and prediction is not only often better, but may have more scope for improvability. An electric supplier could not say when Mary Smith will switch on her oven, but it may know pretty precisely how many kilowatts it must supply at a given time, based on an aggregate analysis of past behavior. Insurance companies know that whether an individual is, say, a smoker or obese matters probabilitistically to his chances of dying. But the company would go broke trying to predict individuals' precise dates of death.[17]

It is important to remember that it is not macroeconomic theory that supervenes on microeconomic theory, but macroeconomic reality that supervenes on microeconomic reality. The disabilities of microeconomic theory thus prove, at most, that there can be no automatic presumption that microeconomics is more basic, because it is more successful, and that macroeconomics is merely heuristic. The critical relationship is the reducibility in principle suggested by relation (5.11) above. To begin to undermine reducibility in the case of macroeconomics, it helps to note a

---

[17] Both these examples are repeated verbatim from Hoover (1995a).

crucial disanalogy with biology. Reduction appeals to biologists because it removes scientifically suspect teleological explanation common in evolutionary biology and other functional accounts. The aim of reduction in economics, however, is precisely the opposite: Macroeconomics appears mechanical and dehumanized, and the point of the program of microfoundations is to reintroduce human decision making as an explanatory element. The point is to recover intentionality.

Kim's analysis posits two levels of properties that are (semantically at least) distinct and then investigates how they must be related if one set is supervenient on the other. Intentionality at the microeconomic level undermines the distinctness of microeconomic properties from macroeconomic properties. Levy's argument (see Section 5.1) that individual economic actors will invariably make reference to social wholes and aggregates is even more fundamental than he imagines. In evaluating the future, individuals must form expectations about real prices and real quantities. Independently of the uncertainty of the future, the Cournot problem implies that it is impracticable to solve good-by-good, price-by-price, period-by-period planning problems in all their fine detail. Practically, the best that one is able to do is to work with aggregates. The information on which these are based is fundamentally monetary. Economic actors must use estimates and expectations of the general price level and real interest rates to form any practical assessment of their situations. Hayek (1979, p. 62) writes:

in the social sciences it is necessary to draw a distinction between those ideas which are *constitutive* of the phenomena we want to explain and the ideas which either we ourselves or the very people whose actions we have to explain may have formed *about* these phenomena and which are not the cause of, but theories about, the social structures.

What Levy's argument demonstrates is that Hayek is mistaken, that how people theorize about the economy *is* constitutive of macroeconomic phenomena.[18] Since people cannot theorize about certain sorts of phenomena without appealing to macroeconomic categories – that are not themselves reducible to microeconomic categories – the Cournot problem introduces analytical constraints, not only in practice, but in principle as well. The distinctiveness of the properties at the microeconomic and macroeconomic levels is breached, undermining Kim's analysis, because complete characterizations of the microeconomic must include characterizations of the macroeconomic on the part of individual agents.

---

[18] In contrast to Hayek, his fellow Austrian-school economists, Mises (1943, p. 252) argues that knowledge of economic theory can prevent the mistaken investments that fuel the business cycle.

To challenge the applicability to economics of the reductionism in principle, implicit in Kim's analysis and in Rosenberg's application of it to biology, does not challenge the notion that macroeconomics supervenes on microeconomics. Kim's analysis is epistemological: It argues that there must be laws that would permit us to draw connections between the micro and macro levels. The point here is ontological: Even though macroeconomics cannot be reduced to microeconomics as the program of microfoundations suggests, the elements of macroeconomics could not exist without the substrate of microeconomic individuals.

## 5.4 TWO ARGUMENTS FOR THE REALITY OF MACROECONOMICS

So far we have argued that the ontological status of macroeconomic entities is problematic in the sense that, like other entities posited by scientific theories, they are not part of our common-sense ontic furniture. Furthermore, the nature of the relationship through which the elements of macroeconomics supervene on the elements of microeconomics precludes direct reduction of the macroeconomic to the microeconomic, even in principle. If macroeconomic entities exist, they cannot be said therefore to exist only derivatively, despite their supervenience on microeconomic entities. It remains to argue directly for the existence of macroeconomic entities.

The first argument is based on the argument from manipulability championed by Ian Hacking (1983, esp. pp. 22–24): "If you can spray them, then they are real." Hacking argues that convincing evidence of the reality of the electron is found in experiments aimed at detecting the existence of free quarks, in which niobium balls are charged by "spraying" them with electrons. The general point is that an entity defined by a scientific theory has real existence when procedures used to manipulate parts of the world outside the domain of the theory are best understood as procedures in which the entity is an instrument or tool. This argument is similar to the "no-miracles" argument for the reality of scientific entities. The best explanation of why theories are predictively successful, including successfully predicting the consequences of using them to design experimental or engineering manipulations of the world is that the entities posited by them in fact exist – anything else would be an inexplicable miracle.

It is common to denigrate the empirical success of economics (see, e.g., Rosenberg 1992, pp. 18, 56, 112, 238, passim). It is true that economics does not have the precision of physics or chemistry, although it is less clearly inferior to meteorology, geology, climatology, parts of biology, and cosmology – to name just a few of the less exact, but nevertheless scientific disciplines. The reputation of economics for predicting poorly arises partly because people seek unconditional forecasts ("what will happen tomorrow?") while economic theories typically predict only conditionally ("tomorrow $X$ will happen if $Y$ happens"). Quantified economic relations are at best locally stable: The precise estimate of the price elasticity of demand for Volvos changes with changes in the range of alternative brands and models, with changes in the proportion of academics to the total population, and with changes in other background conditions. Nevertheless, qualitatively stable relations are well established; for example, demand curves slope down (i.e., when the price of Volvos rises, sales of Volvos fall). And there is often enough local stability that useful quantitative assessments are possible. Can irreducible macroeconomic aggregates be manipulated as well?

The answer seems to be clearly yes. Consider the following example. Almost every macroeconomic theory predicts that sufficiently large expansions of government expenditure will change (probably increase) nominal GDP and the general level of prices.[19] Different theories differ in their precise understanding of the mechanisms. Similarly, no macroeconomic theory disputes the ability of the Federal Reserve to use its ability to supply or remove reserves from the banking system to set the level of the federal funds rate (the rate at which one commercial bank borrows from another overnight). The empirical evidence in support of these propositions is also overwhelming. Now consider two irreducibly macroeconomic aggregate entities: the real rate of interest (i.e., the market rate of interest less the percentage change in the aggregate price level, $\Delta p$) and the yield curve (an aggregate relation portrayed as a graph of market interest rates against time to maturity of the associated bonds). Both the real rate of interest and the yield curve are synthetic aggregates, and both are entities with causal powers in some economic theories. Every macroeconomic theory that I know predicts that actions that increase the general price level or the federal funds rate will shift the yield curve upwards in the short run. And, at least if the changes are unanticipated, increases in the general price level will reduce the level of the real interest rate. The empirical evidence for these effects is overwhelming, and indeed are easily confirmed by anyone willing to read the *Wall Street Journal* regularly for a month. Just like the electron, some macroeconomic aggregates can not only be controlled, but can be used to manipulate other macroeconomic aggregates.

---

[19] The caveat "almost" and the ambiguity over the direction both hinge on the financial market. If the interest elasticity of money demand were zero (empirically a false supposition), there would be no change in prices. If the increase in the demand for money induced by an increase in government bonds financing an increase in government expenditure were large enough (again unlikely), the price level could fall.

Applied to causality, Hacking's and other such arguments from manipulability face the same charge of circularity leveled at analyses of causality that refer to direct control (Chapter 2, Section 3). The defense is also the same. The appeal to manipulability is not intended to provide a reduction of causality or reality to something else. Manipulability provides evidence for the reality of entities (physical or macroeconomic) or of causal relations only in a context of contingently indubitable knowledge. The argument is an abductive or bootstrap argument, the conclusions of which are corrigible and fallible if one is willing to challenge maintained assumptions about the context.

The second argument is related to the first. Leszek Nowak (1980) and others have argued that the principal method of constructing scientific theories is *idealization*. Nowak's (1980, p. 29) paradigm idealization statement is:

If $G(x)$ and $p_1(x) = 0$ and ... $p_{k-1}(x) = 0$ and $p_k(x) = 0$,

then $F(x) = f_k(H_1(x), \ldots, H_n(x))$,                                 (5.12)

where $G(x)$ is the complete theory, $F(x)$ is the idealized theory, $H_i$ ($i = 1, \ldots, n$) denote *primary factors*, and the $p_j$ ($j = 1, \ldots, k$) denote *secondary factors*. An idealized theory is one that picks out the primary factors by setting the secondary factors to extreme values: zero or $\pm\infty$, represented here, without loss of generality, as $p_j = 0$.

Were $G(x)$ a *known* and exhaustively complete theory of the phenomenon within its explanatory range such that one could accurately specify each of the secondary factors that were set aside, then the distinction between primary and secondary factors would in fact be unclear, because our complete knowledge of $G(x)$ would allow us for example to replace (5.12) with

If $G(x)$ and $H_1(x) = 0$ and ... $H_{n-1}(x) = 0$ and $H_n(x) = 0$,

then $F(x) = f_n(p_1(x), \ldots, p_k(x))$.                                 (5.13)

In the case of either (5.12) or (5.13), releasing the idealizing conditions ($p_k(x) = 0$ or $H_i(x) = 0$) allows us to recover the complete theory, $G(x)$. Idealization has been reduced to a fancy name for an arbitrary selection of *ceteris paribus* conditions or to a formal nesting relationship for theories.

Hoover (1994b) argues that in an empirical context, the method of idealization has power only if we recognize that not all of the idealizing conditions can be explicitly stated. The claim to distinguish between primary and secondary factors is then a claim that the primary factors are the *essence* of the matter. Idealized theories thus aim to identify, isolate, and relate the real essences or causally effective capacities of economic reality.[20] The success of such an idealized theory then amounts to an ontological claim for its primary factors.

That Keynesian macroecononomics could be cast as an idealization that employs macroeconomic aggregates essentially is beyond doubt.The major competitor to Keynesian macroeconomics today, new classical macroeconomics, trades on an explicitly microfoundational approach. There is, however, less here than meets the eye. Currently, the most popular new classical macroeconomic theory is embodied in the real-business-cycle model (see Hartley, Hoover, and Salyer 1997; 1998, ch. 1). The proponents of this representative-agent model would like it to be interpreted as an idealization from a complete Walrasian general equilibrium model of the economy in which distributional issues are idealized out of the model so that what remains is a one-agent, one-good, one-price representation of the economy. This would work if the analogue for $G(x)$ in Nowak's schema, the complete Walrasian model (i.e., the "fantasy" model of Chapter 4, Section 4), were both true and known in detail. At least the second condition is false, which undermines the evidential basis for the first condition.[21]

Empirically, far from isolating a microeconomic core, real-business-cycle models, as with other representative-agent models, use macroeconomic aggregates for their testing and estimation. Thus, to the degree that such models are successful in explaining empirical phenomena, it is because they capture the relationships among aggregates, not among individuals. They point to the ontological centrality of macroeconomic, not microeconomic, entities. The appeal to the methods of microeconomics does not in this case amount to the successful implementation of the program of microfoundations, for they are but the simulacrum of microeconomics. The relationship between models that are microeconomic in form and their macroeconomic empirical implementation is metaphorical. The nature of metaphorical connection deserves further exploration. It is enough for the present purpose to understand that, at

---

[20] Cartwright (1983, 1989) argues for realism with respect to causal capacities, but for an instrumentalist interpretation of scientific laws. Laws are either literally false ("the laws of physics lie" – to quote the title of Cartwright's (1983) earlier book) or are merely *phenomenal* – i.e., atheoretic regularities. Hoover (1994b) argues that if idealized models represent essences, then phenomenal laws are necessary bridges to take the place of those secondary factors that cannot in fact be identified explicitly. Mäki (1992) argues that Nowak conflates idealization with *isolation*, which comprises idealization, omission, and other techniques. To apply Mäki's account we would have to say that the omission of secondary factors amounts to a claim that retained primary factors are the essence of the matter.

[21] Hartley et al. (1997, 1998) provide a fuller argument for the ways in which the real-business-cycle models fails to provide genuine microfoundations.

the empirical level, even the new classical representative-agent models are fundamentally macroeconomic in content.

## 5.5  MACROECONOMIC STRUCTURES

The structural account of causality presupposes that there are in fact real entities that may be related in causal structures. We are all familiar with such structures from Hume's examples of billiard balls on the table to the machines, chemical processes, and living things that we encounter in our day-to-day lives. The argument of this chapter is that macro-economics aggregates provide the raw materials for causal structures analogous to these familiar ones. Mäki (1996, sec. 6) argues that the no-miracles argument and other arguments from manipulability cannot be applied successfully to economics, even if they apply to physical sciences. (There may, of course, be other arguments – and Mäki supplies some – for existential beliefs about economic entities.) The conclusion of this chapter is that these reservations cannot be applied generally to economics: *Macro*economics shares characteristics with physical sciences that microeconomics *may* not. In consequence, while there may be differences in detail about the application of the structural account of causality to macroeconomics, there is no objection in principle. The differences in detail between macroeconomics and the physical and biological sciences are considered next.

# 6

# Causality and Macroeconomic Constraints

> *Effect*, n. The second of two phenomena which always appear
> together in the same order. The first, called a Cause, is said
> to generate the other – which is no more sensible than it
> would be for one who has never seen a dog except in pursuit
> of a rabbit to declare the rabbit the cause of the dog.
>
> – Ambrose Bierce, *The Devil's Dictionary*

In Chapter 5, I argued that macroeconomics is a suitable subject for a
structural causal account. In this chapter, I ask, what constraints does the
nature of macroeconomics place on that account?[1]

## 6.1 THE NATURE OF MACROECONOMICS

As we saw in Chapter 5, macroeconomics deals in aggregates. These
aggregates are composed of the behaviors of individuals. Consumption
as reported in the national income accounts, for example, is just the summation of the purchases of a nation's citizens. It is tempting then to
see economic agents as *human molecules* and the relations postulated in
macroeconomic theory or measured in macroeconometrics as the analogues of the ideal gas laws or other macrophysical relations.[2] But there
is a crucial and obvious difference: Molecules do not make choices,
people do; and they do so with reference not just to the immediate past
and their immediate surroundings, but also with reference to future
goals and to global or macro relations (e.g., people use the aggregate
price level to calculate their real wages in striking wage bargains; firms

---

[1] This chapter is a substantially revised and expanded version of Hoover (1993), "Causality and Temporal Order in Macroeconomics or Why Even Economists Don't Know How
to Get Causes from Probabilities," *British Journal for the Philosophy of Science* 44 (4),
693–710, by permission of Oxford University Press.

[2] See Nelson (1992). Koopmans (in Hendry and Morgan 1995, p. 515), using the analogy
of the gas laws, observes that science is possible without microfoundations, but suggests
that economics has an advantage over physics, because we are the "molecules" of the
economy and we know molecular behavior from direct acquaintance.

use information on aggregate GDP in assessing the likely demand for their products). A shorthand term for this feature of macroeconomics is "agency": Unlike gases, which are composed of inert molecules, economic aggregates are constituted by agents.[3] Recognition of an agency problem is the foundation for the research strategy known as the "representative-agent model." An economy is described as if it were populated by a single agent, a Robinson Crusoe whose budget constraint is the entire GDP of the economy.[4]

Robinson Crusoe models gloss over another feature of macroeconomics: the *nonhomogeneity* of economic aggregates. The people who constitute economic aggregates are not alike and do not remain constant in their tastes and circumstances over time. The same numerical value for consumption in the economy as a whole could represent very different patterns of consumption depending on the distribution of income, the demographics of the consumers, and whether it is 1991 or 1941 or 1721. Any stability in such aggregates clearly arises from averaging over behaviors that diverge in fine details. Income studies suggest that the allocation of income into broad categories – food, clothing, housing – may be relatively constant, but allocation into yogurt, beer, books, and motorcars varies considerably over time and between age groups, regions, and social classes.

Greater stability in aggregate relations can no doubt be obtained by accounting for the distribution of income, changing tastes, and so forth. This is the empirical counterpart of the program of establishing microfoundations for macroeconomics. In any practical setting, however, one is still limited to (somewhat finer) aggregates: e.g., accounting for the distribution of income among quintiles of the population may help explain consumption; but the consumption of a fifth of the population is still a nonhomogeneous aggregate.

Pushing the microfoundational program to its logical extreme would require us to account in detail for the economic behavior of each individual and to build up macroeconomic aggregates from there. There is, however, an insuperable difficulty in pursuing such a program: The economy is too complex. It faces what I called in Chapter 5, Section 1, the "Cournot problem." As we saw in the last chapter, the difficulty is

[3] The term "agency" should not be confused here with its use in the context of principal/agent models in microeconomics.
[4] Such single-agent models are typically the only ones called "representative-agent models," but there is no deep difference in principle between such models and others in which a few different types of agents coexist (e.g., overlapping-generations models in which, say, two types of agents – old and young – exist at any time, but in which there are an infinite number of agents over all future time as each young generation becomes old, dies, and is replaced by a younger generation).

not simply the practical one that computers are not now or likely in the foreseeable future to be powerful enough to manage such a reduction of aggregates to their components. More fundamentally, the preconditions for such a reduction do not exist. Neoclassical microeconomics, the economic theory of which the profession is so proud, generally assumes that tastes, knowledge, underlying resources, and other background conditions are either fixed or, at the least, evolve in determinable ways. This is almost surely false. Far from having complete, transitive, and reflexive preferences, people – subject to binding constraints to be sure and not completely inconsistent – choose in whimsical, partially informed, and arbitrary ways. Equally, they choose with respect to relatively subtle changes in background conditions.

The efficiency gains of a free market system arise precisely because of local adaptability, which produces behaviors that, unless viewed from the inside, appear to be random and erratic. The economy is characterized by *informational complexity*, and can be viewed as a giant computer for solving production and allocation problems (Hayek 1937, 1945).[5] One consequence of informational complexity is that the economy is invariably stochastic. Incorporating finer and finer information in the construction of empirical relationships among variables will reduce the residual of unexplained random noise only up to a point. Indeed, a good deal of the stability of aggregates no doubt arises from the mutual canceling out of idiosyncratic behavior to reveal typical or average behavior. This does not suggest that no reduction in the direction of microeconomics is possible, but it does give another reason to think that such a reduction will necessarily be incomplete and that there is probably some optimal level of reduction, which nonetheless involves considerable aggregation.

Recognition of nonhomogeneity and informational complexity reinforces the idea developed in the last chapter that, although macroeconomic reality is tied closely to microeconomic reality, macroeconomics is not reducible to microeconomics. Macroeconomic aggregates are what they are and behave as they do because of the underlying behavior of individual people. One cannot, however, give a complete accounting of macroeconomics from microeconomics alone. Macroeconomics supervenes on, but is not reducible to, microeconomics.

## 6.2 TEMPORAL ORDER

Causal claims in macroeconomics are usually implicit and casual or informal. When they are explicit, they are most frequently justified by

---

[5] The relationship between this description and the position of economists of the Austrian school in the "socialist calculation" debate, as well as to their general "verstehen" approach are obvious; see Hayek (1935a, b, 1940).

an appeal to so-called Granger-causality (Granger, 1969; Sims, 1972). C. W. J. Granger (1980, p. 330) provides a more general definition of cause:[6]

$Y_n$ is said to cause $X_{n+1}$ if $P(X_{n+1} \in A \mid \Xi_n)$

$\neq \text{Prob}\,(X_{n+1} \in A \mid \Xi_n - Y_n)$, for some $A$,

where $X_n$ and $Y_n$ are time-ordered sets of variables defined for time $t = -\infty, \ldots, 0, 1, \ldots, n$, and $\Xi_n$ is the set of nonredundant information available at time $n$. The requirement that the left-hand side simply be unequal to rather than strictly less than the right-hand side suggests that negative relevance may be also be taken into account.

There is a great historical divide in economics between analyses based on process and analyses based on equilibrium. Before the 1940s, macroeconomics was largely the analysis of business cycles, and process analysis, or economic dynamics, held sway. After Keynes's *General Theory* (1936), equilibrium analysis became dominant in macroeconomic theory. The tradition of dynamic analysis was preserved, however, more in Sweden and the United Kingdom than in the United States, as a distinct subfield of econometrics (Morgan 1990, 1991). Granger belongs to that tradition.

Dynamic analysis takes time seriously. If we add to that fact the Humean observation that causes precede effects, we have the basis for Granger-causality. Once we recall, in a world of normal errors at least, that regression is equivalent to estimating conditional probabilities, we also see that Granger-causality employs a sort of screening criterion (see Chapter 1, Section 2): $X$ causes $Y$ if $Y$'s past history does not screen off $X$'s effect on $Y$. In practicable tests, a variable $X$ Granger-causes a variable $Y$ if the error variance of a regression of $Y$ on its own past history and on the past history of $X$ is statistically significantly lower than the error variance of a regression of $Y$ on its own past history alone. There is a large literature on extending Granger-causality from bivariate to multivariate orderings.

We shall examine Granger-causality more carefully in the next chapter. The important point for now is to observe that Granger-causality bears a family resemblance to other probabilistic accounts of causality. Probabilistic accounts stress the patterns of correlation found in empirical data, what Salmon (1984, esp. ch. 2) refers to as the *statistical-relevance basis*. A key conclusion of our analysis up to this point is that, although the statistical-relevance basis contains much useful

---

[6] Granger's notation is changed slightly to keep it consistent with the notation of other chapters.

information, it does not in itself establish the existence or the direction of causal linkages and the useful information that it does carry can be extracted only with additional structural information (also see Salmon 1984, pp. 36–47). Something must be added to any account based on correlations. Salmon (1984, pp. 141 ff.), following Hans Reichenbach, adds the idea of a markable process (see Chapter 4, Section 3, earlier in this book, and Section 6.3 below).[7] Although Nancy Cartwright (1989, sec. 6.7) also appears to find use for the idea of a markable process, she joins Granger, Patrick Suppes (1970), and others in putting extraordinary weight on temporal ordering (Cartwright, 1989, ch. 1). The issue here is whether temporal ordering can bear that weight in a macroeconomic context. And Cartwright's account will serve as a good test case.

Following Herbert Simon, the account of causality defended here resolves the problem of observational equivalence by drawing a distinction between parameters and internally caused variables (see Chapter 2, Section 2, and Chapter 3). Cartwright's solution is quite different, relying on temporal order.

Consider the two systems, analogous to equations (2.9)–(2.12) but involving the random error terms $\varepsilon_i$. The first is

$$\begin{cases} \alpha_{11}x_1 + \alpha_{12}x_2 = \varepsilon_1 \\ \alpha_{21}x_1 + \alpha_{22}x_2 = \varepsilon_2, \end{cases} \tag{6.1}$$

where $x_i$ are the variables of causal interest, and $\alpha_{ij}$ are coefficients whose status as either independent parameters or some combination of independent parameters is in question. If $\alpha_{ij}$ could be interpreted as parameters in the sense of Chapters 2 and 3, then system (6.1) would represent mutual causality. The second is

$$\begin{cases} \beta_{31}x_1 \qquad\quad = \varepsilon_1 \\ \beta_{31}x_1 + \beta_{31}x_2 = \varepsilon_4, \end{cases} \tag{6.2}$$

where again $\beta_{ij}$ are coefficients of questionable status. If $\beta_{ij}$ are parameters, then system (6.2) represents a case of $x_1$ causing $x_2$.

Cartwright cites the econometrician Edmund Malinvaud to the effect that apparent cases of mutual causality between $x_1$ and $x_2$ would turn out with fine enough division of the time line to be cases of $x_{1,t}$ causing $x_{2,t+1}$ causing $x_{1,t+2}$ and so forth (Cartwright, 1989, p. 17). Thus, when a variable is ordered recursively ahead of another, it also occurs before it in time.

---

[7] Salmon (1994) abandons the idea of a markable process as too problematic. His preferred replacement, the idea of the conservation of some quantity over time, appears, superficially at least, to bear a resemblance to the interpretation of marks in terms of variables and genidentity developed in Chapter 4, Section 3.

Contemporaneous causality is ruled out. If all the causal factors are fully specified, then the $\varepsilon_i$ are uncorrelated with each other. In such a system, she shows, observational equivalence is detectable because one cannot take linear combinations of true causal equations and still have the errors in different equations uncorrelated with each other (cf. LeRoy 1995a, pp. 217–218). For example, if system (6.2) represents the true causal order ($\varepsilon_3$ and $\varepsilon_4$ uncorrelated), then one linear transformation converting it to system (6.1) would imply $\varepsilon_1 = (\varepsilon_3 + \varepsilon_4)$ and $\varepsilon_2 = \varepsilon_3$, so that $\varepsilon_1$ and $\varepsilon_2$ would be correlated.

If we accept that causes must precede effects, then Cartwright's solution to the problem of observational equivalence is ontologically satisfactory. It says, arrange the recursive order of the variables of interest in such a way that they both respect time order and have uncorrelated random error terms; and, then, the coefficients will correspond to true parameters. It is epistemologically impossible, however, because the error terms are not directly observed in a manner independent of the supposed causal order. That difficultly to one side, can we accept Cartwright's assumption that causes must precede effects? The three features of macroeconomics already discussed – agency, nonhomogeneity, and informational complexity – undermine causal accounts like Cartwright's based on temporal ordering. Actual macroeconometric models cannot be usefully forced into the mold of temporally ordered causal chains. Consider three problems.

**(1) Frequency of Observation**

Cartwright (1989, p. 17) imagines an economic structure to be a temporally ordered causal chain. This formulation is econometrically too restrictive.

Consider system (6.3), which is the analogue to system (6.2), but with many variables.

$$\begin{cases} x_{1,t} = \sum_{j=1}^{n} \sum_{k=-\infty}^{t-1} \beta_{1j,k} x_{j,k} + \varepsilon_1 \\ x_{2,t+1} = \sum_{j=1}^{n} \sum_{k=-\infty}^{t} \beta_{2j,k} x_{j,k} + \varepsilon_2 \\ x_{3,t} = \sum_{j=1}^{n} \sum_{k=-\infty}^{t+1} \beta_{3j,k} x_{j,k} + \varepsilon_3 \\ \vdots \\ x_{n,t+n-1} = \sum_{j=1}^{n} \sum_{k=-\infty}^{t+n-1} \beta_{nj,k} x_{j,k} + \varepsilon_n \end{cases} \qquad (6.3)$$

Each variable is indexed by a time subscript. Each equation includes all of the variables on the right-hand side that are dated before the variable on the left-hand side.[8] If $\varepsilon' = [\varepsilon_1, \varepsilon_2, \ldots \varepsilon_n]$ is the row vector of random error terms from system (6.3), then $E(\varepsilon\varepsilon') = \Omega$ is the variance-covariance matrix of $\varepsilon_i$. Cartwright's requirement that the $\varepsilon_i$ be uncorrelated is the requirement that $\Omega$ be diagonal, since the off-diagonal elements of $\Omega$ are the covariances that must be zero for the $\varepsilon_i$ to be uncorrelated. Her suggestion is that if all the appropriate causal factors are included on the right-hand sides of the equations in system (6.3), then $\Omega$ will be diagonal by construction.

System (6.3) is very nearly what macroeconometricians refer to as a vector autoregression: Each current variable is regressed on its own past values and the past values of every other variable. In practice, the variance-covariance matrices from vector autoregressions are never diagonal. Why? Why are they not diagonal by construction as they are in Cartwright's account? There must be some specification error. Perhaps we have omitted a causally relevant factor or perhaps we have not allowed for long enough lags.[9]

These are genuine problems, but there is another more troubling one. In Cartwright's account, variables dated the same should not have explanatory power for each other, once past-dated variables are taken into account. But, in fact, they do. Macroeconomic data are reported most often annually or quarterly, not uncommonly monthly, rarely weekly, and extremely rarely daily or more frequently. Prices, interest rates, and stock data are sampled at some particular time of the year, quarter, or month. Flow data (e.g., GDP which equals the production of new goods and services per unit time) adds up all the units occurring during the year, quarter, or month. Thus, GDP for the first quarter is the production on each day of January, February, and March added together. Granger (1969, pp. 377–378) suggests that apparent contemporaneous causality would vanish if data were sampled at fine enough intervals.[10] But such finer and finer intervals would exacerbate certain conceptual difficulties in the foundations of economics. There are hours during the day when there is no production; does GDP fall to nought in those hours and grow astronomically when production resumes? Such wild fluctuations in GDP are economically meaningless. Few goods perish in the instant of their production (electricity is one example); but, if a good endures, it is not new production (and therefore not GDP) but part of

---

[8] Time subscripts are suppressed where no confusion will result.

[9] This is, in part, what is behind the reversal of the Granger-causal ordering of money and income as Sims and others moved from bivariate to multivariate tests of Granger-causality; see Cartwright (1989, pp. 56, 57).

[10] Also Swanson and Granger (1997, p. 358); Breitung and Swanson (1998); and Christiano and Eichenbaum (1987).

the stock of capital. The standard answer to this is to say that GDP is really the flow of services from the stocks of (depreciating) goods. Some goods just depreciate and yield their service up faster than others. There is in practice, however, no way to quantify and measure such flows that suffers from any fewer or less serious conceptual problems than temporal aggregation itself. Economists therefore are unlikely, even in principle, to force macroeconomics into the straitjacket of causal structures that rule out contemporaneous causality.

The ideal gas laws may provide an analogy here as often before. Imagine reducing the number of molecules in a fixed volume until in any easily measurable period only a small number of molecules would erratically strike the pressure gauge built into the container wall. Supposing that the gauge was very sensitive, it would react to irregular transfers of momentum, which would not reflect any stability over time or any similarity to the force felt at any similar size area elsewhere on the container wall. Not only would pressure be hard to measure, it would have a different character altogether than when measurements averaged over large numbers of collisions and the molecules were homogeneously mixed throughout the container.

**(2) Hidden Variables and Temporal Reversal**

Nonhomogeneity and informational complexity complicate any attempts to sample macroeconomic data too frequently. Agency presents its own complications.

Consider a model (similar to the first model in Chapter 3, Section 2) with the following characteristics. (i) The price level rises to make the demand for money equal to the stock of money inherited from the last period. (ii) The demand for money itself depends not only positively on the price level but also negatively on the rate of inflation (the percentage change in the price level), because inflation imposes a real cost on anyone who holds the money while it loses value. (iii) The money supply is set as the sum of a genuine random process and the apparently random process from a deterministic pseudo-random-number generator.[11]

The pseudorandom component in the model is meant to reflect the situation in which the public might have better knowledge of the future course of prices than the econometrician. Were the public ignorant of the deterministic component of the money supply, then money would Granger-cause prices. On the other hand, if the public (but not the econometrician) knew the truth about the pseudorandom component, then prices Granger-cause money. If they knew that the money stock would

---

[11] A formal version of this model is developed in Chapter 7, Section 2.

increase, they would expect prices to rise in future. In the face of expected inflation and the consequent anticipated loss on holding cash, they would, therefore, reduce their current demand for money, which would push current prices up in order to bring the supply of real money balances back into equilibrium with the demand for them. Increases in current prices would help to predict money in future, even though money causes prices in the sense that, in a given causal field, control of the money stock is sufficient to control price changes up to a random error.[12]

It is crucial to this example that the public be better informed than the econometrician. Indeed, one way to think about the issue is that it arises from an omitted third cause. If expectations were directly observable, then an expectations variable would screen off the apparent causal effect of prices on money. The existence of such a variable is problematic. True, people form expectations and act upon them (that is the agency issue), but such expectations do not exist independently of the actions they affect; they are not palpable, like so many pounds of rice bought by a consumer; they are hidden variables. Of course, one could ask people to state their expectations. That, however, would be simply their guess about how they would act or would have acted in a situation that was not yet at hand or had already passed. Such expectations are no more directly observable to individuals than their own preferences and are subject to the same whimsy, arbitrariness, and adjustment to subtle changes in background conditions.

This inflation model provides a macroeconomic illustration of the kind of irreducibly indeterministic common cause highlighted in Cartwright's story of the joint production of an industrial chemical and a pollutant discussed in Chapter 4, Section 3. If anything, the illustration underplays the difficulty we ought to have in macroeconomic cases of finding an expectational variable that acts as an effective screen. We do not in fact have any reason to believe that all individuals know a deterministic factor governing prices in the future. Instead, there is both inhomogeneity and informational complexity: different individuals know different things, infected to varying degrees with random noise. The example works so long as collectively their information is better than the information that the econometrician can represent at an aggregate level.[13] This is once more an example of what I concluded

---

[12] See Hoover and Sheffrin (1992) for a real-world example of such "reverse Granger-causality." Also, recall Kaldor's comments on money not causing Christmas in Chapter, Section 1, note 18.

[13] Jan Schmidt (1998), in an effort to resolve Newcomb's paradox in decision theory, provides a structurally similar story in which a world of microscopic agents can make precise

in Chapter 5 that there is qualitative difference between the microeconomic entity and its apparent macroeconomic counterpart.

The expectations in this model and the models in Chapter 3, Section 2, are macroeconomic and must necessarily be less than the collection of all individual expectations. We cannot hope that any observable expectational variable could serve as a deterministic screen between money and prices. In the models of Chapter 3, I accept the complete unobservability of expectations and solve the expectational terms out of the model in a manner that, analogous to Cartwright's pollution/chemical example, not only acknowledges an irreducible correlation between money and prices, but also introduces an important nonlinearity in parameters. Nonlinearity is characteristic of models with rational expectations or other forward-looking schemas of expectation formation. The strategy of Chapter 3 is an extreme reaction. Better expectational aggregates (e.g., ones based on surveys or ones backed out of term structure or other arbitrage relationships such as the differential between indexed and nonindexed bonds) may well improve causal models. The critical point is that the pursuit of such aggregates could not be perfectly successful in the sense of providing a perfect measure of expectations that would reflect without a random element the microeconomic expectations of each and every agent. If it could, it would eliminate macroeconomics – but there is little risk of that.

### (3) Long-run versus Short-run Causality

Steady states are hypothetical economic configurations in which all short-run variations have stabilized so that prices and interest rates are constant, and stock and flow quantities are either constant or growing at constant exponential rates. Economic theory provides reasonably persuasive accounts of steady states, and the real world provides economic configurations for which steady states are good approximations. Economic theory rarely provides persuasive accounts of short-run transitional phenomena. Steady states are timeless; they are the result of allowing notional time to run on to infinity. In this they are not unlike conceptual devices in physics such as adiabatic expansion – that is, expansion without the transfer of energy. Although timeless, variables in a steady state may be recursively ordered – perhaps in a manner quite different from the short-run temporal ordering.

Consider the following model:

predictions over a short future and communicate them to the agents of the macro world in way that induces a causal reversal at the macro level. Schmidt argues that his story is a genuine case of effects preceding causes. The structural account in the present case, however, says, it only looks that way.

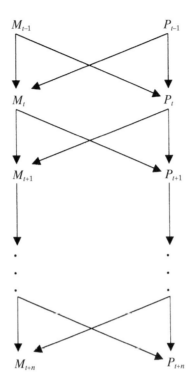

Figure 6.1

$$\Delta P_t = \Delta M_{t-1} + \beta(M_{t-1} - P_{t-1}) + \delta + \varepsilon_t \Big\}$$
$$\Delta M_t = \phi P_{t-1} + \mu M_{t-1} + \tau + w_t, \quad\quad\quad (6.4)$$

where, for any $X$, $\Delta X_t = X_t - X_{t-1}$, Greek letters are parameters, and $\varepsilon_t$ and $w_t$ are uncorrelated random errors.

System (6.4) is an "error-correction" model in which deviations from the steady state are corrected over time. In the short run, $P$ causes $M$ and $M$ causes $P$; but temporal order is respected. Figure 6.1 shows the short-run causal structure. To find the steady state of system (6.4), set all changes to zero and all random shocks to their mean value, also zero. Steady-state values do not refer to particular times, and are thus indicated by variables without time subscripts. The steady-state solution is

$$P = M + \delta/\beta, \quad\quad\quad (6.5)$$

$$M = -\tau/\mu. \quad\quad\quad (6.6)$$

$M$ is recursively ordered ahead of $P$. Despite the absence of a temporal order in the steady state, $M$ causes $P$ in Simon's sense. This seems a natural use of "cause." In the short run, a change to any of the parameters of system (6.4) compels a change to both $M$ and $P$ in a well-defined temporal succession. But the steady-state value of $M$ cannot be affected by the setting of $\delta$ or $\beta$, while any change to its own steady-state value due to a change in $\tau$ or $\mu$ forces the steady-state value of $P$ to change.

Economic theory is largely about steady states. The economic theory of transitional dynamics has little empirical support and carries little conviction among economists. At best, economists have phenomenal laws describing short-run behavior. Very different short-run behaviors are compatible with the same steady states (e.g., if $\phi \equiv 0$ in system (6.4), $P$ would not cause $M$ even in the short run). One might argue that this is just a matter of ignorance; and, that as economics progresses, the transitional details will be filled in, so that steady states are fully explained by the dynamic processes that generate them. Unfortunately, informational complexity and nonhomogeneity again would force an explanation that describes each individual's behavior. Even if that were possible, the explanandum would have shifted to the individual from the macroeconomic variable: Macroeconomics would be denatured.[14]

### 6.3  MARKS AND INTERVENTIONS

The objections to temporal ordering should not be overstated. Knowledge of temporal relationships is often useful in causal inference because of its abductive or bootstrapping character. It is often true that effects follow causes, and in macroeconomics, there are no well-established cases of effects preceding their causes.[15] What we have shown so far is that, to be useful to macroeconomics, a causal account must not depend fundamentally on temporal ordering. There are many cases in which causes and effects must be regarded as simultaneous, not sequential, or in which the question of temporal order cannot arise. The idea of mark transmission as a characteristic property of causal structures and as a means of causal inference suggested by Reichenbach (1956) (and championed by Salmon (1984) and, to a lesser extent, by Cartwright (1993)) is intended to be an alternative to temporal order. Will it work for macroeconomics?

One general objection to mark transmission is that it fails to be an alternative to temporal order, because marking or intervening in a causal structure necessarily refers to time; process presupposes tempo-

---

[14] In the example of the competing polio vaccines in Chapter 4, Section 1, this is the difference between explaining the type-level relative causal efficacies of the vaccines and explaining the token-level effect of an individual person contracting or not contracting polio (cf. Salmon 1984, pp. 272–273).

[15] It is sometimes suggested that the same is not true in physics; see Schmidt (1998).

ral order. Generally, of course, marks are made in temporally continuous processes. But the important point is not the temporal order but the
identity of the marked and unmarked structures. Temporal continuity is
one means of establishing that identity.

But it is not the only way. Consider the example in Chapter 4, Section
3, in which a causal structure involving a man and a mirror in a funhouse
is marked by a fly. If we have two sets of photographs of the man and
the mirror with and without the fly, what matters for our judgment is that
we can group the photographs correctly. Let $A$ be one subsystem. We do
not know whether it is man or mirror, but we must know that, if it is man
in one photo, it is man in the other, and if it is mirror in one, it is mirror
in the other. Similarly for $B$. Equally, we need to know which pair of photographs of $A$ and $B$ are in a *fly-present* state and which are in a *fly-absent*
state. Such judgments may require outside information or may be
implicit in readily observable circumstances. In this example, for instance,
what we know about mirrors reversing images allows us to group the
photographs into $A$ and $B$. If it happens that the fly has in fact landed
on the man's nose, then it is also straightforward to group the photographs into *fly-present* and *fly-absent*. And, if in fact, the fly has landed
on the mirror, which is, say $A$, then we can infer the causal direction from
the mark without even needing to decide which photograph of $B$ is in
the *fly-present* and which in the *fly-absent* state.

The important point is that we have not appealed to time order.
Of course, the inference would have been simplified if we could have
watched the fly landing in real time (or had a film with a clear temporal
direction). Still, temporal order is not of the essence. Watching the
process unfold is a way of convincing ourselves that the identity of the
system has been maintained through a change in an observable variable.
But *change*, which we normally think of as involving time, might here
be given a comparative static or *alternative-universe* interpretation. This
relies, as we argued in Chapter 4, Section 1, on causality being fundamentally a type-level relationship in which alternative realizations of the
same relationship can be considered side by side.

The various examples of mark transmission cited so far have been
physical. Can macroeconomic structures also be marked? Reichenbach's
(1956, pp. 198–199) paradigmatic cases involve a red glass in the path
of white light ray, chalk marks on a billiard ball, the smell of smoke in
an air current, and snow on the roof of a railroad car. What in macroeconomics could be the analogue to such physical marks?

To answer this question, first consider the general features of marking.
In the Cartwright's example (discussed in Chapter 4, Section 3) of the
polluter, we suggested that Cheap-but-Dirty might be identified as the
source of the pollutant through a radioactive mark incorporated into

the causal structure through the use of Carbon-14 into its chemical feed-stocks. The important features of the mark in this case are that it changes a variable in the structure (the presence or absence of radioactivity) without altering the causal structure itself and that the change in the putative effect is traceable to the putative cause. Again, the continuity and identity of the structure between states is the crucial issue. Is it the same isotope in the putative cause and the putative effect? Observing the process unfold or noting spatial continuity is one way of establishing the crucial identity. It is not the only way. Biologists tag fish and animals, release them, and identify them from their tags. Their inference of identity is warranted not by continuous observation, but by a well-warranted collateral belief that it is unlikely the tag could have appeared for any other reason than that they put it there. The baseball that Mark McGwire hit to break Roger Maris's home-run record in September 1998 carried a serial number in invisible ink. The accepted unlikelihood of anyone having independently guessed the serial number, not continuous observation, is what convinces people that the ball on display at the Baseball Hall of Fame is in fact the ball McGwire hit into the stands. It is easy to multiply such cases.

Causal structure is located in the relationships among variables, not in the particular instantiations (within the limits of the causal field) of the parameters. Thus, in macroeconomics, changes of parameters could themselves be viewed as marking a macroeconomic structure, which is continuous before and after marking (or in and out of its marked state). Econometrics describes the statistical relationships among variables. It can be seen as a tool for observing the consequences of particular causal structures, although only in highly special circumstances could we regard this as observing the structures themselves (see Hoover 1994c). Econometric observation can therefore provide evidence of changing parameters – that is, evidence of interventions that mark macroeconomic structures. But econometrics can do only part of the job. Extra-econometric evidence may be needed to convince ourselves that a changed econometric relationship actually corresponds to a mark, a relevant change in parameters, rather than, say, to a change of the causal field or to a failure of observation. To observe a beam of light between a source and a wall through red-tinted glasses would not be to mark the beam, while placing the filter in the line of the beam would. Similarly, some sorts of statistical calculation impose structure on economic relationships that is an artifact of the statistics rather than a property of the data. Distinguishing what is there from what is imposed is a nice problem in statistical and econometric technique.

Population biologists are convinced of their identifications of particular animals and fish because of the extra-statistical aspects of tagging them. They have records of when and how they were marked. Other sciences, including economics, often cannot intervene so deliberately in the processes they wish to observe. There is, nevertheless, often institutional or historical information that suggests that interventions occurred of particular types at particular times. There would be very little doubt, for instance, that a statistical relationship among Federal Reserve policy instruments and the stock of money that was stable up to 6 October 1979 and changed to a new, but also stable, relationship after 6 October 1979 reflected a change in monetary policy (a resetting of the policy parameters) at that date. We would be convinced by such extra-statistical information as the minutes of the Federal Open Market Committee and the public announcements of the Federal Reserve Board, which signaled an intentional intervention in the money-supply process. While purely econometric or statistical information is unlikely to be sufficient to identify interventions or marks, we should not rule out cases analogous to the photographs of the man, the mirror, and the fly in the funhouse in which internal (in this case statistical) features provide the lion's share of the evidence.

In Chapter 8, we shall consider practical aspects of the problem of inferring causal direction.

# 7

# Macroeconometrics and Causality

If all the pens that ever poets held had had the feeling of
their masters' thoughts, they could not write as much solid
fact as you can hold in a pair of calipers.

– Dorothy L. Sayers, *Gaudy Night*

## 7.1 SOME REFLECTIONS ON THE HISTORY OF CAUSALITY IN ECONOMETRICS

Econometrics, statistical tools adapted systematically to the particular requirements of the discipline, is the principal empirical method of economics. By the middle of the 1950s a standard or received view of econometrics was in place and codified in textbooks. As recent histories of econometrics make clear, the field is an old one – in some respects stretching back 350 years to William Petty, Gregory King, and Charles Davenant and the tradition of Political Arithmetic.[1] At least in the early to middle part of the twentieth century, causal analysis was a fundamental organizing principle animating the development of econometrics. Yet, the received view is largely innocent of any discussion of causality. Open any standard econometrics textbook today; if causality is discussed at all, it is as a separable topic – Granger-causality. Causal analysis is no longer the explicit basis for econometric thinking. What happened illustrates the need for a clear conceptual account of the role of causality in

---

[1] Important recent works include Klein's (1997) history of time-series analysis, which starts in 1662 and ends about 1940; Morgan's (1990) history of econometrics, which begins in the mid-nineteenth century and ends in the early 1950s; and Epstein's (1987) history of econometrics, which is restricted to the twentieth century with a focus on the postwar period. In addition, Hendry and Morgan (1995) have put together an anthology of important original sources in the history of econometrics covering essentially the same period as Morgan's history. This anthology is the source for most of the material in this section.

economics. The issues that causal analysis raised in the early development of econometrics remain important, but they have become muddled and hard to see as systematic causal analysis has been expunged from econometric thinking.

There has long existed a tension between econometrics as an instrument of statistical description and econometrics as an instrument of structural articulation. As Mary Morgan (1990) documents, there were two distinct threads in the development of econometrics.

The first is demand analysis. The early attempts to quantify demand curves were structural in the sense that they were rooted in the attempt to articulate and measure theoretically warranted individual and market reactions of quantities to prices and incomes. The first approaches to demand curves were static and timeless. Time entered initially as a nuisance: In order to stabilize the data and to isolate a theoretically acceptable relationship, the econometrician abstracted from time through various techniques to remove trends. It was possible to see the laws of demand as analogues to the ideal gas laws: functional relationships between variables without a causal order. The identification problem was first understood in this context: How is one to isolate the demand curve from data that are generated as an interaction between demand and supply? Solutions to the identification problem involved changing data and so, in a sense, time: Without variation, only a single price/quantity point would be observable, and without independent variation of supply and demand, separate curves could not be isolated. Yet, change of this sort is not fundamentally about process, so time entered only in a fairly impoverished sense. Only later, with the development of cobweb models of agricultural demand and supply, does process begin to appear as important in the demand literature.[2]

The second thread is business-cycle analysis. In attempting to understand the ebb and flow of economic activity, early empirical economists relied on associations among many data that could be discerned informally from tables and graphs. The development of correlation coefficients and other statistical measures marked an important step toward systematizing the mass of available information. Economists wanted to know the causes of cycles; and, even as early as Hume, they were aware that correlation was not causation. Not everyone agreed. At the turn of the twentieth century, Arthur Bowley argued that a high correlation, that is, a correlation coefficient $r > 6[0.67(1 - r^2)/\sqrt{n}]$, where the term in brackets is the probable error of the correlation coefficient itself, did prove causation (Hendry and Morgan 1995, p. 12; also Hooker, p. 122,

---

[2] See Hendry and Morgan 1995, pp. 25–27, who find the cobweb model implicit in work of Henry L. Moore (reprinted as ch. 3 in their anthology), for other references.

fn. 1).[3] Bowley's contemporary, R. H. Hooker (p. 122), explicitly rejected Bowley's criterion and all causal judgments based on correlation alone, suggesting that "[i]n many cases . . . the existence of a causal connection between two phenomena is more clearly demonstrated from mere inspection of diagrams than from mathematical calculation." Such diagrams could not, however, measure the strength of the causal connection, so correlation retained some role. Henry Moore (p. 97) argued that multiple correlation was the practical embodiment of the theoretical economist's *ceteris paribus* condition. It was realized early on that regressions were directional (the regression of $X$ on $Y$ is not the same as the regression of $Y$ on $X$) in a manner that recapitulated causal asymmetry (Hendry and Morgan 1995, p. 12; Persons, p. 138, fig. 8.4; Schultz, pp. 255–256). Many of the issues touched on in noneconometric contexts in earlier chapters were econometric issues in the first half of the twentieth century. Examples include: the role of time (Fisher, pp. 313 317; Tinbergen, p. 400; Orcutt, p. 547); robustness and invariance (Koopmans, p. 280; Frisch, p. 417); the common-cause condition, spurious correlation, and screening (Koopmans, pp. 283–284; Orcutt, p. 548); the need for extra-statistical information for causal inference (Koopmans, pp. 282–283; Wold, p. 464). Although in our earlier treatment we have related these issues to the probabilistic account of causality, most of the econometric discussion was pre-probabilistic. The probabilistic interpretation of econometrics developed simultaneously with causal analysis.

By the early 1930s, demand analysis was becoming more dynamic, and, with the work of Ragnar Frisch and Jan Tinbergen, business-cycle analysis became more structural. Causal issues were now dressed in a structural guise: the meaning of parameters (Hendry and Morgan 1995, p. 61); autonomy (Frisch, p. 417; Tinbergen, p. 422); invariance (Tinbergen, p. 367; Keynes, p. 388; Haavelmo, p. 448; Koopmans 429); and exogeneity (Hendry and Morgan 1995, sec. IX). Structural econometrics, as it is presented in the textbooks, descends directly from the Cowles Commission, which systematized and developed the work of Trygve Haavelmo and Abraham Wald. Its principal legacy is the modern understanding of the econometric identification as a set of theoretically adequate (*a priori*) restrictions on reduced forms that permit the recovery of structural equations from reduced-form estimates. What is now largely forgotten is the degree to which discussion and debate in and about the Cowles Commission was causal. This is clear in Koopmans's (pp. 527–537) discussion of the "causal principle" as the foundation for the classification of variables into exogenous or endogenous.

---

[3] All undated references in this section are to authors and page numbers included in Hendry and Morgan (1995).

The major debate of this period arose from the intersection of the traditions of demand measurement and business-cycle analysis. Despite the inroads of dynamic approaches, the static, equilibrium demand theory suggested that price and quantity stood in a relationship of mutual influence that could be represented by simultaneous equations. Simultaneity is closely related to the identification problem, and business-cycle analysis with its emphasis on dynamics and time suggests a possible solution to it. But is time the essence of causation? In Chapter 6, we examined reasons to doubt that it is. Econometricians of the 1930s and 40s also debated these issues. If time order is rejected as nonfundamental, then how should causal asymmetry be represented? Is mutual causation acceptable? Wold (ch. 41) argued that causes must be asymmetrical and built into economic models before they are estimated. The Cowles Commission was ready to admit simultaneity. Herbert Simon's "Causal Ordering and Identifiability" (1953b), the article that is one of the principal sources for the structural account defended here, was the last gasp of causality in the Cowles econometric tradition. After that, identification became a staple of the received view, but causality is hardly mentioned. Why?

We can offer only conjectures. First, Wold had opposed models involving simultaneity in favor of "explicit causal chains." Wold's causal chains were similar to vector autoregressions or to Nancy Cartwright's time-ordered causal systems (Chapter 6, system (6.3)), except that he permitted contemporaneous variables to be related. But Wold banished simultaneity: If $X_t$ appeared on the right-hand side of a regression with $Y_t$ on the left-hand side, then $Y_t$ must not appear on the right-hand side of a regression with $X_t$ on the left-hand side. Which is cause and which is effect must always be indicated. But Wold lost the debate.

Second, what Simon (1953b) showed was that a linear system of equations was identified if and only if it was causally ordered. This equivalence worked against causal analysis. Identification seemed to be the more pressing problem to econometricians focused on the problems of estimation. Equivalence meant that, in some respects, causality could be ignored without loss. And identification itself had noncausal roots in the problem of the measurement of demand. Causal language simply faded away.

Finally, for reasons that may have to do with larger trends in the philosophy of science, econometricians became shy of anything that smacked of metaphysics – in a sense a return to Hume. Despite being the champion of explicit causal chains, Wold (p. 465) argued that it was better to replace the adjective "causal" with "explanatory." Nor was (or is) Wold alone: Haavelmo (p. 481), Simon (1953a, p. 56), and, more recently, David Hendry (Hendry et al. 1990, p. 184) explicitly deny either the existence of truth or of causal relationship independent of our own causal representations.[4] Why would authors, each of whom subscribes to a conception of econometrics that make most sense in light of a realist metaphysics, be reluctant to endorse a realist interpretation of causality?

One possibility is simply *Zeitgeist*: the logical positivism that dominated the philosophy of science from the 1930s to the 1950s was strongly antimetaphysical. Such intellectual trends tend to diffuse slowly, so that, despite a turn away from the doctrine in philosophy, logical positivism continues to exercise some influence in economics.

A second possibility is the rise of the notion of economic modeling. We take the idea of a model as so central to the practice of economics that we forget that the dominance of model building is relatively new (Hendry and Morgan 1995, p. 68; Morgan 1997, 1999, 2000). Models are self-evidently artifacts, our creations, not given in the world. It is easy to forget that their empirical usefulness is constrained by the need to stand in an appropriately representative relationship with the world.

A third possibility has to do with observational equivalence, which was not only well known to Simon (see Chapter 2 earlier in this book) but to his predecessors and contemporaries as well (e.g., see Frisch, p. 417; Koopmans, p. 551). Koopmans, in particular, was pessimistic about the problem. Orcutt (p. 551) understood, as did Simon, that Koopmans's pessimism was warranted only if the econometrician could not consider interventions that, to use the language of Chapter 2, Section 2, altered parameters. So long as econometricians took a narrow view of the information that they could legitimately bring to bear on quantitative analysis, the resolution of causal questions seemed doubtful and causal language pointless.

After the 1950s, statistical methods in economics divided into two separate streams. The Cowles Commission tradition, now free of causal language, dominated the mainstream textbooks. Wold continued to advocate explicit causal chains into the early 1960s, but Robert Basmann (1965) landed the decisive blow when he showed that any explicit causal-chain model could be recast as an observationally equivalent simultaneous model. Despite the absorption of much of empirical business-cycle analysis into the Cowles Commission framework, the older time-series statistics associated with the atheoretical business-cycle analysis of the first half of the twentieth century developed on a separate track. The work of the statisticians Box and Jenkins (1970) and of the econometricians C. W. J. Granger and Paul Newbold (1977) was particularly influential.

---

[4] By 1966, Simon was more clearly a realist; see Simon and Rescher (1966).

Time-series econometricians revived causality as an important topic in econometrics. The central figure is Granger (1969). Granger suggested a data-based technique for deciding whether two variables were causally linked. Causality was thus reduced to the outcome of a statistical test rather than serving as an organizing category for econometrics in general, as it had in the early history of the discipline. Inevitably, however, the discussions of causality became linked to larger issues. Christopher Sims (1972) popularized Granger-causality tests among economists when he applied them to the causal linkage between money and income. Sims's analysis was equivocal. On the one hand, it appeared to be addressed to the old question, much discussed after Hume (see Chapter 1, Section 1) of whether control over money yielded control over GDP. On the other hand, Sims packaged the test as an effort to determine from the data whether or not they were exogenous in a sense meant to be relevant to the discussions of exogeneity that were important in the structural econometrics of the 1940s and 1950s. Since Sims's (1972) article, many of the issues that were important in the early discussions are on the table once more.

## 7.2 THREE CURRENT ECONOMETRIC APPROACHES TO CAUSALITY

Philosophical questions parallel the old divide between the econometrics of demand-curve measurement and the econometrics of the business cycle, between structural econometrics and descriptive econometrics. Econometrics provides a statistical relevance basis for causal inference. Approaches to causality differ according to how they regard this basis. A *constitutional* account takes the statistical relevance basis to be the product of a causal structure that cannot be directly observed. The causal structure is primary and produces the statistical relevance basis. The causal structure itself may be inferred or (at least) conjectured from that information in combination with other nonstatistical facts. An *informational* account maintains that a certain pattern of empirical relationships in the statistical relevance basis is all that there is to causality. Do we have to make up our minds about which approach is correct? In Chapter 1, we stigmatized the informational account as falling foul of the "epistemic fallacy," yet economists, on the whole, are pragmatic waverers – many hope that we do not, in the end, have to choose. Current approaches to causality in econometrics appeal, to different degrees, to both the informational and to constitutional interpretations of the statistical relevance basis. I shall examine three recent econometric approaches to causality, keeping in mind the distinction between the two interpretations as well as the economist's tendency to muddle them up.

**Granger**

Granger-causality has already been formally defined in Chapter 6, Section 2. The central notion is one of incremental predictability. If a series $Y$ is better predicted by the complete universe of past information than by that universe less the series $X$, then $X$ Granger-causes $Y$. According to the definition, the information set on which conditioning is defined includes all possibly relevant variables and is infinitely extended back into time. Of course, practical implementations must use more limited data sets: a finite number of lags and, often, only a pair of variables. The appeal of Granger-causality is that it can be reduced to a simple econometric test – easily built into econometrics software – so long as one is willing to accept stringent limits on the information set.[5] Granger-causality stands far to the informational side among alternative econometric approaches. The Granger-causality test is meant to define *operationally* what causality is (Granger 1969, 1980, 1998). Yet, as Granger (1995) makes clear, he accepts (implicitly at least) the reality of economic structures and, therefore, the interest of the question, how does Granger-causality relate to economic structure?

As we argued in the last chapter, Granger-causality is a species of the probabilistic approach and subject to all the general objections that can be leveled against it. We cannot, however, dismiss it as an unsuccessful account of causality on those grounds alone. On the one hand, the probabilistic relations that constitute Granger-causality may yield important information for causal judgments even if they do not adequately define them – that is, they may have an informational part to play in causal inference, even if they are not constitutive of causation. On the other hand, since Granger-causality is the economist's favorite notion of causality, it is well to understand its uses and limitations.

Nancy Cartwright (1989, pp. 56–60) sees Granger-causality as essentially an Humean reduction of causality to a pure fact of asssociation (sophisticated correlation). She rejects it for the same reason that she rejects all such approaches (see Chapter 4, Section 3). Granger appeals to an infinite universe of information – explicitly so when he conditions on the infinite past history of variables. In practice, one must pick out a more limited set of *relevant* factors. But what is the operative sense of relevance? If it is *causal relevance*, then Granger's definition of causality is circular. If it is, perhaps, *statistical relevance*, then we have to say exactly how to flesh this notion out. Cartwright worries particularly

---

[5] For example, bivariate Granger-causality tests in which the user sets some finite number of lags can be implemented with a few clicks of the mouse in the popular econometrics software, such as *Econometric Views* (*E-views*) (Lillien, Hall et al. 1998) or *PC-GIVE* (Hendry and Doornik 1997).

about the possibility that in finite samples variables will display conditional correlations that do not correspond to any causal connection. But such problems plague all statistics and do not seem to pose any novel issues in this case. The problem of causal relevance is more pertinent.

In an exact analogy with her criticism of Papineau's claim that multiple regression is an efficacious tool of type-level causal analysis, Cartwright argues that Granger-causality requires the holding fixed *all* causally relevant factors to the beginning of time and that, even if it were possible, this would be an effective strategy only for the determination of token-level causes. But Granger aims to discover type-level causes. Cartwright's central claim is that singular causes are primary. Our response remains what it was in Chapter 4 to Cartwright's earlier analysis. We agree that type-level causal claims presuppose token-level structures; but, within such structures, type-level causal questions can be asked and possibly answered. Appearances to the contrary notwithstanding, Granger does not mean Granger-causality to be a pure test of association with no reference to economic structure.[6]

How, then, does Granger-causality related to economic structure? Consider the following bivariate dynamic, simultaneous system:[7]

$$Y_t = \theta X_t + \beta_{11} Y_{t-1} + \beta_{12} X_{t-1} + \varepsilon_{1t}, \tag{7.1}$$

$$X_t = \gamma Y_t + \beta_{21} Y_{t-1} + \beta_{22} X_{t-1} + \varepsilon_{2t}, \tag{7.2}$$

where $\varepsilon_{1t}$ and $\varepsilon_{2t}$ are each independently, identically distributed random variables with zero means. The coefficients multiplying the $X$s and the $Y$s on the right-hand sides are parameters in the sense used in earlier chapters.

The current values can be solved out of equations (7.1) and (7.2) to yield the reduced forms

$$Y_t = \Pi_{11} Y_{t-1} + \Pi_{12} X_{t-1} + \upsilon_{1t}, \tag{7.3}$$

$$X_t = \Pi_{21} Y_{t-1} + \Pi_{22} X_{t-1} + \upsilon_{2t}, \tag{7.4}$$

where

$$\Pi_{11} = \frac{\beta_{11} + \theta\beta_{21}}{1 - \theta\gamma}$$

---

[6] The best evidence for this is Granger's (1995) criticism of the manner in which the Granger-causality test has been used to draw inferences about exogeneity. He endorses a structural notion of exogeneity, which is discussed more fully in 7.3.

[7] This example is drawn from Jacobs, Leamer, and Ward (1979) and has been widely used to exposit issues related to Granger-causality – see Hoover (1988a), ch. 8, sec. 1; LeRoy (1995a).

$$\Pi_{12} = \frac{\beta_{12} + \theta\beta_{22}}{1 - \theta\gamma}$$

$$\Pi_{21} = \frac{\gamma\beta_{11} + \beta_{22}}{1 - \theta\gamma}$$

$$\Pi_{22} = \frac{\gamma\beta_{12} + \beta_{22}}{1 - \theta\gamma}$$

$$\upsilon_{1t} = \frac{\varepsilon_{1t} + \theta\varepsilon_{2t}}{1 - \theta\gamma}$$

$$\upsilon_{2t} = \frac{\gamma\varepsilon_{1t} + \theta\varepsilon_{2t}}{1 - \theta\gamma}$$

If $\Pi_{12} \neq 0$, then $X$ Granger-causes $Y$; if $\Pi_{21} \neq 0$, then $Y$ Granger-causes $X$. Contrast this with what the formalization of causal order given in Chapter 3 implies: If the parameters in equations (7.1) and (7.2) are defined on nondegenerate sets, then causation is mutual; if $\theta, \beta_{12} \in \varnothing$ and $\gamma \notin \varnothing$ or $\beta_{21} \notin \varnothing$, then $Y$ is a one-way cause of $X$; and if $\gamma, \beta_{21} \in \varnothing$ and $\theta \notin \varnothing$ or $\beta_{12} \notin \varnothing$, then $X$ is a one-way cause of $Y$.

There is no simple relationship between Granger-causality and the structural causality. Suppose that $Y$ is a one-way cause of $X$ in the linear model in equations (7.1) and (7.2).[8] What does it imply about Granger-causality? Inspection of the definitions of the $\Pi_{ij}$ shows that $X$ does not Granger-cause $Y$, since $\Pi_{12} = 0$. In general, it would also seem to imply that $\Pi_{21} \neq 0$ or that $Y$ does in fact Granger-cause $X$. It is these relationships between the two notions of cause that encourage some to believe that Granger-causality is a practical implementation of a structural notion.

Unfortunately, they are not robust. Take the latter, positive relationship: Does structural causality imply Granger-causality? Notice that $\Pi_{21} = 0$ and, therefore, that Granger-causality fails even when $Y$ is a one-way cause of $X$ provided that $\gamma\beta_{11} = -\beta_{21}$. This might appear to be such a special and unlikely condition that it could be dismissed as a "measure-zero" result – a mere curiosum of no practical significance. But that is wrong. There are two cases. If $\beta_{21} = 0$ and either $\gamma = 0$ or $\beta_{11} = 0$, then $\Pi_{21} = 0$. Suppose that this occurs when $\gamma \neq 0$, because $\beta_{21} \in \varnothing$ and $\beta_{11} \in \varnothing$. This corresponds to $Y$ contemporaneously causing $X$, but with lagged $Y$ neither contributing to the own-dynamics of $Y$ nor causing current $X$. This case, then, represents a broad class of potential models, not an incredibly unlikely special case.

---

[8] The illustration is symmetrical: Everything said about the case of $Y$ as a one-way cause of $X$ applies *mutatis mutandis* to $X$ as a one-way cause of $Y$.

The second case occurs in situations of optimal control. It is the dynamic analogue of the case of reverse causality (or endogenous money) discussed in Chapter 2, Section 4. Suppose that $Y$ (e.g., the money stock) is a policy variable used to control $X$ (e.g., GDP). Equation (7.2) can be interpreted as a reaction function, and policy can be described as different choices of its parameters. Suppose, as in fact it is often said to be, that the goal of monetary policy is to reduce the variability of $X$ (Blinder 1998, chapter 1). Policy cannot affect the value of the random-error terms, so the best that can be achieved is to choose $Y_t$ so that the right-hand side of equation (7.2) is zero :

$$0 = \gamma Y_t + \beta_{21} Y_{t-1} + \beta_{22} X_{t-1} \qquad (7.5)$$

or

$$Y_t = -\frac{\beta_{21}}{\gamma} Y_{t-1} - \frac{\beta_{22}}{\gamma} X_{t-1} \qquad (7.5')$$

Comparing equation (7.5′) term by term with the reaction function, equation (7.1), the policymakers should set $\theta = 0$, $\beta_{11} = -\beta_{21}/\gamma$, and $\beta_{12} = -\beta_{22}/\gamma$. Substituting $Y_t$ from equation (7.1) with this parameter settings into equation (7.2) eliminates all the right-hand terms except $\varepsilon_{2t}$, reducing the variability of GDP as far as policy possibly can reduce it. The second of the three parameter choices ensures that $\Pi_{21} = 0$. Just in the case in which $Y$ is being used optimally to control $X$, that is, just when the causal relationship between $Y$ and $X$ is most effectively exploited, the Granger-test indicates no causal connection. This is yet another example in which agency (in this case the relatively uncomplicated fact that policy makers try to do their best) undermines a notion of causality that places (temporally ordered) correlations on center stage. Such examples will recur frequently so long as policymakers pursue optimal policies.

The upshot of these examples is that Granger-causality is not necessary for structural causality. It might appear that Granger-causality is a sufficient condition for structural causality, but this turns out to be true only in the linear case. Consider the case discussed in Chapter 6, Section 2 in which prices appear to Granger-cause money because the public is better able to predict the implications of monetary policy for future inflation than is the econometrician and the public's expectations are unobservable. Nonlinearities of the type introduced by rational expectations undermine the correspondence between Granger-causality and structural causality. A simple variation on the model of the demand for money in a hyperinflation analyzed in Chapter 3, Section 2, shows more formally how this can happen.

The demand for money was given in equation (3.5″), repeated here as

$$m_t - p_t = \mu - \alpha({}_t p_{t+1}^e - p_t) + v_t. \tag{7.6}$$

The current model differs from the earlier model through the addition of a stochastic growth term, $\theta_{t-1}$, to the money-supply rule.

$$m_{t+1} = \lambda + \theta_{t+1} + m_t + \varepsilon_{t+1}. \tag{7.7}$$

$\theta_{t+1}$ is assumed to be an identically distributed serially independent random variable, uncorrelated with any other random term in the model.

If it is assumed that $\theta_{t+1}$ is unobservable at time $t$, then it can be grouped with the error term $\varepsilon_{t+1}$, and the solution to the model for prices repeats equation (3.9):

$$p_t = m_t - \mu + \alpha\lambda + v_t. \tag{7.8}$$

Substitute equation (7.7) lagged once into (7.8) to yield

$$p_t = (1 + \alpha)\lambda + m_{t-1} - \mu + (\theta_t + \varepsilon_t + v_t). \tag{7.9}$$

Equations (7.7) and (7.9) form a system of reduced-form equations. By inspection, it is obvious that money Granger-causes prices, but prices do not Granger-cause money in this system.

But now let us suppose that the public is better informed than the econometrician: The public knows $\theta_{t+1}$ and earlier realizations at time $t$, although not realizations at time $t + 2$ and later, while the econometrician is ignorant of all realizations. A reasonable conjecture for the rate of inflation (analogous to equation (3.8)) is

$$({}_t p_{t+1}^e - p_t) = \lambda + \frac{\theta_{t+1}}{1+\alpha}. \tag{7.10}$$

We confirm that this is the rational expectation of inflation. First, substitute (7.10) into (7.6) and rearrange to get an expression for current prices:

$$p_t = m_t - \mu + \alpha\left(\lambda + \frac{\theta_{t+1}}{1+\alpha}\right) + v_t. \tag{7.11}$$

Next take expectations of actual inflation conditional on information available at time $t$ based on the current and future price levels determined by equation (7.11):

$$E(p_{t+1} - p_t \mid \Omega_t) = E\left( m_{t+1} - \mu + \alpha\left( \lambda + \frac{\theta_{t+2}}{1+\alpha} \right) + v_{t+1} \right.$$

$$- \left( m_t - \mu + \alpha\left( \lambda + \frac{\theta_{t+1}}{1+\alpha} \right) + v_t \right) \Bigg)$$

$$= E\left( m_{t+1} - m_t + \left( \lambda + \alpha\left( \frac{\theta_{t+2} - \theta_{t+1}}{1+\alpha} \right) + v_{t+1} - v_t \right) \right)$$

$$= \lambda + \theta_{t+1} - \frac{\alpha\theta_{t+1}}{1+\alpha} = \lambda + \frac{\theta_{t+1}}{1+\alpha}, \tag{7.12}$$

which is what we conjectured. The terms involving $\theta_{t+2}$ drop out under the expectations operator because $\theta_t$ is mean zero and the public has advanced knowledge of its realizations only one period ahead.

Solve equation (7.11) for $\theta_{t+1}$:

$$\theta_{t+1} = (1+\alpha)\left[ \frac{p_t - m_t + \mu - v_t}{\alpha} - \lambda \right]. \tag{7.13}$$

Substitute equation (7.13) into (7.7), simplify, and rearrange to yield the reduced form for the money stock:

$$m_{t+1} = \left[ \left( \frac{1-\alpha}{\alpha} \right)\mu - \alpha\lambda \right] - \left( \frac{1}{\alpha} \right)m_t + \left( \frac{1+\alpha}{\alpha} \right)p_t - \left[ \left( \frac{1+\alpha}{\alpha} \right)v_t + \varepsilon_{t+1} \right]. \tag{7.14}$$

Thus, even though prices at time $t$ do not cause money at time $t + 1$, according to the structural account, they nonetheless Granger-cause money. The behavior of current prices is a way in which the public's superior knowledge of the future course of money is made observable to econometricians. Current prices serve as a proxy for the value of $\theta_{t+1}$, which the econometricians cannot observe.

In the end, we must conclude that whatever uses Granger-causality has a measure of incremental predictability, it is neither necessary nor sufficient for structural causality in a range of cases important to macroeconomics.

**Glymour, Scheines, Spirtes, and Kelly**

A second econometric approach to causality is based in work of four philosophers and computer scientists, exposited in two books and a series of papers, including one (Glymour and Spirtes 1988) published in the *Journal of Econometrics*. Most of the illustrations of their methods employ data from social sciences other than economics. Recently, however, Norman Swanson and Granger (1997) and

Steven Sheffrin and Robert Triest (1998) applied these methods to macroeconomic problems. The central idea is that the intuitive notion of causal connection can be represented as a diagram or graph (in the most visually appealing version, by variable names connected by arrows in the manner of many of the figures in earlier chapters); and that these may, in turn, be systematically related to observable correlations among the variables. As the name of the earlier of the two books, *Discovering Causal Structure* (Glymour et al. 1987), suggests, the graph-theoretic approach is naturally interpreted as structural. Even so, while they discuss a variety of philosophical issues related to causation, for practical purposes they strike a Humean attitude and are essentially agnostic as to what causality is essentially.[9] The facts of causality are found in the associations among variables, and the graphs serve to summarize some general features of those associations in a manner that corresponds to our causal intuitions. The approach belongs, by and large, to the family of probabilistic approaches to causality discussed in Chapters 1 and 4.[10]

The reader of earlier chapters is already familiar with the idea that causal connections can be indicated graphically using variable names and arrows, that these can be seen as translations of equations, and that, if these equations are regarded as structures generating observable data, they imply in turn the correlations among the variables. In our account, however, the graphs are inessential. As was shown in Chapter 3, the system of equations and, crucially, the identification of some variables as parameters and others as structural variables determines the causal ordering. In Glymour et al.'s approach, the graphs are essential.[11] It is only when the graphs are added to the matrix of correlations that both qualitative causal orders and quantitative measures of the strengths of causal connections are possible. As I suggested earlier (Chapter 2, Section 2), a particular parameterization is the functional equivalent to placing the heads on the causal arrows. The power of the graph-theoretic approach, displayed most clearly in Peter Spirtes, Clark Glymour, and Richard Scheines (1993) and in the closely related work of Judea Pearl and his co-workers, is that they are able to appeal to a well-developed

---

[9] See Woodward (1997, p. 284) commenting on Glymour (1997).

[10] Glymour et al. try to remain agnostic among fundamental theories of causality; nevertheless see Glymour's discussion of Holland (in Holland 1986) in which he provides a counterfactual interpretation of causality. The manner in which Glymour et al. use probabilities epistemically is analogous to other examples of a probabilistic approach (see Chapter 1, Section 2).

[11] Different subsets of the four authors in this research program shall be referred to as Glymour et al. when it is the body of the research program and not a particular work to which we refer.

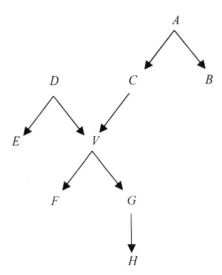

Figure 7.1

body of results in the mathematical field of graph theory to develop their causal analyses.[12]

Glymour et al.'s analysis is sophisticated and their terminology daunting. It is not to our purpose to attempt give a complete account, but merely to suggest the main lines of their approach and to relate it to the structural account and to econometric practice. The essence of Glymour et al.'s approach is found in two axioms: the Causal Markov Condition and the Faithfulness Condition. Consider a variable $V$ in a causal graph. A *directed path* is a chain of arrows linked through variables that are aligned in a uniform direction. The variables that are connected to $V$ through chains of arrows pointing into $V$ are the *ancestors* of $V$; the immediate ancestors are the *parents*. The variables that are connected to $V$ through chains of arrows originating at, and pointing away from, $V$ are the *descendants* of $V$; the direct descendants are the *children*. To illustrate, in Figure 7.1, $A$, $C$, and $D$ are parents of $V$, and $F$, $G$, and $H$ are descendants; while neither $E$ nor $B$ is a parent nor a descendant. The *Causal Markov Condition*, paraphrasing Spirtes et al. (1993, p. 54), says:

*Any variable, V, in a causal graph is, conditional on its parents, independent of all other variables that are neither its parents nor its descendants.*

The Causal Markov Condition is closely related to screening and the common-cause condition, which played so important a role in

[12] Pearl's work with various colleagues is voluminous; see Pearl and Verma (1991), Pearl (1995, 1998a,b) for articles covering some key elements. Pearl (2000) is a treatise covering the range of his work on causality.

probabilistic accounts of causality such as Hans Reichenbach's account. Among other relationships in Figure 7.1, the Causal Markov Condition implies that $D$ screens off $E$ from $V$, that $C$ screens off $A$ from $V$, and that $C$ and $D$ screen off $B$ from $V$.

The *Faithfulness Condition*, again paraphrasing Spirtes et al. (1993, p. 56), says:

*The probability distribution of the variables in a casual graph is* faithful *if, and only if, every conditional independence relationship true in the probability distribution is also implied by the Causal Markov Condition applied to the graph.*

The Faithfulness Condition says that there is a one-to-one mapping between the screening relationships discoverable in the data and those implied by the causal structure of the graph.

The probability distribution of the variables in a graph carries one more dimension of information than the graph, for the graph is supposed to represent the causal structure for all possible values of the variables and all possible correlations among them, whereas the probability distribution permits us to assign numerical values to those correlations.

Correlation is symmetrical. The causal direction between two isolated variables cannot be established using Glymour et al.'s approach. But partial correlation is asymmetrical, and the principles that they use to establish causal direction among three or more variables are easily illustrated. Consider Figure 7.2. If $B$ and $C$ are correlated and the partial correlation of $B$ and $C$ conditional on $A$ is zero, then they conclude that a pattern like graph (i) generated it.[13] If $B$ and $C$ are not correlated, but the correlation of $B$ and $C$ conditional on $A$ is positive, then a pattern like graph (ii) is suggested. Spirtes et al. (1993, p. 48) give an example that illustrates this second situation. Imagine that a light bulb is lit ($A$) only when a battery is charged ($B$) and a switch is on ($C$). If the switch and the charge of the battery are independent, they nevertheless will be correlated conditional on knowing that the bulb is lit; for if one knows that the bulb is lit and that the battery is charged, then the switch must be on.

These triadic relationships are not the only ones implied by the graphs. Glymour et al. analyze four-way relationships as well, and higher-order relationships may also be implied. Consider panel (i) of Figure 7.3. The graph implies four triadic screening relationships: $r_{AC|B} = 0$, $r_{AD|B} = 0$, $r_{AD|C} = 0$, $r_{BD|C} = 0$. Consider the numerators from the formulae that define the middle two vanishing partials:

---

[13] This correlation is written as $r_{B,C|A}$ and is defined in Chapter 4, Section 3, note 18.

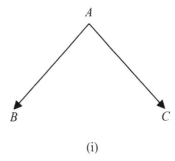

(i)

Figure 7.2

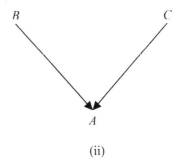

(ii)

$$r_{AD|B} = 0 \quad \text{implies} \quad r_{AD} - r_{AB}r_{BD} = 0, \tag{7.15}$$

$$r_{AD|C} = 0 \quad \text{implies} \quad r_{AD} - r_{AC}r_{CD} = 0. \tag{7.16}$$

Together these imply

$$r_{AB}\, r_{BD} - r_{AC}\, r_{CD} = 0. \tag{7.17}$$

Glymour et al. refer to relationships such as this as *vanishing tetrad differences*. Although observation of a vanishing tetrad difference helps us to order the variables in a graph, it does not place a direction on the arrows of that graph: Panel (ii) in Figure 7.3 is observationally equivalent to panel (i) – it implies precisely the same screening relationships and the same vanishing tetrad difference. In general, Glymour et al.'s approach under the best case permits us to narrow the

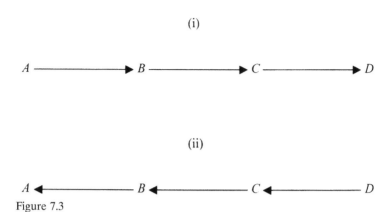

Figure 7.3

class of acceptable graphs, but does not resolve all observational equivalence.

Glymour et al. treat the relationships among variables as deterministic. Therefore, in order to introduce randomness, they presume that every explicit variable has a latent, random variable as a cause. Graphs such as Figures 7.1–7.4 are then seen to be elliptical expressions for more complicated graphs. For example, panel (i) of Figure 7.2 could be expressed more fully as in Figure 7.4, in which the ε are latent, random variables. In general, every explicit variable has a latent, random cause. Glymour et al. permit those causes to be correlated, which, of course, violates the assumptions that we have previously made about the structure of the causal field (see Chapter 2, Section 4, and Chapter 3, Section 1). The conflict can, however, be resolved once the causal graphs are cast into the formalism of Chapter 3; for what Glymour et al. show as linkages among the latent variables can be recast as nonlinear relationships among the explicit variables.

Glymour et al.'s approach is operationalized in computer programs, *Tetrad* (Glymour et al. 1987) and *Tetrad II* (Spirtes et al. 1993). These programs start with the correlation matrix for a set of variables, search for vanishing partial correlations and vanishing tetrad differences, and then suggest the graph that is most "faithful." The algorithms of these programs incorporate many of the graph-theoretic results developed in great detail in their work. The main idea is perhaps more transparent in an economic example that implements their methods using standard econometric tools.

Swanson and Granger (1997) use Glymour et al.'s approach to determine the causal order among the contemporaneous variables of a vector autoregression (VAR). The problem is easily understood with reference

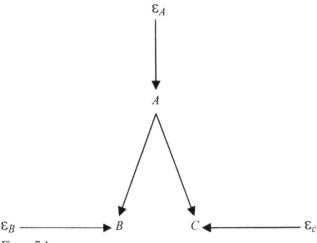

Figure 7.4

to the simple bivariate, dynamic system given in equations (7.1) and (7.2) and their reduced forms, repeated here:

$$Y_t = \Pi_{11} Y_{t-1} + \Pi_{12} X_{t-1} + \upsilon_{1t} \tag{7.3}$$

and

$$X_t = \Pi_{21} Y_{t-1} + \Pi_{22} X_{t-1} + \upsilon_{2t}, \tag{7.4}$$

where

$$\upsilon_{2t} = \frac{\varepsilon_{1t} + \theta \varepsilon_{2t}}{1 - \theta \gamma}$$

$$\upsilon_{2t} = \frac{\gamma \varepsilon_{1t} + \varepsilon_{2t}}{1 - \theta \gamma}.$$

In general, the error terms, $\upsilon_{1t}$ and $\upsilon_{2t}$ are correlated and cannot be viewed as primitive shocks (in the terminology of Chapter 2, they violate the conditions necessary to be impounded in the causal field). The variance-covariance matrix of the system (7.1)–(7.2) can be written as

$$\Omega = \begin{bmatrix} \omega_{11} & \omega_{12} \\ \omega_{12} & \omega_{22} \end{bmatrix}, \tag{7.18}$$

where each of the elements $\omega_{ij}$ are nonzero. If we multiply equation (7.3) through by $\delta = \omega_{12}/\omega_{11}$ and subtract the result from equation (7.4), we have:

$$X_t = \delta Y_t + \rho_2 Y_{t-1} + \rho_2 X_{t-1} + \eta_t, \tag{7.19}$$

where $\rho_1 = \Pi_{21} - \delta\Pi_{11}$, $\rho_2 = \Pi_{22} - \delta\Pi_{12}$, and $\eta_t = \upsilon_{2t} - \delta\upsilon_{1t}$. Now consider equations (7.3) and (7.19) as a system. It is analogous to the system (7.3) and (7.2) with $\theta = 0$, since the variance-covariance matrix of the error terms of (7.3) and (7.19) is

$$\mathbf{N} = E\left[\begin{bmatrix} \varepsilon_{1t} \\ \eta_t \end{bmatrix}\begin{bmatrix} \varepsilon_{1t} & \eta_t \end{bmatrix}\right] = \begin{bmatrix} \omega_{11} & 0 \\ 0 & v^2 \end{bmatrix}, \tag{7.20}$$

where $v^2 = \mathrm{var}(\eta_t)$. The contemporaneous terms of the system (7.3) and (7.19) are causally ordered on Simon's criterion with $Y_t$ causing $X_t$. This manner of imposing causal order on the reduced forms is, however, arbitrary. Had we multiplied equation (7.4) by $\theta = \omega_{12}/\omega_{22}$ and subtracted the result from equation (7.3), we would have ended up with a new equation that, together with equation (7.4) would have been causally ordered with $X_t$ causing $Y_t$ – yet another case of the now familiar problem of observational equivalence.

The VAR methodology can be generalized. Let $\mathbf{Y}$ be a vector of variables. Then a VAR can be written as

$$\mathbf{Y} = \mathbf{A}\mathbf{Y}_{-1} + \upsilon,^{14} \tag{7.21}$$

where the variance-covariance matrix is given by

$$\Omega = E(\upsilon\upsilon'), \tag{7.22}$$

the off-diagonal elements of which are generally not zero. There is a unique upper-triangular matrix, $\mathbf{P}$, such that $\mathbf{P}\mathbf{P}' = \Omega$.[15] Premultiply both sides of (7.21) by $\mathbf{P}^{-1}$ to yield

$$\mathbf{P}^{-1}\mathbf{Y} = \mathbf{P}^{-1}\mathbf{A}\mathbf{Y}_{-1} + \mathbf{P}^{-1}\upsilon = \tilde{\mathbf{A}}\mathbf{Y}_{-1} + \eta. \tag{7.23}$$

The variance-covariance matrix of $\eta$ is

$$\mathbf{N} = E(\eta\eta') = E(\mathbf{P}^{-1}\upsilon\upsilon'\mathbf{P}'^{-1}) = \mathbf{P}^{-1}E(\upsilon\upsilon')\mathbf{P}'^{-1} = \mathbf{P}^{-1}\Omega\mathbf{P}'^{-1} = \mathbf{I}; \tag{7.24}$$

that is, the off-diagonal elements are all zero, and the diagonal elements are normalized by dividing through by their own variances. The error terms are said to be *orthogonalized*. Since $\mathbf{P}^{-1}$ is lower triangular, the variables in equation (7.23) are recursively ordered with each variable in $\mathbf{Y}$ unaffected by the current values of any variable above it in the vector and affecting the current values of all the variables below it. This is an example of a *Wold causal chain*. Block recursive orderings, in which some subgroups of variables in $\mathbf{Y}$ are simultaneous, are also possible. In

[14] This is a first-order VAR, but since any higher order VAR can be recast as a first-order VAR no generality is lost by sticking to this simple case.
[15] This is the Choleski factorization.

this case, **P** would no longer be upper-triangular, although the error terms would be orthogonalized.

Just as in the two-variable case, the causal order is arbitrary. For every different and statistically equivalent order in which the variables are listed in **Y**, there is a different matrix, **P**, and a different Wold causal chain. The puzzling empirical problem is how one might choose between these different causal orders. Swanson and Granger give two illustrations of how to order VARs using Glymour et al.'s methodology. Consider their first example. The data consist of time-series observations on money ($M_t$), consumption ($C_t$), investment ($I_t$), and GDP ($Y_t$). They estimate a VAR-like equation (7.21) and obtain estimates of the error vector $\hat{\upsilon} = [\hat{\upsilon}_M \ \hat{\upsilon}_C \ \hat{\upsilon}_I \ \hat{\upsilon}_Y]'$, where the hats indicate estimates. They then calculate the correlation matrix of the elements of $\hat{\upsilon}$. From this correlation matrix, they are able to calculate all of the partial correlations among the $\upsilon$ variables. They then conjecture a causal order based on treating the lowest absolute partial correlations as the most likely candidates for vanishing partial correlations. From this, they conjecture the following ordering:

$$M_t \to C_t \to I_t \to Y_t$$
$$\uparrow \quad \uparrow \quad \uparrow \quad \uparrow \qquad\qquad (7.25)$$
$$\varepsilon_M \quad \varepsilon_C \quad \varepsilon_I \quad \varepsilon_Y$$

where the $\varepsilon$ variables are the independent random shocks that correspond to random field variables in our own terminology. The reasoning is as follows. There are 12 partial correlations among four variables. The lowest 3 in absolute value turn out to be: (i) $r_{YM|C}$, (ii) $r_{YM|I}$, and (iii) $r_{IM|C}$. From (i) we surmise that $C_t$ screens $Y_t$ from $M_t$, and from (ii) that $I_t$ screens $Y_t$ from $M_t$; so that either (A) $Y_t$—$I_t$—$C_t$—$M_t$ or (B) $Y_t$—$C_t$—$I_t$—$M_t$, where the line without an arrowhead indicates an undirected causal connection. From (iii) we surmise that $C_t$ screens $I_t$ from $M_t$. This argues in favor of order (A). However, the next lowest absolute partial correlations are (iv) $r_{CM|I}$ and (v) $r_{CM|Y}$, which suggest that separately $I_t$ and $Y_t$ screen $C_t$ from $M_t$. Either conclusion contradicts order (A). These correlations are, of course, statistics and subject to sampling error, so such a contradiction is not necessarily fatal. And the next lowest absolute partial correlation is $r_{CY|I}$, which suggests that $I_t$ screens $C_t$ from $Y_t$, a conclusion consistent with order (A). The remaining correlations are larger and are not *prima facie* good candidates for vanishing partial correlations. As noted in the discussion of tetrad differences, vanishing partial correlations and tetrad differences cannot orient the arrows of an order such as (A). Swanson and Granger prefer the order of (7.25) to the reverse order represented by (A) read left to right through an appeal to temporal order: At least one of money, consumption, or investment is a leading indicator for GDP.

Swanson and Granger's next step is to check whether the conjectured causal graph both represents and implies the vanishing partial correlations in the data up to the accuracy of the statistical estimates. To do this they estimate test statistics for the significance of the partial correlations against the null hypothesis that they are zero. To test, for example, $r_{CM|I}$, they regress $\upsilon_C$ on $\upsilon_M$ and $\upsilon_I$. The $t$-statistic on the coefficient on $\upsilon_M$ is their measure of the significance of the partial correlation. They prove that the partial correlation vanishes if, and only if, this coefficient is zero. The causal order (7.25) is the maintained hypothesis. If it is true, variables later in the causal chain cannot screen earlier variables. Therefore, $r_{CI|Y}$, $r_{CM|I}$, $r_{CM|Y}$, and $r_{IM|Y}$ are assumed to be nonzero in order to identify the graph. On that assumption, a regression corresponding to any of these partials, say of $\upsilon_C$ on $\upsilon_I$ and $\upsilon_Y$, would be statistically inconsistent because the true error terms for such a regression would be correlated with the independent variables as the dependent variable is a cause of the independent variables. The partial correlations used to identify the causal structure are, therefore, not tested.

The test statistics are not independent and precise joint distributions of the test statistics are unknown. Using rules of thumb, however, Swanson and Granger conclude that the model implies all of the over-identifying vanishing correlations implied in the data. It also implies one ($r_{CY|I} = 0$) that is not found in the data. Conversely, the data do not imply any vanishing partial correlations that are not represented in the graph.[16]

Spirtes et al. (1993, ch. 4) acknowledge some ways in which their approach can fail, but argue that it has strong heuristic value and that the problems are generally second order. One such problem is already familiar from Chapter 1, Section 2, in the guise of Simpson's paradox. Broadly construed this refers to the fact that conditional correlations that appear in populations may not be evident, or may even be reversed, in subpopulations (see Chapter 1, Section 2).

A second problem occurs with respect to Udny Yule's "nonsense correlations."[17] Elliot Sober (1988, p. 90) gives an example familiar to

---

[16] Swanson and Granger (1997, p. 363) also argue that the data suggest rejecting the null hypothesis that $r_{IM|C} = 0$. Not $r_{IM|C} = 0$ implies not $r_{CM|I} \neq 0$, which would be indirect evidence contradicting one of the four identifying assumptions for the graph. But, as Swanson has acknowledged in private correspondence with the author, he and Granger misread their own $p$-statistics and the evidence is that the null of $r_{IM|C} = 0$ *cannot* be rejected. The corrected information is even more consonant with their conjectured graph: In all, the data is faithful for 11 (not 10, as they say) of the 12 implied partial correlations.

[17] Reprinted in Hendry and Morgan (1995), ch. 9.

philosophers of a correlation between bread prices in England and rising sea levels in Venice. David Hendry gives an example more familiar to economists of the correlation between cumulative rainfall in Scotland and inflation.[18] Each arises because the time-series variables are nonstationary (i.e., the means, and possibly other moments, of their distributions are shifting through time). A time series is integrated of order $d$ (notated $I(d)$) if the $d$th difference of the series is stationary. Any two $I(1)$ series (e.g., inflation, cumulative rainfall, and, most likely, bread prices and sea levels) will be correlated with an $R^2$ approaching unity as time goes to infinity, whether or not there is any causal connection between them. Spirtes et al. (1993, p. 63) argue that this is, again, a case of mixing data from different populations analogous to Simpson's paradox.

In each case, Spirtes et al. fall back on the strategies of the probabilistic approach already familiar from Chapter 1, first, to insist on measuring correlations only in homogeneous populations, and second, to the degree that one is interested in the global outcome and not merely in the subpopulation outcomes to fill in additional details. An additional variable may indicate to which subpopulation any particular member is assigned. This strategy is more appealing as a way of dealing with cases like Simpson's paradox than it is in dealing with nonsense correlations. There may, of course, be some variable that ultimately is a common cause of two trending series: in either Sober or Hendry's examples, global warming, perhaps. But must there be? The examples are chosen precisely to suggest that any common causes are so remote as to be ignorable. Nonsense correlations may arise whenever time series are trending, and such trends arise in all growth processes. Treating each time as in itself an indicator of a different subpopulation fails to do justice to the connections between variables at different times, to the essence of dynamic and growth *processes*. The real problem with these examples is not their causal structure, but the limitations of the model that underwrites the statistical tools applied to them – correlation and regression. Each was developed with explicit or implicit assumptions of stationarity. The recent literature on *cointegration* shows that analogous techniques can be developed in the context of a statistical model that does not assume stationarity.[19] Two or more series are cointegrated if each has the same degree of integration ($d$) and a linear combination of them is

---

[18] Hendry (1980, pp. 17–20) reports regression results which show that the relationship between cumulative rainfall in Scotland and prices is as close (measured by the squared correlation coefficient, $R^2$) and more statistically significant (measured by the $t$-statistics on the estimated coefficients) than that between money and prices,

[19] On cointegration, see Hamilton (1994, ch. 19) and Hendry (1995, ch. 8).

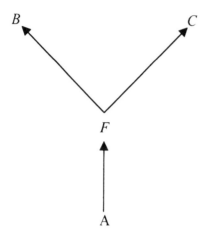

Figure 7.5

stationary (i.e., $I(0)$). It is highly doubtful that bread prices in England and sea levels in Venice or inflation and cumulative rainfall in Scotland are cointegrated.

Setting the question of nonsense correlations to one side, how successful is Spirtes et al.'s argument that failures of the Markov condition can be laid at the door of omitted variables? In Chapter 4, Section 3, we considered Cartwright's example of the polluting chemical factory. This is one of a class of examples that Wesley Salmon (1984, pp. 168–169) refers to as *interactive forks*. In Salmon's example the laws of motion and the configuration of the balls on a pool table imply that the realization of the uncertain event of the eight ball going into the left-corner pocket almost certainly coincides with the cue ball going into the right-corner pocket for a scratch. The common cause, the cue ball striking the eight ball, does not screen the effect of sinking the eight ball from sinking the cue ball. Spirtes et al. (1993, p. 63; cf. Papineau 1991) wish to subsume all such cases to patterns like the one in Figure 7.5. Here the variable $F$ is further information – for example, the exact momentum of the cue ball or, in Cartwright's case, whether the chemical process "fired" or not.[20] Conditional on $F$, $B$ and $C$ are independent, even though they are not conditional on $A$ alone. In economics, variables linked through budget constraints might act similarly.[21]

Must there always be a variable such as $F$? Cartwright says no. Spirtes et al. say almost always. They admit a possible exception from quantum mechanics. The famous thought experiment of Albert Einstein, Boris

---

[20] A number of similar cases were considered in Chapter 4, Section 1.
[21] See Cartwright 1989, p. 117; but also see the discussion of the "Walrasian fantasy" in Chapter 4, Section 4.

Podolsky, and Nathan Rosen proposes that two subatomic particles, say electrons, are emitted from a single source with no angular momentum and travel a long distance in opposite directions.[22] The spin of each particle is measured and, because of the law of conservation of angular momentum, one is measured spin-up if, and only if, the other is measured spin-down. The measurements, therefore, are correlated, and it is natural to look for the common cause. The standard understanding of quantum mechanics rules out the particles even having a well-defined spin until the measurement is actually made, so that it appears that the measurement itself induces the correlation of two causally disconnected events. Einstein, Podolsky, and Rosen suggested, exactly as do Spirtes et al. in other contexts, that there must be an unmeasured conditioning variable (such as $F$) that accounts for the correlation.[23] J. S. Bell demonstrated, subject to certain assumptions, whose validity is still debated, that quantum mechanics violates implications of the existence of such a *hidden* conditioning variable, even though the experimental evidence confirms the correctness of the quantum mechanical measurements. Apparently one must choose between the empirically validated theory and the assumption that there must be a hidden conditioning variable. Most physicists accept the theory.

Spirtes et al. (1993, p. 64) offer a heuristic defense of the Causal Markov Condition that in effect draws the distinction between the weak version of the common-cause condition ("every correlation requires a casual explanation") and the strong version ("common causes screen off the correlations among their effects") (see Chapter 4, Section 3):

> the apparent failure of the Causal Markov Condition in some quantum mechanical experiments is insufficient reason to abandon it in other contexts. We do not, for comparison abandon the use of classical physics when computing orbits simply because classical dynamics is literally false. The Causal Markov Condition is used all the time in laboratory, medical and engineering settings, where an unwanted or unexpected statistical dependency is *prima facie* something to be accounted for.

Just so; but it does raise the question whether other disciplines pose systematic threats to the Causal Markov Condition.

Macroeconomics does pose such threats. In Chapter 5, we argued for the ontological autonomy of macroeconomics from microeconomics. The search for an unmeasured conditioning variable may end in the crossing of the micro/macro border before an appropriate conditioning variable could be located. We saw that to eliminate contemporaneous correlation

---

[22] The summary here is based on Cartwright (1989, pp. 232–233).
[23] Spirtes et al. are not endorsing Einstein, Podolsky, and Rosen's discredited appeal to hidden variables in quantum mechanics, but merely pointing out that analogous situations can occur in unrelated contexts.

among variables in a VAR we might have to take finer and finer temporal cuts of the variables. Variables like GDP, which are necessarily defined over a time interval, lose their distinctive characteristics as the time interval becomes smaller and smaller. Similarly, in the rational-expectations models of Chapter 3 and Section 7.2, the macroeconomic expectations term is homonymous, but not synonymous, with an individual's expectation of a particular price. In fact, rather than treat $_tp_{t+1}^e$ as a latent variable, we replaced it with the nonlinear constraints implied in its elimination from the system of equations. This strategy seems especially reasonable in the case in which we posit that individual information is greater than the econometrician's information. Given the discontinuity between these individual expectations and $_tp_{t+1}^e$, the homonymous macroeconomic variable, it is unlikely that any macroeconomic variable could, even conceptually, remove the informational advantage of individual (microeconomic) agents. Thus, even if $_tp_{t+1}^e$ were replaced through some sort of index of individual expectations or through an estimate based on some independent relationship (a measurement instrument), there would still be a residual informational advantage on the part of individual economic agents. The consequence in the case of Granger-causality was that, even when prices do not cause money structurally, they Granger-cause them. This is a violation of the Faithfulness Condition, since the appropriate causal graph would imply a vanishing conditional dependency that was not found in the data. The considerations of Chapter 5 suggest that this is an insurmountable ontological difficulty. But, even if one quarrels with the ontology, there is little doubt that it is an insurmountable practical problem. The same reasons that suggest to Spirtes et al. that we should continue to rely on the Causal Markov Condition – namely its heuristic power in practice – suggest that we have reason to be skeptical in macroeconomic applications.

As we have seen already, expectations (a product of economic agency) violate Faithfulness in that they imply constraints that fail to appear in the data. We have also seen that agency can result in constraints appearing in the data that are not implied (in general) by the causal structure. Consider Figure 7.6 and a corresponding set of equations:

$$A \Leftarrow \varepsilon_A, \tag{7.26}$$

$$B \Leftarrow \alpha A + \varepsilon_B, \tag{7.27}$$

$$C \Leftarrow \beta A + \gamma B + \varepsilon_C, \tag{7.28}$$

where the $\varepsilon$ variables are independent random-error terms. $B$ can be regarded as a control variable analogous to $M$ in the previous discussion of Granger-causality or in the discussion of reaction functions in Chapter

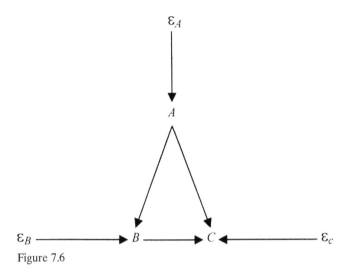

Figure 7.6

2, Section 4. If the object of the control is to minimize the variability of $C$, then the optimal $\alpha = -\beta/\gamma$. Consider when two of the key partial correlations vanish:

$$r_{AC|B} = 0$$

if $r_{AC} - (r_{AB})(r_{BC}) = (\alpha\gamma + \beta)\sigma_A^2 - \alpha\sigma_A^2[\alpha(\alpha\gamma + \beta)\sigma_A^2 + \gamma\sigma_B^2] = 0$     (7.29)

and

$$r_{BC|A} = 0$$

if $r_{BC} - (r_{AC})(r_{AB}) = [\alpha(\alpha\gamma + \beta)\sigma_A^2 + \gamma\sigma_B^2] - \alpha\sigma_A^2(\alpha\gamma + \beta)\sigma_A^2] = 0.$     (7.30)

If $\alpha$ is chosen optimally and $\sigma_B^2 = 0$ – that is, if control is both optimal and precise – then each of these conditions is fulfilled. In that case, using the Causal Markov Condition, we would find that the $B$ screens the correlation of $A$ and $C$ and $A$ screens the correlation of $B$ and $C$. Even more strongly, $C$ would appear to be unconditionally uncorrelated with either $A$ or $C$. This can be seen by substituting (7.27) into (7.28), setting $\alpha$ to its optimal value, and eliminating $\varepsilon_B$ on the ground that its variance has been assumed to be zero. In effect, the data would tell us to erase the causal arrow between $A$ and $C$ as well as that between $B$ and $C$ and to remove the head from the arrow between $A$ and $B$ (since we know that they are correlated but have no third relationship with a third variable that would indicate the alignment of the arrow). This apparently weak causal structure arose just when the causal linkages from $A$ to $B$ and from both to $C$ were being used most effectively to control $C$.

Notice, however, that this would not be the case if control were not precise – that is, if $\sigma_B^2 \neq 0$. An implementation error, noise in the control rule, would permit in principle appropriate causal inferences. But the smaller that $\sigma_B^2$ is, the harder the causal link will be to detect. Spirtes et al. (1993, p. 95) acknowledge the possibility that particular parameter values might result in violations of faithfulness, but they dismiss their importance as having "measure zero." But this will not do for macro-economics. It fails to account for the fact that in macroeconomic and other control contexts, the policymaker aims to set parameter values in just such a way to make this supposedly measure-zero situation occur. To the degree that policy is successful, such situations are common, not infinitely rare.

The approach of Glymour et al. can be viewed as a sophisticated version of a probabilistic account of causality – one that takes notice of the causal structures that generate the probabilistic relations among vari-ables. Probabilistic constraints – vanishing partial correlations and tetrad and higher-order differences – do not exhaust the implications of causal structures. But they do constitute evidence – evidence that must, on a broad interpretation of the common-cause principle, be given a causal explanation. In the right circumstances, this approach is a powerful tool in identifying causal structures. In the somewhat more difficult circum-stances that are natural to macroeconomics, it may nonetheless prove a useful heuristic and an adjunct to other tools.

### LeRoy

The third approach to causality in econometrics, due to Stephen LeRoy (1995a), provides less of a recipe for practical causal ordering of variables than an interpretive basis for assessing econometric policy evaluation. LeRoy's approach is informational in two senses: First, it is more directly about the architecture of economic models than about causal structures thought to subsist in the economy; second, its principal notion is that a cause is a *sufficient aggregator* of information. The general idea is that, given a model, factors outside the model determine the outcomes within the model. Sometimes a variable inside the model carries all the relevant information about some of the outside factors for some other variable. In that case, the first variable is a cause of the second variable.

LeRoy distinguishes between structural and nonstructural variables. *Structural* variables are ones that the modeler chooses to classify as either exogenous or endogenous. An *exogenous* variable is one that is outside the model and subject to direct control. An *endogenous* variable is one that is inside the model and not subject to direct control.

Variables are *nonstructural* if no such classification is made. A *structural model* is one in which at least some of the variables are structural. On this categorization all of the variables involved in the rational-expectations/demand-for-money model used in the discussion of Granger-causality earlier in this chapter are structural; while only the contemporaneous variables in Swanson and Granger's model used to illustrate Glymour et al.'s methods are structural. Yet, both *models* are structural. LeRoy (1995a, pp. 219–221) also discusses the distinctions between parameters and variables frequently met in economics and is at some pains to point out the variability and the inconsistencies of common usage. Nonetheless, he has for some purposes his own preferred usage: First, a coefficient in a model "is a *parameter* if it is structural or a *constant* if it is nonstructural" (LeRoy 1995a, p. 217; emphasis added); and a *parameter* is a variable that does not change in real time (i.e., it may vary between alternative universes or in comparative static exercises, but must not change in a given process) (LeRoy 1995a, p. 225; cf. LeRoy 1995b, p. 241). He acknowledges the distinction popularized in discussions of policy analysis in the new classical macroeconomics between *deep* and *shallow* parameters.

All this makes for a complex and difficult terminological landscape. The essence of LeRoy's points, however, can be made with reference only to the distinction between exogenous and endogenous variables. Exogenous variables, except for the fact that LeRoy makes their status depend on the classificatory decisions of the modeler, are equivalent to the definition of parameters in Chapter 3. Even the exception may not prove to be much of a difference, since LeRoy does not use a notion like our causal field, which involves, in part, pragmatic choices – and, therefore, classification – partly at the option of the investigator.

For LeRoy, a model is a set of functions mapping exogenous into endogenous variables:

$$y_n = f_n(e(y_n)), \quad n = 1, 2, \ldots, \tag{7.31}$$

where the $y_n$ are endogenous variables, and $e(y_n)$ is the smallest set of exogenous variables needed to determine $y_n$.

A variable $y_i$ causes $y_j$ in LeRoy's formalism if, and only if, three conditions obtain:

1. *Strict Inclusion*: $e(y_i) \subset e(y_j)$.
2. *Composition*: if $y_j = f_j(e(y_j))$, then there is a function $g(\bullet)$ such that $y_j = g(f_i(e(y_i)), e(y_i) - e(y_j))$,
3. *Nonconstancy*: the function $g(\bullet)$ is *not* a constant function, where a constant function is defined as follows: $g(\bullet)$ is constant if, $g(y_i^*, e(y_i) - e(y_j)) = $ a constant for all $y_i^* \in y_i$.

The strict inclusion condition carries with it Simon's syntactic definition of cause as (block-)recursive ordering (LeRoy 1995a, pp. 218–219; see also Chapter 2, Section 2). The central idea is that causes determine effects asymmetrically. The nonconstancy condition is introduced largely to solve the problem of causal overdetermination (LeRoy 1995a, p. 214). In Chapter 2, Section 1, we argued that causal overdetermination is unlikely to pose particular problems for macroeconomics. It remains a secondary consideration here.

The distinctive force of LeRoy's schema is found in the composition condition – in the claim that causes are sufficient aggregators of information. Consider the following example from LeRoy (1995a, p. 214):

$$x_{11}y_1 = x_{10},  \tag{7.32}$$

$$x_{21}y_1 + x_{22}y_2 = x_{20},  \tag{7.33}$$

$$x_{31}y_1 + x_{32}y_2 + x_{33}y_3 = x_{30},  \tag{7.34}$$

where the $x$'s are parameters and the $y$'s are variables. For Simon this is clearly a case in which $y_1$ causes $y_2$ and $y_2$ causes $y_3$. But for LeRoy, $y_2$ does not cause $y_3$. To see this, note that $e(y_2) = \{x_{10}, x_{11}, x_{20}, x_{21}, x_{22}\}$ and $e(y_3) = \{x_{10}, x_{11}, x_{20}, x_{21}, x_{22}, x_{30}, x_{31}, x_{32}, x_{33}\}$. In the system, equations (7.32)–(7.34), $y_2$ and $e(y_3) - e(y_2) = \{x_{30}, x_{31}, x_{32}, x_{33}\}$ are insufficient to determine $y_3$. We require knowledge either of all of the elements of $e(y_3)$ or of $y_1$ in addition to $y_2$. The second case implies that $\{y_1, y_2\}$ are joint causes of $y_3$, even though $y_2$ is not a cause on its own. Note that $y_1$ is itself a cause of $y_3$ since $y_1$, equations (7.33) and (7.34) and $e(y_3) - e(y_1) = \{x_{20}, x_{21}, x_{22}, x_{30}, x_{31}, x_{32}, x_{33}\}$ determine $y_3$. Similarly, $y_1$ is a cause of $y_2$.

LeRoy is, of course, free to define "cause" in whatever manner he likes. There is always a danger that a stipulative definition will be applied to situations in which it is not appropriate. And it is reasonable to ask whether this definition captures, as LeRoy clearly intends, the sense of causality usually employed in macroeconomics and ordinary life.

LeRoy's definition of causality is a positive one; roughly: $y_1$ causes $y_2$ if it carries complete information on the $x_i$ that determine $y_1$ and (in part) $y_2$. In contrast, the Simonesque definition that we defend is partly positive ($y_1$ carries *some* nonredundant information from the $x_i$ that determine $y_1$) and partly negative (roughly: $y_2$ does not cause $y_1$ if there exists some setting of the $x_i$ such that $y_2$ changes but $y_1$ does not change). On this basis, $y_2$ causes $y_3$. There are three advantages to our definition. The first is empirical: Singular negatives are demonstrable; universal positives are not. The second is semantic: Our definition captures the conditional nature of causality in which causes are INUS conditions for their effects.

The third is pragmatic, albeit closely related to the second. It can be illustrated by a noneconomic example. Suppose that a bomb with a two-part trigger sits in the corner of a room. The first part is photosensitive; the second part is electrically activated, and the electric mechanism is connected to a wire that runs to a solar cell in the far corner of the room. In the same corner, there is a very bright light, which is initially switched off so that the room is dark. If the light is switched on, the bomb explodes, because the light directly trips the photosensitive part and, by means of the solar cell, generates by means of the solar cell a current that trips the electrical part. Let $y_1$ be the light (a variable with the values *on* and *off*); $y_2$, the electric current (also an *on/off* variable); and $y_3$, the bomb (a variable that takes the values *explodes/does-not-explode*). On LeRoy's definitions, $y_1$ causes both $y_2$ and $y_3$, but $y_2$ does not cause $y_3$. Surely, this is counterintuitive. In common usage, $y_2$ is *a* cause of $y_3$, even though it is not *the* cause of $y_3$. On our definitions, $y_2$ causes $y_3$, despite the fact that $y_2$ does not carry all of the information about $y_1$ relevant to $y_3$: One must know not just that the electricity is on, but also that the light is on to know the state of the bomb. Nevertheless, one must know $y_2$ independently of $y_1$. For example, clipping the electric wire or shielding the bomb from the light stops the bomb from exploding, but intervening in one process has no effect on the other process.[24]

LeRoy (1995a, pp. 217–218) relates causal ordering to econometric estimation. A model is called "complete" if it explains all the correlations among the endogenous variables without appeal to uninterpreted correlations among the exogenous variables. If a linear model is complete and $x$ causes $y$ on LeRoy's definitions, then the conditions of the Gauss-Markov theorem (Theil 1971, pp. 119–121) are met and ordinary-least-squares (OLS) regression will provide unbiased estimates of the strength of the causal linkage. LeRoy suggests that the contrapositive of this result allows one to infer that two variables are not causally related. The idea is that if a linear model is complete and the OLS estimator is biased, then the variables cannot be causally ordered. He provides the following example:

$$x_t = \lambda x_{t-1} + u_t, \tag{7.35}$$

$$u_t = \rho u_{t-1} + e_t, \tag{7.36}$$

where $x_0$, $u_0$, and the $e_t$ are independently distributed exogenous variables. The model is complete. An OLS estimate of equation (7.35) is

---

[24] Talk of intervention raises two points. First, the specification of the problem is elliptical. Nevertheless, it is easy to see that further variables and relations could be introduced that would articulate the scope of possible interventions without stepping outside the model. Second, some notion of intervening seems critical to any realistic account of causality.

biased, because $x_{t-1}$ and $u_t$ are correlated. LeRoy concludes that $x_{t-1}$ does not cause $x_t$.

Notice, however, that equations (7.35) and (7.36) can be rewritten as[25]

$$x_t = (\rho + \lambda)x_{t-1} - \rho\lambda x_{t-2} + e_t,$$
$$= \Pi_1 x_{t-1} + \Pi_2 x_{t-2} + e_t. \tag{7.37}$$

The $\Pi$s can be estimated without bias by OLS, and $\rho$ and $\lambda$ are identified and can be recovered from these estimates.[26] Given $x_1$ as an additional exogenous variable, it would appear that $x_{t-1}$ does cause $x_t$ on LeRoy's definitions.[27] Yet, equation (7.37) is not really a different model than equations (7.35) and (7.36). It is a different representation of the same model.

Part of the problem here is that LeRoy sees causality as a property of the representation, and not a property of the world. This also undermines the epistemic value of LeRoy's observation that causal ordering in complete linear models is related to the unbiasedness of OLS regression. When one knows the model, one can indifferently work out bias or whether particular variables are causally ordered under LeRoy's definitions. But neither the models nor the bias of regressions are facts that the variables wear on their faces. So, starting from the data, there is no way to use the bias or lack of bias of an OLS regression to say anything about causal structure in the world.

### 7.3 EXOGENEITY AND CAUSALITY

In placing emphasis on exogeneity and complete systems of equations, LeRoy again revives the discussion, mentioned in Section 7.1, of causality and exogeneity that was central to the econometric debates of the 1940s and early 1950s and was revived in Sims's popularization of Granger-causality tests in the 1970s. Exogeneity, while a popular notion with economists and econometricians, turns out to be ill-defined in most discussions. It is worth trying to understand the range of the possible meanings and how they relate to econometrics. The best starting point is the magisterial analysis due to Robert Engle, David Hendry, and Jean-François Richard (1983).[28]

---

[25] Lag equation (7.35) one period and subtract the result from (7.35) and substitute from (7.36).
[26] $\lambda$ is the solution to the quadratic equation, $\lambda^2 - \lambda\Pi_1 - \Pi_2 = 0$, and $\rho = \Pi_1 - \lambda$.
[27] Setting aside the vexed question of whether a variable can be properly said to cause later manifestations of itself.
[28] A thorough discussion is found in Hendry (1995, ch. 5), on which much of this section is based.

**Concepts of Exogeneity**

When an economist calls a variable *exogenous*, it implies that the variable is in some sense outside the model. This is often analyzed as if it is a question of the correlation of independent variables with the unobserved error term in a regression. Hendry (1995, pp. 167–168) provides examples of the intrinsic ambiguity of that approach. Instead, Engle et al. define exogeneity as obtaining when information about some variables can be ignored without loss to the question of interest. A sequence of related questions of interest gives rise to a hierarchy of exogeneity concepts.

LeRoy's causality question viewed econometrically amounts to this: When can the process through which an independent variable is determined be ignored for purposes of estimation? In the Engle et al. taxonomy, this is the question of when a variable is weakly exogenous. Another question is, when can the process through which an independent variable is determined be ignored in predicting the future value of another variable? This is the question of when a variable is strongly exogenous. A final question is, when can the regime in which a variable is determined be ignored? This is the question of when a variable is super-exogenous.

The starting point for Engle et al.'s analysis is a complete probabilistic description of the universe of variables – the true *data-generating process* (often abbreviated $DGP$). The data-generating process need not be simple or stable through time, and it is certainly not directly observable. The goal of econometrics is to characterize pieces of the data-generating process in useful ways. And the issue of exogeneity is how small those pieces can be for various purposes. For purposes of exposition, we shall describe tractable data-generating processes as if we knew them. Tractability implies that we have already ignored large chunks of the true data-generating process and have made assumptions about the stability and other desirable characteristics of the remaining bits. We assume that these are legitimate restrictions, recognizing, of course, that in practice their empirical legitimacy would be a critical question.

I shall concentrate on a bivariate case. (The generalization to multivariate cases is obvious.) Define a vector of current-date variables

$$\mathbf{x_t} = \begin{bmatrix} y_t \\ z_t \end{bmatrix}. \tag{7.38}$$

Let $\mathbf{X_{t-1}}$ be the past history of $\mathbf{x_t}$. Then the data-generating process can be written as a conditional probability distribution:

$$D_x(\mathbf{x_t}|\mathbf{X_{t-1}}, \theta), \tag{7.39}$$

where

$$\theta = \begin{bmatrix} \theta_1 \\ \theta_2 \\ \theta_3 \\ \vdots \\ \theta_n \end{bmatrix}$$

are the parameters that govern the form of $D_x(\bullet)$; $\theta \in \Theta$, the parameter space from which the $\theta_i$ are drawn.

Consider a transformation of $\theta$,

$$\phi = f(\theta), \tag{7.40}$$

where $\phi \in \Phi$ is a new parameter space. There can be many such functions, $f(\bullet)$.

It is immediately obvious that Engle et al. use "parameter" in a different sense than either we used it in Chapter 3 or LeRoy uses it in his analysis of causality. For Engle et al. a "parameter" is a quantity, which relative to the variation or covariation of the variables in a particular *representation* of the data-generating process, or some particular subpart of it, is constant. Such a parameter need not be a constant in real time, as LeRoy requires. Whether it is independent of the values of other parameters, as we required in Chapter 3, is a logical and empirical question that bears on the question of exogeneity, as we shall see presently.

Any joint probability distribution can be rewritten as the product of a conditional and a marginal distribution. Consider one parameterized in terms of a partition of $\phi$,

$$\phi = \begin{bmatrix} \phi_1 \\ \phi_2 \end{bmatrix}:$$

$$D_x(\mathbf{x}_t \mid \mathbf{X}_{t-1}, \theta), = D_{y|z}(y_t \mid z_t, \mathbf{X}_{t-1}, \phi_1) D_z(z_t \mid \mathbf{X}_{t-1}, \phi_2). \tag{7.41}$$

Suppose that $\psi$ is a vector of parameters of interest to the economist. Then $z_t$ is *weakly exogenous for* $\psi$ if

    i.   $\psi = g(\phi_1)$ only,

and

    ii.  $\phi_1$ and $\phi_2$ are variation free.

Parameters are *variation free* when the particular value of one parameter in no way restricts the admissible values of the other parameter. In the notation of Chapter 3, Section 1, $(\phi_1, \phi_2) \in \Phi_1 \times \Phi_2$.

Weak exogeneity is similar to LeRoy's definition of causality in that the question it poses is, when can the process that determines one variable be ignored when considering the influence of that variable on another? But it goes beyond LeRoy in making clear the relativity of that question to both the particular parameterization of the data-generating process and to the parameters one seeks to recover. It is necessary for the efficient estimation of a parameter of interest in a conditional model that the conditioning variables be weakly exogenous for parameters of interest.

$\mathbf{X}_{t-1}$ contains the past history of both $y_t$ and $z_t$. In order to use information on $z_t$ and its history to predict future values of $y_t$, it is in general necessary to model the behavior of both $y$ and $z$, even if $z_t$ is weakly exogenous for the parameters of interest in the model of $y_t$ conditional on $z_t$. This is because lagged $y$s are determinants of $z_t$, so that the dynamics of $y$ cannot be described without accounting for the way in which it feeds back on itself through past $z$s. But suppose that lagged $y$s do not, in fact, influence $z_t$, then, we can write the marginal distribution of $z_t$ as

$$D_z(z_t \mid \mathbf{X}_{t-1}, \phi_2) = D_z(z_t \mid \mathbf{Z}_{t-1}, \phi_2), \tag{7.42}$$

where $\mathbf{Z}_{t-1}$ is the past history of $z_t$ and any initial conditions for $y$, call them $y_0$. Equation (7.42) is simply an alternative way of stating that $y$ does not Granger-cause $z$ (see the definition of Granger-causality in Chapter 6, Section 2). A conditioning variable is *strongly exogenous* according to Engle et al. when it is weakly exogenous for the parameters of interest and it is not Granger-caused by the variable one seeks to forecast.

Engle et al. refer to the absence of Granger-causality from a dependent variable to a conditioning variable, the notion of exogeneity popularized by Sims (1972), as *strict exogeneity*.[29] Strict exogeneity is, in itself, not one of their hierarchy of exogeneity concepts (weak, strong, super). Sims showed that if a variable $X$ is strictly exogenous for $Y$, then there is a regression model in which $Y$ is a function of lagged $X$s only and for which the $X$s are not correlated with the error terms, so that estimates of the coefficients on the $X$s are consistent. Sims's result has sometimes been incorrectly interpreted to mean that strict exogeneity supports the consistency of estimation for any model of interest. But, in fact, it is an existence result: There is *some* parameterization for which consistent estimates are guaranteed. If one cannot recover one's parameters of interest from this parameterization – and there is no reason, in general,

---

[29] Interestingly, Granger (1995, p. 230) writes: "I have never equated non-(Granger) causality with exogeneity, even though some later writers incorrectly did do so." He goes on to endorse Engle et al.'s analysis.

to think that one can – then strict exogeneity cannot substitute for weak exogeneity, which is specifically relative to parameterization.[30] Nevertheless, one can regard strong exogeneity as weak exogeneity plus strict exogeneity.

Define an intervention at time $t$ as a vector $\delta_t \in \Delta_t$, a set of possible interventions. Let $\theta_t = h(\theta, \delta_t)$ describe the manner in which $\theta$ varies with $\delta_t$. The parameter vector $\phi_1$ is *invariant* with respect to $\Delta_t$, if $h(\bullet)$ assigns a constant value to $\phi_1$ for each value of $\delta_t$. If $z_t$ is weakly exogenous for $\psi$ and $\phi_1$ is invariant with respect to $\Delta_t$, then $z_t$ is *super-exogenous* for $\psi$ with respect to $\Delta_t$. Super-exogeneity is necessary to support the use of a model to analyze regime changes of the type indexed by $\delta_t$. Whether it is correct to analyze regime changes in the manner envisaged by Engle et al., Lucas, and many other commentators is, in fact, controversial and bears on questions important to causal analysis. We take that question up in the next section. Before that, however, let us consider how these notions of exogeneity work out in some familiar examples.

**The Demand for Money with Extrapolative Expectations**

Begin with a modified version of the model of the demand for money in a hyperinflation discussed in Chapter 3, Section 2. Equation (3.5″) is repeated here as:

$$m_t - p_t = \mu - \alpha({}_t p^e_{t+1} - p_t) + v_t. \tag{7.43}$$

Instead of assuming rational expectations, we assume that expectations of future inflation simply project the current rate of inflation; hence:

$${}_t p^e_{t+1} - p_t = p_t - p_{t-1}. \tag{7.44}$$

Substituting equation (7.44) into (7.43) yields

$$p_t = \left(\frac{1}{1-\alpha}\right)m_t - \left(\frac{\mu}{1-\alpha}\right) + \left(\frac{\alpha}{1-\alpha}\right)p_{t-1} + \left(\frac{1}{1-\alpha}\right)v_t. \tag{7.45}$$

The stock of money is governed by equation (3.6), repeated here as

$$m_t = \lambda + m_{t-1} + \varepsilon_t. \tag{7.46}$$

Equations (7.45) and (7.46) are the data-generating process. Suppose that we wish to estimate $\alpha$ and $\mu$. To follow the format of the preceding exposition, let

$$\mathbf{x}_t = \begin{bmatrix} p_t \\ m_t \end{bmatrix}. \tag{7.47}$$

---

[30] There is a more detailed account of this issue in Hoover (1988a, ch. 8, sec. 1, especially pp. 175–176 and fn. 22).

The joint probability distribution of the data-generating process is

$$D_x(p_t, m_t | \mathbf{X_{t-1}}, _\theta), \tag{7.48}$$

where

$$\theta = \begin{bmatrix} \alpha \\ \mu \\ \lambda \\ \sigma_v^2 \\ \sigma_\varepsilon^2 \end{bmatrix}.$$

The parameters of interest are $\Psi = [\alpha\,\mu]'$. Consider the following reparameterization, $\phi = f(\theta)$:

$$p_t = \Pi_0 + \Pi_1 m_t + \Pi_2 p_{t-1} + \omega_t, \tag{7.49}$$

$$m_t = \Omega_0 + \Omega_1 m_{t-1} + \xi_t. \tag{7.50}$$

Equation (7.49) can be interpreted as the distribution of $p_t$ conditional on $m_t$, and equation (7.50) as the distribution of $m_t$ marginal of $p_t$. Again, sticking to the earlier format,

$$\phi = \begin{bmatrix} \Pi_0 \\ \Pi_1 \\ \Pi_2 \\ \Omega_0 \\ \Omega_1 \\ \sigma_\omega^2 \\ \sigma_\xi^2 \end{bmatrix}$$

$\phi$ can be partitioned as follows:

$$\phi_1 = \begin{bmatrix} \Pi_0 \\ \Pi_1 \\ \Pi_2 \\ \sigma_\omega^2 \end{bmatrix}$$

and

$$\phi_2 = \begin{bmatrix} \Omega_0 \\ \Omega_1 \\ \sigma_\varepsilon^2 \end{bmatrix}.$$

$\phi_1$ and $\phi_2$ are variation free, and $\psi$ can be recovered from $\phi_1$ only:

$$\mu = -\frac{\Pi_0}{\Pi_1} \text{ and } \alpha = -\frac{\Pi_2}{\Pi_1} \text{ or } \alpha = -\frac{\Pi_1 - 1}{\Pi_1}.$$

The two different ways of calculating $\alpha$ constitute an overidentifying restriction that can be tested statistically.

Using Engle et al.'s definitions, $m_t$ and $p_{t-1}$ are weakly exogenous for $\alpha$ and $\mu$. Notice that equation (7.50) involves no lags of $p_t$. Therefore, $p_t$ does not Granger-cause $m_t$, and $m_t$ is strictly exogenous for $p_t$; and, consequently, $m_t$ and $p_{t-1}$ are strongly exogenous for $\alpha$ and $\mu$. Furthermore, if we regard $\lambda$ as a parameter in the control of the monetary authorities and notice that in equation (7.45) none of the bracketed terms involves $\lambda$, we can conclude that $m_t$ and $p_{t-1}$ are super-exogenous for $\alpha$ and $\mu$ with respect to interventions in $\lambda$.

**The Demand for Money with Rational Expectations**

There is a temptation, which is supported by the notion considered and rejected in Chapter 2, Section 6, to regard causality as fundamentally about robustness under interventions, to identify causal order with super-exogeneity. In the case of the demand for money with extrapolative expectations, the causally ordered system is super-exogenous, but another example shows that the actual relationship is more complex.

Consider the model of the demand for money with rational expectations; that is, equations (7.43), (7.46), and equation (3.7) repeated here as:

$$_t p_{t+1}^e = E(p_{t+1} \mid \Xi_t). \tag{7.51}$$

The solution to this model for prices is given in equation (3.9), repeated here as:

$$p_t = m_t - \mu + \alpha\lambda + v_t. \tag{7.52}$$

Analogously to equations (7.49) and (7.50) of the model with extrapolative expectations

$$p_t = \Pi_0 + \Pi_1 m_t + \omega_t, \tag{7.53}$$

$$m_t = \Omega_0 + \Omega_1 m_{t-1} + \xi_t. \tag{7.54}$$

So,

$$\phi = \begin{bmatrix} \Pi_0 \\ \Pi_1 \\ \Omega_0 \\ \Omega_1 \\ \sigma_\omega^2 \\ \sigma_\varepsilon^2 \end{bmatrix}.$$

$\phi$ can be partitioned as follows:

$$\phi_1 = \begin{bmatrix} \Pi_0 \\ \Pi_1 \\ \sigma_\omega^2 \end{bmatrix}$$

and

$$\phi_2 = \begin{bmatrix} \Omega_0 \\ \Omega_1 \\ \sigma_\varepsilon^2 \end{bmatrix}$$

$\phi_1$ and $\phi_2$ are variation free, but weak exogeneity depends on the parameters of interest. If the parameters of interest were $\Psi = [\Pi_0 \; \Pi_1]'$, then $m_t$ would be weakly exogenous for $p_t$ for these parameters. Notice, however, that $m_t$ is not super-exogenous for $p_t$ and $\Psi$ for the policy parameter $\lambda$, since $\Pi_0 = \alpha\lambda - \mu$, which alters with every resetting of $\lambda$.

If, however, the parameters of interest are $\Psi = [\alpha \; \mu \; \lambda]'$, then $m_t$ is not weakly exogenous for $p_t$ and $\Psi$, since these parameters cannot be recovered from $\phi_1$. In general, a systems estimator that simultaneously estimated both $\phi_1$ and $\phi_2$ would be required for efficient estimation of the parameters of interest.

Note that the failure of weak exogeneity, in itself, rules out both strong and super-exogeneity (with respect to $\lambda$). $m_t$ remains strictly exogenous for $p_t$, as $p$ does not Granger-cause $m$.

This example is important as an illustration of a class of models that arises routinely in macroeconomic contexts. Recall from Chapter 3 that on our definitions $m$ is a one-way cause of $p$. Yet, $m$ is not super-exogenous for $p$ for $\Pi_0$ and $\Pi_1$ and with respect to interventions in $\lambda$. This clearly distinguishes causal structure from invariance or robustness. In the example without rational expectations, causal order and super-exogeneity coincide. This is not accidental, but results from the intrinsic linearity in parameters of the underlying structure. The coincidence breaks down in the case with rational expectations because of the non-linearity of the cross-equation restriction. Of course, the failure of super-exogeneity is a failure only with respect to the conditional distribution represented by equation (7.53). Notice that equation (7.54) is invariant with respect to interventions in $\alpha$ and $\mu$. Causal structure governs the transmission of influence. A salient fact about one-way causal order is that influences do not transmit backwards against the arrow of causality. Invariance and robustness are relevant to causal order, but they do not define it. Rather it is the causal order that determines just what the invariance relationships are among variables. So, just as the evidence of conditional probabilities and screening are useful information in causal inference, even though we reject basing a definition of causality upon them, invariance, robustness and super-exogeneity also are sources of relevant information, which must be interpreted in relationship to causal structures.

## 7.4 THE LUCAS CRITIQUE AND CAUSALITY

Robert Lucas's article "Econometric Policy Evaluation: A Critique" is surely the most influential article in macroeconomics in the last quarter of the twentieth century. It played an important role in the development of macroeconometrics and in furthering the program of microfoundations of macroeconomics that has come to dominate disparate schools of macroeconomic thought. And it is subject to a causal interpretation.[31] Lucas's article is offered as general criticism of the manner in which "Keynesian" macroeconometric models of the 1950s to 1970s were used to analyze policy.[32] Broadly stated, Lucas's objection was that the econometric models estimated aggregate relationships that were the result of a complex interaction between individual decisions of consumers and producers and the policy environment; those individual decisions would change whenever the policy environment changed; so one could not expect the estimated aggregate relationships to remain invariant in the face of changing economics policies; and, therefore, such relationships could not be used to provide valid assessments of the effects of new policies. Lucas's solution to the problem of policy evaluation is to model the individual decision-making processes.[33]

[31] On the influence of Lucas's article, see Hoover (1999, introduction); for more general discussions of the Lucas critique and reactions to it, see Hoover (1988a, ch. 8) and Hoover (1992); for a causal analysis of the "Lucas critique," see Hoover (1994c).
[32] The quotation marks indicate that Keynes himself is not actually implicated in this strategy of policy analysis. In fact, Keynes can be considered to be another precursor of Lucas's analysis (see Hoover 1997a, p. 229).
[33] The original article contains no actual econometric applications involving data or estimations. It is unclear whether Lucas regards detailed econometric modeling as a practicable solution. His own econometric work tends to focus on situations in which the considerations of the "critique" can be set aside (see Hoover 1999, introduction). Others (e.g., Hansen and Sargent 1980) have taken the call for a microfoundational approach

Taken this broadly, the "Lucas critique" is uncontroversial and, as he himself understood, does not originate with Lucas but is found in a variety of forms – implicitly and explicitly – among earlier economists and econometricians. In terms of a structural approach to causal analysis, the "critique" can be seen as pointing either to the failure to articulate the true underlying causal structure in econometric modeling or to a failure to confine econometric analysis to situations in which the causal field remains constant. In this broad interpretation, the "critique" raises no conceptual difficulties, only questions of practical, empirical significance.[34]

Lucas's article may also be interpreted more narrowly in a manner of greater programmatic significance for the new classical school of macroeconomics. This interpretation singles out rational expectations as the source of instability of estimated macroeconometric relationships.[35] While Lucas provides his own examples, the point is easily illustrated using the variation on the model of the demand for money already used in Chapters 3 and 6 and in Section 7.3.

Equation (7.45), repeated here, is the price equation when expectations are extrapolative:

$$p_t = \left(\frac{1}{1-\alpha}\right)m_t - \left(\frac{\mu}{1-\alpha}\right) + \left(\frac{\alpha}{1-\alpha}\right)p_{t-1} + \left(\frac{1}{1-\alpha}\right)v_t. \qquad (7.45)$$

It shows that the coefficients that measure the marginal effects of aggregate money and past prices on current prices are actually convolutions of "deep parameters" – $\alpha$ and $\mu$ are the parameters of the underlying demand-for-money function (equation (7.43)), which can be taken as describing individual choice. Policy is described according to equation (7.46), repeated here:

$$m_t = \lambda + m_{t-1} + \varepsilon_t. \qquad (7.46)$$

The important point is that the policy parameter, $\lambda$, plays no part in the price determination equation (7.46). As we saw in the last section, $m_t$ and $p_{t-1}$ are super-exogenous for $\alpha$ and $\mu$ with respect to interventions in $\lambda$. Econometric policy evaluation in this case could legitimately proceed in

to econometrics more seriously; while others (e.g., Sims 1986) have focused on situations in which policy regimes could be regarded as constant and the Lucas critique irrelevant (see Hoover 1988a, pp. 197–202).

[34] In a detailed assessment of the economic literature on the "Lucas critique," Ericsson and Irons (1995) conclude that it is essentially a possibility theorem with little practical significance. See Leeper's (1995) comments on Ericsson and Irons for an opposing view.

[35] On the rational-expectations hypothesis, see Sheffrin (1996) and Hoover (1988a, chs. 1 and 2).

the manner that Lucas attacks. Estimate the reduced form of equation (7.49), repeated here:

$$p_t = \Pi_0 + \Pi_1 m_t + \Pi_2 p_{t-1} + \omega_t. \qquad (7.49)$$

That is, ignore the microeconomic structure of the decision problem reflected in the deep parameters. Assume a path for $m$. Plug that path into equation (7.49) and calculate the path for $p$ on the basis of the estimated values of $\Pi_i$.

Lucas criticizes such policy analysis as violating the fundamental assumption of economic rationality. People who base expectations of future prices on extrapolations of current and past rates of inflation are bound to find their expectations *systematically* falsified whenever inflation is either accelerating or decelerating, as it would when monetary authorities sought, on one hand, to lower unemployment by exploiting the Phillips curve or, on the other hand, to secure price stability. Under the rational-expectations hypothesis, people are modeled as forming expectations consistent with the structural model of the economy, so that the only falsifications of their expectations are *unsystematic* and, therefore, irremediable. In the last section, the price equation with rational expectations was given as:

$$p_t = m_t - \mu + \alpha\lambda + v_t. \qquad (7.52)$$

The policy parameter is an element of the coefficients on its right-hand side. The reduced form of equation (7.52) is repeated here as:

$$p_t = \Pi_0 + \Pi_1 m_t + \omega_t. \qquad (7.53)$$

Lucas maintains that it is wrong to assume a path for $m$, independent of assuming a description of the policy rule that would generate that path – in other words, a path for $\lambda$. Under rational expectations, people act as if they know the underlying policy rule. One cannot successfully follow the strategy of policy evaluation outlined above, since every change in monetary policy (that is, every change in $\lambda$) would alter the $\Pi_i$, causing the true reduced-form equation to shift. As we saw in the last section, $m_t$ is not super-exogeneous for $p_t$ and $[\Pi_0 \ \Pi_1]$ for the policy parameter $\lambda$.[36] Policy analysis could, in principle, be carried on consistently with Lucas's analysis through the joint estimation of the deep parameters of the behavioral equations and the policy rules, provided that they are econometrically identified. Then, the effects of the policy are worked out by

---

[36] The failure of super-exogeneity is such a characteristic feature of the narrow interpretation of the Lucas critique that Favero and Hendry (1992) and Ericsson and Irons (1995, pp. 281–307) have concentrated their analysis of the practical significance of the Lucas critique on demonstrating that there is no failure of super-exogeneity in situations in which Lucas's analysis would require one.

simulating the effect of a change in a policy parameter rather than by assuming a particular path for a policy variable.

Lucas provides a second type of example of unobjectionable policy analysis. While his example focuses on the response of investment decisions to tax policy, the point can be easily illustrated using Hamilton's models of the demand for money under stochastic regime switching developed in Chapter 3. Like the illustration of a one-off regime change analyzed in Lucas's first type of examples, agents with rational expectations integrate the policy behavior of the monetary authorities into their demand for money. But if regimes are changed according to some pattern (in Chapter 3, the growth rate of money switched between zero and λ, following a two-state Markov process), the probabilities of such shifts would be additional factors in their decisions and, therefore, in the pricing equation.

Lucas treats the two types of cases (a one-off change in regime in which agents act as if, once changed, the new regime will be permanently maintained and a regime in which agents act as if the regime may change with definite probabilities) as illustrating the same objection to "Keynesian" policy analysis. LeRoy (1995b) bases his criticism of Lucas's analysis of economic policy evaluation on a distinction between the two types of cases.[37] LeRoy's objection has two planks.

The first is that it is incorrect to describe policy according to a *changing* parameter. In his analysis of causal structure (LeRoy 1995a; see Section 7.2 earlier in this book), LeRoy provides a stipulative definition of "parameter," which includes the requirement that it remain constant in real time.[38] Thus, elements of the model such as λ, the coefficient on money in the policy rule (equation 7.46), are not properly regarded, in LeRoy's view, as parameters, but (implicitly, at least) are actually variables. When policy changes, these coefficients vary; therefore, they are variables. Lucas's first type of example fails to recognize that fact, while his second type does.

LeRoy's second plank rests on the first: the rational-expectations hypothesis requires that the probability of variables changing be an element of people's decision making. If not, then just as people make a systematic error by adopting some form of extrapolative expectations of prices in situations in which the rate of inflation is changing, so, too, people would make systematic errors in assuming that policy was to remain forever constant after each change in the policy rule. In LeRoy's

---

[37] LeRoy's article develops ideas he first suggested in Cooley, LeRoy, and Ramon (1984). For an evaluation of this earlier article, see Hoover (1988a, pp. 192–197).

[38] LeRoy has no objection to comparative static (i.e., counterfactual) exercises in which one contemplates how otherwise identical economies might have been different had a parameter been different.

view, Lucas's second type of example is not subject to the same objection. In models like Hamilton's regime-switching model, the possible policy states are constants, and the constant probabilities of switching between states are incorporated into people's choices.

LeRoy sees his criticism of Lucas as having important implications for policy analysis amounting to a refutation of the narrow form of the Lucas critique. First, since the only sense in which regime changes occur is as switches governed by probabilities, aggregate econometric relationships – structural or reduced-form relationships such as VARs – should already have incorporated the relevant probabilities of switching into the outcomes of individual decision-making processes and, therefore, should provide true estimates whatever regimes are actually realized in any sample period.

Second, Lucas's admonition that proper policy analysis requires a specification of policy rules, not particular paths or policy shock terms, is unwarranted. If policy rules are described by parameters, and parameters never change by definition, then the only way one policy differs from another is through the actual realizations of random processes; and the only way to evaluate its consequences is to conjecture the realized path and work out the implications from the model.

LeRoy's attack on the Lucas critique is a threat to the structural account of causality. We have defined parameters as variables that meet certain independence criteria. And we have used parameters to define causal structure. If parameters are truly unchangeable, this strategy is upset. Another way of looking at the threat is to notice that LeRoy's account attacks the potential instrumentality of the causal structure. How could causal structures be useful as tools or transmission mechanisms of policy if LeRoy's account were correct?

Policy requires a sense of inside and outside: The policymaker looks at the world from a detached perspective, takes actions that possess some degree of independence from the world, and relies on the enduring causal structure of the world to translate those actions – if properly chosen – into desirable outcomes. Similarly, as we argued in Chapter 4, Section 4, causality requires the notion of causal structure, which carries with it the notion of an inside and an outside. A universal determinism is not consistent with causal structure – pragmatically, at least. We argued that nonstochastic indeterminism is essential to causal order. *Nonstochastic indeterminism* refers to change that is unpredictable because it is not governed by rules – neither deterministic nor probabilistic. There must be true innovation. It may be the Lucretian swerve – an unconscious, undeliberate, literally senseless and arbitrary event – or it may be a human decision (such as a policy action), which, in the final analysis, often contains an element of arbitrariness. Human arbitrariness need not imply irrationality. Sometimes actors' reasons are so compelling that choice is forced and predictable. But sometimes not. The typical monetary policy decision of the Federal Reserve – say, the choice to raise interest rates – may be justified and yet not be compelled to be precisely 25 basis points today. It is not rational for Buridan's ass to starve just because he finds himself between two equally desirable piles of hay. Which way he goes is arbitrary.[39]

Many decisions combine predictable and stochastically unpredictable elements. And in economics, Hamilton's regime-switching model may provide a good illustration of such decisions. But that model has parameters in the form of the given switching probabilities. Who chooses those probabilities? Surely, they are the nonstochastically indeterministic choice of the policymakers. One may, of course, reject that conclusion and argue that switches in these probabilities are themselves stochastically indeterministic, governed by higher order probabilities. But, then, who chooses those probabilities? How far can the game of embedding each apparent parameter choice into a stochastic switching model be ramified?

To think that the ramification goes on forever, so that the whole economy is described as a giant supergame with fixed parameters, is another version of the Walrasian fantasy rejected in Chapter 4, Section 4. LeRoy appears to be in the thrall of just such a fantasy. In LeRoy's account, policy is emasculated. Imagine that policy is described by Hamilton's regime-switching model ramified indefinitely.[40] Policymakers can be thought to choose the alternative regimes only if there is some sense in which they could have done differently. The implication of the rational-expectations hypothesis – as LeRoy understands it – is that expectations equal realizations plus an error. In that case, the only unfettered choice is the error, and even the error must obey a stochastic rule. So, for example, the policymaker could not choose a set of positive error terms in order to give the economy a boost, as then the distribution of the errors would be skewed, and the errors themselves would be serially correlated in violation of the rational-expectations hypothesis. Policymakers would lack the potential for useful direction.

LeRoy denies this conclusion. He maintains that the rational-expectations hypothesis means that agents know the true distribution of the variables – as if God had whispered it in their ears. Thus, when policymakers deliver a series of positive errors, so that the realized means and other moments differ from the true population moments,

---

[39] Amartya Sen used to say in his elementary microeconomics lectures in Oxford that Buridan's ass died for revealed preference theory.

[40] Which, by the way, Hamilton himself does not assert.

agents regard the errors as outliers. In a long enough run of coin flips, even a thousand heads in a row should come up rarely. But in what sense is this deliberate policy? If the rational expectation of policy is really based on the true distribution, the policymakers could deliver such a policy *only* as the result of a truly randomized process (e.g., as a fortuitous series of outliers from a random number generator); that is only as the result of a process without choice. Otherwise, the maintained assumption that agents know the true distribution is false.

LeRoy defends his account of policy by arguing that the policymakers do make choices in exactly the same sense that individuals make choices even when we accurately describe those choices as governed by the maximization of utility subject to a budget constraint. It is quite true that from a detached, outsider's perspective we describe consumption choices as determined or modelable. But would we therefore deny that an individual could change his behavior so that the parameters that had previously described his choices have to be replaced by new parameters? Should we say that a policymaker cannot change the parameters that best describe his decision-making process? Just as some situations are best described (even from the outside) as a change of taste, so are some situations described as a change of policy.

The economist describing consumer choice or the policymaker trying to understand the economy on which his policies operate takes an outsider's perspective. When the economist adopts the rational-expectations hypothesis, he analytically transforms the policymaker to the inside of the economy. But this transformation need not be complete. LeRoy sees an incomplete transformation as a failure to apply the rational-expectations hypothesis consistently.

Sargent and Wallace (1976, pp. 180–183) are aware of the sort of argument from consistency that LeRoy offers, but reject it. They treat the rational-expectations hypothesis as fully operational only in a model, up to the limits of practical applicability of that model. The model is, at best, a first approximation to the world.[41] In such an approach, it will make sense to describe policy sometimes as an unexpected, permanent change in parameters, sometimes as regime switching, sometimes as a change in the probabilities of regime switching, and so on. Given that it is a pragmatic decision which of these models to apply, there is no reason why the sudden failure of a model to match reality should not be regarded

---

[41] Sargent and Wallace's explicit endorsement of this view seems consistent with Lucas's views that the rational-expectations hypothesis is best understood as a consistency property of a model, rather than a property of the world, and that rational economic analysis is relevant only to situations of risk and not of uncertainty in Frank Knight's use of those terms (Lucas 1977, p. 15; 1987, p. 13, fn. 4)

as a change in a parameter, which in many cases may be associated with the intention of the authorities to alter policy.

LeRoy's most forceful objection to this pragmatic approach is that, since we have adopted the rational-expectations hypothesis, there can certainly be no virtue in failing to apply it consistently. But this assigns an unjustifiably privileged role to the rational-expectations hypothesis. The rational-expectations hypothesis relies on a notion of economic rationality that, though common enough in economics, does not necessarily correspond closely to the behavior of flesh-and-blood people. There are alternative hypotheses consistent with the minimal formal requirements of rationality as set out in elementary treatises on economic theory. And these alternatives are not without empirical support (see, e.g., Lovell 1986). The persuasive name "rational" should not blind us to the fact that the rational-expectations hypothesis is a contingent hypothesis, not an *a priori* truth.

The strongest justification for the rational-expectations hypothesis is an economic one. There are strong economic incentives for people to remember that policymakers are also economic agents and that their behavior can be understood and that understanding used to improve one's own economic situation. Economic incentives undermine the asymmetry between policymakers and individual economic actors. What is more, there are strong economic incentives to learn from past mistakes. It is unattractive to assume that people persistently make cheaply correctable errors. This would suggest that an account of learning would be central to a complete description of the economic process. Absent such an account, LeRoy's interpretation of the rational expectations hypothesis as the situation in which people know the true probability distribution should be seen merely as an approximation, a convenience relevant in cases in which the learning has been both rapid and effective, but not necessarily relevant under all circumstances. That something works as a good approximation in some circumstances is no reason to turn it into an inviolable principle governing all levels of description. Planets conceived as point masses provide a good first approximation for the solar system and a seriously deficient one for the tides.

The rational-expectations hypothesis is thus too weak a reed to support LeRoy's analysis of policy and his attack on the Lucas critique. What is left, then, is the first plank of his argument: If anything changes it cannot by definition be a parameter. The dictionary does not support LeRoy's definition.[42] Yet, if he insists on stipulating such a definition, then let us choose another name to assign to the variables that map out

---

[42] The *Oxford American Dictionary* defines *parameter* as "a variable quantity or quality that restricts or gives a particular form to the thing it characterizes."

the loci of interventions in a causal structure. Independent of the termi-nology, the substance of LeRoy's claim is that people can and do situate (at least implicitly) all economic changes in a probability distribution. Contrary to the objective approach taken in this book, LeRoy advocates a Bayesian – or, at least, subjectivist – approach to probability. But em-pirical psychology does not support the view that people typically be-have as the Bayesian account suggests. And, of course, there are other approaches altogether. We must regard the Bayesian approach not as a positive description of human behavior, but as a normative doctrine. Economics, of course, has gotten a lot of explanatory mileage *in special situations* out of equating the positive with the normative: The economist assumes that what people in fact do is what they rationally should do. But it is another example of the Walrasian fantasy to assume that, just because such an explanatory trope works in some particular circum-stances, it must be applied universally.

# 8

# Inferring Causal Direction

> "As you say, Pip," returned Mr. Jaggers, turning his eyes upon me coolly, and taking a bite at his forefinger, "I am not responsible for that."
>
> "And yet it looked so like it, sir," I pleaded with a downcast heart.
>
> "Not a particle of evidence, Pip," said Jaggers, shaking his head and gathering up his skirts. "Take nothing on its looks; take everything on evidence. There is no better rule."
>
> – Charles Dickens, *Great Expectations*

In the last chapter we saw that both the approach of Glymour et al. and Granger-causality, like other probabilistic approaches to causal order, were species of the informational account of causality. As such they provide information that may be useful to inferring causal structure. But, as we saw, there are cases that arise in macroeconomic contexts in which the apparently natural interpretation of their conclusions fails to correspond to the true, underlying causal structure. And, even in the best case, the usefulness of tests of Granger-causality is limited by the fact that it presumes that there is no contemporaneous causation; while the usefulness of Glymour et al.'s approach is limited by the fact that often it can only narrow possible causal structures down to an equivalence class in which some important causal arrows could just as easily be reversed. Sometimes, in favorable circumstances, such as controlled experiments or processes for which temporal order is obvious, these limitations are not constraining. Yet in many cases in macroeconomics, we would like to go further and find an empirical approach to resolve observational equivalence within a class possibly narrowed through one of these approaches. One of the strengths of the structural approach to causality is that it provides a conception in which one need not reject alternative approaches out of hand, but may use the information provided by Granger-causality or Glymour et al.'s approach in conjunction with additional information to resolve the issue of causal direction in otherwise observationally equivalent classes.[1] In this chapter we propose an inferential scheme that will sometimes be helpful in resolving observational equivalence. In Chapters 9, 10, and 11, we will see this inferential scheme applied to actual macroeconomic problems.

### 8.1   A SIMPLE LINEAR EXAMPLE

To keep things concrete, consider the problem that shall be investigated in actual cases in Chapter 9: Do taxes, $T$, cause government spending, $G$, $(T \rightarrow G)$? or does government spending cause taxes $(G \rightarrow T)$? It is easy to construct situations in which this question is not resolvable statistically. Consider a simple case in which in the true causal structure government expenditure causes taxes according to the data-generating process:

$$T \Leftarrow \alpha G + \varepsilon, \qquad \varepsilon \sim N(0, \sigma_\varepsilon^2), \tag{8.1}$$

$$G \Leftarrow \beta + \eta, \qquad \eta \sim N(0, \sigma_\eta^2), \tag{8.2}$$

where $N(\cdot, \cdot)$ indicates a normal distribution characterized by its mean and variance; and the $cov(\varepsilon, \eta) = 0$, $E(\varepsilon_t \varepsilon_s) = 0$, and $E(\eta_t \eta_s) = 0$, for $t \neq s$.

Assume that equations (8.1) and (8.2) describe the true, but unobservable, data-generating process. The problem is how to use the data to discriminate between $G$ causes $T$, when $G$ in fact causes $T$, and any alternative causal ordering, when only $G$ and $T$ can be observed.

The reduced forms of equations (8.1) and (8.2) are

$$T = \alpha\beta + \alpha\eta + \varepsilon, \tag{8.3}$$

$$G = \beta + \eta. \tag{8.4}$$

Equations (8.3) and (8.4) describe the joint probability distribution of $T$ and $G$, indicated as $D(T, G)$. Elementary statistical theory tells us that such a joint distribution can be partitioned into a conditional distribution and a marginal distribution in two ways:

$$D(T,G) = D(T|G)D(G) = D(G|T)D(T).$$

Standard formulae can be applied to compute these distributions from equations (8.3) and (8.4).[2]

---

[1] In work-in-progress not yet ready to detail in this volume, Selva Demiralp and I are developing an approach that marries the approaches of Granger, Glymour et al. (or Swanson and Granger) to the methods presented in this chapter.

[2] See e.g., Mood, Graybill, and Boes (1974, ch. 10, sec. 5). In general: Let $\mathbf{x} = [x_1, x_2, \ldots x_n]$ be a vector of variables, each of which is distributed independently multivariate nor-

$$D(T|G) = N(\alpha G, \sigma_\varepsilon^2), \tag{8.5}$$

$$D(G) = N(\beta, \sigma_\eta^2), \tag{8.6}$$

$$D(G|T) = N\left(\frac{\alpha\sigma_\eta^2 T + \beta\sigma_\varepsilon^2}{\alpha^2\sigma_\eta^2 + \sigma_\varepsilon^2}, \frac{\sigma_\eta^2\sigma_\varepsilon^2}{\alpha^2\sigma_\eta^2 + \sigma_\varepsilon^2}\right), \tag{8.7}$$

$$D(T) = N(\alpha\beta, \alpha^2\sigma_\eta^2 + \sigma_\varepsilon^2). \tag{8.8}$$

The parameters of the tax process are $\alpha$ and $\sigma_\varepsilon^2$, and the parameters of the government-spending process are $\beta$ and $\sigma_\eta^2$. Now suppose that we have some way of assigning interventions not to particular parameters (since we do not know the actual causal structure) but to one or the other of the two processes (because we may possess nonstatistical institutional or historical knowledge). For example, suppose that a war changes fundamentally the level or the variability of the government-spending process. Then, either $\beta$ or $\sigma_\eta^2$ changes. In either case, $D(G|T)$ and $D(G)$ will change, as is to be expected. Notice, however, that $D(T)$ will also change, and, crucially, that $D(T|G)$ will remain invariant. Suppose, on the other side, that a major tax reform alters either $\alpha$ or $\sigma_\varepsilon^2$. In either case, $D(T|G)$ and $D(T)$ will change. Notice, however, that $D(G|T)$ will also change, and, crucially, $D(G)$ will remain invariant. The partition of the joint probability distribution $D(T|G)D(G)$ is stable in the sense that interventions in the spending process leave the first term invariant, and interventions in the tax process leave the second term invariant. The alternative partition, $D(G|T)D(T)$, shows no such invariance. The difference arises from the fact that *ex hypothesi*, government spending causes taxes, so that the first partition recapitulates the true, underlying causal structure, while the second partition does not. Had taxes caused government spending in the true, underlying causal structure, these results, of course, would have been reversed.

mal. Define $\mathbf{x}^* = [x_2, x_3, \ldots x_n]$. Let $E(\mathbf{x}) = [\mu_1, \mu_2, \ldots \mu_n]$ be the vector of the means. Let $E(\mathbf{x}'\mathbf{x}) = \Sigma =$

$$\begin{bmatrix} \sigma_{x1}^2 & \Sigma_{12} \\ \Sigma_{12}' & \Sigma_{22} \end{bmatrix},$$

where $\sigma_{x1}^2$ is the variance of $x_1$, $\Sigma_{12} = E(x_1\mathbf{x}^*)$ and $\Sigma_{22} = E(\mathbf{x}^{*\prime}\mathbf{x}^*)$. Then the mean of $x_1$ conditional on $\mathbf{x}^*$ is $\bar{x}_1 = E(x_1|\mathbf{x}^*) = \mu_1 + \Sigma_{12}'\Sigma_{22}^{-1}(\mathbf{x}^{*\prime} - E(\mathbf{x}^{*\prime}))$ The variance of $x_1$ conditional on $\mathbf{x}^*$ is

$$\text{var}(x_1|\mathbf{x}^*) = \frac{|\Sigma|}{|\Sigma_{22}|}.$$

All the calculations of conditional distributions in this chapter are applications of this general formula.

This suggests a general strategy for identifying causal orderings. First, if it is possible to determine from historical and institutional knowledge periods in which there are no important interventions in either the tax or the spending processes, regression equations corresponding to each of the conditional and marginal distributions in equations (8.5)–(8.8) can be estimated and should show stable coefficients. Second, if we can then identify periods in which there are interventions clearly associated with the spending process and periods in which there are interventions clearly associated with the tax process, we can check the patterns of relative stability of the alternative partitions, and, thereby, determine which causal ordering (if any) is consistent with the data.

We can illustrate the problem of observational equivalence and the proposed method for causal inference with a simple simulation experiment. Figure 8.1 is a scatterplot of data for data generated as follows:

$$G = 1 + \eta, \qquad \eta \sim N(0,1), \tag{8.9}$$

$$T = 1 + 2G + \varepsilon, \qquad \varepsilon \sim N(0,1). \tag{8.10}$$

In the diagram, there are two regression lines. One is generated from the regression of $T$ on $G$, the other from $G$ on $T$. The difference between the lines arises because the coefficients of the first regression are chosen to minimize the variance of the errors defined as $T - \hat{T}$, where the hat indi-

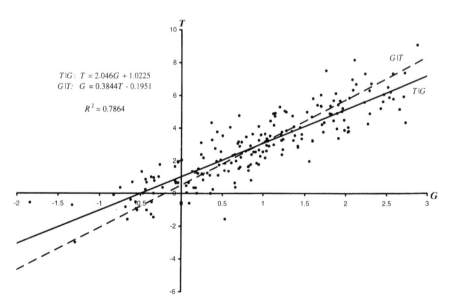

Figure 8.1. The Direction of Regression

cates the estimated value, whereas the coefficients of the second regression are chosen to minimize the variance of the errors defined as $G - \hat{G}$. The covariance between $G$ and the errors in the first regression are necessarily zero, while the covariance between $T$ and the errors in the second regression are necessarily zero. This illustrates that regressions are directional in a manner that corresponds to causal direction. Unfortunately, there is nothing in the statistics that tells us that the data were generated according to equations (8.9) and (8.10) rather than, say, according to equations in which $T$ causes $G$. The evidence for this observational equivalence is found in the measure of the goodness of fit, $R^2$, which is identical in each regression.

Now consider the case in which there is an intervention in the process that governs government expenditure. For the first half of the sample, $G$ is generated by equation (8.9); but for the second half of the sample, it is generated as:

$$G = 2 + \eta, \qquad \eta \sim N(0,1), \qquad (8.9')$$

that is, the mean of $G$ has shifted. Panel A of Figure 8.2 shows the plot of $G$ by observation. Its regression lines, which correspond to the distribution $D(G)$, are measures of the mean of $G$, before and after the intervention. The shift in the mean is clearly visible. Panel B shows the regression of $T$ on $G$ (corresponding to $D(T|G)$) before and after the

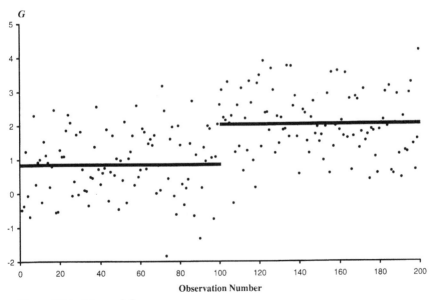

Figure 8.2A. Mean of $G$

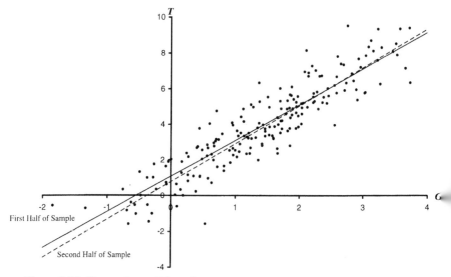

Figure 8.2B.  Regressions of $T$ on $G$

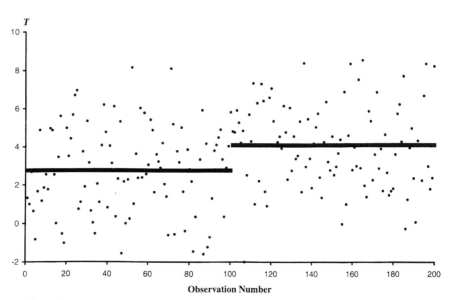

Figure 8.2C.  Mean of $T$

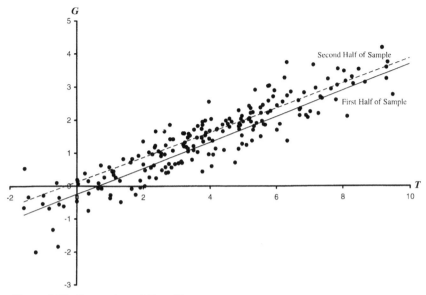

Figure 8.2D. Regression of $G$ on $T$

intervention. The two regression lines line up, showing little shift. Panel C shows the plot of $T$ by observation (corresponding to $D(T)$), while panel D shows the regression of $G$ on $T$ (corresponding to $(D(G|T))$. Both clearly show the shift. This pattern of three unstable and one stable regressions is a characteristic pattern of an intervention in a linear causal structure. The regression that corresponds to the true causal direction is the one that remains stable.

Again, consider the same causal ordering, but let the intervention be in the process that governs taxes. The data for $G$ are generated by equation (8.9); and, for the first half of the sample, the data for $T$ are generated by equation (8.10), while, for the second half of the sample, they are generated as:

$$T = 2 + 2G + \varepsilon, \qquad \varepsilon \sim N(0,1). \qquad (8.10')$$

The four panels of Figure 8.3 represent the same four distributions shown in Figure 8.2. Both panels B and C, the marginal and conditional distributions of taxes, show a shift, as does panel D, the conditional distribution of government expenditure. Panel A, however, shows a very small shift owing to sampling variability.[3] Again, there is a pattern of

---

[3] The reader, of course, is asked to take on faith the claim that the small but visible shift is not a shift of the parameter but the result of randomness in the sample. In formal work, such claims need to be buttressed with statistical hypothesis tests.

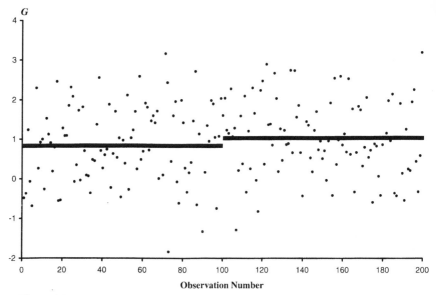

Figure 8.3A.  Mean of *G*

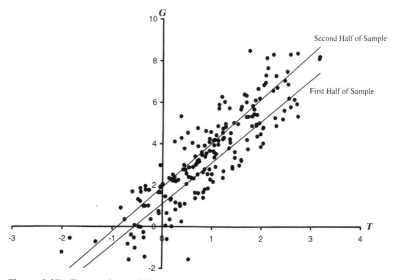

Figure 8.3B.  Regressions of *T* on *G*

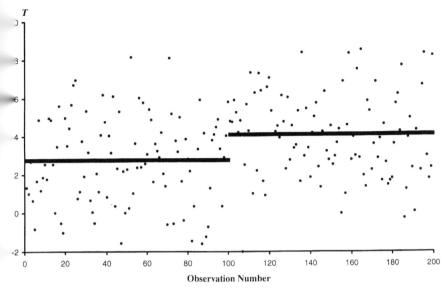

Figure 8.3C. Mean of $T$

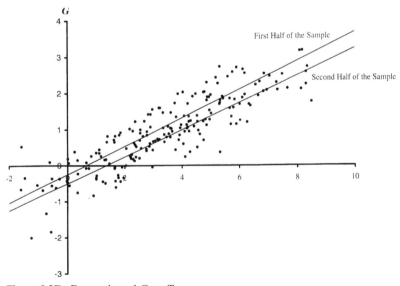

Figure 8.3D. Regression of $G$ on $T$

three unstable and one stable distribution. Again, it is the distribution that corresponds to the true, unobserved causal structure that remains stable. An intervention in either taxes or spending suggests the true causal direction. An intervention in each at different times or different parts of the sample would provide convincing evidence of the true causal structure.

Table 8.1 summarizes the invariance patterns of the simple bivariate example above in the form of a decision algorithm. Table 8.1 is constructed on the assumption that there are no cross-equation restrictions in the data-generating process for the actual data. If there are such cross-equation restrictions as, for example, in the rational-expectations models of Chapter 3, Section 2, or in Robert Barro's (1979) tax-smoothing model, there will be additional complications, which we take up in the next section. We seek to determine the causal order between $G$ and $T$. There are two steps.

**Table 8.1. An Algorithm for Causal Inference**

STAGE 1: IDENTIFICATION

A.  If  (i) There is narrative evidence of an intervention in the $G$ process; and
        (ii) Both $G$ CONDITIONAL and $G$ MARGINAL break statistically,

   Then, there is a genuine intervention in the $G$ process: GO TO STAGE 2.A BELOW.

B.  If  (i) There is narrative evidence of an intervention in the T process; and
        (ii) Both $T$ CONDITIONAL and $T$ MARGINAL break statistically,

   Then, there is a genuine intervention in the $T$ process: GO TO STAGE 2.B BELOW.

STAGE 2: DISCRIMINATION

A.  Interventions in the $G$ Process

| | | T Marginal | |
|---|---|---|---|
| | | Stable | Unstable |
| T Conditional | Stable | $T \perp G$ | $G \Rightarrow T$ |
| | Unstable | $T \Rightarrow G$ | $G \Leftrightarrow T$ |

B.  Interventions in the $T$ Process

| | | T Marginal | |
|---|---|---|---|
| | | Stable | Unstable |
| T Conditional | Stable | $G \perp T$ | $T \Rightarrow G$ |
| | Unstable | $G \Rightarrow T$ | $T \Leftrightarrow G$ |

*Key*: $\Rightarrow$ = "causes," $\Leftrightarrow$ = "mutually causes," $\perp$ = "is causally independent of."

i. First, identify the nature of the break. If both the conditional and the marginal regressions for $G$ (G Conditional and G Marginal) indicate a break statistically and if the narrative evidence supports an intervention in the $G$ process, we identify the break as an intervention in $G$ and proceed to the second stage. Similarly, if both T Conditional and T Marginal break and the narrative evidence supports an intervention in the $T$ process, we identify the break as an intervention in $T$ and proceed to the second stage.

ii. At the second stage, we attempt to discriminate between possible orders. If we identified a $G$ break, we can use the two-by-two table in 2.A. It shows the possible patterns of breaks in the $T$ process and identifies each with a causal order conditional on having previously ascertained that the break was in the $G$ process. So, for example, a pattern of T Conditional stable and T Marginal unstable is consistent with $G$ causing $T$. The table shows all the possibilities. If we identified a $T$ break in the first stage, we can use *mutatis mutandis* the similar two-by-two table in 2.B.[4]

**8.2  NONLINEAR STRUCTURES**

We saw in Chapter 3, Section 2, that macroeconomic models frequently contain nonlinearities due to rational expectations. These nonlinearities complicate the inference of causal direction. The general points are made in the context of a particular economic example – the causal relationship between taxes and government spending that provides part of the rationale for the empirical applications in Chapters 9 and 10.

Consider Robert Barro's (1979) model of tax smoothing.[5] The government is assumed to have rational expectations and to take the path of government spending ($\{G_t\}$, $t = 0, 1, \ldots, \infty$) to be exogenous. The government chooses the path of taxes ($\{T_t\}$) to minimize its expected costs of collection, which are assumed to be quadratic:

$$\min E\left(\sum_{t=0}^{\infty} \beta^t [\mu_1 T_t + \tfrac{1}{2}\mu_2 T_t^2]\right), \qquad 0 < \beta < 1,$$

---

[4] Table 8.1 is incomplete. If both conditions A and B in Stage 1 are fulfilled then causal discrimination is not possible. In such a case, in which every regression breaks and the narrative supports interventions on both sides, it might be that causation is one way in either direction, that causation is mutual, or that there is causal independence — there is simply no way to tell.

[5] Our treatment follows Sargent (1987, ch. 13, sec. 3). This version of the model is tightly parameterized. Roberds (1991) and Hansen, Sargent, and Roberds (1991) discuss tests of intertemporal budget constraints in more general models. These tests, however, do not shed any light on causal issues.

subject to:

$$B_{t+1} = R[B_t + G_t - T_t],$$

$B_t$ bounded for all $t$,

$B_0$ given,

where $R = 1 +$ *the rate of interest* $> 1$ and is taken to be constant.

A necessary condition on the time path of taxes for an optimum is the Euler equation:

$$E_t(T_{t+1}) = -\alpha + (\beta R)^{-1} T_t,$$

$$\alpha = \mu_1 \left[1 - (\beta R)^{-1}\right]\big/ \mu_2, \tag{8.11}$$

where the subscript on the expectations operator indicates that expectations are taken with information available up to time $t$. Assuming that $\beta R = 1$, this condition states that taxes follow a random walk.

To calculate an explicit expression for taxes, it is necessary to specify the stochastic process for government spending. Let this process be given by

$$G_t = \gamma + \gamma(L)\varepsilon_t, \tag{8.12}$$

where $\gamma(L)$ is a polynomial in the lag operator, $L$ (defined so that $L^n x_t = x_{t-n}$), and $\varepsilon_t$ is white noise. Sargent shows that when $\beta R = 1$, this implies that the tax process is given by

$$T_{t+1} - T_t = (1 - 1/R)g(R^{-1})\varepsilon_{t+1}. \tag{8.13}$$

As a specific example, let $g(L) = 1/(1 - \delta L)$. The joint government spending and tax processes are then given by

$$G_{t+1} = \gamma + \delta[G_t - \gamma] + \varepsilon_{t+1}, \tag{8.14}$$

$$T_{t+1} = T_t + [(R-1)/(R-\delta)][G_{t+1} - \delta G_t + (\delta - 1)\gamma] \tag{8.15}$$

where (8.15) is derived by using (8.14) to eliminate $\varepsilon_{t+1}$ from (8.13).

The system of equations, (8.14) and (8.15), is causally ordered with taxes causing government spending. The parameters of the system are presumed to be constant in the derivation. In order to consider interventions, we must be explicit about the possibility of parameter change. To keep things simple, we add a stochastic error term to the tax equation (8.15) and permit its parameters and the parameter $\gamma$ to change. Rewrite equations (8.14) and (8.15) as:

$$G_{t+1} = \gamma_{t+1} - \delta\gamma_t + \delta G_t + \varepsilon_{t+1}, \tag{8.14'}$$

$$T_{t+1} = T_t + [(R-1)/(R-\delta)]$$
$$[G_{t+1} - \delta G_t + \delta\gamma_t - \gamma_{t+1}] + (\gamma_{t+1} - \gamma_t)\omega_{t+1}, \tag{8.15'}$$

where $\omega_{t+1}$ is an independently distributed error term. If $\omega_{t+1}$ is eliminated and $\gamma_t$ set to a constant for all $t$, equations (8.14′) and (8.15′) collapse back to equations (8.14) and (8.15).

To illustrate the problem of causal inference, we simulate the model in equations (8.14′) and (8.15′) (notionally for the years 1800 to 2000) with the following baseline parameterization: $\delta = 0.9$, $\gamma_t = 1$ for all t, $\varepsilon \sim N(0, \sigma_\varepsilon^2)$, $\omega \sim N(0, \sigma_\omega^2)$, $r = 5\%$, $G_{1800} = 1$; and $T_{1800} = 1$. We perform three simulation experiments. We associate these experiments with particular historical events as a mnemonic only; they should not be taken seriously as models of actual events.

**A Spending Intervention without Cross-Equation Restrictions**

Consider an event such as the Civil War. We might think of this as involving an exogenous spending shock: military spending is rising rapidly and without warning. Clearly there are also likely to be changes in revenue collection. The issue is what is the nature of those changes: Is it that taxes will rise to keep up with spending without any modification of the structure of the revenue process, which is what the tax smoothing hypothesis would maintain? Or is it that the spending will open an incipient deficit that can be closed only by structural changes in the revenue process, which is what it means for causal direction to run from taxes to spending (or for both to be causally independent)?

We model the "Civil War" by setting $G_t = 5$ for t = 1861, 1862, . . . 1865. Figure 8.4 shows the path of taxes and spending under this scenario. Notice that although the tax-smoothing model involves cross-equation restrictions in general, none are involved in this simulation, because $G$ is altered by fiat without an intervention in the parameters.[6] This case therefore illustrates the sort of linear causal relationship considered in Section 1 and shows a pattern invariance that occurs even in models that are not forward looking.

To judge the stability of the various marginal and conditional distributions consider plots of the recursive residuals and their ±2-standard-error bands. Recursive residuals are described more fully in Section 8.3. For the moment it is enough to note that a structural break in a regression is indicated when a number of recursive residuals lie outside their standard error bands – a phenomenon often accompanied by a widening of those bands. Figure 8.5A presents the plot of the recursive residuals and their standard errors for the regression of $G_t$ conditional on one

---

[6] This is the type of policy intervention that is consistent with the analysis of policy under rational expectations described in LeRoy (1995b); see Chapter 7, Section 4.

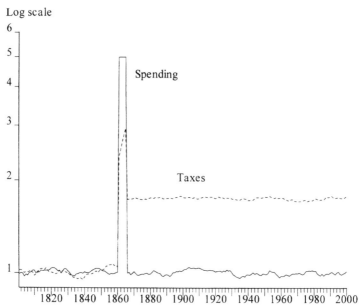

Figure 8.4. A Spending Intervention (the "Civil War") without Cross-Equation Restrictions

lag of itself and on the level and one lag of *T*. Figure 8.5B presents the recursive residuals from the marginal regression for $G_t$ (on its own lag only). Figure 8.5C presents the recursive residuals from the conditional regression for $T_t$, and Figure 8.5D the recursive residuals from the marginal regression. These four figures reveal the characteristic pattern of causal direction running from spending to taxes. Both spending regressions and the marginal regression for taxes show visually obvious structural breaks: Several recursive residuals lie well outside the standard error bands and those bands widen markedly. In contrast, the conditional regression for taxes appears invariant in the face of an intervention in the spending process: The recursive residuals remain within relatively constant standard error bands. (Formal tests of structural stability confirm these visually compelling conclusions.)

### A Spending Intervention with Cross-Equation Restrictions

Consider another spending intervention intended to mimic the permanent increase in the size of government in the New Deal and the aftermath of the Second World War. Here the mean of the spending process is raised in 1930 to a permanently higher level: $\gamma_t = 5$ for

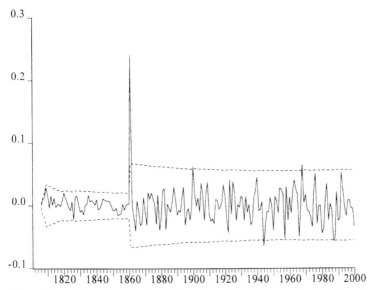

Figure 8.5A. Recursive Residuals from Conditional Regression for Spending for the Case of the "Civil War." Dashed lines are ±2 standard error bands.

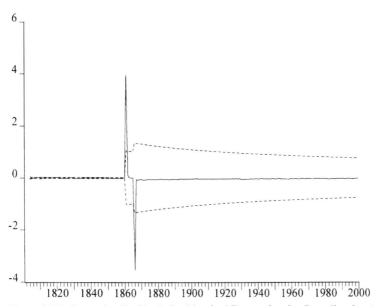

Figure 8.5B. Recursive Residuals for Marginal Regression for Spending for the Case of the "Civil War." Dashed lines are ±2 standard error bands.

*Inferring Causal Direction*

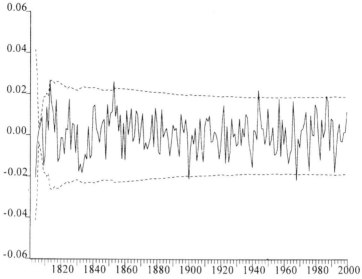

Figure 8.5C. Recursive Residuals for Conditional Regression for Taxes for the Case of the "Civil War." Dashed lines are ±2 standard error bands.

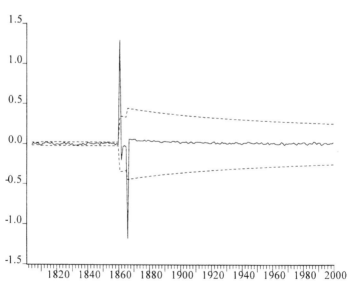

Figure 8.5D. Recursive Residuals for Marginal Regression for Taxes for the Case of the "Civil War." Dashed lines are ±2 standard error bands.

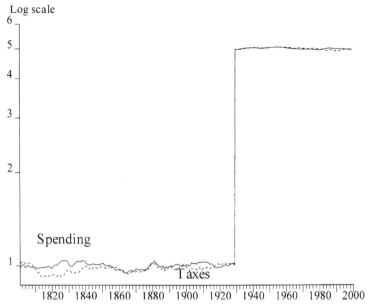

Figure 8.6. A Spending Intervention (the "New Deal") with Cross-Equation Restrictions

$t \geq 1930$. Figure 8.6 presents the paths of taxes and spending under this scenario.[7] Figures 8.7A–8.7D show the recursive residuals and their standard errors from the conditional and marginal regressions for spending and taxes. The two marginal models show the effect of the intervention very crisply. The two conditional models are less dramatic, but show a large outlier at about 1930 and a widening of the standard error bands. Formal tests confirm that there are structural breaks in all four series. This is the characteristic pattern of an intervention in the spending process in a model with cross-equation restrictions in which spending causes taxes: Everything breaks down. This phenomenon vastly reduces the informativeness of a spending break in such a case. It is, for example, impossible on purely statistical grounds to use such a pattern to discriminate among three hypotheses: (a) Spending causes taxes, but there are cross-equation restrictions; (b) there are simultaneous tax and spending interventions; and (c) there is specification error in all of the regressions.

---

[7] This intervention is treated as wholly unexpected and permanent. It is typical of policy interventions as they have been modeled in the aftermath of Lucas (1976) and criticized by LeRoy (1995b); see Chapter 7, Section 4.

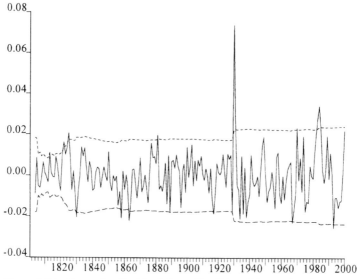

Figure 8.7A. Recursive Residuals from Conditional Regression for Spending for the Case of the "New Deal." Dashed lines are ±2 standard error bands.

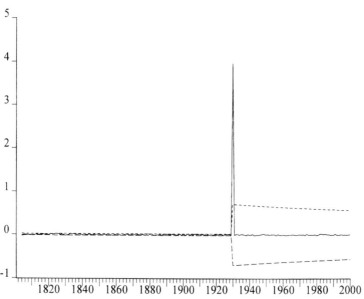

Figure 8.7B. Recursive Residuals for Marginal Regression for Spending for the Case of the "New Deal." Dashed lines are ±2 standard error bands.

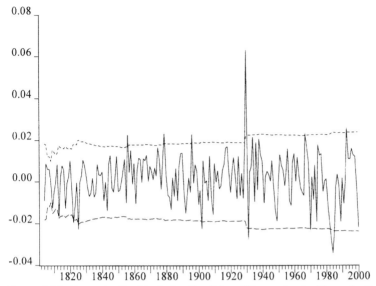

Figure 8.7C. Recursive Residuals for Conditional Regression for Taxes for the Case of the "New Deal." Dashed lines are ±2 standard error bands.

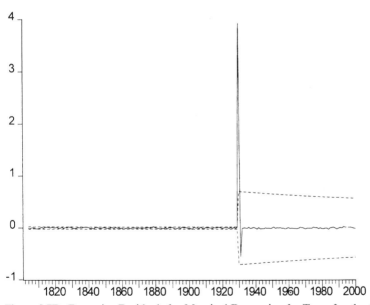

Figure 8.7D. Recursive Residuals for Marginal Regression for Taxes for the Case of the "New Deal." Dashed lines are ±2 standard error bands.

Clearly if the true data-generating process were characterized by cross-equation restrictions and all one had were spending interventions, there would be little to be said about causal order. Fortunately, there are other implications for invariance that are robust to cross-equation restrictions.

## A Tax Intervention with or without Cross-Equation Restrictions

We continue to assume that the data are generated from a tax-smoothing model. An intervention in the tax process that does not directly involve the spending process must affect one of the parameters that is unique to equation (2). Consider a fivefold increase in the standard error of $\omega$ after 1913. (The date is chosen to remind the reader of the institution of the income tax, but no claim is made that this constitutes a serious model of the effect of that intervention.) Figure 8.8 shows taxes and spending under this scenario. Figures 8.9A–8.9D show the recursive residuals and their standard errors from the four conditional and marginal distributions. The two tax regressions clearly show a break about 1913. The two spending regressions show stability. Again these results are confirmed by formal tests. According to the theory of causal inference developed in the paper, this is almost what we should expect with a tax intervention when spending truly causes taxes. The one difference appears to be that we should expect a break in the conditional

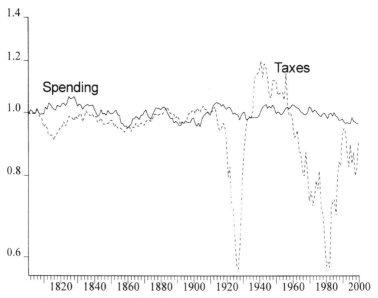

Figure 8.8. A Tax Intervention (the "Income Tax")

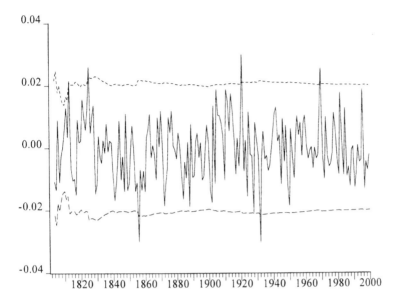

Figure 8.9A. Recursive Residuals from Conditional Regression for Spending for the
Case of the "Income Tax." Dashed lines are ±2 standard error bands.

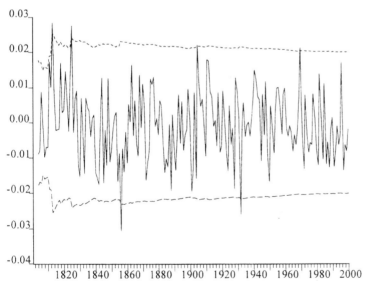

Figure 8.9B. Recursive Residuals for Marginal Regression for Spending for the Case
of the "Income Tax." Dashed lines are ±2 standard error bands.

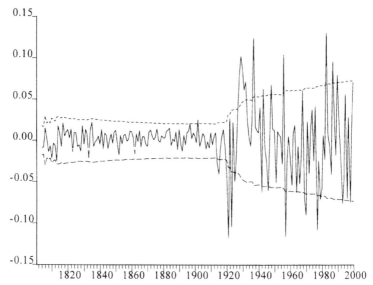

Figure 8.9C. Recursive Residuals for Conditional Regression for Taxes for the Case of the "Income Tax." Dashed lines are ±2 standard error bands.

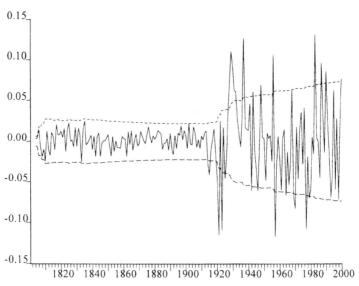

Figure 8.9D. Recursive Residuals for Marginal Regression for Taxes for the Case of the "Income Tax." Dashed lines are ±2 standard error bands.

regression for spending, and we do not see one. This appears to be the result of the fact that the tax intervention is relatively weak; a much larger change in the variance of ω results in a detectable break. The important point, however, is well illustrated by the current case. Since spending causes taxes *ex hypothesi*, an intervention in the tax process that is recursively ordered after spending does not induce a structural break in the regression corresponding to the marginal distribution of spending – despite the presence of cross-equation restrictions. This is a robust characteristic of a causal order from spending to taxes.

These cases illustrate a practical issue in causal inference: It takes a variety of types of interventions to infer causal direction at all reliably. In the case of taxes and spending, interventions in both the tax and the spending processes are needed. Once both sorts of interventions are available, there can be patterns in the data that are inconsistent with proposed causal orderings even in the face of general interdependence and cross-equation restrictions induced by rational expectations. Tax interventions that correspond to structural breaks in the marginal process for government spending, for example, are incompatible with any model in which spending causes taxes and would, therefore, constitute evidence against the tax-smoothing model.

## 8.3  IDENTIFYING INTERVENTIONS

The logic of identifying causal direction is straightforward, but not necessarily easy to implement. It requires that there be distinct interventions that can be assigned to the process for one variable or the other, even though they cannot be assigned to particular parameters governing those variables. In principle, if one knew that the regression equations that were used to characterize the alternative marginal and conditional distributions were correctly specified, identification of an intervention would follow immediately from statistical identification of a structural break. But things are not quite so easy as that. Were one to detect a structural break, it could be because there truly is an intervention in the causal structure or it could be because the initial characterization of the distribution was misspecified. And, when dealing with bivariate relations, one needs some assurance that the source of a structural break is not an intervention in the process of an unaccounted for common cause. To complicate matters further, the statistical analysis of structural break testing, though advancing rapidly, is not always adequate to the sorts of interventions that actually occur. And, finally, one needs to be lucky. A discriminating test occurs when an intervention occurs on one side or the other, but not when interventions occur simultaneously. Thus, some of the most obvious sources of intervention – wars and economic disasters

– are frequently not useful sources of discriminating evidence, because interventions are likely to be widespread, not focused. Equally, if interventions occur too frequently, it is difficult to have any baseline against which one can judge statistically whether there has been any structural break. The methods suggested here may work sometimes, but it is easy to imagine cases in which they would be hopeless as well.

Chapters 9 and 10 represent two previously published empirical studies. Each follows the same general approach to the inference of causal direction. I describe that approach next. It is important to recall, however, that the logic of causal inference described in the last two sections does not imply every detail – especially of the econometric methods employed – and so does not rule out other ways of achieving the same ends. It is also important to recognize that the empirical implementation of the approach is, as the next two chapters make clear, time-consuming and painstaking. As a result, there is no attempt to update these studies, which reflect evolving statistical technology. The statistics described in this chapter are the ones actually used in the subsequent chapters and only brief mention is made of the rapidly evolving techniques for detecting and locating structural breaks.

The first step is to assemble a chronology of potential interventions based on nonquantitative historical and institutional (extra-statistical) evidence.[8] The chronology serves two functions. (1) It divides history into periods that appear to be tranquil, without interventions, and periods in which interventions are likely to have occurred. The tranquil periods form the baseline against which structural breaks are detected and interventions identified. (2) It provides a cross-check to statistical tests. A break detected at a time when no intervention can be identified in the chronology may indicate econometric misspecification. Equally, a break detected statistically and assigned to a different side of the data-generating process from that indicated chronologically raises questions. Consilience of the statistics and the chronology heightens confidence in the correctness of the conclusions drawn.

The second step is to characterize the relevant conditional and marginal distributions for each tranquil period separately. We apply the so-called LSE methodology for econometric specification most closely associated with David Hendry and various colleagues and students.[9]

---

[8] Both studies use time-series data, as is generally true in macroeconomics. There is no conceptual reason, however, that this approach to causal inference could not be applied *mutatis mutandis* to cross-sectional data.

[9] On the details of the LSE methodology, see Mizon (1995), Hendry and Richard (1982), and Hendry (1995). For general defenses of the approach see Hendry (1983, 1987), McAleer, Pagan, and Volker (1985), Gilbert (1986), Phillips (1988). Pagan (1987) surveys the approach and contrasts it with the competing approaches of Sims and Leamer. For more skeptical views, see Faust and Whiteman (1995, 1997) and Hansen (1996).

P. C. B. Phillips (1988, pp. 352–353) provides a succinct description of the main points:

In the Hendry methodology [model selection] involves working back from a general unrestricted dynamic specification towards a parsimoniously reparameterized model whose regressors are temporal transformations that are interpretable in some economic sense and nearly orthogonal. . . . [T]he objective of the Hendry approach is to seek out a single-equation model that is a tentatively adequate, conditional data characterization. Such a model satisfies the following criteria. . . .

(a) The model is coherent with the data (i.e., fits the data up to an innovation that is white noise and, further, a martingale difference sequence relative to the selected data base);
(b) It validly conditions on variables that are weakly exogenous with respect to the parameter of interest;
(c) It encompasses rival models;
(d) Its formulation is consistent with economic theory;
(e) It has parsimoniously chosen and orthogonal decision variables.

Phillips describes a specification search procedure precisely like the one used Chapters 9 and 10. On the basis of econometric theory, he shows that such a search is a practical procedure for reducing a cointegrated system to a single error-correction equation. Comparing Hendry's procedure to the theoretically optimal method for achieving the reduction, Phillips (1988, p. 357) concludes

that the Hendry methodology comes remarkably close to achieving [this] optimal inference procedure. In some cases it actually does so and in other cases it can be further modified to achieve it. . . . These findings can be taken to provide strong support for the Hendry approach.

It remains true, of course, that since high $t$-statistics and other desirable characteristics such as white-noise errors are used to design the regression, these characteristics cannot themselves be used within sample as valid tests. The regressions reported in the second step are *designed* to have desirable properties. To guard against *insidious* data mining, some observations of the baseline period are retained for an out-of-sample stability check. Similarly, the only test statistics from which inferences are drawn directly are either against alternative models or, most important, out-of-sample stability tests in the third step. There is no specification search over these data and, hence, the test statistics bear their usual interpretation.

Some would argue that it would be better to use vector autoregressions (e.g., Sims 1980 and Chapter 7, Section 2) than to follow Hendry's methodology. But this poses serious difficulties. The large number of coefficients to be estimated in a typical VAR would eat up the limited degrees of freedom in our dataset. In addition, such overparameterization usually implies that coefficient estimates are very imprecise, which would reduce the power of tests of structural change. This would pose particular difficulty in this study since detection of changing coefficients is the desideratum of the underlying analysis of causal inference.[10]

To apply the general-to-specific modeling technique, we begin with a deliberately overfitting general dynamic form, a regression of the *level* of the dependent variable on a constant and a number of lags of the dependent variable and the current and a number of lags of the other variables where applicable. Sometimes we refer to an *error-correction* form of these regressions. This is an equivalent reparameterization of the level form that regresses the first *difference* of the dependent variable on a constant and a number lags of the differenced dependent variable, a lagged level of the dependent variable, and (where applicable) the current and several lags of the first difference of the other variables and a lagged level of each of the other variables. These *unrestricted distributed lag regressions* (also known as *autoregressive distributed lag regressions*) are tested for normality of residuals, absence of autocorrelation, absence of autoregressive conditional heteroscedasticity, and coefficient stability. If they pass these specification tests, then they are used as the general form on which further specification is based.

In order to provide more interpretable specifications and to increase the power of structural break tests, we simplify these general forms into more parsimonious representations of the data. The general strategy is to eliminate variables with insignificant $t$-statistics sequentially or to impose other restrictions on estimated coefficients that might be suggested by estimates of the less simplified forms themselves. Each of these new specifications must satisfy the same battery of tests as the unrestricted distributed lag and must, in addition, be a statistically valid restriction of the unrestricted distributed lag regression itself. The simplifications are thus required to carry the same information as the less parsimonious general form. Simplification along any path is complete when no further simplification is possible that does not either violate one

---

[10] Some might prefer an automatic procedure to reduce the VARs to a more parsimonious form; but, given that there are many plausible criteria (e.g., see Box and Pierce 1970, Ljung and Box 1978, Akaike 1973, Schwarz 1978), all the same issues of judgment that an automatic procedure aims to avoid would be reintroduced into the design of the reduction procedure. Relentless application of encompassing tests against seriously maintained rivals provides an *objective* specification test even when an informal reduction procedure is followed (see Mizon and Richard 1986, Hendry and Richard 1987, and Hendry 1988b for details of encompassing and its relation to non-nested hypothesis testing). Hoover and Perez (1999) demonstrate in a Monte Carlo simulation using a stylized version of an LSE general-to-specific specification search that the LSE methods are efficacious at recovering true specifications when they exist.

of the specification tests or is statistically invalid as a restriction of the general form. There may be multiple paths of simplification. A best specification can be chosen from among these terminal specifications (and any other seriously maintained rival specifications that might be offered) using encompassing tests. A specification *encompasses* another if it carries all the information of the other specification and possibly more as well.[11] Whether any terminal specification encompasses another is checked using nonnested hypothesis tests or by nesting both specifications in a joint model and testing for the validity of each as a restriction of the joint model. There are three outcomes: one model may encompass the other or vice versa or neither may encompass the other (i.e., each carries information omitted by the other).

Typically, tests of within-sample stability of the coefficient estimates of the final parsimonious form are used to confirm that the period which was regarded as tranquil on the basis of the chronology is also judged to be tranquil on the basis of statistics.

The third step is to use the parsimonious specifications in the baseline periods to identify structural breaks in the various marginal and conditional distributions. When a period in which we identify interventions is preceded and followed by a tranquil period, then the parsimonious regressions for each tranquil period are used, working forward or backward from the appropriate tranquil period as a baseline for judging structural breaks. When there is only one adjacent tranquil period – for example, at the endpoints of a sample period – then we work in only one direction.

There are two distinct questions relating to relative stability: Does a structural break occur at all? And, given that it occurs, exactly when? A number of formal tests have been developed to answer the first question. The second question remains less well understood, and can, at present, be addressed only with informal methods. Different combinations of a number of tests are used in Chapters 9 and 10. The tests described here are based on recursive estimation, which, starting from a base regression, reestimates the regression adding one period at a time (see Harvey 1990, ch. 2, sec. 6).

### Chow Tests

*(i) Constant-Base Sequential Chow Test*

The test divides the sample into two parts: The first is always the baseline period (hence "constant-base"); the second comprises the

---

[11] On the theory of encompassing, see Mizon (1984), Mizon and Richard (1986), Hendry (1988b, 1995, ch. 14), Hendry and Richard (1987).

observations from the end point of the baseline period to the last observation used in the recursive estimate.[12] Thus, if the baseline period is $N$ observations and the total sample is $K$ observations, the second part starts out as one observation, and increases one observation for each recursive reestimation, until finally there are $K$–$N$ observations. A sequence of $K$–$N$ Chow statistics is then computed.[13]

The sequence of Chow statistics from this test is not independent. Their true distribution has not been worked out. One way of interpreting them, however, as a means of *localizing* a structural break is counterfactually: Suppose that someone challenges us claiming that our baseline regression breaks down at some particular point out of sample; the single Chow statistic out of our sequence for that point is the correct test with a critical value of the size reported in conventional $F$-tables. Thus, as a summary statistic for this test, we report the "break point" – the first time the Chow statistic exceeds its five percent critical value.

*(ii) Constant-Horizon Sequential Chow Test*

The test reports the Chow statistics from splitting the sample at each observation between the end point of the baseline period and the end point of the sample. All $N + K$ observations are always used (hence "constant-horizon").

As with the constant-base test, the Chow statistics in this sequence are not independent. Using the maximum value of these statistics as the indicator of a single, discontinuous change in coefficients is equivalent to Quandt's (1960) maximum likelihood method (see Hansen 1992, p. 519). The distribution of this "max-Chow" statistic is known (see Andrews 1993, Chu 1990, and Kim and Siegmund 1989). As a summary statistic for this test, we report the value and the date of the maximum Chow statistic. Since the natural alternative hypothesis to the null of stable coefficients with the max-Chow test is a single, discontinuous change in the true coefficients, and we have no reason to rule out gradual change or multiple discontinuities, other characteristics of the constant-horizon sequence (such as local maxima) may also be reported.

---

[12] The endpoint may be either the first or last observation in the baseline period depending on whether we are projecting backwards or forwards.

[13] All three recursive Chow tests are based on Chow's first test, which can be computed even when the number of observations in one subsample is less than the number of regressors (Chow 1960, pp. 594–595, 598). Chow tests used for judging within-sample coefficient stability are Chow's more familiar second test, which requires all subsamples to be longer than the number of regressors (Chow 1960, pp. 595–599).

*(iii) One-Step-Ahead Sequential Chow Test*

The test reports the sequence of Chow statistics computed from comparing each recursive estimate to the one that uses just one more observation.

Because the one-step-ahead prediction errors of recursive regressions are independent, each Chow statistic in this sequence is itself independent (Harvey 1990, pp. 54–55). Thus, in large samples using a 5 percent critical value, about 5 percent of the statistics should exceed the critical value. We therefore report the ratio of the number of violations to the total number of statistics in the sequence. To get a further handle on the significance, we also report the value and the date of the maximum one-step-ahead Chow statistic as well as its maximum scaled by its 5 percent critical value. When it is particularly informative, we reproduce the plot of the entire sequence of statistics.

**Plots of Recursive Regression Coefficients**

Practical experience and informal simulations show that visual inspection of plots of recursively estimated regression coefficients against their ±2-standard error bands is often a reliable way to determine the date of a structural break. The standard errors reported are the same as for the corresponding OLS regression, and are used as *informal* guides to sampling variability. Formal tests would have to be constructed along similar lines to Banerjee, Lumsdaine, and Stock (1992), who derive correct asymptotic Dickey-Fuller *t*-statistics for tests of the unit root hypothesis using recursive regressions. Because of the large numbers of plots generated, only the most informative ones are reproduced in later chapters.

**Fluctuation Tests**

Chow tests are based on shifting estimates of the variance of the errors in the regression. Plots of recursive coefficients focus on the shifting parameters of the various distributions directly. But they are informal. *Fluctuation tests* provide a metric for these shifting coefficient estimates. The fluctuation test with an *infinite norm* focuses on that coefficient that shows the largest change one period to the next (Ploberger, Kramer, and Kontrus 1989). C. James Chu (1990) proposes an alternative using the *Euclidean norm*, which is able to consolidate information from all the changing coefficients. Each test compares the coefficient estimates for each recursive regression to those for the whole sample. The reported statistic is the maximum value scaled by its 5 percent critical value (Chu 1990). The fluctuation test with the Euclidean norm is preferred, but it is recommended only when there are five or fewer regressors. In cases in which there are more than five regressors, we substitute the test with infinite norm. In any case, when it is possible to run both tests, they almost always agree.

The number of tests examined of course means that we use no simple, mechanical decision procedure to determine if and when a break occurs. This is appropriate since the nature, timing, and possible multiplicity of interventions in the underlying data-generating process cannot be known *a priori*. This is in the spirit of the pioneering work of Brown, Durbin, and Evans (1975, pp. 149–150):

> the techniques are designed to bring out departures from constancy in a graphic way instead of parameterizing particular types of departure in advance and then developing formal significance tests intended to have high power against these particular alternatives. From this point of view the significance tests suggested should be regarded as yardsticks for the interpretation of data rather than leading to hard and fast decisions.[14]

## 8.4 LINEAR METHODS IN THE CONTEXT OF ENDOGENOUS REGIME SWITCHING

In Chapter 2, Section 6, we argued that structure, and not invariance, was the essence of causality. Yet in this chapter, we have explored a set of methods for resolving questions of causal direction that exploit the patterns of invariance and noninvariance of estimated linear relationships. But there is no reason to restrict causal structures to be linear in parameters.[15] Our notion of causal structure does require the possibility of an intervention – a change of parameters. In Chapter 7, Section 4, we rejected LeRoy's view that it is always possible – indeed logically required – that any apparently changing parameters be seen fundamentally as realizations from a higher order (nonlinear) structure in which the deep parameters are fixed. The rejection was in principle only; for we have no objection, where it is pragmatically useful, to modeling policy as, for example, a regime-switching model such as Hamilton's described in Chapter 3, Section 2. This opens up the linear methods of this chapter to the charge that what they uncover are not really interventions, but stable realizations of a nonlinear system. Where does this leave the inference of causal direction?

Our answer is a pragmatic conjecture. If regime switches are, in fact, rare, they can be treated as if they were true interventions, and the infer-

---

[14] We in fact also examined, but do not report, the cusum and cusum-squared plots developed in Brown et al. (1975). In practice they seemed to be less useful at discriminating between alternative regressions than those tests we do report. Hansen (1990, p. 3 passim), gives theoretical reasons why this should be so.

[15] See Chapter 2, Section 2.

ential methods proposed here should deliver the correct conclusions about causal direction. If, on the other hand, they are frequent, linear methods react to their mean values and variations about the mean are captured in the error terms. The only problematic cases should lie in between these extremes: switches too common and patterned to be seen as singular interventions and too rare to be subsumed to the error term.

To confirm our conjecture and to get some idea of how broad the problematic middle ground might be, we perform a Monte Carlo experiment using the Hamilton regime-switching model calibrated to the actual economy. A set of data is generated from the model described in equations (3.12) and (3.13) in Chapter 3, repeated here as (with the addition of an error term, $\zeta_t$, in the price equation):

$$m_t = s_t \lambda + m_{t-1} + \varepsilon_t, \tag{8.16}$$

where $s_t$ is described by the transition matrix:

|  |  | Regime at time $t+1$ | |
|---|---|:---:|:---:|
|  |  | $s_t = 1$ | $s_t = 0$ |
|  | $s_t = 1$ | $\theta$ | $1 - \theta$ |
| Regime at time $t$ |  |  |  |
|  | $s_t = 0$ | $1 - \omega$ | $\omega$ |

and

$$p_t = -\mu + \frac{\alpha\gamma(1-\omega)}{1-\phi} + m_t + \frac{\phi\gamma}{1-\phi} s_t + \zeta_t. \tag{8.17}$$

Although the data are generated in a nonlinear system, the structural break tests are applied to linear equations:

$$p_t = \Pi_0 + \Pi_1 m_t + \omega_t, \tag{8.18}$$

and

$$m_t = \Omega_0 + \Omega_1 m_{t-1} + \xi_t. \tag{8.19}$$

(These are the same as equations (7.53) and (7.54) in Chapter 7, Section 3.) The true system is stable; but, every time there is a regime change, the linear equations will, in principle, be subject to a structural break. The central question is, how does our ability to detect these breaks vary with the frequency of switches of regime?

The calibration is described in the Appendix to this chapter. The parameters mimic ones that would be found from actual data in the

U.S. economy, except for $\gamma$, the growth rate of the money stock in the high-growth regime. The stability test used is the max-Chow test described in Section 8.3. The critical values and the value of $\gamma$ are chosen in an iterative Monte Carlo process that yields a nominal size of 5 percent when there is no break (i.e., no switch of regime) and an average power of 100 percent against a single break anywhere in the sample. This biases the results in favor of finding structural breaks and underwrites the argument that if breaks are not identified by this test, *a fortiori* they would not be identified by realistically less powerful tests.

Table 8.2 presents the result of 1000 replications each of a sample size of 150 for various combinations of the switching parameters $\theta$ and $\omega$. The higher is $\theta$, the longer on average a high-growth regime will endure, and the less probable switches are to the low growth regime. The higher is $\omega$, the longer on average a zero-growth regime will endure, and the less probable switches are to the high-growth regime. Thus, the number of switches is fewest when both parameters are close to unity (lower right corner of the table) and most numerous when both parameters are close to zero (upper left corner of the table). The table shows that when the average number of switches is low, the test is almost always able to identify correctly whether or not there is a structural break (97.2 percent of the time in the lower right-hand cell). As the number of switches increases, the ability to correctly identify breaks falls rapidly in the direction of type-II error – that is, in the direction of identifying a regime as stable, when in fact it is subject to regime shifts. With as few as 14 switches on average, the proportion of false indications of stability is in excess of 90 percent. Table 8.3 presents the same sort of test for equation (8.19) on the same simulated data.

The practical upshot is that for low-frequency regime changes, the regime changes themselves can be treated as interventions, even though they are, in fact, realizations of a stable super-regime. Causal inferences will be correct, despite the lack of invariance at a fundamental level. For high-frequency regime changes, linear methods will (correctly relative to the super-regime) indicate stability. Only a true intervention in the super-regime parameters – e.g., in $\omega$, $\theta$, or $\gamma$ – would register as an intervention and permit inference of causal direction. The middle ground is not wide in this example, but it is wide enough that there may be some practical cases in which one must attempt to model the nonlinear relationship econometrically if inference of causal direction is to proceed.

**Table 8.2. Identifying Structural Breaks in the Linear Regressions of Prices Conditional on Money Using Data Generated from a Regime-Switching Model**

| | θ | | | | | | | | | | | | | | | | | | | | |
|---|---|---|---|---|---|---|---|---|---|---|---|---|---|---|---|---|---|---|---|---|---|
| | 0.01 | | | 0.05 | | | 0.25 | | | 0.50 | | | 0.75 | | | 0.95 | | | 0.99 | | |
| ω | S | C | T2 | S | C | T2 | S | C | T2 | S | C | T2 | S | C | T2 | S | C | T2 | S | C | T2 |
| 0.01 | 149 | 3.3 | 96.7 | 145 | 2.2 | 97.8 | 128 | 2.8 | 97.2 | 100 | 2.7 | 97.3 | 60 | 1.0 | 99.0 | 14 | 1.3 | 98.7 | 3 | 23.7 | 76.1 |
| 0.05 | 145 | 2.5 | 97.5 | 142 | 1.3 | 96.7 | 126 | 1.8 | 98.2 | 98 | 1.6 | 98.4 | 59 | 1.7 | 98.3 | 15 | 1.9 | 98.1 | 3 | 21.9 | 77.7 |
| 0.25 | 128 | 3.2 | 96.8 | 126 | 1.7 | 98.3 | 113 | 2.2 | 97.8 | 90 | 2.7 | 97.3 | 57 | 2.7 | 97.3 | 14 | 2.4 | 97.6 | 3 | 22.1 | 77.9 |
| 0.50 | 100 | 5.1 | 94.9 | 98 | 3.8 | 96.2 | 90 | 4.7 | 95.3 | 75 | 3.0 | 97.0 | 50 | 2.4 | 97.6 | 14 | 14.5 | 85.5 | 3 | 24.2 | 75.5 |
| 0.75 | 60 | 16.2 | 83.8 | 59 | 14.5 | 85.5 | 56 | 11.7 | 88.3 | 50 | 9.3 | 90.7 | 38 | 8.6 | 91.4 | 13 | 17.3 | 82.7 | 3 | 34.7 | 65.1 |
| 0.95 | 14 | 95.3 | 4.7 | 14 | 95.4 | 4.6 | 26 | 63.3 | 36.7 | 14 | 91.6 | 8.3 | 12 | 88.5 | 11.5 | 7 | 82.4 | 17.6 | 2 | 81.8 | 18.0 |
| 0.99 | 3 | 77.1 | 3.6 | 3 | 76.9 | 3.0 | 3 | 79.5 | 2.7 | 3 | 78.8 | 1.5 | 3 | 76.9 | 0.7 | 3 | 84.3 | 0.9 | 1 | 87.2 | 2.7 |

*Notes:* Data are 1000 replications of the regime-switching model described in the text for each combination of θ and ω. Stability is determined by a max-Chow test with a 5% critical value. Model and critical value calibration are described in the Appendix. θ = the probability of remaining in a low-monetary-growth-rate regime. ω = the probability of remaining in a high-monetary-growth-rate regime. S = average number of *switches*. C = the percentage of replications in which the stability or instability of the linear regression is *correctly* identified. T2 = the percentage of all replications in which the test accepts stability when there are regime switches.

## Table 8.3. Identifying Structural Breaks in the Linear Regressions of Money Marginal of Prices Using Data Generated from a Regime-Switching Model

| | θ | | | | | | | | | | | | | | | | | | | | |
|---|---|---|---|---|---|---|---|---|---|---|---|---|---|---|---|---|---|---|---|---|---|
| | **0.01** | | | **0.05** | | | **0.25** | | | **0.50** | | | **0.75** | | | **0.95** | | | **0.99** | | |
| | S | C | T2 | S | C | T2 | S | C | T2 | S | C | T2 | S | C | T2 | S | C | T2 | S | C | T2 |
| **ω** 0.01 | 149 | 6.5 | 93.5 | 145 | 8.2 | 91.8 | 128 | 9.1 | 90.9 | 100 | 11.4 | 88.6 | 60 | 12.0 | 88.0 | 14 | 10.5 | 89.5 | 3 | 29.3 | 68.4 |
| 0.05 | 145 | 6.8 | 93.2 | 142 | 7.0 | 93.0 | 126 | 8.6 | 91.4 | 98 | 11.6 | 88.4 | 59 | 10.2 | 89.8 | 14 | 10.5 | 89.5 | 3 | 27.2 | 70.6 |
| 0.25 | 128 | 12.0 | 88.0 | 126 | 11.4 | 88.9 | 113 | 11.4 | 88.6 | 90 | 12.3 | 87.7 | 56 | 12.0 | 88.0 | 14 | 10.1 | 88.9 | 3 | 28.5 | 69.5 |
| 0.50 | 99 | 24.1 | 75.9 | 98 | 22.5 | 77.5 | 90 | 20.8 | 79.2 | 75 | 20.0 | 80.0 | 50 | 19.2 | 80.8 | 14 | 20.3 | 79.7 | 3 | 32.5 | 65.9 |
| 0.75 | 60 | 59.4 | 40.6 | 59 | 58.0 | 42.0 | 57 | 52.0 | 48.0 | 50 | 45.9 | 54.1 | 38 | 64.3 | 35.7 | 13 | 86.5 | 13.4 | 3 | 72.6 | 25.4 |
| 0.95 | 14 | 100.0 | 0.0 | 14 | 99.8 | 0.1 | 26 | 94.5 | 5.5 | 14 | 99.1 | 0.8 | 7 | 100.0 | 0.0 | 7 | 100.0 | 0.0 | 2 | 97.8 | 1.6 |
| 0.99 | 3 | 77.7 | 0.0 | 3 | 77.3 | 0.0 | 3 | 79.9 | 0.0 | 3 | 77.8 | 0.0 | 3 | 76.1 | 0.1 | 3 | 82.9 | 0.0 | 1 | 87.3 | 0.5 |

*Notes:* Data are 1000 replications of the regime-switching model described in the text for each combination of θ and ω. Stability is determined by a max-Chow test with a 5% critical value. Model and critical value calibration are described in the Appendix. θ = the probability of remaining in a low-monetary-growth-rate regime. ω = the probability of remaining in a high-monetary-growth-rate regime. S = average number of *switches*. C = the percentage of replications in which the stability or instability of the linear regression is *correctly* identified. T2 = the percentage of all replications in which the test accepts stability when there are regime switches.

*Appendix* 225

## APPENDIX. THE POWER OF STRUCTURAL BREAK TESTS USING A REGIME-SWITCHING MODEL: CALIBRATION AND MONTE-CARLO DESIGN

The Monte Carlo experiment in this chapter is based on equations (8.16) and (8.17). The procedure has two parts: calibration and simulation.

### Calibration

Equation (8.17) is derived in part from

$$p_t = m_t - \mu + \alpha(_t p_{t+1}^e - p_t) + v_t,$$  (8.A.1)

which is a rearrangement of equation (3.5″) from Chapter 3. Calibration proceeds as follows:

C-i. An estimate of $(_t p_{t+1}^e - p_t)$ is formed as the residuals from the regression[16]

$$\log(CPI_t)|constant, \log(CPI_{t-1}), time.$$

C-ii. A regression is then run

$$\log(CPI_t)|constant, \log(M1_t), (_t p_{t+1}^e - p_t).$$

The coefficients in equation (8.A.1) are then chosen as follows:

$\mu = -constant,$

$\sigma_v =$ the standard error of regression, so that $v_t \sim N(0, \sigma_v^2)$

$\alpha =$ the coefficient on $(_t p_{t+1}^e - p_t).$

C-iii. $\sigma_\varepsilon$, which governs the variability of $\varepsilon_t$ in equation (8.16), is obtained as the standard error of regression from

$$\log(M1)|constant, \log(M1_{t-1}), time,$$

so that $\varepsilon_t \sim N(0, \sigma_\varepsilon^2)$. A preliminary value of $\gamma$ is also obtained as the *constant* from this regression.

C-iv. The critical value for the max-Chow test and the value of $\gamma$ are chosen through an iterative process.

    a. The switching parameters are set $\theta = \omega = 0.5$. $\gamma$ is set initially to its value in step (iii). The switching index $s_t$ is initially set to zero. The calibrated versions of equations (8.16) and (8.17) are used to simulate 450 periods of data starting with an initial value $m_0 = \log(M1_{1959.1})$. The last 150 periods of

[16] The data used in the calibration are taken from CITIBASE: the Citibase Economic Database (MicroTSP version), July 1993.

these data are used as a sample that *ex hypothesi* contains no breaks. The max-Chow test is run for equation (8.18) estimated on this sample. The simulation is repeated 1000 times and a distribution is built up of the max-Chow statistics. The critical value is chosen so that the test indicates a break in 5 percent of the runs.

b.  A new set of simulations is performed with, except where noted, the same parameterizations as in (a). A break point is chosen from a uniform distribution defined at random on the interval $[1, 150]$. $s_t = 0$ before this point and $= 1$ after it. The data are again simulated as in (a) and the max-Chow test applied to estimates of equation (8.18) estimated on the simulated sample. This procedure is repeated 1000 times and the average power of the test calculated. The value of $\gamma$ is adjusted and another set of simulations and an average power calculated until the power is 100 percent.

c.  The value of $\gamma$ from (b) is used as a new initial value, and steps (a) and (b) are repeated until $\gamma$ and the critical value of the test converge.

**Simulation**

S-i.  A two-by-two grid is formed as $\theta \times \omega$, where $\theta, \omega \in (0.01, 0.05, 0.25, 0.50, 0.75, 0.95, 0.99)$. Using the previous calibration, except that the switching parameters are now drawn from the grid, 1000 data sets are generated for each element of the grid using procedures analogous to those in step (C-iv).

S-ii.  For each data set at each point in the grid, regression equations corresponding to equations (8.18) and (8.19) are estimated and a max-Chow test run using the critical value from step (C-iv). For each point in the grid, the following are recorded: (1) the average number of switches per data set; (2) the average rate of correct assessments (test indicates stable when actually stable (i.e., there are no switches) and rejects stability when actually unstable (i.e., there are switches); and (3) the rates of type II error (the test indicates stability when actually unstable). The results for equation (8.18) are reported in Table 8.2 in the text and those for equation (8.19), in Table 8.3.

# 9

# Case Study I: The Causal Direction between Taxes and Government Spending in the Postwar Period

> In America where, ever since George Washington, nobody can imagine a king, who is to stop congress from spending too much money. They will not stop themselves, that is certain. Everybody has to think about that now. Who is to stop them.
>
> – Gertrude Stein, "More about Money"

Robert J. Barro's (1979) tax-smoothing hypothesis, described in detail in Chapter 8, Section 1, is the most influential positive theory of deficits in the macroeconomic literature.[1] In it, spending causes taxes: The path of government expenditure is taken to be exogenously given, and taxes are adjusted to minimize distortions while the budget is balanced intertemporally. While the tax-smoothing model is the most popular macroeconomic approach to fiscal policy, it is impossible to say that it is correct *a priori*. It is easy to construct plausible models with other causal orders. This chapter provides an empirical analysis of fiscal policy in the United States in the period after the Second World War that attempts to discriminate among four coarse causal orderings: Spending causes taxes; taxes cause spending; taxes and spending are mutual causes; and taxing and spending are causally independent.

## 9.1 MODELS AND CAUSAL ORDERINGS

### A Model of Expenditure Smoothing

By reversing the roles of spending and taxes in Barro's model, we obtain a model in which taxes are exogenous and the path of spending is "smoothed" to minimize distortions.

---

[1] This chapter is based on joint work with Steven M. Sheffrin (Hoover and Sheffrin 1992), used with permission.

## A Double-Sided Cost-Benefit Model

Both the smoothing models recognize only one source of the costs due to distortions of either taxation or spending, but not both. Spending and taxation may, however, impose costs simultaneously. Assume that welfare is decreasing in taxation at an increasing rate, and also decreasing in the outstanding stock of debt, and that welfare is increasing in spending but at a decreasing rate. Marginal benefits from spending are uncertain as are marginal costs of taxation. Spending and taxes are chosen to maximize expected welfare. To be concrete, let the problem be

$$\max_{T_1, G_1} E_0 \{ (\varepsilon G_1 - \tfrac{1}{2} b G_1^2) - (\eta T_1 + \tfrac{1}{2} e T_1^2) - \tfrac{1}{2} B_1^2 \},$$

where $B_1 = R(B_0 + G_1 - T_1)$, $B_0$ is given, and $\varepsilon'$ and $\eta'$ arc white-noise random shocks with means $\bar{\varepsilon}$ and $\bar{\eta}$.[2]

The levels of spending and taxes can be selected by setting expected marginal costs equal to expected marginal benefits. Thus, the first-order conditions are

$$\bar{\varepsilon} - b G_1 - R^2 (B_0 + G_1 - T_1) = 0 \tag{9.1}$$

$$-\eta + e T_1 + R^2 (B_0 + G_1 - T_1) = 0 \tag{9.2}$$

Equations (9.1) and (9.2) form a simultaneous system. Causation is mutual between $T_1$ and $G_1$.

## A Constant-Share Model

Rather than following any of the three optimizing schemes represented in the three previous models, taxes and spending may be set by rules of thumb as fixed shares of GNP. The target shares need not be coordinated. For example, let

$$G = aY + \varepsilon,$$

and

$$T = bY + \eta,$$

where $Y = $ GNP, and $\varepsilon$ and $\eta$ are white-noise random shocks representing implementation errors. Dividing through by $Y$ yields

$$G/Y = a + \varepsilon', \tag{9.3}$$

[2] Certainty equivalence holds in this model. It is easily adapted to more interesting stochastic environments.

and

$$T/Y = b + \eta', \qquad (9.4)$$

where $\varepsilon$ and $\eta$ are $\varepsilon'$ and $\eta'$ scaled by GNP. Equations (9.3) and (9.4) clearly show that the rates of government spending and taxation are causally independent. Interventions represented by changes in $a$ do not affect $T/Y$, and interventions represented by changes in $b$ do not affect $G/Y$. Yet how far $G$ and $T$ can drift apart in the long run is governed by the difference between $a$ and $b$; and how far they can drift apart in the short run is governed by the variances of $\varepsilon$ and $\eta$.[3]

## 9.2 A CHRONOLOGY OF THE TAX AND SPENDING PROCESSES

To discriminate among the classes of causal orderings represented by these models, we apply the methods of causal inference described in Chapter 8. First, a chronology must be constructed that identifies both stable periods and interventions that can be clearly associated with the tax and spending processes to be identified. A chronology is summarized in Table 9.1. It begins in 1950 and runs until the first quarter of 1989. This corresponds to the sample period for data used in the empirical investigation in Section 9.3. The chronology was prepared by examining standard works on government policy in the political science literature (e.g., John E. Witte, 1985) in advance of econometric examination of the data. It reports only what appear to be the most significant events. There was no guarantee that these would prove to be significant in the econometric investigations or that other events would not be missed.

The history of spending is straightforward. Two wars, Korea and Vietnam, dominate the spending chronology. Their effective starting and ending dates are given in Table 9.1. Two other major events include the rapid growth of entitlements in the 1970s (from 6.2 to 10.2 percent of GNP) and the change in the composition of federal spending towards military spending in the early 1980s.

The history of taxation is somewhat more complicated. Tax bills changing the rates and rules under which taxes are collected come fast and furious throughout the postwar period. But only a few of these bills represent changes of sufficient magnitude or new departures in the character of the tax process to count as important interventions.

---

[3] Neither the double-sided cost-benefit model nor the constant-share model need satisfy the intertemporal budget constraint that is assumed to hold in the two smoothing models. Whether or not such an intertemporal budget constraint holds is an empirical question (see, e.g., Trehan and Walsh 1988).

230 *Case Study I*

**Table 9.1. A Chronology of Taxing and Spending Interventions**

| Year | Events |
|------|--------|
| 1950 | Korean War begins; Excess Profits Tax enacted |
| 1951 | Individual income taxes raised for war finance; Korean War truce talks begin (February) |
| 1953 | Korean War truce signed ends (July); war taxes removed (December) |
| 1964 | Tonkin Gulf Resolution (August); major tax cut |
| 1965 | Major troop buildup in Vietnam begins (July) |
| 1968 | Tax Surcharge enacted |
| 1969 | Surcharge removed; major tax bill; Vietnam troop withdrawals begin |
| 1970 | Build up of entitlements and transfer payments begins |
| 1975 | Tax rebate |
| 1976 | Tax Reform Act |
| 1978 | Revenue Act |
| 1980 | Entitlements stabilize |
| 1981 | Reagan tax cuts |
| 1982 | Cut in budget share of nonmilitary purchases |
| 1986 | Tax reform |

In response to the revenue needs associated with the Korean War, two tax bills were enacted: the Excess Profits Tax of 1950 and the Revenue Act of 1951. The former was a corporate tax increase, while the latter raised individual income tax rates. The Excess Profits Tax was scheduled to expire June 30, 1953. Legislation, however, extended this expiration date until December 31, 1953, which coincided with the expiration date for the individual rate increases in the Revenue Act of 1951.

The next major change in tax code is the tax cut of 1964. This was partially reversed in 1968 with the introduction of a 10 percent tax surcharge aimed at cooling excess demand in the economy. The tax surcharge was removed in 1969 and a major tax bill introduced. A series of tax bills adjusting or modifying the 1969 act were introduced during the remainder of Nixon's presidency.

During the Ford and Carter years, there were several other tax acts. There were tax rebates in 1975, the Tax Reform Act of 1976, and the Revenue Act of 1978. All these acts featured many complex structural changes and typically some individual and corporate tax rate reduction. The revenue changes, however, were relatively small. From 1974.4 to 1980.4, for example, tax revenues grew (including these cuts) at approximately the rate of $45 billion a year. The Joint Tax Committee estimates the effects of the cuts at about $6 billion a year (Witte 1985, p. 164). We tentatively regard these as minor relative to the tax bills associated with the Korean War, the Kennedy administration, and the Reagan administration. Moreover, they should be viewed as partially predictable mechanisms to reduce the large revenues that would flow in automatically from the interaction of the progressive tax system with the lack of indexation for inflation.

On entering office in 1981, Reagan sought a 30 percent cut in income tax rates, finally agreeing with Congress for a 25 percent cut phased in over three years.[4] The central tax reform of the Reagan presidency was the 1986 tax bill. Its provisions included a simplification and reduction of rates, indexing of tax brackets, and abolishing the distinction between capital gains and ordinary income.

Comparing the histories of taxes and spending, we are able to identify two periods in which there do not appear to be any major interventions in either process: 1954–1963 and 1974–1979. These tranquil periods are the starting place for the empirical investigation of the next section.

## 9.3 EVIDENCE

### The Data

Where possible, data are taken from the National Income and Product Accounts. As a first approach, we operate at a highly aggregated level. Taxes are represented by total federal government receipts. Expenditures are total federal outlays net of interest payments. We assume that the levels of taxes and spending are set relative to potential output. Therefore, all variables are scaled by potential output in order to remove common trends.[5] Since we are looking for discretionary changes in policy, we would like to abstract from the effects of inflation and cyclical movements of *GNP* on receipts, and from the effects of automatic stabilizers on expenditure. We, therefore, regressed receipts scaled by potential output on a constant, the current and three lags of the GNP gap (= 1 − (*GNP/potential GNP*)), to capture cyclical effects, and on the current and three lags of inflation (= $\Delta\log(GNP\ price\ deflator)$). The residuals from this regression, *RPOF* (receipts scaled by potential output and filtered) are our tax variable. Similarly, our expenditures variable *XPOF* (filtered expenditures scaled by potential output) is obtained by regressing

---

[4] The 1981 law also included provisions to index tax brackets to be implemented at a later date. Then Secretary of the Treasury Donald Regan remarked: "My favorite part of the tax bill is the indexing provision – it takes the sand out of Congress's sandbox." In the event, these indexing provisions were not implemented.

[5] We adopt the Federal Reserve's measure of potential output, which applies a Kalman filter to an Okun's-law relationship and accounts for changes in productivity (Peter K. Clark 1983). While there are other estimates of potential output, this measure is widely used, and we know of no clearly superior measure.

expenditures scaled by potential output on a constant and the current and three lags of the GNP gap.[6]

**Characterization of Distributions**

The next step is to characterize the conditional and marginal distributions in the tranquil periods identified in Section 9.2. If they have been correctly identified as tranquil, regressions estimated over these periods should be invariant – that is, show stable estimated coefficients.

First, consider regression (ii) in Table 9.2. The low Durbin-Watson statistic on $RPOF$ suggests that $RPOF$ is nonstationary. Differencing once seems to render $RPOF$ stationary as indicated by the Durbin-Watson statistic of 2.43 on $\Delta RPOF$. The $F$-statistic testing the explanatory power of the regressors, which is 10.17 ($F(11,20)$) for the level, drops to 1.08 for the difference. This suggests that none of the regressors has explanatory power for $\Delta RPOF$. The simple fact that the standard deviation of $\Delta RPOF$ is already as low as the standard error of regression for regression (ii) in Table 9.2 further bears this out. A random walk, therefore, seems to be a likely specification. Regression (iii) in Table 9.3 estimates the random-walk specification. The diagnostic statistics reported show that we cannot rule out that the residuals of this regression are normal, conditionally homoscedastic white noise. The Chow test reported in Table 9.3 splits the estimation period in two to check for stability within sample.[7] The random-walk specification is nested in both regressions (i) and (ii) in Table 9.2, and we cannot reject the null hypothesis that it is a valid restriction of them both. Thus a model that is marginal of all expenditure variables and of all but last period's receipt variable appears to adequately characterize $RPOF$.

In the second tranquil period, the story is somewhat different. The standard deviation of the level, $RPOF$, is nearly the same as the standard error of regression (regressions (iii) and (iv) in Table 9.2). According to the $F$-tests, none of the independent variables has any explanatory power for the level or the difference of $RPOF$. $RPOF$ then appears to be stationary rather than a random walk. Regression (v) in Table 9.3 regresses $RPOF$ on a constant and $RPOF$ lagged once. It appears to have stable coefficients and normal, homoscedastic white-noise residuals. It cannot be rejected against regressions (iii) or (iv) in Table 9.2.

---

[6] These adjustments are similar to those used by von Furstenberg, Green, and Jeong (1986, pp. 180–183). Exact sources and definitions are given in the Appendix to this chapter.

[7] This is Gregory C. Chow's (1960, pp. 595–599) second test, the one commonly described in elementary econometrics texts; it is more powerful than Chow's first test, but requires that each subsample have enough degrees of freedom to be estimated separately.

The fact that both the constant and the lagged level term are statistically insignificant confirms the stationary specification. Clearly, then, the specification of the receipts process changes markedly between the first and second tranquil periods, although in neither period are expenditures involved. Even though the coefficient on $RPOF_{-1}$ is insignificant, regression (v) in Table 9.3 is specified so that it nests both the random-walk and the white-noise specifications; this may be helpful in picking up the shift between the two tranquil periods when we turn to out-of-the sample estimates.

Now consider the expenditure regressions in Table 9.2. In the first tranquil period, the Durbin-Watson statistic on $XPOF$ (regressions (v) or (vi) in Table 9.2) is very low, while it is near two on $\Delta XPOF$, suggesting that $XPOF$ is nonstationary. We have already seen that $RPOF$ is nonstationary in the first tranquil period. Together, these facts suggest that $RPOF$ and $XPOF$ may be cointegrated. Regression (i) in Table 9.3 is an error-correction specification in which, in the long run, $XPOF$ must equal $RPOF$.[8] Regression (i) in Table 9.3 appears to be a stable regression with normal, conditionally homoscedastic white-noise errors. It cannot be rejected as a valid restriction of regression (v) in Table 9.2. It will serve as our characterization of the conditional expenditure distribution in the first tranquil period.

Regression (ii) in Table 9.3, which is marginal of all receipts variables, equally well characterizes regression (vi) of Table 9.2. It will serve as the marginal expenditure distribution for the first tranquil period.

As on the receipts side, behavior on the expenditures side changes markedly between the first and second tranquil periods. Although it was derived from an independent specification search, regression (iii) of Table 9.3 has the identical form and, aside from the sign of the constant, quite similar coefficients as regression (ii) of Table 9.3. And it passes the same battery of diagnostic tests. It cannot be rejected as a valid restriction of regression (viii) of Table 9.2 at any conventional level of significance. But, what is more, it cannot be rejected against regression (vii) of Table 9.2. Receipt terms, then, seem to have no explanatory power for expenditures in the second tranquil period.

---

[8] In addition to the informal indicators cited in the text, we have also performed augmented-Dickey-Fuller and Durbin-Watson tests for cointegration between $XPOF$ and $RPOF$. They were inconclusive. In general, given the known low power of these tests in short samples, our informal discussion adopts about the amount of precision possible in the circumstances. In the particular case of regression (i), the high $t$-statistic on the error-correction term (4.88) provides a direct test of the existence of a cointegrating vector between $XPOF$ and $RPOF$. The correct critical values for this $t$-statistic are not conventional, but lie somewhere between those of the Dickey-Fuller test and those of a normal distribution; see Kremers, Dalado, and Ericsson (1989).

Table 9.2. Unrestricted Distributed-lag Regressions

| Regression | Descriptive Statistics | | | | | Regression Summary Statistics | | | | |
|---|---|---|---|---|---|---|---|---|---|---|
| | Dependent Variable | Mean | Standard Deviation | Durbin-Watson | Standard Error of Regression | Sum of Squared Residuals | Normality $\chi^2(2)$ | AR(·) F(·,·) | ARCH(·) F(·,·) | Explanatory Power F(·,·) |
| (i) Receipts Conditional 1955.1–1962.4 | RPOF | 0.0014 | 0.0062 | 0.24 | | | | | | 10.17 (11,20) |
| | ΔRPOF | 0.0005 | 0.0030 | 2.43 | 0.0030 | 0.00018 | 0.30 | 0.17 (4,16) | 0.35 (4,12) | 1.08 (11,20) |
| (ii) Receipts Marginal 1955.1–1962.4 | RPOF | −0.0014 | 0.0062 | 0.24 | | | | | | 21.96 (5,26) |
| | ΔRPOF | 0.0005 | 0.0030 | 2.43 | 0.0030 | 0.00023 | 1.05 | 0.17 (4,22) | 0.61 (4,18) | 1.38 (5,26) |
| (iii) Receipts Conditional 1974.3–1979.2 | RPOF | −0.0030 | 0.0031 | 1.51 | | | | (1)[4] | (1)[4] | 1.08 (11,8) |
| | ΔRPOF | 0.0000 | 0.0038 | 2.58 | 0.0030 | 0.00007 | 0.90 | 0.73 (1,9) | 0.01 (1,8) | 2.00 (11,8) |
| (iv) Marginal Receipts 1975.1–1978.4 | RPOF | −0.0034 | 0.0031 | 1.54 | | | | | | 0.37 (5,19) |
| | ΔRPOF | 0.0002 | 0.0039 | 2.81 | 0.0034 | 0.00012 | 0.31 | 6.56 (1,9) | 3.34 (1,8) | 1.82 (5,10) |
| (v) Expenditure Conditional | XPOF | 0.0360 | 0.0160 | 0.37 | 0.0077 | 0.0012 | 0.37 | 0.18 | 0.26 | 3.08 (11,24) |

| | | | | | | | | | |
|---|---|---|---|---|---|---|---|---|---|
| 1955.1–1962.4 | ΔXPOF | −0.0005 | 0.0097 | 1.75 | | | | (4,16) | (4,12) | 2.67 (11,20) |
| (vi) | XPOF | 0.0360 | 0.0160 | 0.37 | | | | | | 18.60 (5,26) |
| Expenditure Marginal 1955.1–1962.4 | ΔXPOF | −0.0005 | 0.0097 | 1.75 | 0.0080 | 0.0017 | 0.27 | 1.61 (4,22) | 0.19 (2,93) | 3.85 (5,26) |
| (vii) | XPOF | −0.0280 | 0.0190 | 0.24 | | | | | | 5.50 (11,8) |
| Expenditure Conditional 1974.3–1979.2 | ΔXPOF | 0.0001 | 0.0095 | 1.48 | 0.0098 | 0.00077 | 0.99 | 5.75[a] (1,9) | 1.92[a] (1,8) | 0.88 (11,8) |
| (viii) | XPOF | −0.0220 | 0.0160 | 0.30 | | | | | | 7.33 (5,10) |
| Expenditure Marginal 1975.1–1978.4 | ΔXPOF | −0.0005 | 0.0099 | 1.57 | 0.0090 | 0.00082 | 2.40 | 0.07 (1,9) | 0.03 (1,8) | 1.60 (5,10) |

*Notes:* All regressions were run on PC-GIVE, Version 5.0 (Hendry 1989). Conditional regressions correspond to $Y_t = \alpha + \sum_{j=1}^{5} \beta_j Y_{t-j} + \varepsilon_t$, where, when $Y$ = taxes, and vice versa. Equivalent reparameterizations $\Delta Y_t = \alpha$ the marginal regression corresponds to $Y_t = \alpha + \sum_{j=1}^{5} \beta_j Y_{t-j} + \varepsilon_t$, where, $X$ = receipts, $X$ = taxes, and vice versa. The Durbin-Watson statistic is calcualted as DW($X$) $+ \sum_{j=1}^{4} \beta_j' \Delta Y_{t-j} + \sum_{k=0}^{4} \gamma_k' \Delta X_{t-k} + \delta_1 Y_{t-1} + \delta_2 X_{t-1} + \varepsilon_t$, and $\Delta Y_t = \alpha + \sum_{j=1}^{4} \beta_j' \Delta Y_{t-j} + \delta_1 Y_{t-1} + \varepsilon_t$, are also reported. The normality test reported is the Jarque and Bera (1980) test for normal residuals, which $= \sum_{t=2}^{T} (X_t - X_{t-1})^2 / \sum_{t=1}^{T} (X_t - X)^2$, where $X$ is the dependent variable. The $F$-statistics reported are as follows: is distributed as $\chi_{[2]}^2$ under the null hypothesis of normality. The $F$-statistics reported are as follows:

$AR3(\bullet) =$ Lagrange-multiplier test for autocorrelated residuals; the $F$-distribution equivalent is reported, which is distributed $F(\bullet, \bullet)$ under the null hypoth-esis of no residual autocorrelation up to the order indicated by the degrees of freedom in the numerator;

$ARCH(\bullet) =$ Lagrange-multiplier test for autoregressive conditional heteroscedasticity; the $F$-distribution equivalent is reported, which is distributed as $F(\bullet, \bullet)$ under the null of no autoregressive conditional heteroscedasticity up to the order indicated by the degrees of freedom in the numerator;

Explanatory power = $F$-test distributed as $F(\bullet, \bullet)$ under the null hypothesis that all of the regressors are zero.

Degrees of freedom are reported in parentheses.

[a] Calculated over 1974.3–1979.4 because of insufficient degrees of freedom.

235

**Table 9.3. Parsimonious Characterizations of the Conditional and Marginal Distributions**

|  | Regression[a] | | | | |
|---|---|---|---|---|---|
| (i) | | | | | |
| Expenditures | $\Delta$XPOF $= 0.21\,\Delta_4$XPOF$_{-1}$ $- 0.96\,\Delta$RPOF$_{-3}$ $- 0.40$ (XPOF $-$ RPOF)$_{-1}$ $+ 0.016$ | | | | |
| Conditional | $(-0.0005)$ | $(0.057)$ | $(0.41)$ | $(0.082)$ | $(0.0035)$ |
| 1955.1–1962.4 | $[0.0097]$ | $[0.094]$ | $[0.51]$ | $[0.140]$ | $[0.0053]$ |
| (ii) | | | | | |
| Expenditures | $\Delta$XPOF $= 0.30\,\Delta_3$XPOF$_{-2}$ $- 0.40$ XPOF$_{-1}$ $+ 0.015$ | | | | |
| Marginal | $(-0.0005)$ | $(0.085)$ | $(0.10)$ | $(0.0041)$ | |
| 1955.1–1962.4 | $[0.0097]$ | $[0.129]$ | $[0.14]$ | $[0.0051]$ | |
| (iii) | | | | | |
| Expenditures | $\Delta$XPOF $= 0.30\,\Delta_3$XPOF$_{-2}$ $- 0.38$ XPOF$_{-1}$ $- 0.010$ | | | | |
| Marginal | $(-0.0005)$ | $(0.10)$ | $(0.16)$ | $(0.0042)$ | |
| 1975.1–1978.4 | $[0.0099]$ | $[0.06]$ | $[0.16]$ | $[0.0035]$ | |
| | | | | | |
| (iv) | | | | | |
| Receipts | $\Delta$RPOF $= 0.00050$ | | | | |
| Marginal | $(0.0005)$ | $(0.00054)$ | | | |
| 1955.1–1962.4 | $[0.0030]$ | $[0.00054]$ | | | |
| | | | | | |
| (v) | | | | | |
| Receipts | RPOF $= 0.20$ RPOF$_{-1}$ $- 0.0026$ | | | | |
| Marginal | $(-0.0030)$ | $(0.26)$ | $(0.0012)$ | | |
| 1974.3–1979.2 | $[0.0031]$ | $[0.33]$ | $[0.0013]$ | | |

[a] Regressions run on PC-GIVE, Version 5.0. Mean of dependent variable in parentheses and standard deviation in square brackets beneath dependent variable. Standard errors in parentheses and heteroscedasticity-corrected standard errors in square brackets beneath coefficient estimates.
[b] Most statistics as reported in notes to Table 9.2.
[c] Chow test of first half of sample versus second half.

## Observational Equivalence in Practice

At first glance, the regressions reported in Table 9.3 for receipts and expenditures might lead one to conclude that taxes cause spending. This is because receipts seem to be a random walk, while changes in expenditures are driven, in part, by past levels of taxes. It may, therefore, appear that taxes are the driving force in the system. But this presumption would be much too hasty. In fact, Barro's tax-smoothing model, in which spending causes taxes, can lead to estimated regressions similar to those reported in Table 9.3.

**Summary Statistics[b]**

| $R^2$ | Standard Error of Regression | Sum of Squared Residuals | Normality $\chi^2(2)$ | AR (·) F (·,·) | ARCH (·) F (·,·) | CHOW[c] F (·,·) | Nested in UDL (5)[d] F (·,·) |
|---|---|---|---|---|---|---|---|
| | | | | (4) | (4) | | |
| 0.54 | 0.0069 | 0.0013 | 0.45 | 0.70 | 0.18 | 1.82 | 0.36 |
| | | | | (4,24) | (4,20) | (4,24) | (8,20) |
| | | | | (4) | (4) | | |
| 0.38 | 0.0079 | 0.0018 | 0.68 | 0.32 | 0.12 | 2.77 | 0.61 |
| | | | | (4,25) | (4,21) | (3,26) | (3,26) |
| | | | | | 0.05 | | 0.05 |
| | | | | (2) | (3) | | (3,10) |
| 0.44 | 0.0080 | 0.0083 | 3.71 | 0.11 | 0.23 | 1.18 | |
| | | | | (2,11) | (3,7) | (3,10) | 0.26[e] |
| | | | | | | | (9,8) |
| | | | | | | | 1.37 |
| | | | | (4) | (4) | | (5,26) |
| 0.042 | 0.0030 | 0.00029 | 1.01 | 1.36 | 0.68 | 0.010 | |
| | | | | (4,27) | (4,23) | (1,30) | 1.07[f] |
| | | | | | | | (11,20) |
| | | | | | | | 0.34 |
| | | | | (2) | (3) | | (4,10) |
| 0.04 | 0.0031 | 0.00013 | 0.61 | 1.22 | 0.26 | 0.42 | |
| | | | | (2,12) | (3,8) | (2,12) | 0.45[g] |
| | | | | | | | (10,4) |

[d] *F*-test of exclusion restrictions versus corresponding model in Table 9.2.

[e] *F*-test of exclusion restrictions versus regression (vii) (Table 9.2) reestimated over 1975.1–1979.4 to overcome limited degrees of freedom.

[f] *F*-test of exclusion restrictions versus regression (i) (Table 9.2).

[g] *F*-test of exclusion restrictions versus regression (i) (Table 9.2) reestimated over 1975.1–1978.4.

In the tax-smoothing model, taxes follow a random walk. Moreover, taxes will Granger-cause spending if the government uses information other than the past history of spending to forecast future spending. Thus, it would appear that our regressions are potentially consistent with a tax-smoothing world as well.

Before rushing to embrace the alternative causal ordering, spending causes taxes, we note that our regressions do not satisfy one crucial implication of the tax-smoothing model. If current government spending conveys any information about future spending, then the change in taxes should be correlated with the current change in government spending.

However, current expenditure was included as a potential regressor in our model of receipts but was not statistically significant.

This discussion, nonetheless, highlights in a concrete way the general points about observational equivalence made in Chapter 8. To make further progress in discriminating between alternative causal orderings, we turn to an analysis of the stability of the regressions reported in Table 9.3 in the face of interventions.

**Out-of-Sample Projections**

Table 9.4 generally supports our identification of the tranquil periods. Only for the backward projection of the receipts process from the first tranquil period to 1950.1 (projection (viii)) does the sequential Chow test indicate a structural break within the tranquil period. This case will be discussed in due course.

The first three columns of Table 9.5 report the structural breaks we identified in projecting the regressions reported in Table 9.3 out of sample. These results shall be interpreted in Section 9.4. The remainder of this section presents the evidence that supports the entries in Table 9.5. Readers who are willing to take our evidence for these structural breaks on faith should skip immediately ahead to Section 9.4.

*(i) Interventions in the Period 1950–1954*

Projection (viii) (Table 9.4) presents the receipts regression (iii) in Table 9.3 projected backward from the first tranquil period to 1950.1. Although the max-Chow and the fluctuation test do not register any structural break, the one-step-ahead Chow test does, with the sequential Chow test locating the break at 1954.1. The Chow statistic on the one-step-ahead test is probably too large, at 4 times its 5 percent critical value, to be sampling error. Projection (ix), therefore, reruns (viii) but with 1954.1, the date of the maximum observation for the one-step-ahead statistic dummied out. Now the sequential Chow test indicates a structural break at 1951.1. The evidence thus supports two changes in the tax process: 1951.1 and 1954.1.

The break in 1954.1 appears to impinge on the tranquil period identified as 1954.1–1963.4. As we shall see in Section 9.4, this break appears to be associated with the removal of extraordinary tax measures at the end of December 1953. It is, then, hardly surprising that the data do not pick up the break until the first quarter of 1954.

Turn now to the expenditure specification over this same period. Consider first the conditional expenditure specification, regression (i) in Table 9.3. Projection (i) shows that all four tests indicate a break. The sequential Chow test dates a break at 1953.1. The coefficient plot for

**Table 9.4. Tests of Structural Stability**

| Projection | Table 3 Regression | Direction | Projection Period | Max-Chow Test | Fluctuation Test | One-step Ahead Chow Test — Ratio | One-step Ahead Chow Test — Maximum Value | Sequential Chow Test Break Point |
|---|---|---|---|---|---|---|---|---|
| (i) Expenditures Conditional | (i) | Backward | 1954.4–1950.1 | 1.3 | 1.7 | 0.30 | 3.9 | 1953.1 |
| (ii) Expenditures Conditional | (i) | Forward | 1963.1–1975.1 | 1.5 | 4.3 | 0.06 | 1.7 | 1965.1 |
| (iii) Expenditures Marginal | (ii) | Backward | 1954.4–1950.1 | 0.9 | 1.9 | 0.30 | 4.3 | 1953.1 |
| (iv) Expenditures Marginal | (ii) | Forward | 1963.1–1975.1 | 1.6 | 4.9 | 0.06 | 1.5 | — |
| (v) Expenditures Marginal | (iii) | Backward | 1974.4–1962.4 | 0.8 | 2.2 | 0.07 | 1.8 | — |
| (vi) Expenditures Marginal | (iii) | Forward | 1979.1–1989.1 | 0.3 | 0.9 | 0.05 | 2.3 | 1980.4 |
| (vii) Expenditures Marginal | (iii) | Backward | 1983.4–1979.4 | 0.5 | 0.8 | 0.19 | 3.4 | 1982.4 |
| (viii) Receipts Marginal | (iv) | Backward | 1954.4–1950.1 | 0.8 | 0.6 | 0.15 | 4.0 | 1954.1 |
| (ix) Receipts Marginal | (iv) | Backward | 1954.4–1950.1 | 0.9 | 0.6 | 0.16 | 2.0 | 1951.1 |
| (x) Receipts Marginal | (iv) | Forward | 1963.1–1975.1 | 0.2 | 0.6 | 0.15 | 2.3 | 1964.2 |
| (xi) Receipts Marginal | (v) | Backward | 1974.4–1962.4 | 0.7 | 2.0 | 0.12 | 2.7 | 1969.1 |
| (xii) Receipts Marginal | (v) | Forward | 1979.1–1989.1 | 1.7 | 3.3 | 0.05 | 3.9 | — |
| (xiii) Receipts Marginal | (v) | Forward | 1979.1–1989.1 | 2.0 | 4.1 | 0.05 | 1.4 | — |

(omitting 1985.1 & 2)

*Notes:* Test statistics are described in the text. The values of all statistics are expressed as ratios to their 5 percent critical values. For the max Chow tests and the fluctuations tests, the sample period includes the estimation period from Table 9.3 and the projection period. For the one-step-ahead Chow test, the ratio is the number of violations of the 5 percent critical value divided by the number of observations in the projection period. For the sequential Chow test, the break point is the date at which the Chow statistic first exceeded its 5 percent critical value.

240                                                                    *Case Study I*

**Table 9.5. Summary of Structural Breaks**

| Expenditures | | Receipts | |
|---|---|---|---|
| Conditional | Marginal | Marginal | Interventions |
| | | 1951.1 | Korean War tax bills |
| 1953.1 | 1953.1 | | Effective end of Korean War |
| | | 1954.1 | Korean War taxes removed |
| | | 1964.2 | Tax cut |
| 1965.1 | 1965 | | Vietnam War buildup |
| | | 1968 | Tax surcharge |
| | | 1969.2 | Surcharge removed, major tax act |
| | | 1981.2 | Reagan tax cut |
| | 1982.4 | | Reagan military buildup |

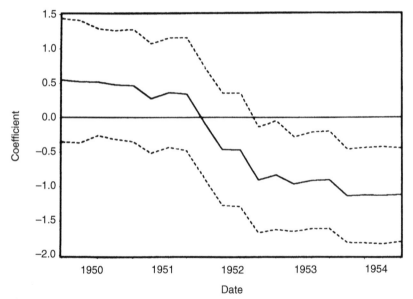

Figure 9.1. Coefficients on $\Delta RPOF_{-3}$ in Projection (i): Regression (I) of Table 9.3 Backward from 1954.4 to 1950.1. Dashed lines are ±2 standard error bands.

$\Delta RPOF_{-3}$ (Figure 9.1) shows that the behavior before 1952.2 is strikingly different from the behavior after 1952.4, even given fairly wide standard error bands.[9] The coefficient plot for the error-correction term, $(XPOF - RPOF)_{-1}$, (not shown) shows a similar break; while the other

---

[9] One should recall that these are not plots of forecasts, but of successive reestimations. The standard error bands, therefore, show ±2 standard errors for each individual esti-

coefficient graphs show no dramatic change, given their standard errors. These seem then to confirm a single break at 1953.1.

Projection (iii) presents the marginal expenditures model over the same period. Except for the max-Chow test, the pattern of the tests is similar to that for the conditional model (projection (i)). Again, this is dramatically reflected in two of the three recursive coefficient estimates (not shown). The plot of the coefficient on $XPOF_{-1}$ shows that it is clearly different before 1953.1 than after 1954.1. The plot of the constant reveals a similar, but less pronounced, pattern.

*(ii) Interventions in the Period 1964–1974*

Projection (i) is the receipts specification (regression (iii) in Table 9.3) estimated for the first tranquil period projected forward to the beginning of the second tranquil period (1975.1). The max-Chow and fluctuation tests indicate no break; but the one-step-ahead Chow does indicate a break, which the sequential Chow test locates at 1964.2. The one-step-ahead Chow statistics indicate a cluster of violations of the 5 percent critical value between 1968 and 1970, which suggests another possible structural break.

Attacking this period from the other side, projection (xi) projects the marginal receipts specification (regression (v) in Table 9.3) backwards from the second tranquil period to the end of the first tranquil period. Now the fluctuation test too indicates a structural break, although it is not located by the one-step-ahead Chow test. The plot of the coefficient on $RPOF_{-1}$ (Figure 9.2) clearly shows that the specification after 1970.2 is different from that before 1969.2. Indeed, one can see from the standard error bands that after 1971.1 the coefficient on $RPOF_{-1}$ is insignificantly different from zero, thus marking the shift in the receipts regression from a random walk in the earlier period to a stationary distribution in the later period. The plot of the constant (not shown) confirms the break. Together, the evidence from forward and backward projections suggests that there is a break about 1964.2 and another about 1969.2. The period between 1964 and 1969 most likely contains other structural breaks, although the precise timing is difficult to determine using our methods.

Now consider the conditional expenditures specification. All four tests (projection (ii)) indicate a structural break possibly at 1965.1. The coefficient plot for $\Delta RPOF_{-3}$ (not shown) indicates that, after 1965.1, the coefficient is insignificantly different from zero. The coefficient plot of the

mate. Thus every estimate after 1952.4 lies completely outside horizontal lines drawn from the standard error bands around the estimate for 1952.1, showing that there is a less than 5 percent chance of the estimates belonging to the same process. Similarly, every estimate before 1952.1 lies outside horizontal lines drawn from the standard error bands around the estimate for 1952.4.

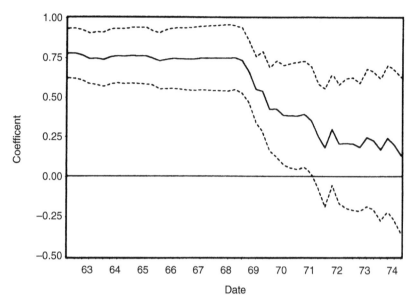

Figure 9.2. Coefficients on $RPOF_{-1}$ in Projection (xi): Regression (v) of Table 9.3 Backward from 1974.4 to 1962.4. Dashed lines are ±2 standard error bands.

error-correction term, $(XPOF - RPOF)_{-1}$, indicates a less sharp but more pronounced break at 1965.1. This pattern is repeated for the constant. The shift in causal structure identified in the initial consideration of the regressions for the tranquil periods is confirmed in these plots. After 1968, only the coefficient on $\Delta_4 XPOF_{-1}$ is always significantly different from zero.

The marginal expenditures specification (projection (iv)) shows a similar pattern, although the one-step-ahead Chow test fails to locate it. The one-step-ahead Chow statistics just barely reject the null of constant coefficients. However, just as for the coefficient on $(XPOF - RPOF)_{-1}$ in projection (ii) the coefficient plot on $XPOF_{-1}$ (Figure 9.3) shows a pronounced break at 1965.1. The constant in projection (iv) behaves similarly. Only the coefficient on $\Delta_3 XPOF_{-2}$ (not shown) never becomes insignificant.

Backward projection (v) of the marginal expenditures specification (regression (iii) in Table 9.3) from the second tranquil period to the beginning of the first tranquil period suggests that the break in the expenditures process can be localized further to 1965. The fluctuation test and the one-step-ahead Chow test indicate a break. The coefficient plot of $\Delta_3 XPOF_{-2}$ (not shown) suggests that the break occurs between 1964.2 and 1965.4. The plots of the other coefficients of the marginal specification indicate similar, though less pronounced, shifts.

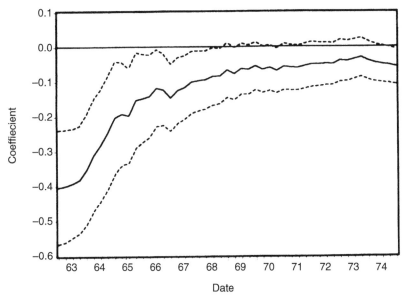

Figure 9.3. Coefficients on $XPOF_{-1}$ in Projection (iv): Regression (ii) of Table 9.3 Backward from 1963.1 to 1975.1. Dashed lines are ±2 standard error bands.

### (iii) Interventions in the Period 1980–1989

The one-step-ahead Chow statistics of the projection of the marginal receipts specification forward to 1989.1 (projection (xii)) shows the Chow statistics for 1985.1 and 1985.2 to be nearly four and nearly two and a half times their 5 percent critical values. Inspection of the plot reveals that these are the only violations. They are probably too high to be dismissed as sampling error. This was at first puzzling, because our initial reading of the historical record suggested no intervention in either tax or spending processes at this date. Looking more closely, however, we discovered that computer malfunction at the IRS delayed payments of tax refunds. Over $6.8 billion of tax refunds were delayed from March to April, i.e., from the first to the second quarter.[10] Once annualized, these huge, but economically meaningless, aberrations in the receipts process easily explain the break discovered.

The receipts specification was re-projected forward dummying out 1985.1 and 1985.2 (projection (xiii)). The fluctuations and max-Chow tests indicate a break, although the sequential Chow test does not locate it. The one-step-ahead Chow tests are borderline. The behavior of the

[10] Clark (1985).

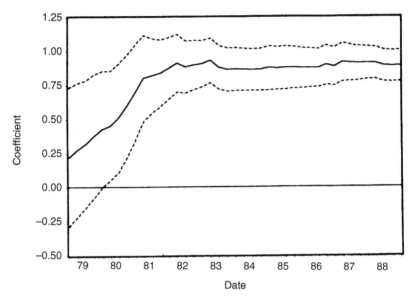

Figure 9.4. Coefficients on $RPOF_{-1}$ in Projection (xiii): Regression (v) of Table 9.3 Forward from 1979.1 to 1989.1. (omitting 1985.1 and 1985.2). Dashed lines are ±2 standard error bands.

coefficient on $RPOF_{-1}$ (Figure 9.4) is distinctly different after 1981.2 and especially after 1982.2 than before 1980.1. The plot of the constant (not shown) shows precisely parallel behavior. Receipts appeared in the second tranquil period to be stationary. After 1982.3, not only is the coefficient on $RPOF_{-1}$ statistically significantly different from zero, it is statistically insignificantly different from one. Once again the receipts process appears to be close to a random walk.

The marginal expenditures specification (projection vi) at best shows borderline rejection of coefficient constancy on the one-step-ahead Chow test only. The plot of the constant (not shown) shows a distinct, although just barely statistically significant, change between 1982.2 and 1982.4. The coefficients on $XPOF_{-1}$ and $\Delta_3 XPOF_{-2}$ indicate parallel, although statistically insignificant, breaks. To confirm this break, the same specification was estimated over 1984.1–1989.1 and projected backward to the end of the second tranquil period (projection vii). The constant-base and constant-horizon Chow tests suggest a break at 1982.4. The plots of the coefficients on the constant and on $XPOF_{-1}$ (not shown) indicate a parallel break; their behavior before 1982.3 is distinctly different from their behavior after 1983.1. Again, similar, but statistically insignificant, changes are indicated for the coefficient on $\Delta_3 XPOF_{-2}$.

## 9.4 INTERPRETATION

The fourth column of Table 9.5 assigns interventions from the chronology presented in Section 9.2 to the most nearly corresponding structural breaks identified statistically in Section 9.3. The chronology and the statistical investigation were conducted *independently*. These are the natural assignments – no attempt was made to search for particular kinds of interventions for particular structural breaks.

A number of features of Table 9.5 deserve notice. First, all of the structural breaks in the expenditures specifications are assigned to interventions in the spending process. Second, in projections from the first tranquil period, when it was possible to estimate both a conditional and a marginal regression for expenditures, both regressions show structural breaks at the same times. These two facts suggest that the breaks are truly in the spending process. Third, although we were not able to specify an independent conditional receipts regression, every break identified for marginal receipts corresponds to an intervention in the tax process.

In addition to the information in Table 9.5, recall that the specification of the tax and spending models changed between the two tranquil periods. In the first period, there was a cointegrated relationship between taxes and spending while in the second tranquil period this relationship disappeared.

These facts first suggest that between the first and second tranquil periods (sometime in the late 1960s or early 1970s) there was a change in the causal field (see Chapter 2, Section 4). The evidence for this is the lack of cointegration between spending and taxes that surfaces in the second period. This means the entire causal relationship between taxes and spending changed between the two periods and causal relationships must be identified within each period.

After the change in the causal field, again some time in the late 1960s or early 1970s, the evidence strongly suggests that *receipts and expenditures are causally independent*. Structural interventions in the spending process, identified by examination of the institutional record, are closely related to structural breaks in the statistical spending process but are not associated with breaks in the marginal receipts process. This implies that spending does not cause receipts. Similarly, structural interventions in the receipts process are associated with breaks in the statistical model for receipts but are not associated with breaks in the marginal model for expenditures. This implies that receipts do not cause expenditures. Thus, we are left with the causal independence of our two series, not unlike the constant-share model in Section 9.1.

Our interpretation of the first part of our sample, before the change in causal field, is a bit more complex. It would appear from Table 9.5 that the same type of causal independence is found in the period 1950–1963 as is found in the later period. Interventions in one process are not apparently associated with breaks in the other process. But this cannot be the complete explanation. If taxes and spending are truly independent processes, why is it that receipts and expenditures appear to be cointegrated in the first tranquil period?

Our preferred resolution of this puzzle is that taxes do cause spending in the first tranquil period, but the Korean War, which jointly affects spending and taxes, masks this relationship in the early part of the sample. Specifically, with the onset of the Korean War, the 1951 tax bills were enacted with built-in expiration dates at the end of 1953. The expiration dates clearly envisaged the end of the conflict by that time. The structural breaks in the tax process are associated with these bills. The war itself formally ended in early 1953, although the fighting ended somewhat earlier. Thus, when the war ended there was no reason not to anticipate that the prior tax increases would expire as scheduled by law. The expenditure break occurs at the end of the Korean War.

This evidence is consistent with the hypothesis that taxes cause spending. Conditional on the war ending, taxes were scheduled to fall by law. Thus, we would anticipate that as the war ended total spending would fall and a break in the spending process would occur. Moreover, since this break occurs in early 1953, we would not expect a further break in the spending process when the tax decrease goes into effect. The scheduled tax decrease was already factored into the prior spending decrease.

It would be somewhat more difficult to argue that spending caused taxes. In that case, as the Korean War ended, we would have anticipated a break in the receipts process, which failed to occur. One could argue that there was a tax decrease already scheduled but the lack of action to move up the expiration date would have to be explained if spending truly caused taxes. One piece of evidence in favor of the spending causes taxes view is that the 1964 tax cut is not directly associated with a break in the spending process. Yet, this observation is potentially contaminated by the rapid onset of the Vietnam War.

Thus, the fact that the breaks in spending are associated with wars (a third cause) in this period makes it difficult to determine the causal direction definitively. The cointegration of spending and taxes clearly points to some causal links. Our preferred explanation is for taxes causing spending. But it would be possible to entertain the alternative model.

**9.5  CONCLUSION**

Three principal conclusions emerged from our causal investigation. First, there was a change in the causal field or causal relation between taxes and spending which occurred sometime in the late 1960s and early 1970s. Second, in the period following the change in the causal field, taxes and spending were causally independent. Finally, in the early period, taxes and spending were causally linked and there is some mild evidence in favor of taxes causing spending.

Scholars of such diversity as Robert E. Lucas and Aaron Wildavsky have also discussed the changes in relationship between taxes and spending at a time similar to that which we uncovered. In a lecture delivered in 1984, but not published until two years later, Lucas (1986, p. 133) noted that

the tendencies towards permanent deficit finance and inflation that have emerged in our economy in the *last fifteen years* have much deeper roots than a succession of transient external shocks and internal mistakes. They arose, I believe, because the implicit rules under which monetary and fiscal policy is conducted have undergone a gradual but fundamental change. [emphasis added]

Lucas clearly suggests that the normative tax-smoothing model in his essay is not an accurate positive description of the fiscal process after the late 1960s.

Wildavsky, a well-known scholar of the budget process, notes a similar phenomenon. In a chapter entitled "The Collapse of Consensus" in his recent book, *The New Politics of the Budget Process* (1988), Wildavsky (p. 120) discusses this change:

Shortly after the standard accounts of classical budgeting were published in the early 1960s – Richard Fenno's *The Politics of the Purse* and the first edition of my *Politics of the Budgetary Process* – that process began to collapse. . . . In retrospect, the pattern is clear; Congress and the Presidents have trouble agreeing.

In Wildavsky's initial book, he had argued that budgeting was incremental, in part, because all parties agreed on the fundamentals and adjustments could be made on the margin. At some point, however, this consensus disappeared.

Our finding that spending and taxes are causally independent in the latter part of the postwar era is intriguing from the standpoint of budgetary history. The period since 1970 has been marked with several major attempts to create causal interdependence through institutional reform. The first major institutional change was the Congressional Budget and Impoundment Act of 1974, which created the budget committees in the House and Senate. These committees were charged to integrate spending and tax decisions. The second major change was the Gramm-Rudman laws, which were again designed to create causal interdependence. Our analysis suggests that institutional reform was undertaken precisely to counteract the lack of causal interdependence between spending and taxes. Moreover, at least by our measures, these reforms were not successful.

From the perspective of comparative politics, the lack of causal ties between taxes and spending is perhaps not that surprising. Compared to parliamentary democracies, the United States has many important actors with divergent interests and agendas. It would be valuable to apply the methods in this paper to countries such as Canada in which budgetary and tax initiatives are more closely tied.[11]

Our results have implications for recent work in the area of fiscal policy. Other economists have considered fiscal policy in more general frameworks than Barro's model. For example, Chari, Christiano, and Kehoe (1990) analyze Ramsey taxation in a real business cycle model with government. Unlike Barro's model, they find that taxes on labor need not follow a random walk. Nonetheless, their model also assumes that government spending is exogenous. Our empirical work suggests that, at least for the United States, this may not be the appropriate assumption.

**APPENDIX. DATA: SOURCES AND DEFINITIONS**

Series run from 1947.1–1989.1. Except where otherwise indicated, primary data are from the National Income and Product Accounts as reported in CITIBASE: Citibank economic database (MicroTSP version) July 1989. The CITIBASE series name is reported where applicable in square brackets.

| | | |
|---|---|---|
| $D752$ | = | dummy variable to account for one-time tax rebate, 1 for observation 1975.2, 0 elsewhere. |
| $EXN$ | = | Nominal Federal government expenditure [$GGFEX$]. |
| $EX$ | = | Real Federal government expenditure: ($EXN/FP$) 100. |
| $FP$ | = | Federal expenditure price deflator [$GDGGF$]. |
| $GAP$ | = | Output gap: $1 - (GNP/PGNP)$. |
| $GNP$ | = | Real $GNP$ [$GNP82$]. |
| $INF$ | = | Inflation rate: ($\Delta\log P$)100. |
| $INTN$ | = | Nominal net interest [$GGFINT$]. |
| $INT$ | = | Real net interest: ($INTN/P$)100. |
| $P$ | = | GNP Deflator [$GD$]. |

---

[11] Hoover and Siegler (2000) apply the same general approach to U.S. data going back to 1789.

$PGNP$ = Potential output: estimated using the methodology of Clark (1983). Observations for 1952.1–1988.4 are from Jeffrey J. Hallman et al. (1989, Appendix A, p. 25); earlier observations are computed recursively according to $PGNP_{t-1} = PGNP_t/1.008467$, where 1952.1 is the initial value for $t$ and 1.008467 is the average quarterly growth factor for $PGNP$ 1952.1–1964.4; the observation for 1989.1 is computed $PGNP_{89.1} = 1.006253909 PGNP_{88.4}$, where 1.006253909 is the average quarterly growth factor for PGNP 1980.1–1988.4.

$RCPN$ = Nominal Federal government receipts [$GGFR$].

$RCP$ = Real Federal government receipts: $(RCPN/P)100$.

$RPO$ = Real Federal government receipts as a share of potential output: $RCP/PGNP$.

$RPOF$ = Real Federal government receipts as a share of potential output filtered to remove inflation and cyclical effects: The reported series is the residuals from the regression of $RPO$ on a constant, the current value and three lags of $GAP$, the current value and three lags of $INF$, and $D752$.

$XPO$ = Real Federal Expenditures net of interest payments as a share of potential output: $(EX - INT)/PGNP$.

$XPOF$ = Real Federal Expenditures net of interest payments as a share of potential output: $(EX - INT)/PGNP$ filtered to remove cyclical effects: The reported series is the residuals from the regression of $XPO$ on a constant and the current value and four lags of $GAP$.

# 10

## Case Study II: The Causal Direction between Money and Prices

Money is a better god than beauty.

– Walker Percy, *The Moviegoer*

### 10.1 DOES MONEY CAUSE PRICES? THE CURRENT DEBATE

This chapter investigates the causal ordering of money and prices in the United States over the period 1950–1985.[1] As we saw in Chapter 1, Section 1, the debate in economics over the causal direction between money and prices goes back at least to David Hume. Although in modern times it had seemed largely settled in favor of the view that money causes prices, the recent interest in real business cycle models has in fact reopened the question. Much of the research into this question has applied tests of Granger-causality. If we take the view that the question of interest is: Supposing the Federal Reserve can control the stock of money, can it thereby also control the level of prices (or the rate of inflation)? Then, as we have seen earlier, another technique is needed. Tests of Granger-causality neither ask nor answer this question (Granger 1980, p. 1).

Although this debate is an old one, it is far from being moribund, having been revived in a surprising quarter. New classical economists are often seen as the successors to monetarism; nevertheless, some new classical economists now doubt the causal efficacy of money over income and, in some respects, over prices. Fischer Black (1970, 1972) and Eugene Fama (1980) have argued that a large portion of the money stock, bank deposits ("inside money"), responds passively to independent changes

---

[1] This case study is reprinted from *Journal of Monetary Economics* 27 (3), Kevin D. Hoover, "The Causal Direction between Money and Prices: An Alternative Approach," pp. 381–423, copyright 1991, with permission from Elsevier Science. It is older than the study presented in the last chapter. It is placed here partly because the other study followed more naturally the tax-and-spend illustration of Chapter 8 and partly because it looks at a somewhat more complex problem than the other study. Being older, however, it does not use some of the statistical techniques employed in the other study.

in economic activity, and that prices are determined almost completely by the amount of currency (and central bank reserves) in circulation ("outside money").[2]

Black and Fama's view favors real business cycle models (e.g., Kydland and Prescott 1982; Long and Plosser 1983), in which all real activity is determined without reference to monetary variables.[3] If real business-cycle models are correct, the correlation between money and nominal income arises because real activity causes money and not because money causes real activity. Robert King and Charles Plosser (1984) present empirical evidence to bolster this claim.

The new classical resuscitation of the notion of an endogenous money stock – a notion that had been peculiarly Keynesian (e.g., Gurley and Shaw 1960; Kaldor 1982) – reopens an issue that many monetarists thought was dormant, if not finally laid to rest. A key event in this long-running dispute is the famous exchange between James Tobin (1970) and Milton Friedman (1970). One piece of common ground between Tobin and Friedman is that both seem to have an implicit notion that causality is not about temporal ordering but about controllability. In contrast to previous empirical investigations of the causal direction between money and prices, the study reported here uses the structural approach that is germane to the question of controllability.

## 10.2 STABLE AND UNSTABLE PERIODS

We begin with the construction of a chronology of potentially important interventions in the money-determination and price-determination processes. Although this chronology is not reproduced here, several points should be noted.[4] First, 1954.1–1966.2 is a tranquil period with no obviously important interventions in either the money-determination or the price-determination process. This period begins after the end of the Korean War and its economic disruptions and ends the quarter before the Federal Reserve's "credit crunch" of 1966.

Second, both the period before this tranquil period, 1950.1–1953.4, and the period after, 1966.3–1985.4, contain important interventions. Some of the important ones in the earlier period are: wage and price controls (1951.1–1953.1); credit controls (1950.3–1952.2); the Fed/Treasury Accord (1951.1) leading to the withdrawal of price supports for government securities and the adoption of the "bills-only" doctrine (finalized

---

[2] Hoover (1988a, ch. 5, and 1988c) presents and criticizes Fama's argument in detail.

[3] For a detailed discussion of these models, see Hoover (1988a, ch. 3), Hartley, Hoover, and Salyer (1997, 1998) and Hartley et al. (1998, chs. 1 and 2).

[4] For a detailed chronology of 1950–1979, see Hoover (1985, ch. 8).

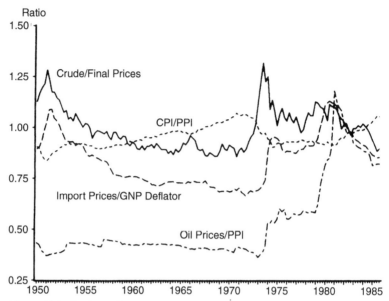

Figure 10.1.  Ratios of Selected Price Indices. Crude prices are Producer Price Index: Crude Materials for Further Processing, and final prices are Producer Price Index: Finished Goods from Producer Price Indexes by Stage of Processing; PPI is the Producer Price Index: All Commodities; oil price is the Producer Price Index: Crude Petroleum, 1982 = 100; CPI is the Consumer Price Index: All Urban Consumers (All Items), 1982–84 = 100. Data are for the last month of the quarter, not seasonally adjusted. Original source: Department of Labor. Import prices and the GNP deflator are the Implicit Price Deflators for Gross National Product and for Imports, 1982 = 100, quarterly, seasonally adjusted. Original source: Department of Commerce. All data are from CITIBASE: Citibank economic database (July 1990).

in 1953.4). In the later period, some important interventions are: the credit crunch and associated policy measures (1966.3); the introduction of lagged reserve accounting (1968.3) and the reintroduction of contemporaneous reserve accounting (1984.1); the Nixon wage/price controls (1971.3–1974.2); the progressive adoption of explicit monetary targets (from 1972.1 on); the introduction of interest-bearing checking accounts (1972.2–1980.1); the experiment with reserve base control (1979.4–1982.3); the oil price shocks (1974.1 and 1979.4); and credit controls (1980.1).

Third, the structure of relative prices changed significantly throughout the 1950.1–1985.4 period. Figure 10.1 plots the ratios of several important price indices. During the tranquil period, these ratios show steady trends. But in the periods before 1954.1 and after 1966.2, the changes are far more erratic, larger, and more rapid.

## 10.3 BASELINE REGRESSIONS

To apply the general-to-specific modeling technique, we begin with an unrestricted distributed lag regression (UDL(5)) of the (log-) levels of money or prices on five lags of themselves and on the current and five lagged values of each of the independent variables (which vary depending upon which conditional or marginal distribution we are estimating) and on a constant and three seasonal dummies (all data are seasonally unadjusted).

Money, interest rates, and prices are represented by quarterly observations of *M1*, the three-month Treasury bill rate, and the consumer price index (*CPI*).[5] These variables are chosen partly for their appropriateness to the problem at hand (*M1* was after all the Federal Reserve's premier monetary aggregate, and the *CPI* is the most publicly visible price index) and partly in order to get consistent data back to 1950 (especially in the case of the Treasury bill rate). The other variables were chosen on the basis of encompassing tests from those suggested by the relevant economic theory.

Currency is within the direct control of the Federal Reserve.[6] Therefore, currency could be a cause of prices but could not be caused by prices (see Section 10.6). Hence, the money variable (*M*) in price regressions is *M1*, which includes currency, and the money variable in money regressions is demand deposits (*DD*), defined as *M1* excluding currency. The complete price regression (1.1 in Table 10.1) is

$$\Delta CPI = 0.18 \; \Delta_4 W_{-1} - 0.0033 \; \Delta SR + 0.0022 \; \Delta_2 SR_{-4}$$
$$[0.039] \qquad [0.0014] \qquad [0.00067]$$
$$- 0.0046 \; \Delta_2 LR_{-4} - 0.0066 \; (CP1 - W)_{-5}$$
$$[0.0027] \qquad [0.013]$$
$$- 0.071 \; CPI_{-5} + 0.16 \; \Delta_2 M_{-1}$$
$$[0.023] \qquad [0.057]$$
$$+ 0.56 + 3 \text{ seasonal dummies.}$$
$$[0.015]$$

$R^2 = 0.86$      AR(4): $F(4,35) = 0.46$
$SER = 0.0022$      ARCH(4): $F(4,31) = 0.19$
Normality: $\chi^2(2) = 1.19$      Nested in UDL(5): $F(22,15) = 1.33$
Chow-1: $F(4,35) = 1.29$      Chow-2: $F(11,28) = 1.42$

---

[5] Natural logarithms of all variables except interest rates are used. Interest rates are pretax in price regressions and after-tax in money regressions. Exact sources and definitions of all the data used in this are found in the Appendix to this chapter.

[6] It is often argued that currency is in practice in the control of the public. This is, however, simply the result of the Federal Reserve's having adopted a fully accommodating reaction function and so does not reverse causality (see Chapter 2, Section 4).

**Table 10.1. Baseline Price Regressions**

| Model | Equation[a] | | | | |
|---|---|---|---|---|---|
| (1.1) Complete: $D(P\|M,r,Z)$ | $\Delta$CPI (0.0037) [0.0037] | $= 0.18\Delta_4W_{-1}$ (0.044) [0.039] | $- 0.0033\Delta$SR (0.0013) [0.0014] | $+ 0.0022\Delta_2$SR$_{-4}$ (0.00079) [0.00067] | $- 0.0046\Delta_2$L (0.0026) [0.0027] |
| | | $- 0.066$(CPI $-$ W)$_{-5}$ (0.017) [0.013] $+ 3$ seasonal dummies | $- 0.071$CPI$_{-5}$ (0.028) [0.023] | $+ 0.16\Delta_2M_{-1}$ (0.062) [0.057] | $+ 0.56$ (0.19) [0.15] |
| (1.2) Marginal of Money: $D(P\|r,Z)$ | $\Delta$CPI (0.0037) [0.0037] | $= 0.11\Delta_2W_{-1}$ (0.060) [0.057] | $+ 0.21\Delta_2W_{-3}$ (0.055) [0.052] | $- 0.0029\Delta$(LR $-$ SR)$_{-4}$ (0.0011) [0.0008] | |
| | | $- 0.0038$LR$_{-4}$ (0.0016) [0.0016] $+ 3$ seasonal dummies | $- 0.030$CPL$_{-5}$ (0.026) [0.027] | $- 0.071$(CPI $-$ W)$_5$ (0.017) [0.016] | $+ 0.41$ (0.17) [0.17] |
| (1.3) Marginal of Interest Rates: $D(P\|M,Z)$ | $\Delta$CPI (0.0037) [0.0037] | $= 0.14\Delta_4W_{-1}$ (0.032) [0.038] $- 0.036$ (0.0062) (0.0052) | $- 0.033\Delta_2\Delta_2M$ (0.012) [0.010] | $- 0.076$(CPI $-$ M)$_{-5}$ (0.013) [0.011] $+ 2$ seasonal dummies | |
| (1.4) Marginal of Interest Rates and Money: $D(P\|Z)$ | $\Delta$CPI (0.0037) [0.0037] | $= 0.20\Delta_4W_{-1}$ (0.046) [0.045] $+ 0.38$ (0.18) [0.19] | $- 0.055$(CPI $-$ W)$_{-5}$ (0.018) [0.017] $+ 3$ seasonal dummies | $- 0.0040$CPL$_5$ (0.026) [0.028] | |

*Notes*: All estimates by ordinary least squares using PC-GIVE, version 5.0.
[a] 50 observations, 1954.1–1966.2. Mean in parentheses, standard deviation in square brackets beneath the dependent variable. Standard errors in parentheses and heteroscedasticity-corrected standard errors in square brackets beneath independent variables.

| | | | | Summary Statistics[b] | | | | |
|---|---|---|---|---|---|---|---|---|
| $R^2$ | SER | RSS | AR(·) $F(\cdot,\cdot)$ | Normality $\chi^2(2)$ | ARCH(·) $F(\cdot,\cdot)F(\cdot,\cdot)$ | CHOW–1 $F(\cdot,\cdot)$ | CHOW–2 $F(\cdot,\cdot)$ | Nested in UDL(5) $F(\cdot,\cdot)$ |
| .86 | 0.0022 | 0.00019 | (4) 0.46 (4,35) | 1.19 | (4) 0.19 (4,31) | 1.29 (4,35) | 1.42 (11,28) | 1.33 (22,15) |
| .84 | 0.0023 | 0.00021 | (4) 0.30 (4,36) | 0.01 | (4) 0.69 (4,32) | 1.48 (4,36) | 0.77 (10,30) | 1.01 (23,17) |
| 0.81 | 0.0024 | 0.00026 | (4) 0.09 (4,40) | 0.47 | (4) 0.63 (4,36) | 0.76 (4,40) | 0.87 (6,38) | 0.40 (23,29) |
| 0.80 | 0.0025 | 0.00027 | (4) 0.71 (4,39) | 1.22 | (4) 0.54 (4,35) | 2.10 (4,39) | 1.04 (7,36) | 0.42 (35,8) |

[b] SER = standard error of regression. RSS = residual sum of squares. AR(·) = test for residual auto-correlation up to order (·); statistic distributed $F(\cdot,\cdot)$. Normality = Jarque and Berra's (1980) test for normal residuals; statistic distributed $\chi^2(2)$. ARCH(·) = Engle's (1982) test for autoregressive conditional het-eroscedasticity up to order (·); statistic distributed $F(\cdot,\cdot)$. CHOW–1 = Chow test of whole sample against a sample shorter by four observations; statistic distributed $F(\cdot,\cdot)$. CHOW–2 = Chow test of whole sample against both half samples.; statistic distributed $F(\cdot,\cdot)$. Nested in UDL(5) = test of reported regression against a vector autoregression including the level and five lags of each basic variable (i.e., without dif-ferences or lags) in the reported regression; statistic distributed $F(\cdot,\cdot)$.

*W* is the wage rate, *SR* a short rate of interest, and *LR* a long rate. Heteroscedasticity-corrected standard errors are shown in square brackets.

This regression is in mixed "levels-and-differences" or "error-correction" form, which permits it to capture short-run behavior while remaining consistent with the degree of cointegration between variables (i.e., with their long-run equilibrium behavior) (see Harvey 1990, ch. 8, sec. 5). The long-run solution is

$$\overline{CPI} = 0.48\overline{W} + 4.1.$$

Neither money nor interest rates appear in the long-run solution. This is because only their differences enter regression (1.1). This form appeared to encompass every rival that included money or interest rates in levels. Originally several additional regressors were considered. Time deposits, labor productivity, the unemployment rate, and unit labor costs were omitted from the specification search because the null hypothesis of no effect of their levels and five lags in UDL(5) could not be rejected at the 5 percent confidence level.

The specification search was conducted retaining four observations for out-of-sample tests of stability. Thus the statistic labeled "Chow-1" reports the test of the constancy of the coefficients of the regression over the period 1954.1–1965.2 against the full sample (1954.1–1966.2). The null hypothesis of constant coefficients cannot be rejected at the 5 percent confidence level. We take this as evidence in favor of the specification, and report only the regression using the full sample.

In addition to this out-of-sample test, the statistic labeled "Chow-2" also reports a within-sample test to buttress the claim that the baseline period is in fact tranquil in the sense that there is no structural change in the regression during it. A standard Chow test is run with the sample divided in half (1954.1–1960.1 and 1960.2–1966.2). Again, the null hypothesis of constant parameters cannot be rejected.

The null hypothesis that this form is a valid restriction of the corresponding UDL(5) cannot be rejected at the 5 percent confidence level (see statistic labeled "Nested in UDL(5)."

In addition, the regression passes a battery of standard diagnostic tests. We cannot reject at the 5 percent level the null of:

  i. autocorrelation up to fourth order (see the statistic labeled "AR");
 ii. autoregressive conditional heteroscedasticity up to fourth order (see the statistic labeled ARCH); or
iii. normality of the estimated residuals (see the statistic labeled "Normality").

We conclude that the complete price regression is tentatively acceptable as a parsimonious representation of the corresponding distribution function. Other, better representations may exist – using additional independent variables or alternative functional forms. If they are truly better, they would have to pass the same battery of tests and encompass the reported regression.

The complete money regression (2.1 in Table 10.2) is

$$\Delta_4(DD\text{–}DPI) = 0.91\ \Delta_4(DD - CPI)_{-1} - 0.26\ \Delta_4\ CPI$$
$$\quad [0.033] \qquad\qquad\qquad [0.075]$$
$$\quad + 1.56\ \Delta CPI_{-4} - 0.012\ \Delta_4\ SR_{-1}$$
$$\quad\ [0.21] \qquad\quad [0.0018]$$
$$\quad - 0.018\ \Delta(LR - SR) - 0.010\ \Delta(LR - SR)_{-3}$$
$$\quad\ [0.0034] \qquad\qquad [0.0045]$$
$$\quad + 0.078\ \Delta_2\Delta GNP_{-2} - 0.0079\ (DD - GNP - CPI)_{-5}$$
$$\quad\ [0.015] \qquad\qquad\quad [0.0060]$$

$R^2 = 0.97$        AR(4): $F(4,38) = 0.66$

$SER = 0.0047$      ARCH(4): $F(4,34) = 0.38$

Normality: $\chi^2(2) = 0.24$    Nested in UDL(5): $F(25,17) = 0.91$

Chow-1: $F(4,38) = 0.96$    Chow-2: $F(8,34) = 2.13$

As with the complete price regression, we cannot reject the null hypotheses that the complete money regression has stable coefficients and white noise errors and is a valid restriction of a more general dynamic form.

The long-run solution is

$$\overline{DD} = \overline{GNP} + \overline{CPI}$$

In other words, money and nominal income are homogeneous of degree one as many theories suggest.

The complete price regression is an estimate of the distribution of prices conditional on money, interest rates, and other variables $(D(P|M, r, Z))$. The complete money regression is an estimate of demand deposits conditional on prices, interest rates, and other variables $(D(DD|P, r, Z))$.

To obtain the various marginal distributions, we omitted the variable with respect to which the distribution was to be marginalized and its lags from UDL(5) and conducted a completely new specification search. Table 10.1 reports the complete price regression as well as marginalizations with respect to interest rates, money, and both interest rates and money. Table 10.2 reports the complete money regression as well as marginalizations with respect to prices, interest rates, and both prices and interest rates. Each of the reported regressions passes the entire

**Table 10.2. Baseline Money Regressions**

| Model | | Equation[a] | | | | |
|---|---|---|---|---|---|---|
| (2.1) | $\Delta_4(DD - CPI)$ | $= 0.91\Delta_4(DD - CPI)_{-1}$ | $- 0.26\Delta_4CPI$ | $+ 1.56\Delta CPL_{-4}$ | $- 0.012\Delta_4SI$ | |
| Complete: | (0.010) | (0.038) | (0.070) | (0.21) | (0.0015) | |
| D(DD\|P,r,Z) | [0.023] | [0.033] | [0.075] | [0.21] | [0.0018] | |
| | | $- 0.018\Delta(LR - SR)$ | $- 0.010\Delta(LR - SR)_{-3}$ | $+ 0.078\Delta_2\Delta GNP_{-2}$ | | |
| | | (0.0037) | (0.0044) | (0.015) | | |
| | | [0.0034] | [0.0045] | [0.015] | | |
| | | $- 0.0079(DD - GNP - CPI)_{-5}$ | | | | |
| | | (0.0065) | | | | |
| | | [0.0060] | | | | |
| (2.2.) | $\Delta_4DD$ | $= 1.00\Delta_4DD_{-1}$ | $- 0.68\Delta DD_{-4}$ | $+ 0.13\Delta_3(1/2GNP + 1/2GNP_{-1})$ | | |
| Marginal | (0.024) | (0.076) | (0.16) | (0.041) | | |
| of Prices: | [0.017] | [0.065] | [0.16] | [0.036] | | |
| D(DD\|r,Z) | | | | | | |
| | | $- 0.0088\Delta_4SR_{-1}$ | $- 0.011\Delta(LR - SR)_{-3}$ | $- 0.0057(LR - SR)_{-5}$ | $+ 0.0046DD$ | |
| | | (0.0016) | (0.0049) | (0.0025) | (0.0010) | |
| | | [0.0013] | [0.0045] | [0.0024] | [0.0010] | |
| | | $+ 3$ seasonal dummies | | | | |
| (2.3) | | | | | | |
| Marginal of | $\Delta DD$ | $= -0.55\Delta DD_{-3}$ | $- 0.098CPL_{-5}$ | | | |
| Interest Rates: | (0.0060) | (0.15) | (0.033) | | | |
| D(DD\|P,Z) | [0.0170] | [0.15] | [0.032] | | | |
| | | $+ 0.12\Delta_4GNP$ | $- 0.35[DD - 1/2(GNP + CPI)]_{-5}$ | $+ 1.28$ | | |
| | | (0.029) | (0.083) | (0.33) | | |
| | | [0.032] | [0.071] | [0.30] | | |
| | | $+ 3$ seasonal dummies | | | | |
| (2.4) | | | | | | |
| Marginal of | $\Delta DD$ | $= 0.21\Delta DD_{-1}$ | $+ 0.0078DD_{-1}$ | $+ 0.082\Delta GNP$ | | |
| Prices and | (0.0060) | (0.13) | (0.0011) | (0.053) | | |
| Interest Rates: | [0.0170] | [0.14] | [0.0010] | [0.055] | | |
| D(DD\|Z) | | | | | | |
| | | $- 0.19\Delta GNP_{-4}$ | $+ 3$ seasonal dummies | | | |
| | | (0.051) | | | | |
| | | (0.044) | | | | |

[a] See notes to Table 10.1.

| | | | AR(·) $F(\cdot,\cdot)$ | Normality $\chi^2(2)$ | ARCH(·) $F(\cdot,\cdot)$ $F(\cdot,\cdot)$ | CHOW–1 $F(\cdot,\cdot)$ | CHOW–2 $F(\cdot,\cdot)$ | Nested in UDL(5) $F(\cdot,\cdot)$ |
|---|---|---|---|---|---|---|---|---|
| | **SER** | **RSS** | | | | | | |
| | | | (4) | | (4) | | | |
| 7 | 0.0047 | 0.00093 | 0.66 | 0.24 | 0.38 | 0.96 | 2.13 | 0.91 |
| | | | (4,38) | | (4,34) | (4,38) | (8,34) | (25,17) |
| | | | (4) | | (4) | | | |
| 98 | 0.0050 | 0.00099 | 0.37 | 1.00 | 1.08 | 0.90 | 1.21 | 0.80 |
| | | | (4,36) | | (4,32) | (4,36) | (10,30) | (17,23) |
| | | | (4) | | (4) | | | |
| .93 | 0.0054 | 0.0012 | 1.14 | 0.27 | 2.34 | 1.48 | 0.87 | 0.53 |
| | | | (4,38) | | (4,34) | (4,38) | (8,34) | (13,21) |
| | | | (4) | | (4) | | | |
| .91 | 0.0057 | 0.0014 | 0.95 | 2.37 | 0.93 | 1.40 | 1.74 | 1.11 |
| | | | (4,39) | | (4,35) | (4,39) | (7,36) | (8,35) |

The top of the table reads: **Summary Statistics**[b]

[b] See notes to Table 10.1.

battery of specification tests described in detail for the complete price regression.

Among the additional variables, interest rates are singled out for special treatment because of the possibility, especially given the *modus operandi* of monetary policy, of substantial interaction between money and interest rates. So, even though no full investigation of the causal direction between interest rates and either money or prices will be undertaken, regressions of both these variables marginal of interest rates are reported.

## 10.4 DIGRESSION: REACTION FUNCTION OR CAUSAL RELATION?

Regressions 2.1 and 2.3 in Table 10.2 have prices as independent variables. The existence of policy reaction functions that change from time to time does not itself pose a problem for our method, but may in fact supply the very sorts of interventions in the money-determination process that yield useful information for causal inference. Still, we must rule out the possibility that the only reason prices ever appeared as independent variables in money regressions was merely because the Federal Reserve had an inflation target and adjusted the money supply in response to price information. Further examination of the baseline regressions suggests that this is not the case.

A "screening" argument, such as we have met in earlier chapters, is relevant here. A Federal Reserve reaction function would have to run from prices through its directly controlled instruments (reserves, the discount rate, and the Federal funds rate) and, finally, through the effects of these instruments on the banking system and the public to the stock of deposits. In that case, if prices were to appear in the money regressions, it would be because prices were proxying for the Federal Reserve's policy instruments. If that were so, then the relationship between demand deposits and these instruments should be closer and more direct than that between demand deposits and prices. If this proves not to be so, we can fairly rule out the reaction function story.[7]

Table 10.3 presents tests of whether adding Federal Reserve policy instruments to those baseline regressions that include prices as regressors makes any difference. The policy instruments are total reserves, the discount rate, and the Federal funds rate. Because the Federal funds rate is available only after 1955.1, all three instruments could be included only if the regression began in 1956.2 (allowing for five lags), two years after the beginning of the baseline period. Therefore, one set of regressions is run over 1956.2–1966.2. The other set uses only total reserves, omitting

---

[7] Cagan (1965, pp. 235–239) employs a similar argument in his study of the money supply.

**Table 10.3. Encompassing Tests for Policy Reaction Functions**

| Regression | | | | | |
|---|---|---|---|---|---|
| 2.1 | 2.3 | plus | Additional Variables | over | Sample Period |
| 1.49 | 1.60 | | Total Reserves | | 1954.1–1966.2 |
| $F(6, 36)$ | $F(6, 36)$ | | | | |
| 1.70 | 2.12 | | Total Reserves, | | 1956.2–1966.2 |
| $F(18, 15)$ | $F(18, 15)$ | | Discount Rate, | | |
| | | | Federal Funds Rate | | |

*Notes*: Each regression adds the current level plus five lags of the noted variables to one of the regressions in Table 10.2 and tests their joint significance. Critical values: $F_{.95}(6, 36)$ = 2.37, $F_{.95}(18, 15)$ = 2.35.

both interest rates, because it is the interaction of the Federal funds rate and the discount rate that is relevant to bank borrowing decisions. It runs the entire baseline period, 1954.1–1966.2.

In no case can we reject the hypothesis at the 5 percent confidence level that the policy instruments may be excluded from the baseline regressions (2.1 and 2.3) plus policy instruments. The baseline regressions therefore *parsimoniously encompass* the less restricted regressions in which they are nested. According to a theorem reported by Hendry and Richard (1987, sec. 6–8) they in turn encompass any regressions *minimally nested* in the less restricted regression.[8] Hence, regressions 2.1 and 2.3 encompass every regression that adds any linear combination of the policy variables to them. The policy variables therefore appear to be redundant, and it is unlikely that prices in 2.1 and 2.3 are related to deposits simply because of a policy reaction function.[9]

## 10.5 OUT-OF-SAMPLE PROJECTIONS

### Backward Projections: 1953.4–1950.1

Table 10.4 presents some summary statistics from the sequential Chow tests projecting the regressions in Table 10.1 backward to 1950.1.

[8] One regression *parsimoniously encompasses* another if it encompasses the other and is nested within the other (Hendry and Richard 1987). Two regressions are *minimally nested* in a third if no variable can be omitted from the third without one or both of the first two failing to be nested in the resulting regression.
[9] An even better test would compare 2.1 and 2.3 not to themselves augmented by the policy variables but to the appropriate UDL(5) augmented by the policy variables. Unfortunately, given only 50 observations in the baseline period, degrees of freedom become a problem.

**Table 10.4. Chow Tests of Structural Stability: Projections Backward 1953.4 to 1950.1**

| | Chow Tests | | | | |
| | Constant Base | Constant Horizon | | One-step Ahead | Scaled |
| Projection of | Break Point$^a$ | Maximum (Date) | Ratio$^b$ | Maximum (Date) | Maximum$^c$ (Date) |
|---|---|---|---|---|---|
| (4.1) Prices Complete (Regression 1.1) | 1952.3 | 24.0 (1951.2) | 0.31 | 92.5 (1951.1) | 22.9 (1951.1) |
| (4.2) Prices Marginal of Money (Regression 1.2) | 1952.3 | 28.8 (1951.2) | 0.31 | 104.5 (1951.1) | 25.9 (1951.1) |
| (4.3) Prices Marginal of Interest Rates (Regression 1.3) | 1952.3 | 44.2 (1951.2) | 0.44 | 108.5 (1951.1) | 27.0 (1951.1) |
| (4.4) Prices Marginal of Money & Interest Rates (Regression 1.4) | 1952.3 | 31.3 (1951.2) | 0.31 | 97.2 (1951.1) | 24.2 (1951.1) |
| (4.5) Money Complete (Regression 2.1) | 1950.2 | 13.6 (1950.2) | 0.25 | 13.6 (1950.1) | 3.4 (1950.1) |
| (4.6) Money Marginal of Prices (Regression 2.2) | 1950.3 | 4.9 (1950.4) | 0.19 | 9.4 (1950.3) | 2.3 (1950.3) |
| (4.7) Money Marginal of Interest Rates (Regression 2.3) | * | 2.9 (1950.2) | 0.00 | 3.5 (1953.1) | 0.9 (1953.1) |
| (4.8) Money Marginal of Prices & Interest Rates (Regression 2.4) | 1951.3 | 2.6 (1952.1) | 0.13 | 6.5 (1951.4) | 1.6 (1951.4) |

*Notes*: Each projection begins with the baseline regression indicated in parentheses and extends the sample starting date backwards one period at a time, reestimating using recursive least squares from 1953.4 to 1950.1 (12 additional observations beyond the baseline sample). The three indicated types of Chow tests are calculated at each step.

$^a$ "Break Point" is the date at which the Chow statistic first exceeded its 5 percent critical value.

$^b$ "Ratio" is the number of violations of the 5 percent critical value divided by the number of observations in the projection period.

$^c$ "Scaled Maximum" is the maximum of the Chow statistics when computed as ratios to their 5 percent critical values.

* Never rejects at the 5 percent critical value.

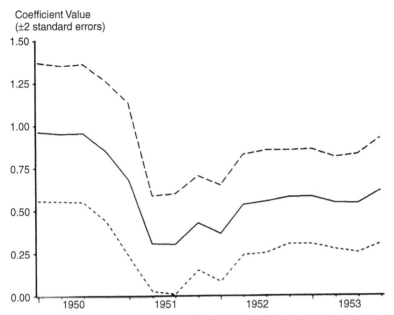

Figure 10.2. Constant in Regression (1.1) Recursively Estimated Backward from 1953.4 to 1950.1 (Projection 4.1). Read from right to left.

The striking thing about the projections of price regressions (4.1–4.4) is their similarity. It is clear, particularly from the one-step-ahead Chow tests, that stability can be rejected in this period for all the price regressions. The break points for the constant-base Chow tests occur at 1952.3 in every case. The maxima for the constant-horizon Chow tests occur at 1951.2 in every case. Figure 10.2 is a typical coefficient plot from the price regressions. The behavior of the constant in the conditional price regression (projection 4.1) is clearly different before 1951.2 than after 1952.2. Plots of the remaining coefficients (not shown) in the four price regressions tell the same story. A few show little change relative to their standard errors; and a few pick up the change only at 1951.2; but most show structural breaks precisely parallel to those in Figure 10.2.

None of the regressions is obviously more stable than the others, and none shows any obvious structural break not common to all of the others. This suggests that we have identified interventions in the price-determination process – a conclusion supported by the institutional record. The structural break at 1951.1 corresponds exactly to the imposition of wage and price controls during the Korean War,

Coefficient Value
(±2 standard errors)

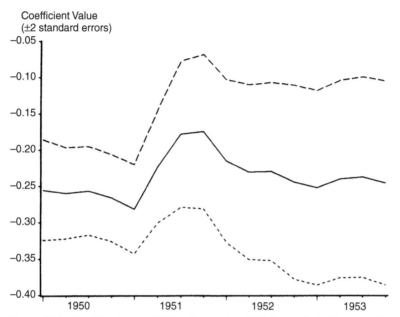

Figure 10.3. Coefficient on $\Delta_4 CPI$ in Regression (2.1) Recursively Estimated Backward from 1953.4 to 1950.1 (Projection 4.5). Read from right to left.

and the break at 1952.2 corresponds to the dismantling of those controls.[10]

The projections of the money regressions (4.5–4.8) tell a different story. The one-step-ahead Chow tests reject parameter stability for every money regression *except* projection 4.7, money marginal of interest rates. While on the constant-base Chow tests the other projections reach break points between 1950.2 and 1951.3, parameter constancy is never rejected for projection 4.7. Similarly, while the constant-horizon Chow statistics for the other regressions reach maxima 1.2 to 3.4 times their 5 percent critical values between 1950.2 and 1952.1, projection 4.7 shows only a borderline rejection at 1953.3 at exactly the 5 percent critical value; parameter stability can be rejected nowhere else.

Most of the coefficients in projection 4.5, the conditional money regression, show some fluctuations but would not be judged unstable

---

[10] The process of dismantling wage and price controls began in 1952.1. Although it did not officially end until 1953.1, it effectively ended in 1952.4 with the resignation of the industrial members of the Wage Board in protest over the board's failure to prevent an increase in wages in the steel industry. See Council of Economic Advisers (1951–1953).

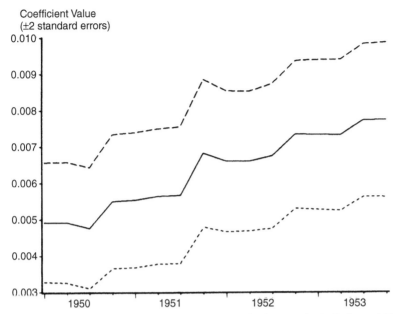

Figure 10.4. Coefficient on $DD_{-1}$ in Regression (2.4) Recursively Estimated Backward from 1953.4 to 1950.1 (Projection 4.8). Read from right to left.

given their standard errors. The coefficient on $\Delta_4 CPI$ (Figure 10.3) however, clearly changes between 1951.3 and 1951.1. The coefficient on $\Delta CPI_{-4}$ (not shown) is similar.

In contrast, the coefficients in projection 4.6, money marginal of prices, appear to be stable within relatively large standard-error bands. The coefficients on $\Delta(LR - SR)_{-3}$ and $(LR - SR)_{-5}$ become insignificant near the beginning of the sample. Thus, even though stability is clearly rejected on the Chow tests, it shows up as a general increase in the variance not in a well-defined shift in the means of the coefficients.

Figure 10.4 shows that the coefficient on $DD_{-1}$ in projection 4.8, money marginal of prices and interest rates, shifts gradually but significantly over the projection period. There is no single date that can be localized as the point of structural breakdown. The coefficient on $\Delta GNP_{-4}$ (not shown) behaves similarly. The remaining coefficients are stable given their standard errors.

Figure 10.5 shows the coefficient on $CPI_{-5}$, the *most* unstable coefficient from projection 4.7, money marginal of interest rates. Except for the borderline significant shift between 1953.3 and 1953.1, the coefficient is stable and well determined statistically. The remaining coefficients (not shown) are even more stable.

Coefficient Value
(±2 standard errors)

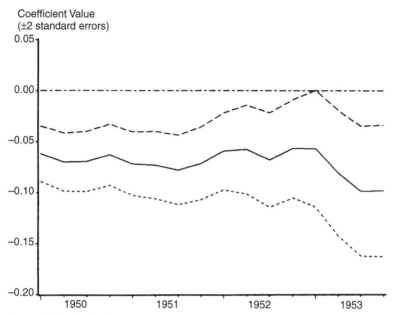

Figure 10.5. Coefficient on $CPL_5$ in Regression (2.3) Recursively Estimated Backward from 1953.4 to 1950.1 (Projection 4.7). Read from right to left.

Credit controls were imposed in 1950.3, tightened in 1951.1, and removed gradually over 1951.4 to 1952.2 (Council of Economic Advisers 1950–53). When added to the fact that marginalizing with respect to interest rates is stabilizing, these interventions in the interest-rate-determination process suggest that regression 2.3 should be regarded as the conditional model. In that case, the fact that its projection (4.7) is stable, while marginalizing further with respect of prices (projection 4.8) reintroduces instability, appears to provide precisely the sort of discrimination between a conditional and marginal model needed to indicate causal direction. The timing of the structural breaks in projection 4.8 is unclear. If, however, we judge by the constant-base Chow test, then the break at 1951.3 corresponds approximately to the introduction of wage and price controls. Precise timing may be unclear in this case because the structure of relative prices changed significantly and continuously over this period – especially with a major boom and bust in commodity prices and different degrees of stringency in wage and price controls. Figure 10.1 shows dramatic shifts in relative prices just at the points at which the price regressions show structural instability. The rise in the *PPI* relative to the *CPI* and oil prices in 1951.1 and its recovery in 1952.4 is compatible with a wage and price regime that controlled retail prices more

F-statistic
(scaled by 5% critical value)

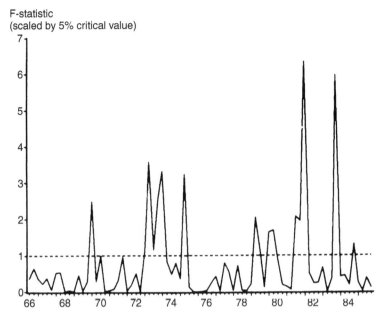

Figure 10.6. One-step-ahead Chow Statistics from the Recursive Estimation of Regression (1.1) Forward from 1966.3 to 1985.4 (Projection 5.1).

stringently than wholesale prices and became gradually less stringent over time (Council of Economic Advisers 1951, pp. 144–146). The rise in import and crude prices relative to the prices of final goods may reflect controls as well, but mostly reflects an exogenous boom in world commodity prices. Not all of these changes would necessarily show up as dramatic breakdowns of *CPI* regressions. Yet they may still have had major differential effects on the alternative money regressions. The weight of evidence on the basis of general stability is in favor of the view that prices cause money and interest rates do not: Money regressions become more stable if interest rates are omitted and less stable if prices are omitted.

**Forward Projections: 1966.3–1985.4**

Table 10.5 presents summary statistics from the sequential Chow tests based on projecting the regressions in Table 10.1 forward over 1966.3 to 1985.4.

Consider first the price regressions (projections 5.1–5.4). The one-step-ahead Chow statistics indicate that none of the regressions is stable across the entire projection period. Figure 10.6 is a plot of the one-step-ahead Chow statistics for projection 5.1, the complete price regression.

**Table 10.5. Chow Tests of Structural Stability: Projections Forward from 1966.3 to 1985.4**

| | | Chow Tests | | | | |
|---|---|---|---|---|---|---|
| | | **Constant Base** | **Constant Horizon** | | **One-step Ahead** | **Scaled** |
| | | **Break Point**[a] | **Maximum (Date)** | **Ratio**[b] | **Maximum (Date)** | **Maximum**[c] **(Date)** |
| 5.1 | Prices Complete (Regression 1.1) | 1970.3 | 10.0 (1969.4) | 0.20 | 24.8 (1982.1) | 6.3 (1982.1) |
| 5.2 | Prices Marginal of Money (Regression 1.2) | 1973.2 | 8.4 (1972.4) | 0.22 | 15.5 (1974.1) | 3.9 (1974.1) |
| 5.3 | Prices Marginal of Interest (Regression 1.3) | 1967.1 | 13.5 (1971.2) | 0.24 | 48.6 (1983.4) | 12.4 (1983.4) |
| 5.4 | Prices Marginal of Money & Interest (Regression 1.4) | 1973.3 | 10.4 (1972.4) | 0.22 | 21.9 (1983.4) | 5.6 (1983.4) |
| 5.5 | Money Complete (Regression 2.1) | 1966.3 | 6.1 (1966.3) | 0.20 | 32.3 (1981.2) | 8.2 (1981.2) |
| 5.6 | Money Marginal of Prices (Regression 2.2) | 1966.3 | 5.1 (1978.1) | 0.17 | 31.0 (1981.2) | 7.9 (1981.2) |
| 5.7 | Money Marginal of Interest Rates (Regression 2.3) | 1967.3 | 6.1 (1967.1) | 0.19 | 11.9 (1975.4) | 3.0 (1975.4) |
| 5.8 | Money Marginal of Prices & Interest Rates (Regression 2.4) | 1966.3 | 5.3 (1974.4) | 0.24 | 18.2 (1979.2) | 4.6 (1979.2) |

*Notes*: Each projection begins with the baseline regression indicated in parentheses and extends the sample starting date forwards one period at a time, reestimating using recursive least squares from 1966.3 to 1985.4 (78 additional observations beyond the baseline sample). The three indicated types of Chow tests are calculated at each step.
[a] "Break Point" is the date at which the Chow statistic first exceeded its 5 percent critical value.
[b] "Ratio" is the number of violations of the 5 percent critical value divided by the number of observations in the projection period.
[c] "Scaled Maximum" is the maximum of the Chow statistics when computed as ratios to their 5 percent critical values.

It shows the particular difficulty of fitting the periods from 1973 to 1975 and 1979–1984. Inspection of the analogous plots for the other price regressions (not shown) reveals that this is a common feature.

The fact that all price regressions show a similar pattern suggests a break in the price-determination process. One might think that Nixon's price controls could explain the earlier break; but the timing is not quite right. Phase three of the price controls, which *relaxed* controls somewhat, was adopted in 1973.1, and phase two, which was stricter, was reimposed in 1973.2. If the common structural breaks in the price equations are to be attributed to price controls, why is there no indication of a common break corresponding to the introduction of the stricter phase one (1971.3) or phase two (1971.4)?

A more likely source for these common breaks, which seems to correspond more closely to the apparent timing, is the massive change in the structure of relative prices associated with the oil price increase starting 1974.1 and the somewhat earlier commodity price boom. Figure 10.1 shows massive changes in the ratios of import prices to the GNP deflator and in crude to final goods prices that correspond closely to the indicated structural breaks and can be construed to be violations of the *ceteris paribus* conditions implicit in the *CPI* equations estimated here.

A similar explanation would easily account for the later break. Oil prices rose massively beginning in mid-1979, peaked in 1981.3, and fell substantially until the end of our sample. There were, to be sure, events in the monetary sector – particularly the Federal Reserve's changes in operating procedures in 1979 and 1982 – that might also be thought of as sources of such structural breaks, but for the fact that the breaks are common across all four price regressions.

Although it seems clear that there are interventions in the price-determination process that are common across price regressions, it is still possible to discriminate among them. Figure 10.6 shows that the complete price regression probably breaks down before 1973.1 as well. Inspection of the plots of the one-step-ahead Chow statistics for the other price regressions (not shown) reveals that the regression marginal of interest rates (projection 5.3) shows signs of structural break not only before the first common break (1973.1–1975.2) but after it as well. The regressions marginal of money (projection 5.2) and of money and interest rates (projection 5.4) show no signs of breaks other than the two common breaks.

Using the length of time beyond the baseline period before a constant-base Chow test indicates rejection as one measure of general stability suggests that the price regression marginal of money and interest rates (projection 5.4) is the most stable, followed by that marginal of money (projection 5.2) and the complete price regression (projection 5.1), with that marginal of interest rates the least stable. The maxima of the constant-horizon Chow statistics can be ranked by date identically.

Figure 10.7 plots the constant from the complete price regression (projection 5.1). It shows a pattern common to most of the coefficients in all of the price regressions: a hump that peaks about 1972.4. Judging

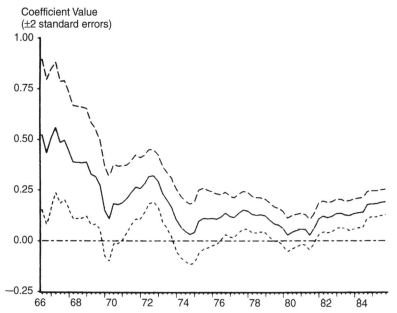

Figure 10.7. Constant in Regression (1.1) Recursively Estimated Forward from 1966.3 to 1985.4 (Projection 5.10).

by the standard error bands, the constant is clearly different after 1975.2 than before 1973.1, and clearly different at 1985.4 than at 1979.1. This is typical of other coefficients in other projections, and confirms our general conclusions about interventions in the price-determination process. Figure 10.7 also shows, however, that the behavior of the constant in the complete-price regression is different before 1969.1 than after 1970.1. The coefficient on $\Delta_2 M_{-1}$ in projection 5.1 (not shown) is similar. The coefficient on the error-correction term, $(CPI-M)_{-5}$, in projection 5.3 (Figure 10.8) shows a somewhat earlier but similar shift in behavior. The constant in projection 5.3 is similar. Inspection of the coefficient plots for the remaining regressions indicates nothing similar.

The evidence therefore suggests that there are two common interventions in the price-determination process, and that regressions which include money show structural breaks even before the first intervention. Both examination of coefficient plots and more general measures of structural stability confirm that the omission of money from price regressions is stabilizing.

The forward projections of the money regressions (5.5–5.8) are somewhat trickier to interpret than those for the price regressions. The one-step-ahead Chow statistics indicate that none of the four is stable. The

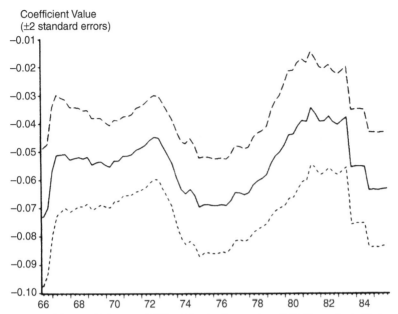

Figure 10.8. Coefficient on $(CPI - M)_{-5}$ in Regression (1.3) Recursively Estimated Forward from 1966.3 to 1985.4 (Projection 5.3).

maxima for the statistic for both the complete money stock (projection 5.5.) and the regression marginal of prices (projection 5.6) occur at 1981.2 and are twice as large as the maxima for the other two regressions and 6 to 15 times as large as the statistics for the other two regressions at 1981.2. This is suggestive of instability associated with the interest-rate-determination process, since only projections 5.5 and 5.6 include interest rates. Figure 10.9, which plots the coefficient on $\Delta_4 SR_{-1}$ in projection 5.5, makes the point dramatically. The coefficient shows two distinct breaks; the second one coincides with maximum for the one-step-ahead statistic. The plot of the coefficient on $\Delta_4 SR_{-1}$ for projection 5.6 (not shown) is nearly identical. The other coefficients on interest rate variables in those regressions show similar though less dramatic behavior. Such instability, common to money regressions both with and without prices as a conditioning variable, suggests that, as with the backward projections, we should regard the regression of money marginal of interest rates as the conditional distribution.

The constant-base Chow tests place a break point for the regression of money marginal of interest rates (projection 5.7) at 1967.3. The Chow tests reject constancy at increasingly high levels for every period thereafter. For the regression of money marginal of prices and interest rates

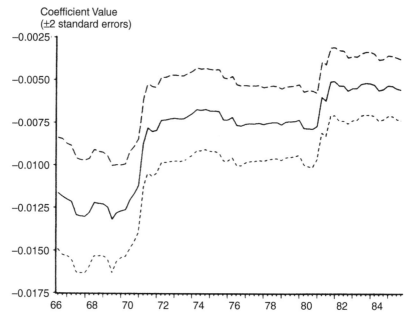

Figure 10.9. Coefficient on $\Delta_4 SR_{-1}$ in Regression (2.1) Recursively Estimated Forward from 1966.3 to 1985.4 (Projection 5.5).

(projection 5.8), constancy is rejected immediately at 1966.3 and at increasingly high levels for every period but one thereafter. The constant-base Chow tests for the other two money regressors also reject stability in 1966.3 and thereafter.

Clearly the omission of interest rates is a stabilizing factor. The structural break in three of the regressions at 1966.3 suggests that a shock to the interest-rate-determination process is the source. This would clearly need further confirmation from a study of interest-rate regressions, although this is outside the scope of our current study. The institutional record suggests that this is a plausible hypothesis. The Federal Reserve instituted a "credit crunch" in 1966.3, driving interest rates up to the point that regulation Q ceilings on savings and time deposits were binding. The scope of regulation Q ceilings was widened to cover savings and loan deposits. Banks were urged to restrain loan supply. And special rules were adopted for the administration of the discount window. By 1967.2, the credit crunch was over, and special arrangements were dismantled (Wojnilower 1980; Board of Governors 1967–1968).

The fact that all regressions indicate a structural break by 1967.3 suggests that the source of the instability is the money-determination process.[11] It is more difficult to find a likely source for this break in the institutional record. However, it should be noted that the credit crunch itself was a watershed. Before the 1966.3, regulation Q had been allowed to bind only sporadically, when monetary policy was tight. Afterwards, regulation Q was binding most of the time until it was finally eliminated in the mid-1980s.

The different performance of projections 5.7 and 5.8 before 1967.3 favors the view that omitting prices from a money regression is destabilizing. But this is a weak reed. The coefficient plots provide additional evidence. Figure 10.10 plots the coefficient on the error-correction term,

[11] It will surely occur to many readers that the period of the "missing money" in which U.S. money stock equations break down is not until 1973, so that the breakdown of the regressions reported here might be simply misspecification. Furthermore, some authors (e.g., Baba et al. 1992 and Rose 1985) report parameter constancy even across the 1973 period. It should be recalled that the original Goldfeld (1976) missing-money paper as well as Baba et al., Rose, and the survey by Gordon (1984) estimate up through 1973. The most compelling evidence for misspecification rather than structural break would be to show that there exists an encompassing regression that remains stable across the periods that we have identified as structural breaks. Direct comparison of any of these studies with ours is not easy since they all take $M1$ rather than its demand deposit component to be the dependent variable and they all use information outside of our baseline period in formulating their models. Because of the difficulties of obtaining the precise data and other relevant information, we do not attempt to reproduce all of the studies. But to illustrate that the existence of these "stable" regressions is not necessarily evidence against our results, consider Rose's (1985, p. 446) equation 7 and his version of Goldfeld's equation (Rose 1985, p. 441, eq. 2). I was unable to obtain the original data from the author; and, instead, had to follow the indications in his data appendix and use published sources. The Goldfeld equation shows roughly the right magnitudes on the coefficients and all the right signs, but has a standard error of regression substantially less than that reported by Rose. Rose's own equation shows roughly the correct magnitudes and signs for most regressors, but the cointegration term is positive rather than negative, and its standard error of regression is somewhat higher than reported by Rose. (On the difficulties of replication of econometric results, see Dewald, Thursby, and Anderson 1986). When the Goldfeld model is reestimated over the baseline period, it can be rejected against the corresponding UDL(5) with $F(20, 27) = 2.42$. Rose's model cannot be rejected against UDL(5) with $F(17, 23) = 1.85$. Direct comparison with our regressions in Table 10.2 is not possible since the dependent variables are different. It is worth noting, however, that both the Goldfeld and Rose regressions have higher percentage standard errors than any of our money regressions, and that both reject stability on the Chow test at 1966.3, like all of the regressions reported in Table 10.4, except money marginal of interest rates. When Chow tests are run for later periods, Goldfeld's equation shows stability up to 1973.4 – i.e., until the period of the missing money; while Rose's is stable up to 1979.2, which is compatible with what Rose himself reports. It therefore appears that both equations provide further evidence of a structural break at 1966.3 in equations like our complete money stock, and this despite the fact that Rose's equation appears to be stable across the period of the missing money when its initial estimation period ends in 1973.4.

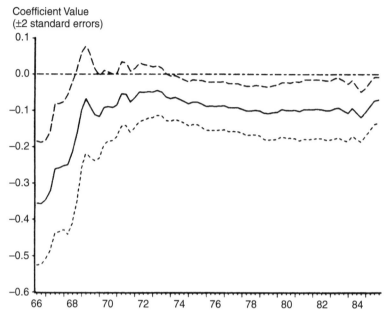

Figure 10.10. Coefficient on $(DD - \frac{1}{2}(GNP + CPI)_{-5})$ in Regression (2.3) Recursively Estimated Forward from 1966.3 to 1985.4 (Projection 5.7).

$(DD - \frac{1}{2}(GNP + CPI)_{-5})$, from the regression of money marginal of interest rates (projection 5.7). The plot clearly reflects the structural break common to all the money regressions early on. After 1969.2, however, the coefficient is very stable. Every coefficient but one in projection 5.7 shows analogous behavior. The exception is the coefficient on $\Delta DD_{-3}$ (not shown), which again shows the early common structural break but then drifts toward statistical insignificance over the sample.

In contrast, Figure 10.11 shows that the coefficient on $\Delta DD_{-1}$ from the regression marginal of prices and interest rates (projection 5.3) drifts around over sample. Casual visual inspection suggests that its most dramatic change occurs in early 1974, about the time of the oil crisis. The plots of the coefficients in projection 5.8 are again, with a single exception, analogous. The coefficient on $\Delta GNP$ (not shown) is fairly stable albeit with large standard errors, while, far from dramatic, the evidence favors the view that the omission of prices is destabilizing.

**Patterns of Stability**

Taking all the evidence together from the two sets of recursions, a consistent and surprising pattern emerges: Money regressions marginal of

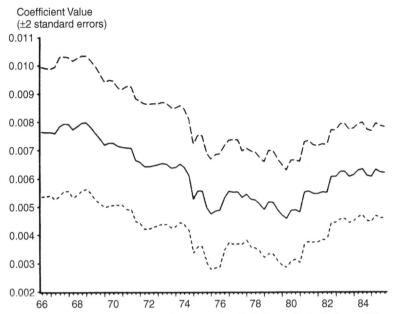

Figure 10.11. Coefficient on $DD_{-1}$ in Regression (2.4) Recursively Estimated Forward from 1966.3 to 1985.4 (Projection 5.8).

prices are less stable than money regressions conditional on prices, and price regressions marginal of money are more stable than price regressions conditional on money. On balance, this supports the view that prices cause money, and that money does not cause prices.

The projections of price regressions in both periods before and after the baseline seem clearly to reflect known interventions in the price-determination process. While there appears to be little evidence to discriminate among the price regressions in the earlier period, there is some evidence in the later period to suggest that marginalizing with respect to money is stabilizing at precisely the points at which the money regressions indicate a common intervention. The interaction of interest rates with the other variables in the price regressions appears complicated and potentially confusing. It is certainly worthy of further detailed investigation.

In contrast, the evidence of the money regressions appears more clear cut: Marginalizing with respect to interest rates stabilizes the projections, and further marginalizing with respect to prices destabilizes the projections. This is most clear-cut in the earlier period in which there do not appear to be any interventions in the money-determination process to muddy the waters. In the later period, the balance of evidence clearly supports this view, although the fact that there appears to be a common monetary intervention early in the projection period makes interpretation somewhat more difficult.

### 10.6  DOES *CURRENCY* CAUSE PRICES?

The money variable in our price regressions is the Federal Reserve's *M1*. Theoretical work by Fama (1980) and empirical work by King and Plosser (1984) suggest that although demand deposits do not influence prices, currency does. If they are correct, using *M1* as the money variable may mask the causal role of currency. To check whether we have been misled, the complete price equation was reestimated over the original baseline period (1954.1–1966.2) with the current and five lags of currency as additional regressors. The test of whether or not they are statistically significant is a test of the restriction that currency and demand deposits enter the complete price equation with the same coefficients. With $F(6,33) = 0.54$, the null of common coefficients cannot be rejected at any conventional level of significance. It would appear, therefore, that we are correct to treat *M1* as a whole and not to separate out the influences of demand deposits and currency. The evidence against money causing prices is thus also evidence against currency causing prices.

### 10.7  SUMMARY AND CONCLUSIONS

What economists, statisticians or, for that matter, laymen mean when they ask, "does *A* cause *B*?" is fraught with difficulty. One thing that seems often to be meant, however, is, were one to make *A* happen, would *B* also happen? Does control of the supply of money give us control of prices as well? The structural approach to causality is well adapted to addressing this question.

Applying our general strategy to money, prices, and interest rates in the United States from 1950 to 1985 produces a somewhat surprising result: The evidence supports the view that prices cause money, and not that money causes prices.

The limited scope of the investigation may be questioned. If only the range of possible causal interactions had been expanded to include more fully the role of interest rates or the role of real variables and so forth, the results might have been different. To this criticism, there is no answer except that every study must be circumscribed. In the case of interest rates, for example, to have investigated their role as fully as we have money and prices would have more than doubled the size of the investigation. And while the precise role of interest rates remains unclear, the evidence is that whether or not interest rates are included, money regressions are more stable with prices as regressors than without, and price regressions are more stable without money as regressors than with. Our main conclusions seem to be robust. The limited nature of the present investigation simply calls for further research along these same lines – a highly desirable thing in itself.

Our results are clearly antimonetarist. But they are also limited. Monetarism can be thought of as a set of beliefs: The money supply is exogenous and in the control of the central bank; the demand for money is stable; money is neutral in the long run; and the short-run channels connecting money to prices and output are direct and not mediated through financial markets (see Friedman 1974; Friedman and Schwartz 1982, ch. 2).

This study does not directly address controllability of the money supply; that would require examination of the causal links between the Federal Reserve's instruments – reserves, the discount rate, and the federal funds rate – and the monetary aggregates, such as *M1*.

Many studies, not just ours, have given reason to doubt that money-demand functions are stable (e.g., Judd and Scadding 1982). Our preferred partition of the joint probability distribution of money and prices involves a price regression with money not appearing as a regressor. The preferred money regression includes prices but not interest rates as regressors. Regression 2.3, which omits interest rates, shows a long-run price elasticity with respect to nominal income of only one-half, rejecting neutrality.

Finally, and most directly, our results point to an absence of a *direct* causal linkage between money and prices, which clearly contradicts strict monetarism. Notice, however, that we have not thoroughly examined the linkages between real GNP and money and prices, and we have only partly examined the linkages between interest rates and money and prices. It is therefore possible to maintain that our results are correct but that money affects prices through indirect channels. Such a position might be called monetarist by some, but it certainly is not the classic monetarism of Milton Friedman.

Details aside, the central claim of monetarism is often painted with a broad brush: "The central fact is that inflation is always and everywhere a monetary phenomenon. Historically, substantial changes in prices have always occurred together with substantial changes in the quantity of money relative to output." (Friedman 1968a, pp. 105–6; cf. Lucas 1977, pp. 232–33). Although our study covers a limited period and lacks the historical sweep of Friedman and Schwartz's (1963a, 1982) research, it is consistent with the monetarist observation, although not with the monetarist interpretation of that observation. Our preferred causal ordering (prices cause money; money does not cause prices) would generate a consistently high correlation between money and prices in the long run.

Everyone, including Friedman, recognizes that one cannot infer causal direction from such a correlation. Friedman and Schwartz examined the consistently high correlation of money and prices across large institutional changes. But, hitherto no one has examined the *relative* stability of alternative conditional and marginal distributions, which provides a basis for discriminating between a high correlation due to money causing prices and one due to prices causing money.

Our results partly, although not completely, support the views of some advocates of real business cycles. Like them, we find that prices (nominal income) do not cause demand deposits (inside money). Unlike them, we do not find evidence that currency (outside money) causes prices.

The empirical results presented in this and the previous chapter are substantive. They also, and perhaps more importantly, illustrate one sort of evidence interpretable in the light of the structural approach to causality. Clearly, there is more work to do on the causal linkages among macroeconomic variables; and, clearly, other sorts of evidence may be causally relevant. But the evidence of the three case studies is that this is one fruitful way to proceed.

**APPENDIX. DATA: SOURCES AND DEFINITIONS**

The basic regression variables used in this chapter are defined as follows:

$CPI$ = $\log(PRICE)$
$DD$ = $\log(M1 - CASH)$
$GNP$ = $\log(NOMGNP/PRICE)$
$LR$ = $100[\log(1 + (LONG/100)\ TAX)]$ for money regressions; and
    = $LONG$ for price regressions (i.e., $LR$ is an after-tax rate in the money regressions and a before-tax rate in the price regressions)
$M$ = $\log(M1)$
$SR$ = $100[\log(1 + (SHORT/100)\ TAX)]$ for money regressions; and
    = $SHORT$ for price regressions (i.e., $SR$ is an after-tax rate in the money regressions and a before-tax rate in the price regressions)
$W$ = $\log(WAGE)$

The source variables for the regression variables follow. All variables are quarterly and not seasonally adjusted. Where the original sources give monthly data, averages of monthly data are used.

*CASH*: "Currency component of the Money Stock"
Billions of dollars
1948–1985

Board of Governors of the Federal Reserve System, *Banking and Monetary Statistics* 1941–1970, p. 20, Table 1.1B, "currency component" column for 1948–1958; *Money Stock Revisions*, March 1986, Table 4 for 1959–1985.

*CORP*: "Corporate bonds, Moody's Aaa"
Percent per annum
1948–1985
Board of Governors of the Federal Reserve System, Banking and Monetary Statistics, 1941–1970, p. 720, Table 12.12A, for 1948–1970; Board of Governors of the Federal Reserve System, *Annual Statistical Digest*, 1970–1979, p. 162, Table 22A, line 33, for 1971–1979; *Annual Statistical Digest* 1980, p. 76, Table 25A, line 33, for 1980; *Annual Statistical Digest* 1981, p. 80, Table 26A, line 34, for 1981; Board of Governors of the Federal Reserve System, *Federal Reserve Bulletin*, (68)4, April 1982, p. A27, Table 1.35, line 34, for Jan.–Mar. 1982; (68)7, July 1982, p. A27, Table 1.35, line 34, for Apr.–June. 1982; (68)9, Sept. 1982, p. A27, Table 1.35, line 34, for Jul.–Aug. 1982; (69)1, Jan. 1983, p. A28, Table 1.35, line 34, for Sept.–Dec. 1982; *Annual Statistical Digest* 1983, p. 84, Table 25A, line 35, for 1983; *Annual Statistical Digest* 1984, p. 75, Table 22A, line 35, for 1984; *Federal Reserve Bulletin*, (71)6, June 1985, p. A24, Table 1.35, line 35, for Jan.–Mar. 1985; (71)10, Oct. 1985, p. A24, Table 1.35, line 35, for Apr.–Jul. 1985; (71)12, Dec. 1985, p. A24, Table 1.35, line 35, for Aug. 1985; (72)3, Mar. 1986, p. A24, Table 1.35, line 35, for Sept.–Dec. 1985.

*LONG*: "Three-to-Five year issues"
Percent per annum
Monthly and Quarterly
Seasonally (TSP) and Nonseasonally Adjusted
1948–1985
Board of Governors of the Federal Reserve System, *Banking and Monetary Statistics* 1941–1970, p. 694, Table 12.7A, for 1948–1970; Board of Governors of the Federal Reserve System, *Annual Statistical Digest* 1970–1979, p. 162, Table 22A, line 28, for 1971–1979; *Annual Statistical Digest* 1980, p. 76, Table 25A, line 28, for 1980; *Annual Statistical Digest* 1981, p. 80, Table 26A, line 29, for 1981; Board of Governors of the Federal Reserve System, *Federal Reserve Bulletin* (68)4, April 1982, p. A27, Table 1.35, line 29, for Jan.–Mar. 1982; (68)7, July 1982, p. A27, Table 1.35, line 29, for Apr.–June. 1982; (68)9, September 1982, p. A27, Table 1.35, line 29, for Jul–Aug. 1982, (69)1, January 1983, p. A28, Table 1.35, line 29, for Sept.–Dec. 1982; *Annual Statistical Digest* 1983, p. 84, Table 25A, line 30, for 1983; *Annual Statistical Digest* 1984, p. 75, Table 22A, line 30, for 1984; *Federal Reserve Bulletin*, (71)6, June 1985,

p. A24, Table 1.35, line 30, for Jan.–Mar. 1985; (71)10, October 1984, P. A24, Table 1.35, line 30, for Apr.–Jul. 1985; (71)12, December 1985, p. A24, Table 1.35, line 30, for August 1985; (72)3, March 1986, p. A24, Table 1.35, line 30, for Sept.–Dec. 1985.

$M1 = M1O - 2.4$ for 1948.1–1958.4

$= M1N$ for 1959.1–1985.4

($2.4 billion is the difference between $M1O$ and $M1N$ at 1959.1)

*M1N* "M1: currency, travelers checks, demand deposits, and other checkable deposits."

Billions of dollars

1959–1985

Money Stock measures and Liquid Assets, Table 1, for 1959–1985.

*M1O*: "Money supply, total" (Old measure)

Billions of dollars

1948–1970

Board of Governors of the Federal Reserve System, *Banking and Monetary Statistics* 1941–1970, p. 20, Table 1.1B, for 1948–1970.

*MUNI*: "State and Local government bonds, Moody's Aaa"

Percent per annum

1948–1985

Board of Governors of the Federal Reserve System, *Banking and Monetary Statistics*, 1941–1970, p. 720, Table 12.12A, for 1948–1970; Board of Governors of the Federal Reserve System, *Annual Statistical Digest*, 1970–1979, p. 162, Table 22A, line 29, for 1971–1979; Annual Statistical Digest 1980, p. 76, Table 25A, line 29, for 1980; *Annual Statistical Digest* 1981, p. 80, Table 26A, line 30, for 1981; Board of Governors of the Federal Reserve System, *Federal Reserve Bulletin*, (68)4, April 1982, p. A27, Table 1.35, line 30, for Jan.–Mar. 1982; (68)7, July 1982, p. A27, Table 1.35, line 30, for Apr.–Jun. 1982; 68(9), Sept. 1982, p. A27, Table 1.35, line 30, for Jul.–Aug. 1982; (69)1, Jan. 1983, p. A28, Table 1.35, line 30, for Sept.–Dec. 1982; *Annual Statistical Digest* 1983, p. 84, Table 25A, line 31, for 1983; *Annual Statistical Digest* 1984, p. 75, Table 22A, line 31, for 1984; *Federal Reserve Bulletin*, (71)6, June 1985, p. A24, Table 1.35, line 31, for Jan.–Mar. 1985; (71)10, October 1985, p. A24, Table 1.35, line 31, for Apr.–Jul. 1985; (71)12, December 1985, p. A24, Table 1.35, line 31, for August 1985; (72)3, March 1986, p. A24, Table 1.35, line 31, for Sept.–Dec. 1985.

*NOMGNP*: "Gross National Product"

Billions of dollars

1948–1985

U.S. Department of Commerce, Survey of Current Business 66(7), July 1986, pp. 406–410, Tables 9.1.

PRICE: "Consumer price index for all urban consumers"
Index: 1967 = 100
1948–1985
U.S. Department of Commerce, Bureau of Economic Analysis, *Business Conditions Digest*, (25)4, April 1985, p. 101, for 1951–1984; U.S. Department of Commerce, *Survey of Current Business*, 66(2), p. S-5, for 1985.

*TAX = MUNI/CORP*

SHORT: "Three-month T-bills, market yield"
Percent per annum
1948–1985
Board of Governors of the Federal Reserve System, *Banking and Monetary Statistics* 1941–1970, p. 694, Table 12.7A, for 1948–1970; Board of Governors of the Federal Reserve System, *Annual Statistical Digest* 1970–1979, p. 162, Table 22A, line 13, for 1971–1979; *Annual Statistical Digest* 1980, p. 76, Table 25A, line 13, for 1980; *Annual Statistical Digest* 1981, p. 80, Table 26A, line 14, for 1981; Board of Governors of the Federal Reserve System, *Federal Reserve Bulletin*, (68)4, April 1982, p. A27, Table 1.35, line 14, for Jan.–Mar. 1982; (68)7, July 1982, p. A27, Table 1.35, line 14, for Apr.–June. 1982; (68)9, September 1982, p. A27, Table 1.35, line 14, for Jul–Aug. 1982; (69)1, January 1983, p. A28, Table 1.35, line 14, for Sept.–Dec. 1982; *Annual Statistical Digest* 1983, p. 84, Table 25A, line 15, for 1983; *Annual Statistical Digest* 1984, p. 75, Table 22A, line 15, for 1984; *Federal Reserve Bulletin*, (71)6, June 1985, p. A24, Table 1.35, line 15, for Jan.–Mar. 1985; (71)10, October 1985, p. A24, Table 1.35, line 15, for Apr.–Jul. 1985; (71)12, December 1985, p. A24, Table 1.35, line 15, for August 1985; (72)3, March 1986, p. A24, Table 1.35, line 15, for Sept.–Dec. 1985.

WAGE: "Average hourly earnings excluding overtime per production worker on payrolls of manufacturing estab., total"
Dollars
1948–1985
United States Department of Commerce, Bureau of Economic Analysis, *Business Statistics*, 1979 ed., p. 228, for 1948–1974; 1982 ed., p. 170, for 1975–1978, and p. 54 for 1979–1982; U.S. Department of Commerce, Survey of Current Business, (64)1, January 1984, p S-12, for 1983; (65)1, January 1985, p. S-12, for 1984; (66)2, February 1986, p. S-12, for 1985.

All data for Figure 10.1 are from CITIBASE: Citibank economics database 1946–1988.04, New York, Citibank, N.A.

All data are quarterly and not seasonally adjusted. Where the original data are monthly, the data used are for the last month in the quarter.

*CPI*: "Consumer Price Index: All Urban Consumers: All Items," Series *PZUNEW*

*CRUDE PRICES*: "Producer Price Index: By Stage of Processing: Crude Materials for Further Processing," Series *PWCMP*

*FINAL PRICES*: "Producer Price Index: By Stage of Processing: Finished Consumer Goods," Series *PWF*

*GNP DEFLATOR*: "Implicit Price Deflator for GNP," Series *GD*

*IMPORT PRICES*: "Implicit Price Deflator for Imports," Series *GDIM*

*OIL PRICE*: "Producer Price Index: Selected Commodity Groupings: Crude Petroleum," Series *PW561*

# 11

## Causality in Macroeconomics

> Well, you can't see elec-a-tricity a movin' on the line.
> How in the world can you doubt it, when you can see it
> shine.
> When you get salvation, the spirit you can feel.
> Don't have to have nobody to tell you that it's real.
>
> – Jimmy Murphy, "Electricity" – a Bluegrass song

In the front material of *The Seven Pillars of Wisdom*, T. E. Lawrence remarks

Half-way through the labour of an index to [*The Seven Pillars*] I recalled that I had never used the index of a book fit to read. Who would insult his *Decline and Fall* by consulting it just upon a specific point?

He then offers the reader a synopsis as an adequate fingerpost to his complex history of the Arab Revolt. For myself, I feel about synopses – at least the ones that form the final chapter of a complicated work – in much the same way that Lawrence felt about indexes. Yet, we are far down river from Hume, and an empirical case study hardly seems like the fitting end to our journey. To restate the main themes of the book in a short compass might better mark our resting place and give the reader some aid in placing the various passages and detours of the journey into a connected vista.

Hume the philosopher was a causal pessimist – skeptical of any claim that we could ever know what causality is "in the objects." Hume the macroeconomist was a causal optimist, ready to use causal language and causal knowledge to guide policy. We have sided throughout this book with the optimistic Hume. Our position stands in contrast to much of the post-Humean tradition, which holds that, if cause is ineffable in itself, perhaps it can be reduced to something, such as the facts of probabilistic association, that we understand better. Our argument is that the

reductionist program is not tenable. The reductionist literature on causality has been shaped by a set of causal intuitions that suggest corrections
and revisions to any causal reduction that is felt to go wrong. These intuitions are the shadow of the idea of causal structure. Causal structures
are revealed in the way things work. The causal reductionist account
envisages a world populated by Hume's peasants who know only that
the watch does not work; the structural causal account is populated by
Hume's artisans, who if they do not know for sure that it is a grain of
sand that has stopped the movement of the watch, at least seek answers
of that sort.

   We take the idea of structure to be the fundamental notion of causality. It is its essence, not a reduction: The causal relations among the
elements of a structure are what they are and not another thing – not
constant conjunction, not probabilities, not time order, not incremental
predictability, not noninvertible functional relations. They are what
Hume identified as the necessary connections between things. Hume's
mistake was in thinking that we could know nothing about that connection absent a sensory experience of it. There are other ways to learn than
by direct acquaintance, and we have ideas about, and knowledge of,
many things that we have never sensed: "You don't have to see elec-a-
tricty a movin' on the line. . . ." And, indeed, we know a great deal about
the electron, though no one has ever seen one.

   The two principal questions of the book are:

   • First, how can the notion of structure be articulated adequately to
     make explicit the implicit causal account that shaped so many
     reductive efforts?
   • And, second, how does causality fit into macroeconomic analysis?

The questions are not independent. Our concern with the second question conditioned our answer to the first. Economists and econometricians
use the language of equations and variables. The account of causal order
developed by Herbert Simon and extended in the early chapters is
appealing in large measure because it uses economists' language. There
are other ways to make many of the same points. For example, the graph-
theoretic accounts of Judea Pearl and Clark Glymour *inter alia* provide
powerful tools for relating structural ideas to their implications for probabilistic relations.

   Knowledge of causal structures tells us when and to what degree probability, time order, invariance, controllability, and related notions often
connected with causality are the consequences of particular causal
relationships and when they are likely to mislead. In a practical sense,
though, one must really know something about particular causal structures; to go beyond broad generalities, one must possess detailed subject-

matter knowledge. Hence the interest in the second principal question concerning the place of causality in macroeconomics.
There are two further related questions:

• First, can there be a causal structural account of macroeconomics? (That is, are there elements of the macroeconomy that could serve as causes and effects?)
• And, second, what constraints does macroeconomics place on usable characterizations of causality?

Our answer to the first question sails into the teeth of an intellectual gale. Most economists believe that macroeconomics is methodologically and ontologically reducible to microeconomics. We maintain that the arguments for microfoundations for macroeconomics are unsound, resting on equivocations and false analogies. But the strongest argument is the utter failure to carry out the program of microfoundations. The closest that macroeconomics has come to microfoundations is in the representative-agent model, broadly conceived to include all models that reduce economic actors to a small number of types and economic quantities to macroeconomic aggregates. The representative-agent model assumes away the central problem of the microfoundation program – namely, how to connect the behaviors of individuals to the behavior of measured macroeconomic aggregates – and then declares it solved. The representative-agent model is an implicit concession, a capitulation, to the impossible goal of the microfoundational program.

The mainspring of the insistence on microfoundations – despite the hackneyed formulations – is not "methodological individualism." The more reflective macroeconomists are fully aware that the representative agent is a sleight of hand in the microfoundational shell game. Rather, the insistence on microfoundations is grounded in ontological individualism. The economy comprises individuals who, it is thought, must be responsible for the properties of the macroeconomic aggregates. The aggregates could not be fundamental.

Our strategy is to use the philosophical concept of supervenience in a novel, antireductionist way. We concede that the macroeconomic aggregates supervene on microeconomic entities in the sense that any time the micro entities had exactly the same configuration (in the same context), the macro entities would also be the same. Yet, reduction of macro to micro is not possible. The macroeconomic aggregates have emergent properties that, of their nature, cannot belong to microeconomic entities. These properties give the aggregates an external, objective existence – they are independent of individual human minds and of the representations of economic theory. And genuine causal relationships worthy of scientific study connect them.

The nature of macroeconomic structures places limits on the strategies of causal inference. The use of a policy instrument to control a target aggregate, for example, can render screening relations (the causal Markov condition) uninformative about causal structure. And, even where this does not occur, conflicting causal relationships may prove to be observationally equivalent with respect to screening. Nonhomogeneity and informational complexity can reverse or eliminate the apparent temporal priority of cause and effect, so that Granger-causality tests and other tests based on time order fail to identify the true causal structure.

The methods of causal inference developed in this book mainly address the problems of observational equivalence and apparent time reversal – that is, the situations in which the approaches of Granger and Glymour et al. are most likely to fail to isolate the true causal structure. Those methods can be seen as asking, "what implications does a causal structure have for the observed correlations among variables?" and then attempting to work backwards from those correlations to infer the underlying structure. Our methods ask, "what implications does a causal structure have for the observed invariance of the conditional and marginal probability distributions of variables?" and then work backwards from the patterns of invariance to infer the underlying structure. These methods depend crucially on the distinction between parameters and variables that is essential to the Simonesque characterization of causality developed in the book. Changes in parameters and their practical analogue, and changes in policy regime or institutional arrangements, generate the changing patterns of invariance that reveal causal structure.

As a practical matter, the invariance methods explored in the last three chapters are strongest when only the causal direction between two variables is in question. The challenge for the future is to combine the leading idea of these methods with the leading ideas of Granger and Glymour et al., which, though they cannot resolve every interesting causal question, are more adaptable to the degree of causal complexity often faced in real macroeconomic structures.

The river that started with Hume rolls on, and we have yet to reach its mouth.

# Bibliography

Akaike, H. (1973) "Information Theory and an Extension of the Maximum Likelihood Principle," in B. N. Petrov and F. Csaki (eds.), *Second International Symposium on Information Theory*. Budapest: Akademiai Kiade, pp. 267–281.

Amemiya, Takeshi. (1985) *Advanced Econometrics.* Oxford: Blackwell.

Anderson, John. (1938) "The Problem of Causality," in *Studies in Empirical Philosophy*. Sydney: Angus Robertson, 1962.

Andrews, Donald W. K. (1993) "Tests for Parameter Instability and Structural Change with Unknown Change Point," *Econometrica* 61(4), 821–856.

Baba, Yoshihisa, David F. Hendry, and Ross M. Starr. (1992) "The Demand for M1 in the U.S.A.," *Review of Economic Studies* 59(1), pp. 25–61.

Banerjee, Anindya, Robin L. Lumsdaine, and James H. Stock. (1992) "Recursive and Sequential Tests of the Unit-Root and Trend-Break Hypotheses: Theory and International Evidence," *Journal of Business and Economic Statistics* 10(3), 271–287.

Barro, Robert J. (1979) "On the Determination of Public Debt," *Journal of Political Economy* 87(5, part 1), 940–971.

Basmann, R. L. (1965) "A Note on the Statistical Testability of 'Explicit Causal Chains' Against the Class of 'Interdependent' Models," *Journal of the American Statistical Association* 60(312), 1080–1093.

Basmann, R. L. (1988) "Causality Tests and Observationally Equivalent Representations of Econometric Models," *Journal of Econometrics*, Annals, vol. 39, 69–101.

Bell, Eric T. (1937) *Men of Mathematics*. New York: Simon and Schuster.

Bhaskar, Roy. (1975) *A Realist Theory of Science*. Leeds: Leeds Books.

Bickel, Peter, Eugene Hammel, and J. William O'Connell. (1977) "Sex Bias in Graduate Admissions: Data from Berkeley," in William Fairley and Frederick Mosteller (eds.), *Statistics and Public Policy*. Reading, MA: Addison-Wesley, pp. 113–130.

Black, Fischer. (1970) "Banking and Interest Rates in a World without Money," in Fischer Black, *Business Cycles and Equilibrium*. Oxford: Basil Blackwell, 1987, ch. 1.

Black, Fischer. (1972) "Active and Passive Monetary Policy in a Neoclassical Model," in Fischer Black, *Business Cycles and Equilibrium*. Oxford: Basil Blackwell, 1987, ch. 2.

Blaug, Mark. (1992) *The Methodology of Economics: Or How Economists Explain*. Cambridge: Cambridge University Press.

Blaug, Mark. (1995a) "Is the Quantity Theory of Money True?" in Kevin D. Hoover and Steven M. Sheffrin (eds.), *Monetarism and the Methodology of Economics: Essays in Honour of Thomas Mayer*. Aldershot: Edward Elgar, pp. 49–72.

Blaug, Mark. (1995b) "Why Is the Quantity Theory of Money the Oldest Surviving Theory in Economics?" in Mark Blaug et al., *The Quantity Theory of Money: From Locke to Keynes and Friedman*. Aldershot: Edward Elgar, pp. 27–49.

Blinder, Alan S. (1998) *Central Banking in Theory and Practice*. Cambridge, MA: MIT Press.

Board of Governors of the Federal Reserve System. (1967–1968) *Annual Report*. Washington, DC.

Boland, Lawrence. (1979) *The Foundations of Economic Method*. London: George Allen and Unwin.

Box, George E. P., and Gwilym M. Jenkins. (1970) *Time Series Analysis: Forecasting and Control*, 1st edition. San Francisco, Holden-Day (3rd edition with Gregory C. Reinsel. Englewood Cliffs, NJ: Prentice Hall, 1994).

Box, George E. P., and D. A. Pierce. (1970) "Distributions of Residual Autocorrelations in Autoregressive Integrated Moving Average Models." *Journal of American Statistical Association* 65(332), 1509–1526.

Breitung, Jörg, and Norman R. Swanson. (1998) "Temporal Aggregation and Causality in Time Series Models," unpublished typescript, Humboldt University and Pennsylvania State University, March.

Brown, R. L., J. Durbin, and J. M. Evans. (1975) "Techniques for Testing the Constancy of Regression Relationships over Time," *Journal of the Royal Statistical Society*, Series B, 37(2), 149–192 (with discussion).

Bunge, Mario. (1963) *The Place of the Causal Principle in Modern Science*. Cleveland, OH: Meridian Books.

Cagan, Philip. (1956) "The Monetary Dynamics of Hyperinflation," in Milton Friedman (ed.), *Studies in the Quantity Theory of Money*. Chicago: University of Chicago Press, pp. 25–117.

Cagan, Philip. (1965) *The Determinants of the Money Stock in the United States, 1875–1963*. New York: National Bureau of Economic Research.

Calomiris, Charles W., and Christopher Hanes. (1995) "Historical Macroeconomics and American Macroeconomic History," in Kevin D. Hoover (ed.), *Macroeconometrics: Developments, Tensions and Prospects*. Boston: Kluwer, pp. 351–416.

Cartwright, Nancy. (1979) "Causal Laws and Effective Strategies," *Nous* 13(4), 419–437.

Cartwright, Nancy. (1983) *How the Laws of Physics Lie*. Oxford: Clarendon Press.

Cartwright, Nancy. (1989) *Nature's Capacities and Their Measurement*. Oxford: Clarendon Press.

Cartwright, Nancy. (1993) "Marks and Probabilities: Two Ways to Find Causal Structure," in F. Stadler (ed.), *Scientific Philosophy: Origins and Development*. Dordrecht: Kluwer, pp. 113–119.

Cartwright, Nancy. (1994) "Fundamentalism vs. The Patchwork of Laws," *Proceedings of the Aristotelian Society*, 279–292.

Cartwright, Nancy. (1997) "Where Do Laws of Nature Come From?" *Dialectica* 51(1), 65–78.

Cartwright, Nancy. (1999) *The Dappled World*. Cambridge: Cambridge University Press.

Cat, Jordi. (1998) "The Physicists' Debates on Unification in Physics at the End of the 20th Century," *Historical Studies in the Physical Sciences* (2), 253–299.

Chari, V. V., Lawrence J. Christiano, and Patrick J. Kehoe. (1990) "Optimal Taxation of Capital and Labor Income in a Stochastic Growth Model," Federal Reserve Bank of Minneapolis Working Paper No. 465, September.

Chow, Gregory C. (1960) "Tests of Equality between Sets of Coefficients in Two Linear Regressions," *Econometrica*, 28(2), 591–605.

Christiano, Lawrence T., and Martin Eichenbaum. (1987) "Temporal Aggregation and Structural Inference in Macroeconomics," *Carnegie-Rochester Conference Series on Public Policy* 26, 63–130.

Chu, C. James. (1990) *The Econometrics of Structural Change*. Unpublished doctoral dissertation, Department of Economics, University of California, San Diego.

Clark, Lindley, Jr. (1985) "Positive Reading: Despite New Statistics, Analysts See Economy Continuing to Expand," *Wall Street Journal*, Eastern edition, 6 May, p. 1.

Clark, Peter K. (1983) "Okun's Law and Potential GNP," unpublished paper, Board of Governors of the Federal Reserve System, June.

Cogan, John F. (1993) "Federal Budget," in David R. Henderson (ed.), *The Fortune Encyclopedia of Economics*. New York: Warner Books, pp. 243–247.

Cohen, Morris R., and Ernest Nagel. (1934) *An Introduction to Logic and Scientific Method*. London: Routledge & Kegan Paul.

Cooley, Thomas F., Stephen F. LeRoy, and Neil Raymon. (1984) "Econometric Policy Evaluation: A Note," *American Economic Review* 74(2), May, 467–470.

Council of Economic Advisers. (1950–1953) *The Economic Situation at Mid-year*. Washington, DC: Government Printing Office.

Cournot, Augustin. (1838/1927) *Researches into the Mathematical Principles of the Theory of Wealth*, Nathaniel T. Bacon (trans.). New York: Macmillan.

Dewald, William G., Jerry G. Thursby, and Richard G. Anderson. (1986) "Replication in Empirical Economics: The *Journal of Money, Credit and Banking* Project," *American Economic Review* 76(4), 587–603.

Duesberg, Peter H. (1996) *Inventing the AIDS Virus*. Washington, DC: Regnery.

*Economist*. (1997) "Bird Vision: Ultrasexy," *Economist* 9, August.

*Economist*. (1998) "Whose Body of Evidence? (Standards for Forensic Scientists)," 348(8076, July 11), 78–81.

Eells, Ellery. (1991) *Probabilistic Causality*. Cambridge: Cambridge University Press.

Ellis, Brian. (1966) *Basic Concepts of Measurement*. Cambridge: Cambridge University Press.

Engle, Robert F., David F. Hendry, and Jean-François Richard. (1983) "Exogeneity," *Econometrica* 51(2), 277–304.

Epstein, Roy J. (1987) *A History of Econometrics*. Amsterdam: North-Holland.

Ericsson, Neil, and John Irons. (1995) "The Lucas Critique in Practice: Theory without Measurement," in Kevin D. Hoover (ed.), *Macroeconometrics: Developments, Tensions and Prospects*. Boston: Kluwer, pp. 263–312.

Fama, Eugene. (1980) "Banking in the Theory of Finance," *Journal of Monetary Economics* 6(1), 39–57.

Faust, Jon, and Charles H. Whiteman. (1995) "Commentary [on Grayham E. Mizon, 'Progressive Modeling of Macroeconomic Times Series: The LSE Methodology']," in Hoover (1995b), pp. 171–180.

Faust, Jon, and Charles H. Whiteman. (1997) "General-to Specific Procedures for Fitting a Data-Admissible, Theory-Inspired, Congruent, Parsimonious, Encompassing, Weakly-Exogenous, Identified, Structural Model to the DGP: A Translation and Critique," *Carnegie-Rochester Conference Series on Economic Policy*, Vol. 47, December.

Favero, Carlos, and David F. Hendry. (1992) "Testing the Lucas Critique: A Review," *Econometric Reviews* 11(3), 265–306.

Feigl, Herbert. (1953) "Notes on Causality," in Herbert Feigl and Mary Brodbeck (eds.), *Readings in the Philosophy of Science*. New York: Appleton-Century-Crofts, pp. 408–418.

Feynman, Richard. (1995) *Six Easy Pieces: Essentials of Physics Explained by Its Most Brilliant Teacher*. Reading, MA: Addison-Wesley.

Fisher, Irving. (1911/1931) The Purchasing Power of Money. New York: Macmillan.

Forster, Malcolm R. (1997a) "How to Reduce Cause to Probability," unpublished typescript, Department of Philosophy, University of Wisconsin, 6 July.

Forster, Malcolm R. (1997b) "Causation, Prediction, and Accommodation," unpublished typescript, Department of Philosophy, University of Wisconsin, 26 December.

Frassen, Bas van. (1977) "The Pragmatics of Explanation," *American Philosophical Quarterly* 14(2), 143–150.

Friedman, Milton. (1953) "The Methodology of Positive Economics," in *Essays in Positive Economics*. Chicago: Chicago University Press, pp. 3–43.

Friedman, Milton. (1955) "Leon Walras and His Economic System: A Review Article," *American Economic Review*, 45(5), 900–909.

Friedman, Milton. (1956) "The Quantity Theory of Money: A Restatement," in Milton Friedman (ed.), *Studies in the Quantity Theory of Money*. Chicago: Chicago University Press.

Friedman, Milton. (1968a) *Dollars and Deficits: Inflation, Monetary Policy and the Balance of Payments*. Englewood Cliffs, NJ: Prentice Hall.

Friedman, Milton. (1968b)"The Role of Monetary Policy," *American Economic Review* 58(1, March), 1–17.

Friedman, Milton. (1970) "Comment on Tobin," *Quarterly Journal of Economics* 82(2), 318–327.

Friedman, Milton. (1974) "A Theoretical Framework for Monetary Analysis," in Robert J. Gordon (ed.), *Milton Friedman's Monetary Framework*. Chicago: University of Chicago Press, pp. 1–62.

Friedman, Milton, and Anna J. Schwartz. (1963a) *A Monetary History of the United States, 1867–1960*. Princeton: Princeton University Press.

Friedman, Milton, and Anna J. Schwartz. (1963b) "Money and Business Cycles," *Review of Economics and Statistics* 45(1, part 2: supplement), in Milton Friedman, *The Optimum Quantity of Money and Other Essays*. Chicago: Aldine, 1969, pp. 189–236.

Friedman, Milton, and Anna J. Schwartz. (1982) *Monetary Trends in the United States and the United Kingdom: Their Relation to Income, Prices and Interest Rates, 1867–1975*. Chicago: University of Chicago Press.

Furstenberg, George M. von, R. Jeffrey Green, and Jin-Ho Jeong. (1986) "Tax and Spend, Or Spend and Tax?" *Review of Economics and Statistics* 68(2), 179–188.

Gilbert, Christopher L. (1986) "Professor Hendry's Econometric Methodology," *Oxford Bulletin of Economics and Statistics* 48(3), 283–307.

Glymour, Clark. (1980) *Theory and Evidence*. Princeton: Princeton University Press.

Glymour, Clark. (1997) "A Review of Recent Work on the Foundations of Causal Inference," in Vaughn R. McKim and Stephen P. Turner (eds.), *Causality in Crisis? Statistical Methods and the Search for Causal Knowledge in the Social Sciences*. Notre Dame, IN: Unversity of Notre Dame Press, pp. 201–248.

Glymour, Clark, Richard Scheines, Peter Spirtes, and Kevin Kelly. (1987) *Discovering Causal Structure: Artificial Intelligence, Philosophy of Science, and Statistical Modeling*. Orlando: Academic Press.

Glymour, Clark, and Peter Spirtes. (1988) "Latent Variables, Causal Models and Overidentifying Constraints," *Journal of Econometrics* 39(1/2), 175–198.

Goldfeld, Stephen M. (1976) "The Case of the Missing Money," *Brookings Papers on Economic Activity*, No. 3, 683–730.

Good, I. J. (1961) "A Causal Calculus – I," *British Journal for the Philosophy of Science* 11(44), 305–318.

Goodman, Nelson. (1965) *Fact, Fiction and Forecast*, 2nd edition. New York: Bobbs-Merrill.

Gordon, Robert J. (1984) "The Short-run Demand for Money: A Reconsideration," *Journal of Money, Credit and Banking* 16(4), 403–434.

Gramlich, Edward M. (1989) "Budget Deficits and National Saving: Are Politicians Exogenous?" *Journal of Economic Perspectives* 3(2), 23–35.

Granger, C. W. J. (1969) "Investigating Causal Relations by Econometric Models and Cross-Spectral Methods," in Robert E. Lucas, Jr. and Thomas J. Sargent (eds.), *Rational Expectations and Econometric Practice*. London: George Allen and Unwin, 1981, pp. 371–386.

Granger, C. W. J. (1980) "Testing for Causality: A Personal Viewpoint," *Journal of Economic Dynamics and Control* 2(4), November, 329–352.

Granger, C. W. J. (1995) "Commentary [on Stephen F. LeRoy, 'Causal Orderings'']," in Kevin D. Hoover (ed.), *Macroeconometrics: Developments, Tensions and Prospects*. Boston: Kluwer, pp. 229–234.

Granger, C. W. J. (1998) "Granger Causality," in John B. Davis, D. Wade Hands, and Uskali Mäki (eds.), *The Handbook of Economic Methodology.* Aldershot: Edward Elgar, pp. 214–216.

Granger, C. W. J., and Paul Newbold. (1977) *Forecasting Economic Time Series,* 1st edition. New York: Academic Press (2nd edition 1986).

Gurley, John, and Edwin Shaw. (1960) *Money in a Theory of Finance.* Washington, DC: Brookings Institution.

Hacking, Ian. (1983) *Representing and Intervening.* Cambridge: Cambridge University Press.

Hahn, Frank H. (1965) "On Some Problems of Proving the Existence of Equilibrium in a Monetary Economy," in Frank H. Hahn and F. P. R. Brechling (eds.), *The Theory of Interest Rates.* London: Macmillan, pp. 126–135.

Hallman, Jeffrey J., Richard D. Porter, and David H. Small. (1989) "M2 per Unit of Potential GNP as an Anchor for the Price Level," Board of Governors of the Federal Reserve System Staff Paper No. 157, April.

Hamilton, James D. (1994) *Time Series Analysis.* Princeton: Princeton University Press.

Hamilton, James D. (1995) "Rational Expectations and the Econometric Consequences of Changes in Regime," in Kevin D. Hoover (ed.), *Macroeconometrics: Developments, Tensions and Prospects.* Boston: Kluwer, pp. 325–345.

Hamminga, Bert, and Neil B. De Marchi (eds.). (1994) "Idealization VI: Idealization in Economics." *Poznań Studies in the Philosophy of the Sciences and Humanities,* vol. 38. Amsterdam: Rodopi.

Hammond, J. Daniel. (1992) "An Interview with Milton Friedman on Methodology," in W. J. Samuels (ed.), *Research in the History of Economic Thought and Methodology,* vol. 10. Greenwich, CT: JAI Press, pp. 91–118.

Hammond, J. Daniel. (1996) *Theory and Measurement: Causality Issues in Milton Friedman's Monetary Economics.* Cambridge: Cambridge University Press.

Hansen, Bruce I. (1990) "Testing for Structural Change of Unknown Form in Models with Non-stationary Regressors," University of Rochester, Department of Economics, Working Paper.

Hansen, Bruce E. (1992) "Testing for Parameter Instability in Linear Models," *Journal of Policy Modeling* 14(4), 517–533.

Hansen, Bruce E. (1996) "Methodology: Alchemy or Science?" *Economic Journal* 106(438, September), 1398–1431.

Hansen, Lars Peter, and Thomas J. Sargent. (1980) "Formulating and Estimating Dynamic Linear Rational Expectations Models," *Journal of Economic Dynamics and Control,* 2(1), 7–46.

Hansen, Lars Peter, Thomas J. Sargent, and William T. Roberds. (1991) "Time Series Implications of Present Value Budget Balance and of Martingale Models of Consumption and Taxes," in Thomas J. Sargent, Lars Peter Hansen, John Heaton, and Albert Marcet (eds.), *Rational Expectations and Econometrics.* Boulder, CO: Westview, pp. 121–162.

Hardy, Thomas. (1874) *Far from the Madding Crowd.*

Harris, James F., and Kevin D. Hoover. (1980) "Abduction and the New Riddle of Induction," *The Monist* 63(3), 329–341.

Hartley, James E. (1997) *The Representative Agent in Macroeconomics*. London: Routledge.

Hartley, James E., Kevin D. Hoover, and Kevin D. Salyer. (1997) "The Limits of Business Cycle Research: Assessing the Real Business Cycle Model," *Oxford Review of Economic Policy* 13(3), 34–54.

Hartley, James E., Kevin D. Hoover, and Kevin D. Salyer (eds.). (1998) *Real Business Cycles: A Reader*. London: Routledge.

Harvey, Andrew C. (1990) *The Econometric Analysis of Time Series*, 2nd edition. Cambridge, MA: MIT Press.

Hausman, D. M. (1992) *The Inexact and Separate Science of Economics*. Cambridge: Cambridge University Press.

Hausman, D. M. (1998) *Causal Asymmetries*. Cambridge: Cambridge University Press.

Hayek, F. A. von. (1935a) "Socialist Calculation I: The Nature and History of the Problem," in *Individualism and the Economic Order*. Chicago: University of Chicago Press, 1948, pp. 119–147.

Hayek, F. A. von. (1935b) "Socialist Calculation II: The State of the Debate," in *Individualism and the Economic Order*. Chicago: University of Chicago Press, 1948, pp. 148–180.

Hayek, F. A. von. (1937) "Economics and Knowledge," in *Individualism and the Economic Order*. Chicago: University of Chicago Press, 1948, pp. 119–147.

Hayek, F. A. von. (1940) "Socialist Calculation III: The Competitive Solution," reprinted in *Individualism and the Economic Order*. Chicago: University of Chicago Press, 1948, pp. 181–208.

Hayek, F. A. von. (1945) "The Use of Knowledge in Society," reprinted in *Individualism and the Economic Order*. Chicago: University of Chicago Press, 1948, pp. 77–91.

Hayek, F. A. von. (1979) *The Counter-Revolution in Science: Studies in the Abuse of Reason*, 2nd edition. Indianapolis: Liberty Press.

Hempel, Carl. (1945) "Studies in the Logic of Confirmation (I)," *Mind* 54(1), 1–26.

Hendry, David F. (1980) "Econometrics: Alchemy or Science?" *Economica* 47(188), 387–406.

Hendry, David F. (1983) "Econometric Modelling: The Consumption Function in Retrospect," *Scottish Journal of Political Economy* 30(3), 193–220.

Hendry, David F. (1987) "Econometric Methodology: A Personal Viewpoint," in Truman Bewley (ed.), *Advances in Econometrics*, vol. 2. Cambridge: Cambridge University Press, pp. 29–48.

Hendry, David F. (1988a) "The Encompassing Implications of Feedback versus Feedforward Mechanisms in Econometrics," *Oxford Economic Papers* N.S. 40(1), 132–149.

Hendry, David F. (1988b) "Encompassing," *National Institute Economic Review* (August), 88–92.

Hendry, David F. (1989) *PC-GIVE: An Interactive Econometric Modelling System*. Oxford: University of Oxford.

Hendry, David F. (1995) *Dynamic Econometrics*. Oxford: Oxford University Press.

Hendry, David F. (1997) "On Congruent Econometric Relations: A Comment."
*Carnegie-Rochester Conference Series on Public Policy*, Vol. 47, 163–190.
Hendry, David F., and Jurgen A. Doornik. (1997) *PcGive/PcFiml 9.0 Professional
for Windows* [Econometric Software and Manual]. London: International
Thomson Business Press.
Hendry, David F., Edward E. Leamer, and Dale J. Poirier. (1990) "The ET
Dialogue: A Conversation on Econometric Methodology," *Econometric
Theory* 6(2), 171–261.
Hendry, David F., and Mary S. Morgan (eds.). (1995) *The Foundations of Econo-
metric Analysis*. Cambridge: Cambridge University Press.
Hendry, David F., and Jean-François Richard. (1982) "On the Formulation of
Empirical Models in Dynamic Econometrics," *Journal of Econometrics,
Annals* 20(1), 3–33.
Hendry, David F., and Jean-François Richard. (1987) "Recent Developments in
the Theory of Encompassing," in B. Cornet and H. Tulkens (eds.), *Contribu-
tions to Operation Research and Econometrics. The XXth Anniversary of
CORE*. Cambridge, MA: MIT Press.
Hesslow, G. (1976) "Discussion: Two Notes on the Probabilistic Approach to
Causality," *Philosophy of Science* 43(2), 290–292.
Holland, Paul W. (1986) "Statistics and Causal Inference [with discussion],"
*Journal of the American Statistical Association* 81(396), 945–960.
Holt, Jim. (1997) "Parallel Worlds" [book review]," *Wall St. Journal*, 7 August.
Hoover, Kevin D. (1984) "Two Types of Monetarism," *Journal of Economic
Literature* 22(1), 58–76.
Hoover, Kevin D. (1985) *Causality and Invariance in the Money Supply Process*,
unpublished doctoral dissertation, Trinity term (Oxford University).
Hoover, Kevin D. (1988a) *The New Classical Macroeconomics: A Sceptical
Inquiry*. Oxford: Basil Blackwell.
Hoover, Kevin D. (1988b) "On the Pitfalls of Untested Common-factor
Restrictions: The Case of the Inverted Fisher Hypothesis," *Oxford Bulletin of
Economics and Statistics* 50(2), 125–138.
Hoover, Kevin D. (1988c) "Money, Prices and Finance in the New Monetary
Economics," *Oxford Economic Papers* N.S. 40(1), 150–167.
Hoover, Kevin D. (1990) "The Logic of Causal Inference: Econometrics and
the Conditional Analysis of Causality," *Economics and Philosophy* 6(2),
207–234.
Hoover, Kevin D. (1991) "The Causal Direction between Money and Prices:
An Alternative Approach," *Journal of Monetary Economics* 27(3), 381–
423.
Hoover, Kevin D. (1992) "The Rational Expectations Revolution: An Assess-
ment," *Cato Journal* 12(1), 81–96.
Hoover, Kevin D. (1993) "Causality and Temporal Order in Macroeconomics or
Why Even Economists Don't Know How to Get Causes from Probabilities,"
*British Journal for the Philosophy of Science* 44(4), 693–710.
Hoover, Kevin D. (1994a) "Six Queries about Idealization in an Empirical
Context," *Poznán Studies in the Philosophy of Science and the Humanities*, vol.
38. Amsterdam: Rodopi, pp. 43–53.

Hoover, Kevin D. (1994b) "Econometrics as Observation: The Lucas Critique and the Nature of Econometric Inference," *Journal of Economic Methodology* 1(1), 65–80.

Hoover, Kevin D. (1994c) "Pragmatism, Pragmaticism, and Economic Method," in Roger E. Backhouse (ed.), *New Directions in Economic Methodology*. London: Routledge.

Hoover, Kevin D. (1995a) "Why Does Methodology Matter for Economics?" *Economic Journal* 105(430, May), 714–734.

Hoover, Kevin D. (1995b) "Comments on Cartwright and Woodward: Causation, Estimation and Statistics," in Daniel Little (ed.), *On the Reliability of Economic Models: Essays in the Philosophy of Economics*. Boston: Kluwer, pp. 75–90.

Hoover, Kevin D. (1995c) "Is Macroeconomics for Real?" *Monist* 78(3), 235–257.

Hoover, Kevin D. (1997a) "Is There a Place for Rational Expectations in Keynes's *General Theory*," in G. C. Harcourt and P. A. Riach (eds.), *A "Second Edition" of The General Theory*. London: Routledge, pp. 219–237.

Hoover, Kevin D. (1997b) "Econometrics and Reality," Working Paper, Department of Economics, University of California, Davis.

Hoover, Kevin D. (ed.). (1999) *The Legacy of Robert E. Lucas, Jr.*, three volumes. Aldershot: Edward Elgar.

Hoover, Kevin D., and Stephen J. Perez. (1994a) *"Post Hoc Ergo Propter Hoc* Once More: An Evaluation of 'Does Monetary Policy Matter' in the Spirit of James Tobin," *Journal of Monetary Economics* 34(1), 47–73.

Hoover, Kevin D., and Stephen J. Perez. (1994b) "Money May Matter, But How Would You Know?" *Journal of Monetary Economics* 34(1), 89–99.

Hoover, Kevin D., and Stephen J. Perez. (1999) "Data Mining Reconsidered: Encompassing and the General-to-Specific Approach to Specification Search," *Econometrics Journal* 2(2), 167–191.

Hoover, Kevin D., and Steven M. Sheffrin. (1992) "Causation, Spending and Taxes: Sand in the Sandbox or Tax Collector for the Welfare State?" *American Economic Review* 82(1), 225–248.

Hoover, Kevin D., and Mark V. Siegler. (2000) "Taxing and Spending in the Long View: The Causal Structure of U.S. Fiscal Policy," *Oxford Economics Papers* 52(4), 745–773.

Hume, David. (1739) *A Treatise of Human Nature*. Page numbers refer to the edition by L. A. Selby-Bigge. Oxford: Clarendon Press, 1888.

Hume, David. (1754) (a) "Of Money," (b) "Of Interest," (c) "Of the Balance of Trade," in *Essays: Moral, Political, and Literary*. Page numbers refer to the edition by Eugene F. Miller. Indianapolis: Liberty Classics, 1985.

Hume, David. (1777) *An Enquiry Concerning Human Understanding*. Page numbers refer to the edition by L. A. Selby-Bigge, *Enquiries Concerning Human Understanding and Concerning the Principles of Morals*, 2nd edition. Oxford: Clarendon Press, 1902.

Humphreys, Paul. (1989) *The Chances of Explanation: Causal Explanation in the Social, Medical, and Physical Sciences*. Princeton: Princeton University Press.

Irzik, Gürol. (1996) "Can Causes Be Reduced to Correlations?" *British Journal for the Philosophy of Science* 47(2), 249–270.

Jacobs, Rodney L., Edward E. Leamer, and Michael P. Ward. (1979) "Difficulties in Testing for Causation," *Economic Inquiry* 17(3, July), 401–413.

Janssen, Maarten. (1993) *Microfoundations: A Critical Inquiry*. London: Routledge.

Jarque, C. M., and Anil K. Berra. (1980) "Efficient Tests for Normality, Homoscedasticity and Serial Independence of Regression Residuals," *Economic Letters* 6(3), 255–259.

Jeong, Jinook, and G. S. Maddala. (1993) "A Perspective on Application of Bootstrap Methods in Econometrics," in G. S. Maddala, C. R. Rao, and H. D. Vinod (eds.), *Handbook of Statistics*, vol. 11. Amsterdam: Elsevier Science Publishers, 1993.

Johnston, J. (1972) *Econometric Methods*, 2nd edition. New York: McGraw-Hill.

Judd, John P., and John L. Scadding. (1982) "The Search for a Stable Money Demand Function: A Survey of the Post-1973 Literature," *Journal of Economic Literature* 20(3), 993–1024.

Kaldor, Nicholas. (1970) "The New Monetarism," *Lloyd's Bank Review*, No. 97, July, 1–18.

Kaldor, Nicholas. (1982) *The Scourge of Monetarism*. Oxford: Oxford University Press.

Katzner, Donald W. (1983) *Analysis without Measurement*. Cambridge: Cambridge University Press.

Keynes, John Maynard. (1930/1971) *A Treatise on Money*, vol. 1 (*The Pure Theory of Money*). London: Macmillan.

Keynes, John Maynard. (1936) *The General Theory of Money, Interest and Prices*. London: Macmillan.

Kim, H. J., and D. Siegmund. (1989) "The Likelihood Ratio Test for a Change Point in Simple Linear Regression," *Biometrika* 76(3), 409–423.

Kim, Jaegwon. (1978) "Supervenience and Nomological Incommensurables," *American Philosophical Quarterly* 15(2), 149–156.

King, Robert G., and Charles I. Plosser. (1984) "Money, Credit and Prices in a Real Business Cycle," *American Economic Review* 74(3), 363–380.

Kirman, A. P. (1992) "Whom or What Does the Representative Agent Represent?" *Journal of Economic Perspectives* 6(2), 117–136.

Klein, Judy L. (1997) *Statistical Visions in Time: A History of Time Series Analysis, 1662–1938*. Cambridge: Cambridge University Press.

Kremers, Jeroen J. M., Juan J. Dalado, and Neil R. Ericsson. (1989) "The Power of Cointegration Tests," unpublished typescript, Board of Governors of the Federal Reserve System.

Kydland, Finn E., and Edward C. Prescott. (1982) "Time to Build and Aggregate Fluctuations," *Econometrica* 50(6), 1345–1369.

Lachmann, Ludwig. (1976) "On the Central Concept of Austrian Economics: Market Process," in Edwin G. Dolan (ed.), *The Foundations of Austrian Economics*. Kansas City, MO: Sheed and Ward, pp. 126–132.

Laidler, David. (1991) "The Quantity Theory Is Always and Everywhere Controversial – Why?" *Economic Record* 67(199, December), 289–306.

Laplace, Pierre S. (1812) *Essai Philosophique sur les Probabilités*. Paris: Courcier.
Leeper, Eric. (1995) "Commentary [on Ericsson and Irons, 'The Lucas Critique in Practice: Theory without Measurement']," in Kevin D. Hoover (ed.), *Macroeconometrics: Developments, Tensions and Prospects*. Boston: Kluwer, pp. 313–324.
LeRoy, Stephen F. (1995a) "Causal Orderings," in Kevin D. Hoover (ed.), *Macroeconometrics: Developments, Tensions and Prospects*. Boston: Kluwer, pp. 211–228.
LeRoy, Stephen F. (1995b) "On Policy Regimes," in Kevin D. Hoover (ed.), *Macroeconometrics: Developments, Tensions and Prospects*. Boston: Kluwer, pp. 235–252.
Levy, David M. (1985) "The Impossibility of a Complete Methodological Individualist: Reduction When Knowledge Is Imperfect," *Economics and Philosophy* 1(1), 101–108.
Lillien, David M., Robert E. Hall, et al. (1998) *Eviews 3.0* [Econometric Software and Manual]. Irvine, CA: Quantitative Micro Software.
Ljung, G. M., and G. E. P. Box. (1978) "On a Measure of Lack of Fit in Time Series Models," *Biometrika* 65(2), 297–303.
Locke, John. (1690) *An Essay Concerning Human Understanding*.
Long, John B., Jr., and Charles I. Plosser. (1983) "Real Business Cycles," *Journal of Political Economy* 91(1), 39–69.
Lovell, Michael C. (1986) "Tests of the Rational Expectations Hypothesis," *American Economic Review* 76(1), 110–124.
Lucas, Robert E., Jr. (1976) "Econometric Policy Evaluation: A Critique," in Karl Brunner and Allan H. Meltzer (eds.), *The Phillips Curve and Labor Markets*. Carnegie-Rochester Conference Series on Public Policy, vol. 1, Spring. Amsterdam: North-Holland, pp. 161–168.
Lucas, Robert E., Jr. (1977) "Understanding Business Cycles," in Robert E. Lucas, Jr., *Studies in Business-Cycle Theory*. Oxford: Blackwell, 1981, pp. 215–239.
Lucas, Robert E., Jr. (1980) "Methods and Problems in Business Cycle Theory," *Journal of Money, Credit and Banking* 12(4, part 2, November), 696–715. Reprinted in Lucas, *Studies in Business-Cycle Theory*. Oxford: Blackwell, 1981, pp. 271–296.
Lucas, Robert F., Jr. (1986) "Principles of Fiscal and Monetary Policy," *Journal of Monetary Economics* 17(1), 117–134.
Lucas, Robert E., Jr. (1987) *Models of Business Cycles*. Oxford: Blackwell.
Mackie, John L. (1980) *The Cement of the Universe: A Study in Causation*, 2nd edition. Oxford: Clarendon Press.
Mäki, Uskali. (1992) "On the Method of Isolation in Economics," *Poznań Studies in the Philosophy of Science and the Humanities*, vol. 25, pp. 289–310.
Mäki, Uskali. (1996) "Scientific Realism and Some Peculiarities of Economics," in R. S. Cohen, R. Hilpinen, and Qui Renzong (eds.), *Realism and Anti-realism in the Philosophy of Science*. Dordrecht: Kluwer, pp. 427–447.
Marshall, A. (1920) *Principles of Economics: An Introductory Volume*, 8th edition. London: Macmillan.

McAleer, Michael. (1997) "Pictures at an Exhibition: The Experiment in Applied Econometrics Conference, Tilburg, The Netherlands, 1996," *Journal of Economic Surveys* 11(4), 419–432.

McAleer, Michael, Adrian R. Pagan, and Paul A. Volker. (1985) "What Will Take the Con out of Econometrics?" *American Economic Review* 75(3), 293–307.

Mesarovic, Mihajlo D. (1969) "Mathematical Theory of General Systems and Some Economic Problems," in H. W. Kuhn and G. P. Szegö (eds.), *Mathematical Systems and Economics I*. Berlin: Springer Verlag, pp. 93–116.

Mill, John Stuart. (1851) *A System of Logic, Ratiocinative and Deductive: Being a Connected View of the Principles of Evidence and the Methods of Scientific Investigation*, 3rd edition, vol. I. London: John W. Parker.

Mises, Ludwig von. (1943) "'Elastic Expectations' and the Austrian Theory of the Trade Cycle," *Economica* NS 10(3), 251–252.

Mises, Ludwig von. (1949/1966) *Human Action: A Treatise on Economics*, 3rd edition. Chicago: Henry Regnery.

Mizon, Graham E. (1984) "The Encompassing Approach in Econometrics," in D. F. Hendry and K. F. Wallis (eds.), *Econometrics and Quantitative Economics*. Oxford: Basil Blackwell, pp. 135–172.

Mizon, Graham E. (1995) "Progressive Modelling of Economic Time Series: The LSE Methodology," in Kevin D. Hoover (ed.), *Macroeconometrics: Developments, Tensions and Prospects*. Boston: Kluwer, pp. 107–170.

Mizon, Graham E., and Jean-François Richard. (1986) "The Encompassing Principle and Its Application to Testing Non-nested Hypotheses," *Econometrica* 54(3), 657–678.

Mood, Alexander M., Franklin A. Graybill, and Duane C. Boes. (1974) *Introduction to the Theory of Statistics*, 3rd edition. London: Macmillan.

Moore, Basil J. (1988) *Horizontalists and Verticalists: The Macroeconomics of Credit Money*. Cambridge: Cambridge University Press.

Moore, Geoffrey H., and Victor Zarnowitz. (1986) "The Development and Role of the National Bureau of Economic Research's Business Cycle Chronologies," in Robert J. Gordon (ed.), *The American Business Cycle: Continuity and Change*. Chicago: University of Chicago Press, pp. 735–779.

Morgan, Mary S. (1990) *The History of Econometric Ideas*. Cambridge: Cambridge University Press.

Morgan, Mary S. (1991) "The Stamping Out of Process Analysis from Econometrics," in Neil de Marchi and Mark Blaug (eds.), *Appraising Economic Theories: Studies in the Methodology of Research Programs*. Aldershot: Edward Elgar.

Morgan, Mary S. (1997) "The Technology of Analogical Models: Irving Fisher's Monetary Worlds," *Philosophy of Science* 64(4), S304–S314.

Morgan, Mary S. (1999) "Learning from Models," in Morgan and Margaret Morrison (eds.), *Models as Mediators*. Cambridge: Cambridge University Press, pp. 347–388.

Morgan, Mary S. (2001) "Models, Stories, and the Economic World," in Uskali Mäki (ed.), *Fact and Fiction in Economics: Models, Realism, and Social Construction*. Cambridge: Cambridge University Press, forthcoming.

Nagel, Ernest. (1961) *The Structure of Science: Problems in the Logic of Scientific Explanation*. London: Routledge and Kegan Paul.

Neftçi, Salih, and Thomas J. Sargent. (1978) "A Little Bit of Evidence on the Natural Rate Hypothesis from the U.S.," *Journal of Monetary Economics* 4(2), 315–319.

Nelson, A. (1992) "Human Molecules," in Neil De Marchi (ed.), *Post-Popperian Methodology: Recovering Practice*. Dordrecht: Kluwer, pp. 113–133.

North, Douglass C. (1966) *The Economic Growth of the United States, 1790–1860*. New York: Norton.

Nowak, L. (1980) *The Structure of Idealization: Towards a Systematic Interpretation of the Marxian Idea of Science*. Dordrecht: Reidel.

Owens, David. (1992) *Causes and Coincidences*. Cambridge: Cambridge University Press.

Pagan, Adrian. (1987) "Three Econometric Methodologies: A Critical Appraisal," *Journal of Economic Surveys* 1(1), 3–24.

Papineau, David. (1985) "Probabilities and Causes," *Journal of Philosophy* 82(2), 57–74.

Papineau, David. (1989) "Pure, Mixed and Spurious Probabilities for a Reductionist Theory of Causation," in Philip Kitcher and Wesley Salmon (eds.), *Scientific Explanation*, vol. 13 of *Minnesota Studies in the Philosophy of Science*, Minneapolis: University of Minnesota Press, pp. 307–348.

Papineau, David. (1991) "Correlations and Causes," *British Journal for the Philosophy of Science* 42(3), 397–412.

Pearl, Judea. (1995) "Causal Diagrams for Empirical Research" (with commentary and reply), *Biometrika* 82(4), 669–710.

Pearl, Judea. (1998a) "Graphs, Causality, and Structural Equations Models," *Sociological Methods and Research* 27(2), 226–284.

Pearl, Judea. (1998b) "Graphical Models for Probabilistic and Causal Reasoning," in D. M. Gabbay and P. Smets (eds.), *Handbook of Defeasible Reasoning and Uncertainty Management Systems*. Kluwer: Dordrecht, vol. 1, pp. 367–389.

Pearl, Judea. (2000) *Causality: Models, Reasoning, and Inference*. Cambridge: Cambridge University Press.

Pearl, Judea, and Thomas Verma. (1991) "A Theory of Inferred Causation," in J. A. Allen, R. Fikes, and E. Sandewall (eds.), *Principles of Knowledge Representation and Reasoning: Proceedings of the 2nd International Conference*. San Mateo, CA: Morgan Kaufmann, pp. 441–452.

Peirce, Charles S. (1934) *Collected Papers of Charles Sanders Peirce*, vol. 6, Charles Hartshorne and Paul Weiss (eds.). Cambridge, MA: Belnap Press.

Phillips, Peter C. B. (1988) "Reflections on Econometric Methodology," *Economic Record* 64(187), 344–359.

Ploberger, Werner, Walter Kramer, and Karl Kontrus. (1989) "A New Test for Structural Stability in the Linear Regression Model," *Journal of Econometrics* 40(2), 307–318.

Popper, Karl. (1972) *Objective Knowledge: An Evolutionary Approach*. Oxford: Clarendon Press.

Potter, Simon M. (1995) "Nonlinear Models of Economic Fluctuations," in Kevin D. Hoover (ed.), *Macroeconometrics: Developments, Tensions and Prospects*. Boston: Kluwer, pp. 325–345.

Pratt, J. W., and Robert Schlaifer. (1984) "On the Nature and Discovery of Structure," with discussion, *Journal of the American Statistical Association* 79(385), 9–33.

Quandt, Richard. (1960) "Tests of the Hypothesis That a Linear Regression System Obeys Two Separate Regimes," *Journal of American Statistical Association* 55(290), 324–330.

Redhead, Michael. (1987) *Incompleteness, Nonlocality, and Realism: A Prolegomenon to the Philosophy of Quantum Mechanics.* Oxford: Clarendon Press.

Reichenbach, Hans. (1956) *The Direction of Time.* Berkeley and Los Angeles: University of California Press.

Robbins, L. (1935) *An Essay on the Nature and Significance of Economic Science.* London: Macmillan.

Roberds, William T. (1991) "Implications of Expected Present Value Budget Balance: Application to Postwar U.S. Data," in Thomas J. Sargent, Lars Peter Hansen, John Heaton, and Albert Marcet (eds.), *Rational Expectations and Econometrics.* Boulder, CO: Westview, pp. 163–176.

Romer, Christina D., and David H. Romer. (1989) "Does Monetary Policy Matter? A New Test in the Spirit of Friedman and Schwartz," in Olivier Blanchard and Stanley Fischer (eds.), *NBER Macroeconomics Annual,* vol. 4. Cambridge, MA: MIT Press, pp. 121–170.

Romer, Christina D., and David H. Romer. (1994) "Monetary Policy Matters," *Journal of Monetary Economics* 34(1), 75–88.

Rose, Andrew K. (1985) "An Alternative Approach to the American Demand for Money," *Journal of Money, Credit and Banking* 17(4), 439–455.

Rosen, Deborah. (1982) "A Critique of Deterministic Causality," *Philosophical Forum* 14, 101–130.

Rosenberg, Alexander. (1985) *The Structure of Biology.* Cambridge: Cambridge University Press.

Rosenberg, Alexander. (1992) *Economics: Mathematical Politics or Science of Diminishing Returns?* Chicago: Chicago University Press.

Russell, Bertrand. (1918) "On the Notion of Cause," in Russell, *Mysticism and Logic.* London: Allan and Unwin, pp. 180–208.

Salmon, Wesley. (1984) *Scientific Explanation and the Causal Structure of the World.* Princeton: Princeton University Press.

Salmon, Wesley. (1994) "Causality without Counterfactuals," *Philosophy of Science* 61(2), pp. 297–312.

Samuelson, Paul A., and Ryuzo Sato. (1984) "Unattainability of Integrability and Definiteness Conditions in the General Case of Demand for Money and Goods," *American Economic Review* 74(4), 588–604.

Sanford, David H. (1976) "The Direction of Causation and the Direction of Conditionship," *Journal of Philosophy* 73(8), 193–208.

Sanford, David H. (1988) "Can There Be One-way Causal Conditionship?" *Synthese* 76(3), 397–408.

Sanford, David H. (1989) *If P then Q.* New York: Routledge.

Sargent, Thomas J. (1976) "The Observational Equivalence of Natural and Unnatural Rate Theories of Macroeconomics," *Journal of Political Economy* 84(3), 631–640," reprinted in Robert E. Lucas, Jr., and Thomas J. Sargent (eds.),

*Rational Expectations and Econometric Practice.* London: Allen and Unwin, 1981.

Sargent, Thomas J. (1987) *Macroeconomic Theory,* 2nd edition. Boston: Academic Press.

Sargent, Thomas J., and Neil Wallace. (1976) "Rational Expectations and the Theory of Economic Policy," *Journal of Monetary Economics* 2(2), 169–183.

Schmidt, Jan Hendrik. (1998) "Newcomb's Paradox Realized with Backward Causation," *British Journal for the Philosophy of Science* 49(1), 67–88.

Schwarz, Gideon. (1978) "Estimating the Dimension of a Model," *Annals of Statistics* 6(2), 461–464.

Sheffrin, Steven M. (1996) *Rational Expectations,* 2nd edition. Cambridge: Cambridge University Press.

Sheffrin, Steven M., and Robert K. Triest. (1998) "A New Approach to Causality and Economic Growth," unpublished typescript, University of California, Davis.

Simon, Herbert A. (1953a) "On the Definition of the Causal Relation," in Simon, *Models of Man.* New York: Wiley, 1957, ch. 3.

Simon, Herbert A. (1953b) "Causal Ordering and Identifiability," in Simon, *Models of Man.* New York: Wiley 1957, ch. 1.

Simon, Herbert A. (1955) "Causality and Econometrics: Comment," *Econometrica* 23(2), 193–195.

Simon, Herbert A., and Yumi Iwasaki. (1988) "Causal Ordering, Comparative Statics, and Near Decomposability," *Journal of Econometrics* 39(1/2), 149–173.

Simon, Herbert, and Nicholas Rescher. (1966) "Causes and Counterfactuals," *Philosophy of Science* 33(4), 323–340.

Simon, Julian L. (1970) "The Concept of Causality in Economics," *Kyklos* 23(2), 226–254.

Simpson, E. H. (1951) "The Interpretation of Interaction in Contingency Tables," *Journal of the Royal Statistical Society, Series B* 13(2), 238–241.

Sims, C. (1972) "Money, Income and Causality," in Robert E. Lucas, Jr., and Thomas J. Sargent (eds.), *Rational Expectations and Econometric Practice.* Allen and Unwin, 1981, pp. 387–403.

Sims, Christopher A. (1980) "Macroeconomics and Reality," *Econometrica* 48(6), 1–48.

Sims, Christopher A. (1986) "Are Forecasting Models Usable for Policy Analysis?" *Federal Reserve Bank of Minneapolis Quarterly Review* 10(1, Winter), 2–15.

Sober, Elliot. (1987) "The Principle of the Common Cause," in J. Fetzer (ed.), *Probability and Causality.* Dordrecht: D. Reidel, pp. 211–228.

Sober, Elliot. (1988) *Reconstructing the Past.* Cambridge, MA: MIT Press.

Spirtes, Peter, Clark Glymour, and Richard Scheines. (1991) "From Probability to Causality," *Philosophical Studies* 64(1), 1–36.

Spirtes, Peter, Clark Glymour, and Richard Scheines. (1993) *Causation, Prediction, and Search.* New York: Springer-Verlag.

Spohn, Wolfgang. (1983) "Probabilistic Causality: From Hume via Suppes to Granger," in M. C. Galavotti and G. Gambetta (eds.), *Causalità e Modelli Probabilistici.* Bologna: CLUEB, pp. 69–87.

Stabile, Donald R., and Jeffrey Cantor. (1991) *The Public Debt of the United States: An Historical Perspective, 1775–1990.* New York: Praeger.

Strotz, Robert H., and Herman O. A. Wold. (1960) "Recursive vs. Nonrecursive Systems: An Attempt at Synthesis," *Econometrica* 28(2), 417–427.

Studenski, Paul, and Herman Krooss. (1952) *Financial History of the United States.* New York: McGraw-Hill.

Suppes, Patrick. (1970) "A Probabilistic Theory of Causality," *Acta Philosophica Fennica*, fasc. XXIV.

Swamy, P. A. V. B., and George S. Tavlas. (1995) "Random Coefficient Models: Theory and Applications," *Journal of Economic Surveys* 9(2), 165–196.

Swanson, Norman R., and Clive W. J. Granger. (1997) "Impulse Response Functions Based on a Causal Approach to Residual Orthogonalization in Vector Autoregressions," *Journal of the American Statistical Association* 92(437), 357–367.

Temin, Peter. (1976) *Did Monetary Forces Cause the Great Depression?* New York: Norton.

Theil, Henri. (1971) *Principles of Econometrics.* New York: Wiley.

Trehan, Bharat, and Carl E. Walsh. (1988) "Common Trends, the Government Budget Constraint, and Revenue Smoothing," *Journal of Economic Dynamics and Control* 12(2/3), 425–444.

Tobin, James. (1970) "Money and Income: Post Hoc Ergo Propter Hoc?" *Quarterly Journal of Economics* 82(2), 301–317.

Tooke, Thomas. (1844) *An Inquiry into the Currency Principle: The Connection of the Currency with Prices and the Expediency of a Separation of Issue from Banking*, 2nd edition. London: Longman, Brown, Green and Longmans. Reprinted as no. 15 in Series of Reprints of Scarce Works on Political Economy, London School of Economics and Political Science, London, 1959.

Tooke, Thomas, and William Newmarch. (1838–1857) *A History of Prices: And of the State of Circulation from 1792–1856*, vols. I–VI. Introduction by T. E. Gregory. New York: Adelphi, 1928.

Tooley, Michael. (1987) *Causation: A Realist Approach.* Oxford: Clarendon Press.

Turner, Thomas H., and Charles H. Whiteman. (1981) "Econometric Policy Evaluation Under Rational Expectations," *Federal Reserve Bank of Minneapolis Quarterly Review* 5 (Spring/Summer), 6–15.

United States Bureau of the Census. (1975) *Historical Statistics of the United States, Colonial Times to 1970.* Washington, DC: U.S. Department of Commerce, Bureau of the Census.

Webber, Carolyn, and Aaron Wildavsky. (1986) *A History of Taxation and Expenditure in the Western World.* New York: Simon and Schuster.

Weidner, Richard T., and Robert L. Sells. (1973) *Elementary Classical Physics*, vol. 1. Boston: Allyn and Bacon.

Weintraub, Roy. (1979) *Microfoundations: The Compatibility of Microeconomics and Macroeconomics.* Cambridge: Cambridge University Press.

Wildavsky, Aaron. (1988) *The New Politics of the Budgetary Process.* Glenview, IL: Scott, Foresman.

Williams, Donald. (1953) "The Elements of Being," *Review of Metaphysics* 7(2), 171–192.

Witte, John F. (1985) *The Politics and Development of the Federal Income Tax*. Madison: University of Wisconsin Press.

Wojnilower, Albert M. (1980) "The Central Role of Credit Crunches in Recent Financial History," *Brookings Papers on Economic Activity* (2), 277–326.

Wold, Hermann. (1960) "A Generalization of Causal Chain Models," *Econometrica* 28(2), 443–463.

Woodward, James. (1995) "Causation and Explanation in Linear Models," in Daniel Little (ed.), *On the Reliability of Economic Models: Essays in the Philosophy of Economics*. Boston: Kluwer, pp. 9–62.

Woodward, James. (1997) "Causal Models, Probability, and Invariance," in Vaughn R. McKim and Stephen P. Turner (eds.), *Causality in Crisis? Statistical Methods and the Search for Causal Knowledge in the Social Sciences*. Notre Dame, IN: University of Notre Dame Press, pp. 265–316.

Yule, G. Udny. (1903) "Notes on the Theory of the Association of Attributes in Statistics," *Biometrika* 2(2), 121–134.

Zellner, Arnold A. (1979) "Causality and Econometrics," in Karl Brunner and Allan H. Meltzer (eds.), *Three Aspects of Policy Making: Knowledge, Data and Institutions*, Carnegie-Rochester Conference Series on Public Policy, vol. 10. Amsterdam: North-Holland, pp. 9–54.

# Index

aggregates, economic: informational complexity of, 131–40; nonhomogeneity of, 130–40

aggregates, macroeconomic: composition of, 128–31; general price level and GDP as, 112–19, 125; natural, 113; properties of, 285–6; real rate of interest, 125; supervenience on microeconomics, 119–24; synthetic, 113–14, 119, 125; yield curve, 125

antimonetarism, 46–9

arbitrage doctrine (Hume), 3–5

asymmetry: of causality (Hausman), 81–7; in cause, 34; from parameterization, 85; as property of causal direction, 69

Banerjeee, Anindya, 219

Banking School, Britain, 7

Barrie, J. M., 108

Barro, Robert J., 200–202, 227, 236–7

Bell, J. S., 167

Bhaskar, Roy, 22

Bierce, Ambrose, 129

Black, Fischer, 250–1

Blaug, Mark, 110–11

bootstrapping (Glymour), 42n12

boundary conditions, 44–5

Bowley, Arthur, 145

Box, George E. P., 148

Brown, R. L., 220

Bunge, Mario, 22

business-cycle analysis, 145–6

Cagan, Philip, 64

Cartwright, Nancy, 15–17, 52–6, 75–6, 89–101, 103–4, 106, 127n20, 133–5, 141, 150–1, 166

causal capacities: as dispositions, 100; emergence of, 100; invariance of, 54–8; locality feature of, 100–101

causal chains: temporally ordered, 134–6; of Wold, 147, 162–4

causal direction: addressed by Granger-causality, 26; approach to inference of, 214–15; in causal order, 34–41; Hume's view of, 13; identification of, 213; linearities and nonlinearities to infer, 194–213; between money and prices, 250; probabilistic accounts with known, 25

causal field: as background of standing conditions, 45; normative or legal use of, 31; parameters in, 45; variables in, 43–6, 50–1

causal graph: triadic screening relationships of variables, 158–60; variable relationships in Causal Markov Condition, 157–8; variable relationships in Faithfulness Condition, 158–9; variables outside causal structure on, 45–6

causal intuition, 22

causality: asymmetry of (Hausman), 81–7; causal structure of, 186; conditional analysis of (Mackie), 29–34; constitutional account of, 149; counterfactual nature of, 102; criterion of constant conjunction in, 14; direct and indirect, 69; history in econometrics of, 144–9; Hume's contribution to idea of, 2–13, 23, 29, 49, 54, 88, 91, 99, 108, 283–4; informational account of, 149; involving probability, 53; LeRoy's definition, 172, 177; long- and short-run, 138–40; mechanisms in Hume's discussions of, 3–5, 11; mutual

macroeconomic structures: change of
parameters in, 142; limits on causal
inference with, 286
Mäki, Uskali, 109, 112, 113, 127n20, 128
mapping: of causally ordered system,
62–3
mark transmission: in causal process,
96–8, 103; examples of, 141; general
features of, 141–2; objection to,
140–1; as property of causal structures,
140
Marshall, Alfred, 7, 109–10
Mesarovic, Mihajlo, 61
microeconomics: defined, 108; neoclassical,
131; supervenience of macroeconomics
on, 119–24
microfoundations program for
macroeconomics, 109–12; pushed to
extreme, 130–1; in schools of
macroeconomic thought, 182;
unsoundness of, 285
Mill, John Stuart, 44
Mises, Ludwig von, 123n18
monetarism: antimonetarism, 46–9; causal
analysis of, 48; components of, 277;
doctrine of, 46; interpretation of money
and price relationship, 277; modern
argument over, 1
money: causal direction between prices
and, 250; endogenous, 46
Moore, Henry, 146
Murphy, Jimmy, 283
Myrdal, Gunnar, 7

Newbold, Paul, 148
Newcomb, Simon, 7
Nixon Administration price controls
(1971–3), 268–9
nonlinearities: of capacities, 56; in causally
ordered structures, 64–8; common-
cause conditions, 91–6; extension of
Simon's causal analysis to cases of, 60;
in inferring causal direction, 201–13; in
parameters and variables, 60; in
rational expectations models, 138, 153,
201; in relation between structural and
Granger-causality, 153–5
Nowack, Leszek, 126, 127

Ohlin, Bertil, 7
Orcutt, Guy, 148
Owens, David, 71n1

Paasche index, 116
Papineau, David, 53, 90–1, 94, 99
parameterization: of data-generating
process, 177; defined, 62

parameters: altering, 38–9; as boundary
conditions, 44–5; in causal structure, 59,
61–3; constant, 44–5; deep and shallow,
171; distinct from variables, 39–40;
distinctions between variables and
(LeRoy), 171, 176; under rational
expectations, 68; uses (Engle, Hendry,
Richard), 176–7
Pearl, Judea, 156–7, 284
Peirce, Charles S., 42n12, 54
Percy, Walker, 250
Phillips, P. C. B., 215
Plosser, Charles, 276
Podolsky, Boris, 166–7
Popper, Karl, 8, 10
Postulate of Independence, or Empty
World Postulate, 107n36
Postulate of Prepotence, 107n36
prices: causal direction between money
and, 250; in Walrasian fantasy of
economics, 102
probabilities: distribution of variables in
Faithfulness Condition, 158; limited
dependent variables approach to
introduce, 52–3; probabilistic accounts
of causality, 14, 22, 25; probabilistic
causality in Humean tradition, 13–22;
probabilistic conjunctions in causality,
49
probabilities in causally ordered systems:
error-in-equations approach to
introduce, 50–1, 53; errors-in-variables
approach to introduce, 51, 53;
random coefficients model to
introduce, 51–4
properties: of causal structures, 140; of
macroeconomic aggregates, 285–6;
temporally localized, 84–5

Quandt, Richard, 218
quantity theory of money (Hume), 3, 5
Quine, Willard, 8

randomness: random coefficients
model, 51–2; in variable relationships,
160
rational-expectations hypothesis: in
Barro's tax-smoothing model, 200–202,
227, 236–7; economic justification for,
189; hypotheses alternative to, 189;
LeRoy's interpretation of, 187–9;
nonlinearities introduced by, 153–4;
parameters under, 68; treatment by
Sargent and Wallace, 188
rational-expectations model: causal
structure in, 64–6; nonlinearities in,
138, 153, 201

For EU product safety concerns, contact us at Calle de José Abascal, 56–1°,
28003 Madrid, Spain or eugpsr@cambridge.org.

www.ingramcontent.com/pod-product-compliance
Ingram Content Group UK Ltd.
Pitfield, Milton Keynes, MK11 3LW, UK
UKHW042211180425
457623UK00011B/162